EAT AND BE SATISFIED

A Social History of
Jewish Food

JOHN COOPER

𝒜

JASON ARONSON INC.
Northvale, New Jersey
London

This book was set in 9 pt. Bookman by Lind Graphics of Upper Saddle River, New Jersey, and printed by Haddon Craftsmen in Scranton, Pennsylvania.

Library of Congress Cataloging-in-Publication Data

Cooper, John, 1935–
    Eat and be satisfied : a social history of Jewish food / John Cooper.
      p. cm.
    Includes bibliographical references and index.
    ISBN 0-87668-316-2
    1. Food in the Bible. 2. Jews—Dietary laws. 3. Jews—Food—
History. 4. Cookery, Jewish—History. I. Title.
BS680.F6C66   1993
296.7'3'09—dc20   92-45772

Manufactured in the United States of America. Jason Aronson Inc. offers books and cassettes. For information and catalog write to Jason Aronson Inc., 230 Livingston Street, Northvale, New Jersey 07647.

EAT
AND BE
SATISFIED

Dedicated to the memory
of my father, Isaac Cooper (1900–1974), and
my mother, Kitty Cooper (1900–1991)

CONTENTS

ACKNOWLEDGMENTS

During the writing of this book, I have sought the advice and assistance of members of both the Jewish community and the community of food historians. While the history of gastronomy may now be a trendy subject, it is not a rigid discipline and its practitioners generously share their ideas and knowledge with one another.

I would like to thank Herr Ulf Löchner for sending me copies of recipes from Old German cookery books, Dr. Claudio Benporat for enlightening me about the Renaissance recipes, and William Woys Weaver for unraveling the geneaological connection between bagels and pretzels. Alan Davidson has answered endless queries as to the "Who's Who" of food historians, probably without realizing they were coming from the same person.

There are also those such as Professor Barbara Kirshenblatt-Gimblett, Josephine Bacon, and Valerie Mars, who straddle the diverse worlds of Jewish food scholarship and culinary history. Professor Kirshenblatt-Gimblatt's research on Jewish cookery books has opened new doors for me. To Valerie Mars and Dr. Jonathan Weber I owe gratitude for organizing the First Oxford Symposium on Jewish Food in 1989 and for encouraging me to sort out my jumbled ideas on east European Sabbath dishes. To Josephine Bacon I am grateful for a stimulating course of lectures on Jewish food history at the Spiro Institute and conversations that forced me to clarify my own hypotheses on Jewish culinary trends and to deepen my researches. Moreover, I owe her further special thanks for her skills as a professional translator in vastly improving my translation of the thirteenth-century Spanish and North African Jewish food recipes rescued from obscurity by Professor Lucie Bolens. My thanks to Professor Bolens for allowing me to utilize her French version of these recipes.

At the start of the project, Rabbi Dr. Norman Solomon guided me through rabbinic texts, and Mr. Bernard Jacob graciously lent me a succession of books from his library as well as adding his comments to some of the early drafts of my chapters. As the project expanded, Rabbi Samuel Rodrigues-Pereira aided my stumbling through rabbinic texts.

My warm thanks to all these gentlemen. I should like to acknowledge the help of the late Hanoch Fischer, the late Rose Teper, and the late Solomon Cikurel, as well as Chaim Berlin, Aubrey Silverstone, Carole Malkin, Dr. Isaac Gottlieb, Luce Ronan, Michael Teper, Chaim Klein, Emma Klein, Ethel Levine, Naim Dangoor, and Monique and Eldad Neumark.

My sincere thanks to the librarian at Jews' College, London, Ezra Kahn, who took such trouble to assist me, to Roy Segal of the Leo Baeck Library, and the staffs of both the Jewish National Library and the H.U.C. Library in Jerusalem.

My deep gratitude to Arthur Kurzweil for his initial confidence in my project, and my special appreciation to the editors Muriel Jorgensen and Janet Warner for their hard work in editing and preparing the manuscript.

On a more personal note, I am very grateful to my brother, Rabbi Dr. Martin Cooper, who was a never-ending source of encouragement and without whose help my book would not have found a publisher. My thanks also to my mother-in-law, Flower Elias, and her sister, my aunt, Mercia Mansfield, for their support and constant willingness to search for source material for me. In fact, the whole of my extended family network provided various bits and pieces of invaluable information, for which I extend my heartfelt thanks.

My mother, Kitty Cooper, took a great interest in this book over the whole ten years from its inception to its completion. Although she died just before its acceptance for publication, she always had complete faith in its success.

To my wife, Judy, who put a shotgun to my head to finish this project and who polished more than one clumsy sentence, my warm and loving thanks. To my children, Flower and Zaki, who were both amused and bored by my obsession with Jewish food, my affectionate thanks for all their help and for being available when the word processor would not obey my commands.

INTRODUCTION

The history of Jewish food was an area of research pioneered by scholars in Vienna, a city that was itself an intellectual hothouse in the early decades of this century. Outstanding contributions were made by Samuel Krauss (1866–1948) in a chapter on the food of the Jews in the Roman and Babylonian empires in his *Talmudische Archeologie* (1910–1912) and in his wide-ranging survey "Aus der Jüdischen Volksküche" (1915). Max Grunwald (1871–1953), the founder of the study of Jewish folklore, contributed "Aus dem Jüdischen Kochbuch" in 1920 and touched again on the subject of Jewish food in his book *Vienna* (1936), one of a series of volumes on different Jewish communities. Grunwald was a rabbi in Vienna from 1903 to 1933, but earlier, while serving in Hamburg, he established the *Mitteilungen zur Jüdischen Volkskunde,* the first Jewish folklore journal, and later Jewish folklore societies in Hamburg and Vienna jointly sponsored it.[1]

In the polyglot Austrian Empire and in its atrophied successor state, Jewish intellectuals studied not only their history, but their total social system, folklore, and customs to see how they differed from those of other nationalities and to define themselves. One of the areas on which they focused was the distinctive culinary tradition of the Jews. The challenges of modernization not only affected the Jews in Austria, however, but also those in Poland, where Yehuda Zlotnik, born 1887 and like Grunwald a rabbi, published *Yiddishe Maykholim* in Warsaw in 1920. It was written under the pseudonym of Yehuda Elzet because it was considered somewhat frivolous for a rabbi to write works on Jewish folklore. Both Max Grunwald and Yehuda Zlotnik were busy rabbis, concentrating on the needs of their communities, even if Zlotnik later followed a career in Jewish education. Both were ardent Zionists who eventually settled in Israel. We can appreciate how their interest in Jewish folklore was a facet of their Jewish nationalism and how the study of ethnic food helped to demarcate more clearly the boundaries between the Jewish and the Gentile worlds and was at the same time a conscious endeavor to preserve Jewish food traditions that were disappearing.[2]

Similarly, Samuel Krauss had a yeshiva education, although he supplemented it by study in the rabbinical seminary and at the University of Budapest; he, too, had a strong Zionist orientation, being the author of a popular work that demonstrated the unbroken presence of the Jews in the Holy Land. He was on the staff of the rabbinical seminary in Vienna from 1906, rising to become its head in 1932, while he published his major contribution on Jewish food in Max Grunwald's folklore journal, the *Mitteilungen.*

Jewish food research languished for almost forty years. When it was revived, its center of study shifted to the United States, where Jews and Jewish learning benefited from the expansion of the universities after the Second World War. It received a fresh stimulus from Mordecai Kosover in his book *Yiddishe Maykholim* published by Yivo in 1958, a detailed study based on a remarkable knowledge of rabbinic sources in which he surveyed in considerable historial depth east European Jewish foods made from flour. Kosover had the same background as did his predecessors Grunwald and Zlotnik, being steeped in traditional Jewish learning after having studied in a *yeshivah* and spending some time in Palestine, where he wrote a volume on Arabic elements in Palestinian Yiddish. His philological researches on Jewish food were extended in new directions by Marvin Herzog, who brought out *The Yiddish Language in Northern Poland: Its Geography and History* in 1965. Herzog showed how the variants in certain foods, such as gefilte fish with and without sugar, followed the same boundaries as did the Polish and Lithuanian Yiddish dialects. Today there is a big project under way to devise a cultural atlas of Ashkenazi Jewry, in which the variations in the preparation and names of Jewish food in the different regions where Yiddish was spoken will be carefully mapped and discussed. Next, a number of classic nineteenth-century Jewish cookery books were reprinted by Jewish women, who were partially influenced by the feminist movement and who were determined to retrieve the role of their mothers and grandmothers. Among these women three must be singled out: Josephine Bacon for reprinting Esther Levy's *Jewish Cookery Book* (1871)and Edouard de Pomiane's *The Jews of Poland Recollections and Recipes* (1929) and Ruth L. Gales and Lila T. Gold for producing a facsimile edition of *The Jewish Manual* (1846).

In the United States Barbara Kirshenblatt-Gimblett, a Yiddish scholar with a background in anthropology, has initiated the careful analysis of Jewish cookery books. Whereas most of the Jewish cookery books published in England and Germany in the nineteenth century were kosher, she observed, the American cookery books, except for a few such as Mrs. Esther Levy's *Jewish Cookery Book,* published in 1871 in Philadelphia, contained mostly recipes that were *treyf.* The

American cookery books, such as *Aunt Babette's Cook Book* (1889), while providing traditional German-Jewish recipes for the festivals, were deliberately *treyf*, including dishes with shrimps, oysters, ham, and bacon. Nonetheless, an important lacuna is the lack of any edited editions of the German-Jewish cookery books, starting with I. Stolz's *Kochbuch der Israeliten* (1815), nor has there been any study of an eighteenth-century Yiddish manuscript housed in the Jewish Museum in Prague. Mention should also be made of John M. Shaftesley's multifaceted paper entitled "Culinary Aspects of Anglo-Jewry" (1975), which gave the original impetus to the study of Jewish cookery books.[3]

Another topic that deserves investigation is the surprising number of Jewish recipes contained in the later editions of a classic eighteenth-century English work, Hannah Glasse's *Art of Cookery Made Plain and Easy* (1781). Some of the recipes appear to point to a Spanish or Portuguese Jewish origin and were probably related by the wives of wealthy Sephardic merchants. The recipes to which I am referring are the Jewish method of stewing green peas in oil reminiscent of Spanish cuisine, and marmalade of eggs made from the yolks of twenty-four eggs beaten for one hour, after which they were stirred with sugar and pounded almonds before being mixed with orange peel and citron to form cakes in the shape of birds, fish, and fruit. There were also recipes for preserving beef and salmon "the Jew's way," which would enable the food to keep for long voyages to the West and East Indies as well as another recipe for dressing haddock in a Jewish style.[4]

Reading Fernand Braudel's *Capitalism and Material Life 1400–1800* when it was published in England in 1973 was both stimulating and exhilarating, as it appeared to open fresh vistas on claimed and uncharted territory; in particular, his highlighting of the crucial role of the daily bread in the global diet and his insistence on the carnivorous diet of Western man must be stressed. The *Annales*, the journal of the French historical school, was inundated with articles on food, particularly in the 1970s, including Jean Soler's seminal article from a structuralist viewpoint that was entitled "The Semiotics of Food in the Bible" and was akin to the research of Mary Douglas. In 1979 Alan Davidson and other enthusiasts in England launched *Petits Propos Culinaires*, an international periodical devoted to the history of food; *The Journal of Gastronomy* was established in the United States in 1984, while the distinguished historian of France Theodore Zeldin promoted the Oxford Symposium on Food in the 1980s. During the late 1970s and 1980s, Claude Lévi-Strauss, through his *Origins of Table Manners*, inspired many followers, among others prompting Joëlle Bahloul to write a study of the food of the Algerian Jews from a structuralist viewpoint. Food has become an important field of study, even if it is often a fringe subject as far as universities are concerned.[5]

This work endeavors in some measure to utilize and to integrate the research on Jewish food from rabbinic sources and from the Jewish cookery books with the accumulated evidence of modern, secular research on the history of food in general. We open our account with a discussion of biblical food between the seventeenth century B.C.E. and 586 B.C.E. and concentrate on *la longue durée,* the long-term trends. We attempt to reconstruct the biblical diet over the course of many centuries by comparing it with the food patterns of surrounding nations in the ancient world and with the sustenance of the Ethiopian and Yemenite Jews in more recent times; but archaeological evidence and the scrutiny of the etymology of key food terms are not neglected. We also try to differentiate between the repast of the elite and the food of the masses, a theme to which we constantly return throughout this volume.

We next turn to a consideration of the Dietary Laws and show how they grew in importance after the Babylonian Exile, and we also try to explain the separation of dairy food and meat dishes, but because of limitations of space we do not analyze the reasons for the ban on the consumption of non-Jewish bread, milk, and wine during the medieval period and later; nor do we have the space to consider in detail the variations in the communal customs of waiting for different lengths of time before consuming a milk dish after eating meat.

We have provided a two-chapter treatment of food in the talmudic era between 330 B.C.E. and the fifth century of the common era. One chapter surveys daily food, and we try to disentangle the differences between the diet of the Jews of Palestine influenced by Rome and that of the Babylonian Jews that followed local patterns or borrowed from the cuisine of Iran. The other chapter covers the Sabbath and festival foods, and among the topics that are explored are the eating of warm food on the Sabbath and the possible symbolic meaning of both the *Kiddush* ceremony and the fish served for dinner on Friday night, as the one had messianic undertones, while the other was a portent of resurrection after death. Moreover, we consider the way the Passover service at home after the destruction of the Temple was transformed under Roman influence into a symposium, instead of being a shared meal of the Paschal sacrifice.

We move on to a survey of Jewish food in the Middle Ages, first discussing the typical medieval dishes and foods of the European Jews and those in Islamic lands; and we then examine the Sabbath and the festival foods of the same communities, paying special attention to the evolution of *cholent* and *hamin,* the Sabbath food *par excellence.* We next shift our attention to the cuisine of the Sephardim, the Spanish and Portuguese Jews, although as yet the contours of this field of research are still being delineated by Dr. David M. Bunis. However, I had hoped to include further material on the cuisine of Moroccan Jewry on the one hand, and the Syrian and Iraqi communities on the other, but because of the paucity of research by indigenous Jewish food historians from these countries and the lack of sufficient background material with historical depth on the Arab cuisines of each individual country, I decided that the results of my research were not yet ripe for presentation. Nonetheless, readers can gain much from Joëlle Bahloul's masterly study of Algerian Jewish food from the viewpoint of a structuralist anthropologist. We finally consider the daily and Sabbath festival foods of east European Jewry, based on the pioneering researches of Yehuda Zlotnik and Mordecai Kosover, and try to supplement it with material gleaned from non-Jewish sources.

1

BIBLICAL FOOD

INTRODUCTION

To evaluate the diet of the Israelites, we must in the first instance
compare it with the food eaten by other nations in the ancient world
and with the diet of the less sophisticated Jewish communities in the
modern world. The authors of a masterly study of Egyptian food
asserted that the protein-rich meats and fish were more readily available to the wealthy ruling elite and the priests and that cereals,
vegetables, and fruit together with fermented beverages represented
the staple items of the diet of the masses.[1]

Henri Limet has reconstructed the diet of the Sumerians at the end
of the third millennium B.C.E. At this time in Mesopotamia there was a
huge production of barley for bread and beer, but little wheat and
emmer were milled. The large, flat cakes of barley, consumed by the
common people, resembled the bread (*hobes*) prepared by the Arabs
today. Finer kinds of bread were enjoyed by the upper class, who
utilized better-quality flour and mixed the dough with sesame oil, lard,
or "mutton butter." Moreover, the common people relished the consumption of soups with a starch or flour base, prepared with chick-
peas, lentils, barley flour, or emmer flour. As the soups were sometimes made with hulled barley, they may have resembled the *burghul*
dish of Syria or the *kishk* soup made in other parts of the Middle East.
The Sumerian diet was principally vegetarian, consisting of cereals
and more rarely legumes, which provided protein and carbohydrates,
while other nutritive benefits were provided by the intake of fats and
oils. According to A. Leo Oppenheim, leguminous plants were not of
great dietary importance in Mesopotamia. Some milk was consumed,
as was a large variety of cheese, including white cheese, sharp and
sweetened cheese, and a fresh cheese, although we would surmise that
most of the different kinds of cheese were reserved for upper-class
gourmets. Apples, pears, grapes, figs, pistachio nuts, pomegranates,
and possibly plums were grown, but dates were still scarce and did not
figure as yet in the diet of the peasants. Here as elsewhere meat was

1

consumed primarily by the affluent, although the peasants had access to fish, which were plentiful in the canals, and the peasants may have eaten poultry as well.[2]

Limet characterized the diet of the Sumerian peasantry as "frugal." Grain was the staple food of the majority of the population, whether it was eaten raw, roasted, in porridge, or baked into loaves and flans. Because this largely cereal diet was insipid, Oppenheim stressed how seeds, such as watercress, mustard, cumin, and coriander, and vegetables, such as leek, garlic, and onion, together with salt were used to enliven the diet. Jean Botérro, while admitting that the haute cuisine of spicy stews or platter of birds was reserved for the upper class, believed that the good taste and recipes of the chefs filtered downward, so that it was a myth that the Mesopotamian peasantry were ever reduced to "chewing dull pottages."[3]

In Greece during the heroic age the diet was mainly vegetarian, including barley bread, porridge, and broths of beans and pulses, but the warriors were allowed to indulge their craving for meat. Later, white bread baked with wheat replaced the loaves of barley, and the wealthier members of the population dined on salted fish and a large variety of vegetables, although among the privileged the use of pulses fell into disfavor. The chief food of the ancient Roman farmers was a thick porridge made with wheat or beans called *puls,* and this together with the addition of hard, flat bread called *libum* and vegetables such as beets, beans, turnips, and onions constituted the bulk of the diet. With the expansion of the Roman Empire, the rich developed a taste for white bread and pastries, fish, meat, and game. Recently, scientists have analyzed the contents of Roman latrines at a fort in Scotland, recovering wheat debris similar to those found in wholemeal bread after its passage through the digestive tract. The scientists suggested that a higher proportion of the food was from fruits and vegetables rather than from meat than had previously been thought to be the case, and they concluded that this pointed to "primarily a vegetable diet."[4]

Turning to modern Jewish communities, we can also learn much from the dietary habits of the Yemenite Jews during the nineteenth century and the Ethiopian Jews in more recent times. According to Jacob Sapir, who visited Yemen in the mid-nineteenth century, the Jews commenced their meal with a dish of vegetables and seeds, from which everyone helped himself or herself, and this served as the hors d'oeuvre. Every day the Jews ate freshly baked bread made from barley or wheat that was "soft, warm and thin." Interestingly enough, Sapir used the biblical term *rakikim* (wafers) to describe the bread. The Yemenite Jews dipped the bread into a strong sauce called *hilbeh,* the ingredients of which included fenugreek seeds, black pepper, caraway seed, cardamon, coriander leaves, and garlic, and which was so sharp that it burned the tongue and lips. Moreover, Sapir declared that "their food is of one kind and it is not mixed like the Babylonians" (the Iraqi Jews). Each course comprised a single meal. So, too, it has been pointed out that the Bemba, a Southern Bantu people, refused to mix their food and despised the Europeans, who ate two or three different dishes at one sitting. Erich Brauer asserted that the Yemenite Jews in the towns hardly ever tasted meat, apart from on the Sabbath and the festivals.[5]

When Dr. Isaac Gottlieb visited the Ethiopian Jews in recent decades, he discovered that their eating habits were similar to those of the Yemenite Jews. During the week a sponge bread called *injedra* was consumed twice a day, and it was likewise dipped into a spicy mixture composed of garlic and onions, which was known as *teff.* By dipping the bread that was eaten into a sharp, spicy sauce, the Ethiopian Jews were able to digest vast quantities of a boring carbohydrate with ease and were able to subsist on a monotonous diet. At this meal the Falashas drank a beer called *talla,* again a very nutritious food, or sipped some coffee. The amounts of bread and beer consumed remind one of the dietary regime of the ancient Babylonians. By contrast, on the Sabbath the Ethiopian Jews dined on black bread cut into cubes with goat's meat or chicken. Both the Yemenite and the Ethiopian Jews lived on a boring diet during the week, consisting principally of bread and a piquant sauce that helped the stodgy and gritty bread to slide down their throats. We may confidently apply our conclusions concerning the ancient world and our observations on the diet of the Yemenite and Ethiopian Jewish communities to the data in the Bible concerning the food of the Israelites.[6]

THE DIET OF THE ISRAELITES

Meat

In ancient Israel the majority of the population lived on a diet of barley bread, vegetables, and fruit, supplemented by milk products and honey, which was used as a universal sweetener. Unless a family belonged to a section of the small priestly elite or court circles, meat was rarely eaten but was consumed at festive meals or tribal gatherings when the participants were given a share of the sacrificial feast, usually a portion of a domestic animal such as a goat or a sheep. Meat was prepared by boiling in water with seasonings, by roasting, baking, or frying. The most commonly mentioned form of meat in the Bible was that of a goat or kid, not that of a sheep, which was regarded as being a more valuable animal. The goat was still the most popular milk- and meat-producing animal in Palestine in the 1930s, when the Arab peasants and bedouin maintained 440,000 goats as against 253,000 sheep. In ancient times the fat tail of sheep, which sometimes weighed as much as 15 pounds, was looked upon as a delicacy that was, for instance, offered to Saul by Samuel's cook (1 Samuel 9:24); even today it is prized as a special treat by Jews from the oriental communities. Calves that had been fattened in stalls provided a meat that was particularly savored by the wealthy in ancient Israel. The prophet Amos denounced those members of the elite "who loll on beds inlaid with ivory and sprawl over your couches feasting on lambs from the flock and fatted calves . . ." (Amos 6:4). According to the Book of Kings (1 Kings 4:22–24), "Solomon's provision for one day was thirty kor of flour and sixty kor of meal, ten fat oxen and twenty oxen from the pastures and a hundred sheep, as well as stags, gazelles, roebuck and fattened fowl." So, too, the Mishnah informs us that there was a special Temple medical officer who attended to bowel sickness, caused, according to the commentators, by the priest's overindulgence in meat (*Shekalim* 5:1).[7]

Bread

But now we must turn our attention to the diet of the Israelite peasant. In Deuteronomy 8:8 there is a list of seven basic agricultural products of ancient Israel: wheat, barley, figs, grapes, olives, pomegranates, and honey. More frequently, the Bible mentions the three staple products of corn, wine, and oil, on which the Israelite population depended for its subsistence. "If ye shall hearken diligently to my commandments . . . I will give the rain of the land in its season . . . that thou mayest gather in thy corn, thy wine and thine oil. . . . But if ye turn aside and serve other gods and worship them . . . he will shut up the heaven, that there be no rain, and that the land yield not her fruit" (Deuteronomy 11:13–31). Many centuries later the prophet Hosea admonished his wife, who exclaimed, "I will go after my lovers; they give me my food and drink, my wool and flax, my oil and my perfumes," and chided her that "it is I who gave her corn, new wine and oil" (Hosea 2:5 and 8). Louis Rabinowitz suggested that the three staple items of the people's diet described in the Bible, namely *dagan* (grain), *tirosh* (choice wine), and *yitzhar* (refined oil), all contributed to a balanced diet. The corn provided carbohydrates, the wine vitamins, and the oil fats. Later, blessings over bread and wine were incorporated into Jewish religious ritual, particularly at Sabbath meals, and were adapted by the Church into the Eucharist ceremony. The French historian George S. Duby has pointed out that partly under the influence of the Christian church the area of cultivation of corn and wine in Europe expanded because of the importance attached to these products in Christian ritual. So, in a subtle manner the Bible influenced the pattern of agricultural production in Europe, particularly in the Mediterranean area, and the landscape that emerged from it.[8]

What were the cereal crops that the Israelites cultivated to bake their bread? Professor Yehuda Feliks has drawn attention to an interesting passage in Isaiah, chapter 28, in which the prophet describes the agricultural year of the Israelite peasant farmer. According to this interpretation, verse 25 refers to five kinds of cereal, three being species of wheat, *hittah* (hard wheat and bread wheat), *nisman* (spelt wheat), and *kussemeth* (emmer or rice wheat), and two being species of barley, *se'orah* (barley) and *sorah* (two-eared barley). The Authorized Version of the Bible distinguished references to wheat, barley, and rye in this verse, without any enumeration of the various strains of wheat and barley discerned by Feliks, although the translation of *kussemeth* as rye is clearly incorrect, as this crop did not grow at all in ancient Israel. Nor have any traces of spelt been found by archaeologists excavating strata connected with ancient Israel. Perhaps Professor Feliks' translation is forced in this respect, but in excavations two- and four-rowed barley have been discovered together with the species of wheat referred to in the Bible as *hittah* and *kussemeth*. Indeed, Aaron Aaronsohn in 1906 discovered a species of *kussemeth* growing wild in Israel, wrongly concluding that this was the ancestor of all domestic strains of wheat. The Israelite farmer also sowed the ground with *ketzah* (fennel) and *kammon* (cumin), spices that were added to the dough to improve the taste of bread. In addition to beating, Isaiah enumerated four methods of threshing: treading by a horse, a toothed threshing sledge, a cartwheel, and a roller sledge. All the implements were pieces of advanced agricultural technology that were introduced into Egypt and the Roman Empire only in Hellenistic times. It appears that the Israelite peasant farmers were in advance of their neighbors, while in all probability their bread was superior as well. Articles of food such as wine, lentils, and oil were stored in pottery vessels in certain areas of the Israelite houses, and pits for storing grain were commonly dug into the ground, sometimes to a depth of twenty feet.[9]

The Bible mentioned the most primitive method of preparing corn, which was to roast ears of grain in a fire, thereby making parched corn, a process known in Arabic as *friké*, a food that is still widely utilized as a substitute for bread in the Middle East. This form of food was the ancestor of the bread we eat today, for Lévi-Strauss has pointed out that roasting rather than boiling was the earliest form of cooking food. In Leviticus 2:14 it is stated that "if you bring a meal offering of the first fruits to the Lord, you shall bring new ears parched with fire, grits of the fresh grain, as your meal offering of the first fruits." After a hard winter the unripe kernels of grain (Hebrew *aviv*) would be toasted when the groats would be most nutritious, thus permitting a harvest a month early. Second, the ears of grain, when they had changed in color from green to a riper hue (Hebrew *karmel*, Leviticus 23:14) could be consumed raw or roasted to make a gruel. Third, the fully matured wheat known as *kali* in Hebrew could also be roasted, after which it could be munched in the field by harvesters or could be transported over longer distances (1 Samuel 17:17 and Ruth 2:14). Finally, apart from the parched grain we have just mentioned, there was a process in which the ripe grains of wheat could be cooked and left to dry in a cloth in a sheltered place in the sun to make burghul (Hebrew *riffot*), which was eaten as a porridge or made into flour.[10]

In the biblical period the Israelites baked dough directly on sand or on heated stones covered with glowing ashes (1 Kings 19:6 and Isaiah 44:19), just as Turkish soldiers in the sixteenth century baked their bread in the ashes of a camp fire. When Israel Abrahams traveled in Palestine in the late nineteenth century he enjoyed the hospitality of the bedouin near Modin and

> was given some native bread for breakfast. I was very hungry, and I took a large and hasty bite at the bread, when lo! my mouth was full of gravel. They make the bread as follows: One person rolls the dough into a thin round cake (resembling a *matzah*), while another person places hot cinders on the ground. The cake is put on the cinders and gravel, and an earthenware pot is spread over all, to retain the heat. Hence the bread comes out with fragments of gravel and cinder in it.

Thus the maxim in Proverbs 5:17 that "bread gained by fraud is sweet to a man, but afterwards his mouth will be filled with gravel." Further, peasant bread in Yugoslavia in the 1920s was made from poorly cleansed grain ground in hand mills and inadequately sifted. The resulting bread, indigestible for the modern palate, was found to be inadequately leavened and to contain 1.75 percent of sand, derived partly from the grain and partly from the millstone. According to the *Jewish Encyclopedia*, the bread was sometimes placed by Arabs on heated stones under the earthenware pot, while dung fuel was heaped around it and kindled. Possibly Ezekiel was referring to such a technique when he remarked that the Lord permitted him to use cow dung rather than human excrement to bake his bread (Ezekiel 4:12–15).[11]

There were two more advanced methods of baking bread practiced by the Israelites. One was to bake bread in a griddle or frying pan made of clay, although by the time of Ezekiel in the sixth century B.C.E. they were made of iron (Ezekiel 4:3). The same technique was later adopted by the Arabs. Hannah Trager, recalling her childhood in Palestine during the 1880s, declared that she "went into the tent of our Arab woman and watched her making barley bread. She mixed the meal with water, rolled it out and laid it in a round tin on the smouldering charcoal. In a few minutes she turned it over and it was soon done. She made about twenty such cakes. . . ." The other method was to use an earthenware oven, the *tanur* (Hebrew from the Akkadian *tinuru*), with an opening at the bottom to enable a fire to be kindled, in which a fire was lit until it was sufficiently hot or alternatively cakes of dung fuel were left to glow in the oven. Then the dough was stuck to the heated inner walls of the oven until the bread was baked. The Yemenite Jews still bake their bread in a similar fashion to their biblical ancestors, by heating an earthen oven with embers, putting the dough in the oven, and then extinguishing the fire before baking; or they bake their cakes on a griddle, a round iron plate that they place in some embers.[12]

According to the *Encyclopaedia Britannica*, "Breads of the Middle East and India, though yeast-leavened, are apt to be dry flatbreads," a statement that needs to be qualified, as the bedouin still tend to use unleavened bread made of barley meal. But whereas barley meal can easily be baked into flat cakes of unleavened bread, wheat flour requires a leavening agent if it is to be baked into a palatable loaf. From Leviticus chapters 2, 7, and 23 we learn that the Israelites prepared these cakes with cereals, oil, and salt, sometimes adding a leavening agent but sometimes omitting this ingredient. According to Alexis Soyer, the Israelites probably learned the trick of preparing leaven from the Egyptians. The substance called *seor* "was, perhaps, flour diluted with water left to go sour. Pliny assures us that of all means employed by the ancients to render bread savoury and light, this is the most simple and easy." Nonetheless, Naum Jasny has concluded that although leavened bread was mentioned by the Greek writer Cratinus the Elder in the fifth century B.C.E., its use "spread immensely slowly . . . Little, if any, bread was leavened in Italy and probably in Greece when the Christian era started." During the period when man was a primitive hunter, he naturally imbibed salt with raw meat, which he ate, but when farming became a settled way of existence it became a physiological necessity for man to add salt to his cereal diet. As in the rest of the ancient world, barley was the principal cereal used to make bread in Israel in the biblical period, as can be seen in the dream of one of Gideon's soldiers, who dreamed that a cake of barley bread rolled into the Midianites' camp and toppled a tent (Judges 7:13; 2 Kings 4:22).[13]

The Greek word *maza* was probably connected with the Hebrew term *matzah* in its meaning of barley (Assyrian: *massartu* = "Staples set in a household for specific periods to be processed by its craftsmen," and Old Babylonian: *ma-as-sa-ar-tum* = barley). Martin Bernal in *Black Athena* (1987) has shown the Phoenician and Egyptian underpinnings of Greek language and culture, which the majority of the scholars of classical civilization have chosen to ignore. "*Maza*, the standard food of the Greeks, was barley very coarsely ground with nothing removed, mixed with water and cooked, probably in a container on an open fire, or . . . dried on the fire . . . *maza* was apparently similar to the Rumanian *mamalyga* of today. . . ." Did the ancient Israelites have such a porridge? The answer is, probably. While the Bible is silent, apart from the phrase *hallot matzot* (Leviticus 2:4), unleavened barley cakes, which may be distinguishing different types of *matzah*, the archaeologist may one day be able to supply us with a more definite answer about *matzah* porridge, although this would still tell us little as to the frequency of its use.[14]

In ancient Mesopotamia there was a choice of more than three hundred kinds of bread, and in spite of a more limited choice in ancient Israel, there was still a considerable variety of bread. It is likely that the Israelite loaves resembled Arab *hobes* bread, being in the form of a round, flat loaf. Common expressions for bread were the Hebrew words *uggah* (cake), coming from the root "to be round" (Genesis 8:6 and 1 Kings 19:6) and *kikkar* (round) used to describe a loaf of a similar shape. The latter was perhaps derived from the Assyrian *kukku*, meaning bread made with excellent flour and noble oil. The term *rakik* (Hebrew) (wafer) referred to a very slim loaf that was perhaps similar in appearance to modern Iraqi bread, as a tenth-century Iraqi manuscript mentioned a large rolling pin to produce the thin *rikak* (Arabic) bread. Whereas the crisp, wafer bread was made in a griddle, a soft, moist bread was prepared in a pan. Other loaves, which were heart-shaped like a certain Mesopotamian bread, were designated by the term *levivah* from the Hebrew word for heart.[15]

In the Bible there was a commandment that whenever the Jews ate bread, they were to set aside a thick loaf (*hallah*) as a gift to the Lord from the first of the dough, just as grain from the threshing floor was offered at the annual harvest (Numbers 15:20). A thick loaf was bestowed on the priests as a gift in contradistinction to the offering of the thin wafer bread. Such thick loaves of bread were found during excavations at Gezer in ancient Israel, although it is true that they were not round in shape. All the loaves offered to the priests were made with choice flour (*solet*), inaccurately translated in the past as fine flour but meaning the hard grains of flour left after the milling of wheat—the semolina. This gives us an insight into the baking techniques of ancient Israel and shows how even the upper class had to suffice with low-grade breads. Although the law of *hallah* applied only to Palestine, the rabbis ordained that it was to remain in force beyond the borders of this land. The etymology of the word *hallah* has been traced to the Hebrew root for hollow and pierce, indicating how the portion of *hallah* was torn from the freshly kneaded dough. Because the portion of dough from the baking of bread can no longer be given to a priest, it is cast into a fire by Jewish bakers and by orthodox women when they bake their own bread.[16]

In the Tabernacle the priests arranged the twelve loaves of show-bread (*lehem hapanim*) in two rows on the altar and renewed the loaves every Sabbath (Leviticus 24:5–8). According to Josephus, this bread, which was unleavened, was heaped into two piles of six loaves in the Temple, with one loaf leaning against another. The Mishnah tells us that the loaves of showbread were made in a mold so as to preserve their perfect shape (*Menahot* 11:1), while excavations in Israel from the Middle Bronze Age period between 2100 and 1550 B.C.E. have uncovered special round perforated baking trays designed to prevent bread sticking to them. So, too, the Babylonians offered to the gods various sweet unleavened cakes of wheat called *akalu*, which they laid before the gods on tables in sets of twelve, as this number has a sacred significance. The Hebrew phrase *lehem hapanim* had its counterpart in the Assyrian term *akal pânu*, although David's eating the bread of display while fleeing from his enemies attests to the antiquity of the practice in ancient Israel. In the Temple all the meal offerings were unleavened except the thank-offering cakes and the two loaves that were baked for Shavuot. From a representation of the showbread table on a two-drachma coin minted during the Bar-Kochba revolt it appears that the table had arched rims to prevent the showbread from falling off.[17]

Pulse

Bread was in the biblical phrase the staff of life, but next in importance in the diet of the biblical age was pulse, such as lentils, beans, and peas, which could be made into a pottage or used to supplement bread in various ways. If such a diet is to be efficient, the cereals and pulse must be eaten together at the same meal, as cereals are low in lysine, in which pulse is rich. Only in this way can humans ensure that they are obtaining the eight essential amino acids that are utilized as building blocks for protein. Nonetheless, meat and fish are a much easier source of protein, but we have already seen how meat formed only a small part of the diet of the mass of Israelite peasantry. We would add that fish was not eaten in much quantity before the talmudic age, as the Israelites infrequently controlled the Mediterranean coast, and their fishing was confined to the Sea of Galilee.

At the beginning of the second millennium Sinhue, an Egyptian noble, described Palestine prior to the Israelite conquest. "Figs and grapes were abundant and the land had more wine than water; it was rich in honey and oil, and its trees were laden with fruit; it had barley and wheat and countless cattle." Moreover, the letter of Aristeas written in the second century B.C.E. gives a vivid description of the agricultural productivity of ancient Israel, thereby revealing the chief foods that were eaten, but the description also holds true of an earlier age. "The land is thickly planted with multitudes of olive trees, with crops of corn and pulse, with vines too, and there is abundance of honey. Other kinds of fruit trees and date palms cannot be compared with these. There are cattle of all kinds in great quantity and a rich pasturage for them."[18]

It is interesting to note how many of the different varieties of pulse were first cultivated in the ancient Near East, either in the Land of Israel or in the area adjoining it. Lentils, which are mentioned four times in the Bible, appear to have been domesticated in the Near East, where carbonized seeds have been discovered dating from 7000 or 6000 B.C.E. Likewise, the wild ancestor of the broad bean (*Vicia faba* L.) may also have originated in the Levant, as Israeli archaeologists have found seeds at a neolithic site in Lower Galilee that have been carbon dated to the period 6840 ± 50 B.C.E., while the broad bean is mentioned in the Bible (2 Samuel 17:27–29). Although the Bible made no reference to the common garden pea, it was, according to Michael Zohary, undoubtedly cultivated by the Israelites. Chick-peas were originally domesticated in Turkey, but carbonized remnants of chick-peas that have been dated to the Bronze Age have been found in Arad in the Negev. In many respects the food of the Israelite peasants seems to have resembled the diet of the medieval west European peasantry, which consisted principally of cereals and pulse.[19]

During the Israelite period, cooking pots were made of earthenware and were placed on clay stands built in a horseshoe shape, the opening being used to light the fire under the pot, or food was cooked in pots suspended from tripods. Both stews (*nezid*) and soups (*marak*) of pulse and other vegetables were prepared in these vessels, while garlic and onions were probably used in a similar way by the Babylonians to add flavor to the resulting dish. Through improved archaeological techniques and thanks to the porosity of these pots, it may be possible one day to evaluate accurately their past contents and to gain knowledge of the recipes of the Israelite peasant. So far, we do not know for certain whether the equivalent of *hummus*, a spread made from pureed chick-peas, or of the Egyptian *fool midammis*, a broad bean seasoned and simmered, existed in ancient Israel. Even more important, we cannot state for certain how often during the week a hot meal was cooked by the Israelite peasants. If we are to judge by the emphasis in the talmudic age on preparing hot dishes for the Sabbath, the inevitable conclusion must be that the Israelite peasants did not taste hot food every day. Confirming this was the rabbinic assumption that Gentiles also did not enjoy cooked dishes daily, because their ordinary cookery pots were not in frequent use.[20]

Vegetables

With the exception of pulse, vegetables played a minor role in the diet of the ancient Israelites. There were no root vegetables such as turnips, beets, and cabbages, nor were cucumbers, lettuce, or tomatoes known. A good idea of the food predilections of the Israelites can be gleaned from a much-quoted passage in Numbers 11:5, and the same food and seasonings, apart from fish, continued to be popular after the conquest of Eretz Israel: "We remember the fish, which we were wont to eat in Egypt for naught, the cucumbers, and the melons and leeks, and the onions and the garlic." The translation of the Hebrew word *kishuim* as cucumbers is an anachronism, however, as they were unknown to the ancient Egyptians. The Hebrew word referred to another member of the gourd family, identified by Zohary as the muskmelon (*Cucumus melo* L.) and by Feliks as chate melon, while the Hebrew word *avatihim* should be translated as watermelon, not melon. The view of medieval Jewish scholars and certain modern scholars identifying the *kishuim* of the Israelites with the Egyptian cucumber (*faqqus*) is somewhat dubious. During the biblical age, many of the pot herbs grew wild and were collected by the Israelite peasants for salads and soups, just as they are gathered today by the small Arab cultivators. Among the wild herbs that were selected were the garden rocket (2 Kings 4:39–40), mallow that was used in a famous soup from medieval times in Egypt, where it was called Jew's mallow (Job 6:6–7), dwarf chicory, and reichardia; the latter were bitter herbs classified in Arabic as *mureir* and in Hebrew as *merorim* and that were eaten with unleavened bread at Passover. Likewise, from a passage in Ruth, it appears that the Israelites dipped bread in vinegar to give it extra relish (Ruth 2:14). Bread eaten with onions formed the basic diet of the ancient Egyptians, while Herodotus claimed that the pyramids were built by laborers living on "radishes, onions and leeks." Without doubt, the Israelite peasants consumed their barley bread with similar tasty vegetables, and perhaps dipped it in oil as well as vinegar to aid the digestive process.[21]

Fruit

Olives and grapes remained important fruits in the biblical age, but the olives were utilized solely for the oil and the grapes principally for the wine and juice that was extracted from them. Moses bestowed a blessing on the tribe of Asher, which settled in the area later known as Upper Galilee, declaring that "he shall dip his foot in oil" (Deuteronomy 33:24), and the area became famous for its abundant production of olive oil throughout Israel's history. By far the most popular fruit was the fig, which was often eaten in the form of dried cakes, while early-ripening figs were regarded as a delicacy because of their sweetness. Particularly in winter, cakes of dried figs were regarded as a useful source of food; hence it was stated that Abigail sent David a present that in part consisted of two hundred cakes of dried figs, a pointer to their significance (1 Samuel 25:18). Unlike figs, dates were scarcely mentioned in the Bible, apart from a few references, especially to Jericho as "The City of Palms" or "Palm City," and were probably more valued for the juice that was extracted from them than as a source of food. Other fruits named in the Bible, such as the pomegranate, the sycamore fig that was consumed by the poor, and possibly the apple, were produced in limited quantities. The Bible also referred to a number of nuts, such as the almond, pistachio, and walnut. Date stones have been found in many strata at Jericho, particularly around 1600 B.C.E. and earlier, while R. S. Stewart Macalister discovered pomegranate rinds at Gezer in the layers of the Bronze Age (3000–2000 B.C.E.), and similar finds were made by Kathleen M. Kenyon in Canaanite Jericho.[22]

Despite doubts as to whether the fruit designated by the Hebrew word *tapuach* should be identified with the apple and not with some other fruit such as the apricot, both the leading experts Zohary and Feliks claim that the accepted identification is correct. This is partly because the Arabic word *tuffah* specifically referred to the apple tree and the ancient Egyptian papyri from the reign of Rameses II (1298–1235 B.C.E.) clearly show apple trees from the Nile delta and partly because all the incidental descriptive details contained in the biblical and rabbinic passages relating to the *tapuach* confirm the correctness of this identification. Moreover, Asaph Goor cited the Harris Papyrus, which demonstrated that the Egyptians imported raisins, pomegranates, carobs, and apples from the Holy Land from 1150 B.C.E. Incidentally, it was the Renaissance painters who first invented or popularized the notion that the tree of knowledge in the Garden of Eden was an apple tree.[23]

Beer and Wine

Barley was domesticated in the sixth millennium B.C.E., and the brewing of beer may have originated shortly after this. Malting the grain was the first process in beer production and was achieved by allowing the grains to germinate. Whereas beer was a popular drink in Mesopotamia 3,000 years ago, wine pressed from grapes was reserved for kings and noblemen until 1000 B.C.E. Spiced pomegranate juice mentioned in the Song of Songs also appears to have been an exotic and expensive drink. Although many examples of beer mugs with strainers to prevent roughage from pouring out have been found in those parts of Israel where the Philistines settled, the finds of such mugs have been sparse in the Israelite areas, an indication that the population were not frequent beer drinkers such as the Mesopotamians or Egyptians. Since the original center of viticulture was in Syria, the production of wine flourished in Israel, where the hill country was well suited to the cultivation of the vine, and grape wine was the favorite beverage of the ancient Israelites. Several different kinds of wine were mentioned in the Bible, including sparkling wine (Psalm 75:9), wine of Helbon, a place near Damascus (Ezekiel 27:18), and spiced wine (Song of Songs 8:2). However, the term *shechar* in the Bible (Deuteronomy 14:26) was related to the Akkadian word *sikaru* meaning date wine, a potent and widely consumed liquor in Egypt and Mesopotamia; in the latter country date wine eclipsed beer in popularity in the period 1700 to 600 B.C.E. It is doubtful whether the translation of *shechar* in the Authorized Version of the Bible as strong wine is correct. Added support for this interpretation that *shechar* means date wine comes from the Talmud, where the Aramaic word *shechar* is used to describe liquor produced from fermented dates, figs, or barley, but not from grapes.[24]

Milk and Honey

A well-known phrase in Bible is the promise to the children of Israel that they would inherit "a land flowing with milk and honey"; we must now turn to an elucidation of its meaning. According to Nogah Hareuveni, to prophets the phrase suggested a land overgrown with wild vegetation and not agricultural land that could easily be cultivated (Isaiah 7:21–24). It was a challenge to nomads to become farmers and skilled cultivators. From the milk, which was provided by goats rather than by cows, the population derived additional sources of fats and protein. Our view as to the importance of goats is supported by a talmudic legend which concluded that the spies' report of the condition of the land of Israel was not exaggerated, "for honey flowed from the trees under which the goats graze, out of whose udders poured milk, so that both milk and honey moistened the ground." In the ancient Near East only sour milk called *laban* was drunk, and fresh milk was rarely consumed. So too, the Israelites, like the bedouin, kept their milk in skin containers, and when these were emptied pieces of curdled milk still adhered to the walls of the bag, causing any fresh milk that was added to turn sour (Judges 5:25). Butter was made in churns, examples of which have been found dating from the fourth century B.C.E. in Beersheba, and the clarified butter that was in liquid form was used for cooking. *Himetu*, an Akkadian parallel form of the Hebrew *hemah*, has been translated as *ghee*, an Indian term, or was the equivalent of the Arabic word *samnah*. Whereas cheese was scarcely mentioned in the Bible, the only references being to hard cheese, *gevinah*, in Job 10:10, and to a soft cheese, *harizei halav*, or curds, elsewhere, there were many detailed discussions on the subject of cheese in the Talmud that proves this item was added to the diet of the Jewish people at a later date.[25]

The principal source of honey in ancient Israel was not the product of wild bees, as honey obtained from this source was a rarity, but was usually extracted in the form of a thick syrup from grapes, figs, and dates. The Jerusalem Talmud in *Bikkurim* 1:3 specifically stated "honey that is dates." This syrup is known as *dibs* in Arabic and was no doubt similar to the date syrup or *hullake* that the Jews from the Middle East utilize on Passover, instead of the *haroset* eaten by the Ashkenazim on the same festival. It has been pointed out that the biblical expressions "honey out of the crag" (Deuteronomy 32:13) and "honey out of the rocks" (Psalm 81:16) refer to the honey of the fig tree that grew in such places. Wild bees commonly made their nests in rocks, however, and there is a cave painting from Spain showing prehistoric honey gatherers scaling rocks to collect honey, so that these passages may refer to this method of collecting honey, a viewpoint supported by modern anthropological evidence. According to D'vora Ben Shaul, the ancients "perfected techniques of heating the rock with fire and then dowsing it with cold water to split the rock, drilling with primitive drills and smoking the bees out if possible"; and there are still colonies of wild bees in Israel. Further, it has been argued that honey from domesticated bees was first mentioned in 2 Chronicles 31:5 under the category "produce of the field," although this was a source of honey that was to become significant later. A nineteenth-century volume on Palestine described the hives of the Arab peasants that were conceivably of ancient design. "They are cylinders of basket-work, covered inside and outside with a plaster of mud, and are placed one over the other horizontally, and then roofed with thatch. . . . In due time the clay at one end is removed, and the honey is drawn out with a hook." There was good reason for this biblical emphasis on the abundance of honey in Israel because the sugar was an important complementary calorie source and a substitute for fats.[26]

Manna and Quails

The Children of Israel, during their years of wandering in the wilderness, were sustained on manna and for a short while had their craving for meat satisfied by the provision of quails. From the time of St. Anthony (c. 250–355 c.e.), the monks of the monastery of St. Catherine's in Sinai believed that the biblical manna was a sweet, sticky substance secreted by insects onto tamarisk trees that grew in the region. More recently F. S. Bodenheimer ascertained that *man* was a general term used by Arabs for plant lice, whereas the honeydew they secrete was called *man-es-simma* (the manna of heaven). In Kurdistan a harvest of thousands of kilograms of man was gathered in June and July of each year. The honeydew that was collected was used to prepare a popular delicacy sold in the bazaars of Baghdad under the name of *man*. This is not a cogent explanation, as the quantities produced in Sinai are small and can hardly be substituted for bread, unlike the biblical manna; nor does the secretion of the insects possess all the features of the biblical manna that "was like coriander seed, white; and the taste of it was like wafers made with honey." Manna has also been identified with a lichen, *Lecanora esculenta*, a plant organism composed of fungus and alga, but as this species has never been found in Israel, the hypothesis is equally unconvincing.[27]

Large flocks of quail regularly migrate from northern countries to Africa in the autumn and return northward in the spring. Flying across the Mediterranean they often become exhausted and are easily caught in nets in Sinai. Until the 1930s and 1940s millions of quails were seized in this fashion, although since then their numbers have been depleted. Maimonides noted that "many people who indulge greatly in eating quail meat develop cramps in the muscles because of the hellebore which is the nourishment of the quail . . ."; other modern research indicates that the quail acquire toxic agents in a different way, so this may account for the illness of the Israelites when they overindulged in the eating of quail in the wilderness.[28]

Conclusion

The daily diet of the Israelite peasantry in the biblical period consisted chiefly of bread, the staff of life, parched corn, and pulse, while unlike the surrounding nations probably cheese was eaten in small quanti-

ties, and more definitely beer was an item absent from their menu.
Even if the preparation of cooked food was not a daily occurrence,
beans and lentils must have been cooked in pots on stands several
times a week, just as "Jacob gave Esau bread and pottage of lentils . . ." (Genesis 25:29–34). Curdled goat's milk was drunk from time
to time; but fruit, apart from figs and to a lesser extent grapes and
watermelons, was eaten infrequently. Meat was an even rarer item,
being reserved for special occasions. Much fruit and vegetables were
consumed raw, as cooked food was something of a treat. Despite Jean
Botérro's defense of the diet of the ancient Mesopotamian peasantry,
the daily diet of the bulk of the Israelite population must have been
tasteless and monotonous but perhaps enlivened with the vinegar and
the dash of salt they added to the food. As Job said, "Is tasteless food
eaten without salt?" (Job 6:6).

At Yale three Babylonian tablets dating from 1700 B.C.E. have recently
been deciphered that have been found to be the oldest extant collection
of culinary recipes. They reveal that the ruling elite in Mesopotamia
almost 3,700 years ago possessed a cuisine with an amazing degree of
sophistication; unfortunately a large number of technical terms cannot
be understood, making it difficult to reconstruct the dishes because the
actual consistency of the ingredients in the dishes appears to be
beyond our comprehension. Like the Mesopotamians, the ancient
Israelites were accustomed to add onion, garlic, and leek to their stews
and soups to give them a succulent flavor. On the one hand, the
Mesopotamian collection of recipes has demonstrated that the cuisine
of the royal courts in the Near East was already elaborate and sophisticated 700 years prior to the inauguration of the Israelite monarchy in
1020 B.C.E., so it is fair to assume that dishes of a similar complexity
must have been served at the tables of King Solomon and his successors; and we know that in an earlier age Samuel had a cook who
prepared sumptuous dishes for some thirty guests (1 Samuel 9:22–24).
Further, King David's officials, who were in charge of the wine cellars,
the wild olives and sycamore figs, the oil stores, and cattle were named
in 1 Chronicles 27:27–31, and it is almost certain that the royal kitchen
had an equally complex organization. On the other hand, the recipes in
the Yale collection show that milk and blood were added by the
Mesopotamians to their meat stews and in this respect the cuisine of
the Israelites under the influence of the Dietary Laws must have been
fundamentally different and unlike that of their neighbors.[29]

2

THE DIETARY LAWS

INTRODUCTION

The rabbis regarded the Dietary Laws as divine statutes that had to be obeyed and that were not open to human understanding; other Jewish authorities believed that the reasons for the Dietary Laws could be examined, even if no completely plausible explanations could be proffered. Philo (c. 30 B.C.E.–40 C.E.), an Alexandrian Jewish philosopher, suggested:

> The lawgiver sternly forbade all animals of land, sea or air whose flesh is the finest and fattest, like that of pigs and scaleless fish, knowing that they set a trap for the most slavish of the senses, the taste, and that they produce gluttony, an evil dangerous to both soul and body, for gluttony begets indigestion, which is the source of all illnesses and infirmities. . . . Yet there is a midway path . . . between rigorous austerity and voluptuous practice. He relaxed the overstrained and tightened the law, allowing them to eat the gentler tame animals which live on the fruit of the earth and do not attack the life of others, and forbidding them vile carnivorous beasts.

Philo discerned a symbolic message behind the permission granted to the Jews to eat animals that chewed the cud and that possessed cloven hooves. For instance, man increased in wisdom only as he repeated and chewed over what he studied. So, too, it was argued in the letter of Aristeas, another Alexandrian thinker, that all our actions must make exact ethical distinctions and be directed toward righteousness, something about which the cloven-hoofed animals symbolically reminded us. Early rabbinic literature and the New Testament on the whole, however, rejected the allegorical explanations of the Alexandrian Jewish philosophers. Nonetheless, the symbolic explanation of the basis of the Dietary Laws has been developed by modern anthropologists with great intellectual élan, particularly by Jean Soler and Mary Douglas, and we shall shortly survey their ideas.[1]

17

Maimonides (1135–1204), who was both a physician and a rabbinic expert, in his *Guide of the Perplexed* agreed that the biblical laws of *kashrut* were designed "to train us in the mastery of our appetites" but thought there was a valid hygienic explanation for the rules. "All the food which the Torah has forbidden us to eat has some bad and damaging effect on the body. . . ." The pig was prohibited because it was "very dirty and feed on dirty things . . . the law requires that one remove filth out of sight even in the field and in a military camp . . . and all the more within cities. Now if swine were used for food, market-places and even houses would be dirtier than latrines. . . . You know the dictum: the mouth of a swine is like walking excrement. . . ." So, too, Maimonides declared that "the fat of the intestines, too, makes us full, spoils the digestion, and produces cold and thick blood. . . . Blood, on the one hand, and carcasses of beasts that have died, on the other, are also difficult to digest and constitute a harmful nourishment. . . ." Nachmanides (1194–1268) followed this line of thinking, commenting on Leviticus 11:9:

> Now the reason for specifying fins and scales is that fish which have fins and scales get nearer to the surface of the water and are found more generally in fresh water areas. . . . Those without fins and scales usually live in the lower muddy strata which are exceedingly moist and where there is no heat. . . . They breed in musty swamps and eating them can be injurious to health.

Another medieval authority repudiated such an explanation, stating: "The dietary laws are not, as some have suggested, motivated by therapeutic considerations, God forbid! Were it so, the Torah would be denigrated to the status of a minor medical treatise and worse."[2]

THE STRUCTURALIST APPROACH: MARY DOUGLAS AND JEAN SOLER

In the first chapter of Genesis, the diet of mankind at the dawn of history was deemed to be vegetarian, and although meat eating was not specifically forbidden, its prohibition should be inferred (U. Cassuto). "Behold, I have given you every plant yielding seed which is upon the face of all the earth and every tree with seed in its fruit; you shall have them for food" (Genesis 1:29). God's food according to Jean Soler are living creatures that were consumed in the form of sacrifices, while edible plants constituted the food of man. It is interesting that some of the Church fathers adopted this view that Adam was not permitted to eat meat; and, for instance, Theophilus asserted that "there were no carnivorous animals before Adam's fall." At the time of the Flood there was a new dispensation for mankind. "Every moving thing that lives shall be food for you; as I gave you green plants, I give you everything" (Genesis 9:3). If, however, man was to avail himself of this concession, he was to refrain from eating the blood of slaughtered animals (Genesis 9:4), as blood incorporates the life force, which if eaten by man, according to Soler, would make him God's equal; but surely it was also forbidden in line with rabbinic argument because it reduced man to the level of animals and made him aggressive and lusting after the blood of his fellow men. Therefore, there was an absolute prohibition on the eating of blood.[3]

During the wanderings of the children of Israel in the wilderness the Torah continued to hold meat eating in low esteem despite the concession that had been allowed to human frailty after the Flood. We can best see this in the passages concerning the gathering of manna, the ideal nourishment, and the criticism of the Israelites for feasting on quails. The Lord told Moses that the Israelites would eat flesh for "a whole month, until it comes out of your nostrils, and it be loathsome unto you . . ." (Numbers 11:20).

Under Moses the eating of meat continued to have a stigma attached to it, but a distinction was made between clean animals, which it was permissible to eat, and unclean animals, which were forbidden as food. In three separate passages in the Bible the Dietary Laws were linked to the concept of holiness (Exodus 22:30, Leviticus 11:44–45, and Deuteronomy 4:21). Here Mary Douglas was elaborating on a passage in an earlier study by Professor Siegfried Stein, who stated that "the Holiness of God is said to be the determining cause of the legislation [relating to the Dietary Laws], the holiness and separateness of the people is its purpose." According to Douglas,

> Holiness is exemplified by completeness. Holiness requires that individuals shall conform to the class to which they belong. And holiness requires that different classes of things shall not be confused. . . . To be holy is to be whole, to be one; holiness is unity, integrity, perfection of the individual and of the kind. The dietary rules merely develop the metaphor of holiness on the same lines.

Each creature had to be perfect in its own element: animals on earth, fish in water, and birds in the sky, thereby tying the classification of animals as food to the opening account in the Bible of the Creation. Here is the originality of the approach of Mary Douglas and Jean Soler. Moreover, the Jews were commanded to be a "kingdom of priests" and all the Dietary Laws were equally applicable to the whole Jewish people. Unlike for the Egyptians, there were not special dietary regulations applicable merely to priests and null and void for the rest of the population.[4]

All clean animals had to be herbivorous and to live off vegetation. To ensure this, they had to chew the cud, have a divided hoof, and be cloven-footed, since hoofed creatures have not the means of seizing prey and must, therefore, subsist on a vegetarian diet. Both Douglas and Soler stressed in different ways how the Israelites, who were originally sheep and goat pastoralists, used these domestic animals as models to which all other animals permissible as food had to conform. Additionally, these animals had to be slaughtered by severing the major blood vessels in the neck, a method known as *shechitah,* and by salting the meat of the slaughtered animal to drain off the remaining blood. Carnivorous animals were doubly unclean as food as they fed on other living creatures; there could be no atonement by offering their blood in a sacrifice and thereby desacralizing them and making them into a permitted source of food. According to Soler, pigs and boars had hoofed feet and were herbivorous, but they did not chew the cud and for this reason failed to qualify as permitted food. Less convincing is the argument of Douglas, who suggested that the Israelites based their typology of permitted animals on the distinctive characteristics of the cow, sheep, and goat or on their wild equivalents and that the wild boar failed to find a place in the latter class. Douglas has been criticized for using both the categories in Leviticus, animals that are cloven-footed and chew the cud, to distinguish between clean and unclean animals and those in the Creation account in Genesis, where each creature has to be perfect in its own sphere, when there does not appear to be a complete congruence between the two sets of concepts. Both pigs and camels were actual quadrupeds walking on the earth, but were nonetheless not kosher animals.[5]

Fins and scales ensured that fish had a proper means of locomotion in water and were, therefore, permitted food, but shellfish were forbidden as they had legs like a beast and could live in more than one element. Birds had to fly through the air if they were to be a permissible source of food and could not live for much of their time in another element such as water. That is why such birds as the heron and swan were a prohibited source of food, while other birds that lived off prey and were carnivorous, such as the eagle, were also forbidden. Locusts, which moved like four-legged animals, were a permitted source of food and were particularly valued by the Yemenite Jews, who staged hunts for the big red and yellow locusts that were also occasions for courting; and Jews in the ancient community of Djerba in Tunisia happily consumed locusts until the eighteenth century. Elsewhere, the eating of locusts was banned by Jewish authorities because they claimed that the species of locust allowed by biblical law could not be clearly distinguished. Later, rabbinic authorities used these dietary regulations as a frame of reference to decide whether or not a new domestic species of animal or bird was kosher; for instance, in the seventeenth century there was a vigorous debate on the merits of the turkey. Despite these concessions to human weakness, the Torah and the prophets came down firmly in favor of a vegetarian diet. Indeed, Isaiah looked forward to a messianic age when "the lion shall eat straw like the ox," when, in fact, there would be no carnivorous animals.[6]

A variant of the Mary Douglas-Jean Soler hypothesis has been presented by Michael Carroll, who emphasized the distinction drawn by Lévi-Strauss between nature and culture. Carroll has argued that the insects mentioned in Leviticus 11:29–30 that invaded the home, such as moths, which gnawed clothes, and those insects, such as bees, gnats, and hornets, that attacked humans were forbidden as food by the Dietary Laws, precisely because they had escaped from nature and invaded the realm of man (culture). Similarly, carnivorous birds and animals confused the distinction between nature and culture, as meat eating was only appropriate for humans, after the special dispensation granted to them. Nonetheless, Carroll's theory has been criticized as being weak with regard to its coverage of water creatures, as it was not clear how shellfish and other creatures that lived in the water blurred the distinction between culture and nature.

THE ECOLOGICAL APPROACH: MARVIN HARRIS

Another approach to the Dietary Laws is the ecological one that has recently been championed by Marvin Harris. He asserted that many ancient states gave the highest priority to the production of cereal crops and vegetables, as the calorie return from them was ten times greater than that obtainable from animal production and could support a larger population. Remains of the domesticated pig have been uncovered in Neolithic villages throughout the Middle East. At Atlit-Yam, an 8,000-year-old Neolithic village near Haifa has been excavated under the sea, and among the wild animals consumed by its inhabitants were the gazelle, the deer, and the pig. Similarly, at the prehistoric town of Ain Ghazal, some 9,000 years old near Amman in Jordan, it has been found that 45 species of wild animal were eaten, but especially several kinds of gazelle and the pig, besides cattle. At the Middle Bronze Age (2100–1550 B.C.E.) sites of Emek Refaim in the suburbs of Jerusalem and of Sasa in Upper Galilee the bones of pigs (at

Sasa 11 percent of the bones), sheep, goats, and a small number of cattle have been revealed. Both these sites still dated from a period prior to the Israelite conquest of Canaan. According to Marvin Harris, the natural habitat of the pig was the forest, riverbanks, and the edges of swamps, where it could find a plentiful supply of tubers, roots, fruit, and nuts. Unlike cattle, sheep, or goats, pigs could not adequately digest husks, stalks, leaves, and grass, and their milk was not so useful. Nor could pigs regulate their bodily temperatures by internal means, as they are unable to sweat and have to rely on an external source of moisture; or if this is not available, they utilize their own feces and urine to keep cool. Hence their propensity to disease, although this is denied by Marvin Harris, who asserted that cattle transmit equally lethal diseases. Harris has further claimed that the taboos against pig eating among the Jews were a response to population pressures in the ancient Near East, where the raising of pigs became too costly; that in the dynastic period in Egypt there was increasing prejudice against its consumption; and that after 2400 B.C.E. pork became taboo in Mesopotamia and was no longer relished.[7]

In criticism of this ecological theory, it could be said that recent archaeological evidence has shown that despite priestly taboos the production of pigs was widespread throughout the cities of ancient Egypt, such as Memphis, Rameses, and Armana, and that even pigpens were provided to keep the pigs cool. The lower classes in Egypt ignored these dietary prohibitions, which were probably observed by the priests and the aristocracy. Herodotus wrote that "pigs are considered unclean. If anyone touches a pig accidently in passing, he will at once plunge into the river, clothes and all, to wash himself; and swineherds, though of purely Egyptian blood, are the only people in the country who never enter a temple, nor is there any intermarriage between them and the rest of the community. . . ." Whereas pig raising flourished in Mesopotamia under the Sumerians, pork was no longer eaten when the Semites became predominant in the area, so that the decline of pig production must be linked to cultural and religious ideals. Similarly, Owen Lattimore suggested that as the Philistines ate pigs and shellfish, the Israelites, who wished to maintain their cultural independence and distance as a people, had strict prohibitions against the consumption of these foods. Likewise, the Mongol rulers had imposed strict taboos against eating pig and fish to prevent their people's absorption by the Chinese. On the other hand, it has been argued that the law codes in the Pentateuch showed no special aversion for the pig; it was merely one among many prohibited species. Another flaw in this ecological theory is that the pig was prohibited among the Israelites, who lived in the Judean and Samarian hills where extensive forests still existed in Gilead and Bashan east of the

Jordan, but flourished among the Philistines, who dwelt on the fertile coastal plain, when according to the ecological theory the reverse situation should have been the case. After recent excavations at Ashkelon, it was reported that "the Philistine stratum had already revealed considerable remains of pigs, something not found in the Israelite settlements of the time, even though, says [Professor] Stager [of Harvard], the wooded hills offered better conditions for pig-raising than the coastal plain." More and more the weight of the evidence points to cultural influences as being of paramount importance in the adoption of the Dietary Laws, not the environment that varied markedly in the ancient Near East.[8]

What further light do recent archaeological excavations in Israel shed on this subject? On Mount Ebal, Israeli archaeologists have discovered an important center of the Israelite settlement period dating from the thirteenth century to the twelfth century B.C.E. Among the bones discovered near the altar were those of animals designated as clean in the Bible, namely cattle, sheep, goats, and fallow deer. Israelites partially succumbed to the pressures of their neighbors, however, and did not always eat ritually pure food. In 1983, when Yigal Shiloh excavated the City of David, he found evidence of the bones of both wild and domesticated pig and catfish, another nonkosher item, all of which were probably eaten by the Jewish inhabitants of the city. The only other plausible explanation for this is that the food was consumed in the households of foreign merchants or mercenaries living in Jerusalem. Again, when Yigael Yadin excavated an Israelite citadel at Hazor that was overwhelmed by the Assyrian army in the eighth century B.C.E., he was surprised to discover the bones of a partially domesticated species of pig that may have been left by the victorious Assyrian army but that may have been tasted by the Israelites. Literary evidence supports the view that the priests and prophets had to battle to convince the Israelite population to forsake the heathen cults and the forbidden foods that were associated with them. According to George Heider, Israelite law forbade the consumption of pork because its ritual eating was connected with participation "in the Canaanite cult of the dead." The wild boar was considered to be a sacred animal in the Syrian and Phoenician cults, while the Egyptians under the influence of Phoenician cultic practice sacrificed pigs to Dionysus and the Moon. The Greeks were similarly swayed, according to Herodotus, who was born between 490 and 480 B.C.E. Isaiah, in texts that have been dated after 550 B.C.E., exclaimed that the Lord was provoked by the renegades, who ate "swine's flesh, and broth of abominable things in their vessels" (Isaiah 65:2–4). The prophet warned that "they that sanctify themselves, and purify themselves in the gardens behind one tree in the midst, eating swine's flesh, and the abomination, and the mouse, shall be consumed together, saith the Lord" (Isaiah 66:17).[9]

THE RITUAL SLAUGHTER OF ANIMALS: SHECHITAH

The slaying of domestic animals in the Bible was denoted by the use of two terms, zebah (zibu, the old Babylonian word for cooked meat offered to the gods), meaning to slaughter or to slaughter for sacrifice, and sht, meaning to butcher, which some scholars have interpreted as referring to profane slaughter. To be able to participate in a feast at which meat was eaten, the ancient Israelites had to slaughter an animal on an altar, which was regarded as the Deity's table. The blood, the life-essence of the slaughtered animal, was poured onto the altar's sides, representing a return of the blood to the Lord, who could alone bestow on mankind a gift of meat from the animal's carcass. Moreover, it was ordained in Leviticus chapter 17 that so long as certain parts of its fat were burnt on the altar and its blood was also sprinkled on the altar an animal merely had to be slaughtered near to an altar at the entrance to the Tent of Meeting. Unless these requirements were meticulously observed, the participants at the feast were regarded as "eating meat together with the blood" or "eating the blood," both of which were serious infringements of the divine order. If these requirements were not met, "blood shall be imputed unto that man; he hath shed blood; and that man shall be cut off from among his people" (Leviticus 17:4). There was an even earlier warning in Genesis, where it was said: "You must not, however, eat flesh with its life-blood in it" (Genesis 9:4).[10]

Further, when King Saul was informed that his army was butchering slaughtered cattle on the ground, he was concerned because "they ate [flesh] with the blood," which caused great offense to the Lord, and he ordered his soldiers to slaughter the cattle on a rock, which served as an improvised altar (1 Samuel 31–35). Among ancient peoples the absolute prohibition in Israel against the tasting of blood was unique, although there were limited examples of this in the Graeco-Roman world, but not among the Babylonians.[11]

In Deuteronomy chapter 12 it was decreed that sacrifices were to take place only at one central shrine, later the Temple. "But whenever you desire, you may slaughter and eat meat in any of your settlements, according to the blessing which the Lord has granted you. The unclean and the clean may partake of it, as of the gazelle and deer" (Deuteronomy 12:15). So too, Ezekiel denounced "the eating [of meat] on mountain tops," that is, on rival shrines outside Jerusalem. The killing of animals for domestic consumption was legalized, provided that nobody "partook of the blood; you shall pour it out on the ground like water" (Deuteronomy 12:16).

We previously mentioned the term *sht*, which appeared 79 times in the Bible, although somewhat surprisingly not in Deuteronomy at all. The key to this seeming incongruity lies in Deuteronomy 12:21, where it was stated that "if the place where the Lord has chosen to establish his name is too far from you, you may slaughter any of the cattle or sheep that the Lord gives you, as I have instructed you; and you may eat to your heart's content in your settlements." It has been suggested by Jacob Milgrom that the correct interpretation of this passage was that the technique of profane slaughter should follow the already established method of sacrificial slaughter, a point with which early rabbinic commentators were in agreement, as witness the Sifre's comments on the same verse. Moreover, according to Milgrom, the Hebrew term *sht* is similar to Arabic words meaning to "slit the throat" and "throat"; and the true meaning of the Hebrew word was probably "slaughtering by cutting the throat." If this is the case, the ritual slaughtering of cattle, sheep, and goats may be traced back to the earliest periods of Israel's history. Reflecting the tradition in Deuteronomy, the Mishnah pronounced that "all may slaughter and at any time and with any implement," which included a hand-sickle, a flint, or a reed knife, but not with "a reaping-sickle or a saw or teeth or the finger-nails. . . ." The Mishnah further stipulated that for slaughtering to be correct, both the gullet and the windpipe of the animal had to be cut, so that the principal blood vessels were severed (*Hullin* 2:4).[12]

Nonetheless, birds in the biblical period were not always treated as being on the same level as domestic animals; hence in Leviticus 5:8 it was stated that a priest, when sacrificing a turtledove or a pigeon, could pinch the head of the bird at its nape without severing it. This verse was elucidated by a rabbinic discussion in the Mishnah. "If he slaughtered [by cutting] at the back of the neck, what he slaughters is invalid, but if he wrung off [the head of the bird] from the back of the neck, it is valid" (*Hullin* 1:4). Moreover, R. Judah b.Ila'i says: "[Not] unless he cut through the veins [of the neck of the bird]. [If he cut through only] the half of either [the windpipe or the gullet] of a bird . . . what he slaughters is invalid; but if [he cut through] the greater part of one in a bird, and the greater part of them both in a beast, what he slaughters is valid" (*Hullin* 2:1). Further, in Leviticus 17:13, it was decreed that when an Israelite or a stranger hunted an animal or a bird that was permissible to eat, he should "pour out its blood and cover it with earth."

The rabbis harmonized and clarified these anomalies by extending the method of ritual slaughter, *shechitah*, ordained by the Oral Law to all categories of clean animals and birds. Henceforth, birds could no longer be slaughtered by merely having their necks pinched, nor could animals be trapped as game. Under rabbinic law following the passage in Leviticus, the blood of game and birds had to be covered with earth and ashes, but this rule did not extend to the blood of cattle. In Leviticus 22:8 it was declared that a priest was not to partake of the flesh of an animal that had died (*nevelah*) or was torn by beasts (*trefah*), while similar sentiments were voiced by Ezekiel (Ezekiel 44:31). In Exodus 22:30 and Deuteronomy 14:21, however, this pro-hibition was extended to all the Israelites, as witness the passage in Exodus we have just cited: "You shall be men holy to Me: you must not eat flesh torn by the beasts [*trefah*] in the field; you shall cast it to the dogs." In the Mishnah, these key terms were redefined. "That which becomes invalid through its manner of slaughter is *Nevelah;* but if the manner of slaughter was proper and some other matter rendered it invalid, it becomes *Trefah*" (*Hullin* 3:1). According to the Mishnah in tractate *Hullin,* it was mainly defects in the organs, particularly the lungs in cattle, and limbs that rendered an animal *trefah.*[13]

Further, the Torah prohibited Israelites from consuming the fat of an animal, although the fat of game and birds was not forbidden. Hence the later popularity of goose fat as a cooking medium among Jews in Eastern Europe. "And the Lord spoke to Moses, saying: Speak to the Israelite people thus: You shall eat no fat of ox or sheep or goat. . . . If anyone eats the fat of animals from which offerings by fire may be made to the Lord, the person who eats it shall be cut off from his kin" (Leviticus 7:22–25). The fat of any animals that had been sacrificed in the Temple was regarded by the rabbis as forbidden fat, as it was originally burnt on the altar. Most of this prohibited or hard fat that was layered was located in the hindquarters of the animal and could be removed only by a process known as porging. The distinguished Venetian rabbi Leon of Modena (1571–1648) wrote:

> Jews do not eat the fat of beef, lamb or goat . . . and therefore they use all care in taking away all the fat and this sinew out of all the beasts they eat. Whence it is, that in many places in Italy and Germany especially, they do not eat the hindquarters; because this sinew is in them, and a great deal of fat, which requires much exactness to be taken away clean; and there are but a few that can do it as it should be.

Whereas in the medieval Rhineland the consumption of certain cate-gories of suet was permitted, in the Slavonic lands from where the rabbinic traditions of Polish Jewry were derived this was banned. It is interesting to note that Mrs. Esther Levy's *Jewish Cookery Book* published in Philadelphia in 1871, which followed the rules of *kashrut* and which was based on the cuisine of German Jewry, had a recipe for a Purim pudding made with suet. Although the Bible seemed to imply that the fat tail of sheep was a forbidden category of food (Leviticus 3:9), among the oriental Jews the rabbis permitted the tails of nonsacrificial sheep to be eaten, while the Karaites followed a strict biblical interpretation and banned the consumption of this delicacy. Both the fifth-century writer Herodotus and the Mishnah mentioned special carts used by shepherds to support the heavy tails of sheep and keep them intact (*Shabbat* 5:4).[14]

Moreover, because of Jacob's fight with the angel and the injury to his thigh in combat, the sciatic nerve or tendon was prohibited as food (Genesis 32:33). In addition, as part of the process of *shechitah*, the blood was removed from the animal by the excision of the large veins and of certain bloody tissues, while later the meat was salted to drain away any remaining blood.[15]

THE EXTENSION OF THE DIETARY LAWS

Ezra and Nehemiah and the later prophets, Haggai, Zechariah, and Malachi, all books written after the return of the Jewish people from the Babylonian Exile after 538 B.C.E., stressed the fundamental importance of a self-imposed segregation of Jews from the foreign elements that had settled in Judah; a strict observance of the priestly dues, gifts, and tithes that were delivered to or collected for the Temple; and a scrupulous adherence to the laws of ritual purity, perhaps under the influence of Parsiism. Ezra warned that the people, including the priests and the Levites, had not "kept themselves apart from the foreign population and from the abominable practices . . ." (Ezra 9:1); further they were advised that "the land which you are entering and will possess is a polluted land, polluted by the foreign population with their abominable practices, which have made it unclean from end to end" (Ezra 9:11). Around 460 B.C.E. Malachi, the last of the prophets, denounced his countrymen because "the table [altar] of the Lord is polluted, and the fruit thereof, is contemptible" (Malachi 1:12).

The more the Temple cult developed over the next couple of centuries, the more the regulations concerning ritual purity flourished, with the consequence that strangers were excluded. A late passage in Isaiah as well in other prophets emphasized this theme: "Awake, awake; put on thy strength, Zion; put on thy beautiful garments, Jerusalem, the holy city: for henceforth there shall no more come into thee the

uncircumcised and the unclean" (Isaiah 52:1). According to Max
Weber, "In Israel, originally ritualistic segregation from strangers was
totally absent. . . . The casuistic elaboration of their dietary and butchering ritual falls only into late antiquity, but basically goes back to the
exilic priestly teaching." Moreover, Nehemiah made the leaders of the
population undertake an oath not to intermarry, to keep the Sabbath,
and "to bring to the priests the first kneading of our dough, and the
first fruit of every tree, of the new wine and of the oil, to the store-rooms
in the house of our God; and to bring to the Levites the tithes from our
land, for it is the Levites, who collect the tithes in all our farming
villages" (Nehemiah 10:37).[16]

One of the chief points of conten-tion between the Jews and the
Philistines, who were of Greek origin, as evidenced by their mono-
chrome earthenware, which was like Mycenaean pottery, was the
attempt to halt the introduction of Greek cults in Judaea. At this stage,
although the Jews were rebuked for sacrificing pigs in imitation of the
Philistines, other cultic malpractices were also flayed by the prophets.
All the relevant passages in the Bible relating to this strife appear to
cluster in the period between the sixth and the fourth centuries B.C.E. It
has been suggested that Zechariah chapters 9–14 were tacked onto the
book in the mid-fourth century B.C.E. Here the prophet declared that
". . . I will cut off the pride of the Philistines. And I will take away the
blood out of his mouth, and the detestable things from between his
teeth . . ." (Zechariah 9:6–7). This prophecy was a stern invitation to
the Philistine strongholds of Askelon, Ashdod, Gaza, and Ekron to
observe the Dietary Laws and appears to echo late passages in Isaiah
chapters 65 and 66, which we quoted earlier. The criticisms of Isaiah
and Zechariah of their neighbors presaged the much sharper conflict
between the Maccabees and the later more robust Hellenizers.[17]

Unlike their oriental neighbors, the Jewish people absorbed Greek
philosophy and science without abandoning their own cultural independence and identity as a nation. According to the Book of Maccabees, "Burnt offerings, sacrifices, and libations in the temple were
forbidden; sabbaths and feast days to be defiled. Altars, idols, and
sacred precincts were to be established; swine and other unclean
beasts to be offered in sacrifice. . . . Yet many in Israel found strength
to resist, taking a determined stand against eating unclean food" (1
Maccabees 1:45–62). Further:

> The Gentiles filled the temple with licentious revelry; they took their
> pleasure with prostitutes . . . in the sacred precincts. They also
> brought forbidden things inside, and heaped the altar with impure
> offerings prohibited by the law. . . . On the monthly celebration of the
> king's birthday, the Jews were driven by brute force to eat the entrails

of the sacrificial victims; and on the feast of Dionysus they were forced
to wear ivy-wreaths and join the procession in his honour" (2 Maccabees 6:4–7).

The Second Book of Maccabees spoke of the heroic action of Eleazar,
"one of the leading teachers of the law, a man of great age and
distinguished bearing. He was being forced to open his mouth and eat
pork, but preferring an honourable death to an unclean life, he spat it
out and voluntarily submitted to the flogging, as indeed men should
act who have the courage to refuse to eat forbidden food even for the
love of life" (2 Maccabees 6:18–28). Clearly, it appears that Antiochus
attempted to establish the worship of the Queen of Heaven in the
Temple as well as the cult of Dionysus, which alarmed the Jews. In
particular the sacrifice of pigs was associated with Dionysian rites.[18]

Similarly, during the struggle against Rome, Josephus recounted
that the Essenes "were racked and twisted, burnt and broken, and
made to pass through every instrument of torture to induce them to
blaspheme their lawgiver and eat some forbidden thing: yet they
refused to yield to either demand. . . . Smiling in their agonies . . . they
cheerfully resigned their souls, confident that they would receive them
back." So, too, Ernest Weisenberg has shown how the Romans, when
they were besieging Jerusalem in 70 c.e., instead of a suitable sacrificial
animal, exchanged by a subterfuge two pigs for baskets of gold for the
daily *Tamid* offering in the Temple. This was a calculated insult to
undermine the morale of the Jewish defenders, and from that date
onward the offering of the *Tamid* sacrifice in the Second Temple, the
focal point of Jewish national resistance, ceased. That was why,
according to the Mishnah, the rabbis responded by proclaiming that "a
Jew must not rear pigs anywhere" (*Bava Kamma* 7:7).[19]

Both the Books of the Apocrypha, some of which were written before
the revolt of the Maccabees, and the Book of Daniel, which was
composed in 166–165 b.c.e., the date of its inception, stressed the
importance of refraining from partaking of Gentile food and of adhering
to the Dietary Laws. We are told, "But Daniel purposed in his heart that
he would not defile himself with the portion of the king's meat, nor
with the wine which he drank. . . . Thus Melzar took away the portion
of their meat, and the wine that they should drink; and gave them
pulse" (Daniel 1:8, 16). Similar sentiments were voiced in the Greek
Additions to Esther: "I, thy servant, have not eaten at Haman's table;
I have not graced a banquet of the king or touched the wine of his
drink-offering . . ." (Esther 14:17). Even earlier than Daniel, and
perhaps as early as the fourth century b.c.e., Tobit declared that "after
the deportation to Assyria when I was taken captive and came to
Nineveh, everyone of my kindred and nation ate gentile food; but I

myself scrupulously avoided doing so" (Tobit 1:10). Again, in the Book
of Judith, a work composed between the fourth and second centuries
B.C.E., it was related that "Holophernes then commanded them to bring
her in where his silver was set out, and he ordered a meal to be served
for her from his own food and wine. But Judith said 'I will not eat any
of it, in case I should be breaking our law' " (Judith 12:2). Earlier,
Judith "gave her maid a skin of wine and a flask of oil; then she filled
a bag with roasted grain, cakes of dried figs and the finest bread . . ."
(Judith 10:5). So, too, when Judas the Maccabee escaped into the
desert with nine companions, "They remained living on what vegetation they found, so as to have no share in the pollution" (2 Maccabees
5:27). Jubilees, which was written before the revolt of the Maccabees,
summed up the position in Jewish law from a radical viewpoint:
"Separate thyself from the nations, do not eat with them, do not act
according to their deeds, and do not associate with them, because their
work is uncleanliness, all their ways are contamination, detestation
and abomination. They slaughter their sacrifices to the dead and pray
to demons" (Jubilees 22:16).

What conclusions are to be drawn from these passages in the
Apocrypha and how are they to be linked with the new framework for
the Dietary Laws outlined in the Mishnah? We would suggest that the
basic issues are the choice of clean animals for consumption, which
had to be slaughtered in accordance with the laws of *shechitah* and the
strict regulations governing the ritual purity of grain, oil, and wine, the
essential products of the land of Israel that were brought as tribute to
the Temple. As far as wine was concerned, the Torah asked, "Where
are their gods, the rock in whom they trusted; who did eat the fat of
their sacrifices and drank the wine of their drink offering?" (Deuteronomy 32:37, 38). Perhaps the rabbinic law reflects not only the
abhorrence of wine associated with pagan ritual, but a positive evalu-
ation of the ritual purity of wine in later rabbinic doctrine because the
Kiddush ceremony or its predecessor had already evolved by the first
or second century B.C.E. in response to the challenge of Dionysian
ideology. So, too, apart from earlier hints in the Book of Judith,
Josephus asserted that the Jews refrained from consuming Gentile oil
in the days of Seleucus Nicator, while the state was compelled to advise
its cities to pay its Jewish citizens money in place of a gift of oil.
Josephus also attacked John of Gischala, one of the rebel leaders, for
making excessive profits out of the sale of kosher olive oil to Syrian
Jews, showing that the regulations for pure olive oil had spread to
communities outside Judaea and must have antedated the Eighteen
Ordinances by many years. With the fresh emphasis on the sanctity of
the Sabbath, kosher oil was required for lighting the Sabbath and
Hanukkah lamps (*Bava Kamma* 6:6). Further, the subjects of the

heroic stories in the Apocrypha are role models, indicating how one should act when offered ritually unclean food by non-Jews. This does not mean that all sections of the population, apart from the pietists, accepted these rules as the norm during the revolt of the Maccabees, and there must be a suspicion that the tightening of these regulations was rejected by the Sadducees and some of the plebian masses.[20]

Within two centuries the bulk of Judaean society accepted the ban on commensality with Gentiles. Thus, when Felix sent priests to Rome to plead their cause before Nero, they lived on a diet of figs and nuts. In the first century of the common era, the preoccupation of certain rabbinic sages with the regulation of purity and tithed food eaten in their exclusive dining clubs presupposes that most Jews were now eating separately from Gentiles; for what would otherwise be the point of this further differentiation among Jews by establishing special table fellowships among selected companions, *haverim,* if there had not already been a preliminary closing of the ranks against Gentiles. We can view this from another angle. The Jewish apostle Peter's "custom had been to eat with pagans, but after certain friends of James arrived he stopped doing this . . ." (Galatians 2:12). In sum, because non-Jews were excluded from the Temple cult and from sharing the sacrificial feast after the offering on the altar, on the same basis Jews and Gentiles could not dine at the same table/altar and participate in a common meal.[21]

According to the Mishnah, bread, wine, oil, cheese, stewed or pickled vegetables containing wine or vinegar, minced fish, and under certain conditions milk obtained from or prepared by Gentiles were forbidden, yet a further ramification of the Dietary Laws (*Avodah Zarah* 2:3, 5, 6). Heinrich Graetz asserted over a century ago that the rabbinic School of Shammai, which he identified with the ultra-Zealots, passed the Eighteen Ordinances in 66 C.E., prohibiting Jews from buying wine, oil, bread, and other items of food from their Gentile neighbors. Although the supporters of Hillel, who were politically moderate, rejected these extreme measures, they were forcibly coerced into accepting them by the militants. The Israeli historian Gedaliah Alon declared, however, that the prohibition of non-Jewish bread, wine, and oil was observed long before the advent of the Hasmoneans, but that the halachah was not universally adhered to. According to Alon, there was a long-held national concept of Gentile uncleanliness, stemming from the automatic pollution of idol worshippers. The Mishnah forbade various foods of Gentiles, who were idol worshippers, because in their persons they were inherently unclean and defiled the food they produced. In the same way, the Mishnah prohibited the sale of cattle to Gentiles to prevent them from sacrificing the animals to idols. Later, this ban on a wider range of Gentile foods was explained by emphasizing that the foods might have absorbed forbidden substances from the walls of vessels owned by non-Jews or as a means of preventing intermarriage. A variant of Alon's interpretation is provided by Martin Goodman. For instance, he mentioned that Jews in the talmudic era deliberately pierced cooking pots if they became contaminated with unclean food so they could no longer be used. Hence, these ever-stricter regulations against pollution by Gentiles according to Goodman showed an "intensification" of the distrust of Gentile rule that led to the revolt against Rome in 66–70 c.e. On the other hand, Jacob Neusner focused on the increasing social differentiation among Jews when he argued that a section of radical priests and laymen tried to eat their meals at home in the same conditions of cultic cleanliness as food was eaten in the Temple. Hence, wheat, oil, and wine, the foods that were offered on the altar, were kept in a state of holiness and separateness to avoid contamination and to keep them away from the sources of death and extinction, such as the dead, blood, and flux.[22]

We now have some archaeological evidence relating to the consumption of wine. Excavations in the storerooms near Herod's palace at Masada have revealed fragments of Roman bottles, amphorae, of wine from Italy with a date on them that corresponds to the year 19 b.c.e. The markings are clear evidence that the wine was imported from Italy and that Herod had no compunction against drinking the wine of Gentiles. In the Hellenistic towns of Judaea and in the Lower City of Jerusalem, where the Seleucid garrison was stationed, many jar handles of wine imported from Rhodes have been found, whereas in the Upper City of Jerusalem few such handles have been discovered, as ritually observant Jews during the Hasmonean period regarded such foreign wine as impure. However, Nachman Avigad, the excavator of the Upper City of Jerusalem, admitted that the inhabitants of one Jewish house appeared to have been imbibers of Italian wine, concluding that there have always been less-orthodox Jews. What this evidence seems to indicate is that Herod's Court and certain members of the Judaean aristocracy had no qualms about drinking non-Jewish wine, but that by the beginning of the first century c.e. sections of the upper class as well as the Pharisees already adhered to the notion of drinking only Jewish wine, although there was always a tough working-class group in the towns who were none too scrupulous in their choice of ritually pure wines. A Palestinian text between 270 and 370 c.e. stated: "It happened once that a band of 'no-goods' were sitting around drinking wine half-way through the night. But they did not get [properly] drunk. Wine was brought to them, and they said to the wine-server (waiter): 'We want wine mixed with wine!' " A later letter was sharply critical of Jewish shellfishers from Alexandria who drank beer in Crusader taverns in Acre, and we can surmise that they probably drank wine as well.[23]

Finally, E. P. Sanders has argued that there was a considerable overlapping between the ritual slaughtering techniques of the Jews and the sacrificial procedure of the ancient Greeks. Hence, while almost all Jews refrained from eating pork or shellfish, there must have been many who would not have been too careful when consuming meat at a Gentile friend's home so long as it was not obviously from a tainted source. Sanders asserted that in some Mediterranean cities during the first century of the common era, it was possible for Jews in theory to purchase the meat of suitable animals, animals that had not been sacrificed to an idol and from which the blood had been drained. So, too, we have already noted that there were assimilated groups of Jews in the ancient world who drank wines of every description, whether or not they were kosher. Even so, Sanders exaggerates the consistent elements and uniformity in the Greek code relating to the sacrifice and butchering of animals, as they differed widely in the city-states. Further, he ignores the Jewish objection to consuming the forbidden fat of an animal and the exact, fixed systematic nature of the Jewish rules pertaining to ritual slaughter that were outlined in the Mishnah. Sometimes the heart, while still beating, was torn out from an animal by the Greeks. Sanders also fails to take into account that on Sabbaths and festivals the bulk of the Jewish population feasted on poultry and not on red meat, and it is doubtful whether the Greeks had strict rules for the slaughter of birds.[24]

True, the Eighteen Ordinances proclaimed shortly before the outbreak of the War with Rome in 66 c.e. reinforced and extended the existing regulations against the consumption of Gentile food; yet the economic boycott of the essential food products of the Gentiles, such as oil and bread, was impossible to sustain after the defeat of Bar Kochba in 135 c.e. and the shrinking of the Jewish population in Palestine. It was declared in the Talmud that Jews risked their lives trying to obtain kosher oil from the Judaean hill country, as the area was inhabited by hostile elements; and so around the thirties and forties of the third century c.e., Judah II Nesia, the grandson of Rabbi Judah the Prince, relaxed the ban on the consumption of Gentile olive oil. Further, the prohibition against eating non-Jewish bread was lifted at the same time, particularly in the coastal cities where Jews had settled after the destruction of the Temple. "Rabbis of Caesarea in the name of R. Jacob bar Aha [said]: 'Even in accord with the position of him who permits [using bread prepared by Gentiles] this is on condition that [it is purchased] from a baker [and not from a householder]' " (*Avodah Zarah* 2:8).[25]

Both Judaism and Hinduism were influenced by Persian religious ideals, particularly the concepts of purity and impurity in relation to food. For several centuries before the common era, Brahmans already applied strict rules to prevent members of their order from being contaminated by contact with polluted humans, animals—such as the dog and domestic pig—or by impure food itself. Among the Brahmans, a person, when eating, had to be in a state of ritual purity, for which he bathed himself beforehand, and he then dined in a square in the kitchen isolated from intruders. Here, there seems to be a parallel with the priestly order and their imitators in Judaism, who partook of the sacrificial meal and even the daily fare in a state of ritual purity by frequently immersing themselves in water, as attested to by the archaeologists' discovery of a multitude of domestic baths from first-century Palestine. Equally, Judaism and Hinduism shared an interdiction on marriage with outsiders, which appears to be structurally linked to the dietary regulations. On a visit to India, I noticed that at a Hindu wedding the bridegroom stamped on a small pot full of grain, which he broke, just as the Jewish bridegroom stamps on a glass under the bridal canopy. Despite this apparent convergence of ancient Judaism and Hinduism, the Jews did not develop a system of castes. Unlike the situation in India, where the Aryans had conquered an indigenous population from whom they continued to stand aloof, the Jews had become a homogenous nation during the talmudic era; and monotheism, unlike polytheism, prevented class division from hardening into castes. With the destruction of the Temple in 70 C.E. certain of the ritual notions concerning food that were connected with the priesthood, such as the importance paid to the correct tithing of food, were undermined. With the disappearance of the Jewish state there was no chance of the Jewish population splitting into specialized occupations with no mobility between them such as in the Hindu caste system. Without a state, there could be no Jewish military caste; and without the ownership of land, there could be no despised peasant caste.[26]

THE SEPARATION OF DAIRY FOOD AND MEAT DISHES

There is a prohibition first proclaimed in Exodus 23:19 and repeated in Exodus 34:26 and Deuteronomy 14:21 against seething a kid in its mother's milk, from which the rabbis deduced the rule of separating meat and milk dishes. The rabbis imposed a ban on eating such dishes together, cooking them together, or deriving any benefit from them.

Moses Maimonides (1135–1204), the great medieval Jewish halachic authority, first suggested that the cooking of a kid in its mother's milk was a pagan cultic practice. He was followed by such later commentators as Don Isaac Abarbanel (1437–1509) and Obadiah Sforno (1475–1550). Apart from an Ugaritic inscription with an incomplete text, there is no evidence to support such a theory. The text has been translated as "coo[k] [a ki]d in milk, a lamb in butter." Critics of this reconstruction have pointed out that a word that has been taken to be a synonym for a kid may really be referring to a plant such as coriander, while the verb translated as seething may really mean slaughtering, and the Ugaritic passage does not mention the crucially important mother's milk for the kid. A different interpretation of the passage was offered by A. Caquot and M. Sznycer, who translated it as "coriander in milk, mint in curds."[27]

Philo (20 B.C.E.–40 C.E.) first suggested that the ban on seething a kid in its mother's milk was intended to outlaw cruelty, in which he was followed by the Church father Clement of Alexandria and the great Jewish commentator Ibn Ezra (1092–1167) and by David Kimchi (1160–1235). Robertson Smith pointed out the similar compassionate rules in the Bible prohibiting the killing of a parent and its young on the same day as well as the slaughter of a female bird sitting with its young. So, too, Menahem Haran recently declared that the prohibition was connected in the Book of Exodus with the feast of the ingathering, the festival of Tabernacles, the time of the year when the first lambs and kids were born in Israel. Tabernacles was "the most exuberant . . . of the pilgrim feasts, celebrated with much food and drink and the choicest of delicacies," and at such time of rejoicing the Israelites were enjoined to act humanely by not seething a kid in its mother's milk.[28]

Louis Finkelstein asserted that the rabbis first extended this prohibition to include cooking in the milk of goats other than the mother of a kid and finally went further by banning the cooking of the meat and milk of any cattle in one pot. Onkelos, who lived between the second and sixth centuries of the common era, paraphrased the Bible into Aramaic, rendering the Hebrew text with the words, "Ye shall not eat flesh and milk," which shows that the general prohibition against the consumption of meat and milk was established by this relatively late date. Vestiges of earlier practices still survived in Galilee, however, where as late as the second century C.E. Rabbi Jose still permitted the consumption of fowl cooked in milk, and the Mishnah declared that "no flesh may be cooked in milk excepting the flesh of fish and locusts. . . . It is forbidden to cook or to benefit at all from the flesh of a clean beast together with the milk of a clean beast; but it is permitted to cook or to benefit from the flesh of a clean beast. R. Akiba says: Wild animals and birds are not [included in the prohibition] . . ." (*Hullin* 8:1

and 4). Similarly, the Ethiopian Jews, the Falashas, who were cut off from the mainstream of Judaism at an early date, mix meat and milk but adhere to the biblical injunction of not seething a kid in its mother's milk.[29]

There is another possible explanation that may account for the separation of meat and milk dishes. It was stated in the Mishnah that "if three men have eaten at a table and have not spoken over it words of Torah, it is as though they had eaten of sacrifices to the dead . . ." (Avot 3:3). H. C. Brichto suggested that the reference to ". . . sacrifices to the dead, makes it clear that the meal partaken of is one which features meat." Moreover, a passage in the Babylonian Talmud clarified these remarks, when discussing a verse in Ezekiel. "[This verse] begins with 'the altar' and concludes with 'the table.' Rabbi Johanan and Resh Lakish both expound: While the Temple was in existence it was the altar which made atonement for a person. Now it is a person's table which makes atonement for him" (Hagigah 27a). With the destruction of the Temple, Brichto asserted that the "human table" was substituted for "the table/altar of God." While the Temple stood and sacrifices of meat were offered on the altar, sacrifices of fermented substances were forbidden. "No cereal offering which you shall bring to the Lord shall be made with leaven; for ye shall burn no leaven nor any honey as an offering by fire to the Lord" (Leviticus 2:11). According to Jean Soler, "A fermented substance is an altered substance, one that has become other. Fermentation is the equivalent of blemish." On the other hand, meat was a primary substance suitable for the sacred cuisine offered to the Lord, but if it was consumed with milk, a substance liable to curdle, particularly in the hot Mediterranean lands, its consumption would be spoiled. Symbolically, meat served on the altar/table could not be eaten with a substance liable to ferment, such as milk, which was unworthy of a place on the altar/table.[30]

Again, according to Robertson Smith, many preliterate "peoples regard milk as a kind of equivalent for blood. . . ," while the Talmud declared that when the blood of a pregnant animal "decomposed" it became milk; thus when meat and milk were boiled together in a pot, this caused the milk to change and become blood. So, too, the belief persisted in medieval lore that human blood and milk were made up of the same substance. Indeed, Dr. Harlow Davis observed that "to those persons who think that the taste of blood must be nauseating, I may add that with eyes closed it is practically impossible to tell the difference between the blood, and milk warm from the cow." Although flesh seethed in sour milk was a common Arab dish, the symbolism that linked milk and blood made it anathema to the Jew; nor could meat and milk/blood be mixed in one dish or at one meal and be served on the altar/table.[31]

3

EVERYDAY FOOD IN THE TALMUDIC AGE

BREAD AND GRAIN

In this chapter we shall examine the food eaten by the Jews in Palestine and Babylonia between 330 B.C.E. and 500 C.E., although we shall sometimes look back a few centuries earlier. Louis Ginzberg observed that bread was the "main dish of a poor man's food," both during the week and on Sabbaths and festivals. Hence the rabbinic ruling following the school of Hillel that if a person said a blessing over bread, he did not need to make a further blessing over side dishes, as bread constituted the bulk of the poor man's food. We must now ascertain how the Jews of that age ate their bread. In the talmudic tractate *Berakhot* we find the first clue, when "Raba b. Samuel said in the name of R. Hiyya: The one who is about to break the bread is not permitted to do so before salt or relish is placed before each one" (*Berakhot* 40a). R. Huna in a famous talmudic passage quoted in the *Haggadah* declared after the opening of his house, "Whosoever is in need let him come and eat" (*Taanit* 20b). Although the Talmud commented that the invitation was made whenever R. Huna had a meal, what the expression literally means is whenever he partook of *wrapped bread.* In the Mishnah the statement was made, "On all the nights we dip once; this night twice" (M. *Pesahim* 10:4), showing that it was then customary to dip food at all meals. Rav decided that an *eruv* of olive and onions had to be sufficient in quantity to provide a relish for bread for meals; similarly, there had to be a sufficient quantity of vinegar to dip in it the usual amount of vegetables consumed with bread in the course of two meals (*Eruvin* 29a). If we compare the eating practices of the Jews in the talmudic era with those of the Ethiopian Jews today or those in Yemen in the nineteenth century, we can appreciate that the wrapped bread with or without a filling of herbs was dipped into salt or a sharp relish to make it more palatable. By the

37

tenth century the Siddur of Saadia declared that "on all nights we do not dip and this night we dip," demonstrating that Arab cuisine under Persian influence had become sophisticated and that dipping was no longer practiced at every meal.[1]

During the talmudic age, bread was chiefly made "from the five species of grain," that is, from both hard wheat (*Triticum darum*) and bread wheat (*Triticum vulgare*), spelt wheat, rice wheat, from six- or four-rowed barley and from two-rowed barley. Professor Yehuda Feliks has pointed out that Rashi's identification of spelt wheat (*shippon*) with rye is incorrect, as this plant was not then grown in Israel, nor was the translation *shibboleth shu'val* (two-rowed barley) as oats accurate because this alleged identification was based on an anachronism. During the talmudic age, bread was also made from millet (*peragim*), sorghum (*doh'n*), and rice, which the Talmud classified as summer crops, and in addition from lentils. Sorghum and millet grow in the semiarid regions of the earth and are the fourth most widely cultivated crops today after wheat, rice, and maize. Although R. Johanan was of the opinion that rice should be added to the five species of grain and be subject to the same laws, his view was rejected; but there were places in Babylonia where *hallah* was separated from dough made of rice, since it was the staple food (*Pesahim* 50b, 51a).[2]

In mishnaic times or in the first two centuries of the common era, wheat replaced barley as the cereal most commonly utilized in baking bread, while barley was relegated to a more lowly position for use as fodder for animals and for making poor man's bread, the true bread of affliction. Anan, the Karaite founder, interpreted the biblical injunction that unleavened bread must be the bread of poverty to mean that it must be exclusively made of barley, as he considered that eating unleavened wheat bread was as sinful as consuming leaven. In the Bible, however, barley was not considered inferior to wheat as food, apart from one passage, in which it suggested, "barley for the horses and the swift steeds" in King Solomon's stables (1 Kings 5:8). In the talmudic tractate *Sotah* 9, it was asked why a wife suspected of adultery had to bring an offering of barley flour. The answer was because she had fed her lover on the choicest of dainties, "she was obliged to bring an offering of animal fodder." Moreover, the Talmud explained the phrase in Isaiah that "ye shall be fed with the sword" as meaning that the people would draw their nourishment from "hard-baked barley bread" (*Kiddushin* 62a). In a rabbinic source the question and answer were posed, "Why do you eat barley? Because I have no wheaten bread" (*Sifre Numbers* 49), and it is clear that in the talmudic age barley had come to be regarded as the food of poor men, together with coarse flour and bran. So, too, R. Hisda, a third-century Babylonian sage, declared that "when one can eat barley bread but eats wheaten bread he violates, thou shall not destroy," meaning that the person was wastefully extravagant (*Shabbat* 140b). During the siege of Jerusalem, a wealthy woman called Martha sent her servant to buy fine white flour and when that was not available, ordinary white flour. As the servant continued to return empty-handed, Martha sent him out to buy in turn poor quality flour and finally barley flour. Here we clearly have a guide to the different qualities of flour that were then utilized for baking bread. Similarly, in ancient Greece and Rome, apart from the earliest periods of their history, barley bread was eaten by the poor and by slaves.[3]

During the talmudic age, Magen Broshi estimated that bread comprised 53 to 55 percent of the calories in the diet eaten by women each day. For parallels we turn to sixteenth-century Antwerp, where 49.4 percent of a family's total income was spent on the purchase of food; even today the Arab population of Samaria and Judea obtain 48 percent of their calories from the consumption of cereals. In contrast, until recently, in West Germany families spent only a third of their income on food, of which 6 percent was devoted to the purchase of bread and other items of bakery. Further, Broshi estimated that the caloric intake of a woman during the talmudic age using a measure of one *seah* to thirteen *liters* was 3,032 calories, but Feliks believed that the ancient Jewish measure, a *seah*, was the equivalent of 8.565 liters, giving a smaller daily calorie intake of 1,874, which appears more plausible. In sixteenth-century Antwerp, the daily caloric intake per head was 2,440 calories, while today the daily recommended caloric intake for a woman is between 1,540 and 2,220 calories, depending on her age.[4]

In the talmudic age, a wife was expected to do a large number of chores for her husband: "she grinds flour, bakes, launders, cooks, feeds her child, makes the beds, and works with wool. If she brought him one female slave [on her marriage], she is free from grinding, baking and laundering; two slaves, she does not have to cook or feed her child. . . ." (M. *Ketubbot* 5:15). According to Saul Lieberman, in Palestinian villages hand mills were common, while in the more developed towns the use of the rotary mill was widespread; but in Babylonia, which was under the Persian sphere of cultural and technological influence, according to Julius Newman a great quantity of grain was ground in water mills. The housewife in Palestine, particularly in the villages, needed to grind the corn for three hours before daybreak to obtain sufficient flour for making bread for a family of five or six persons. In the larger towns, the housewives already took their wheat to professional millers to be ground into flour, as they were to do again in medieval Egypt, and sent the dough to a bakery, where it was baked in a large oven; but perhaps from the time of Nehemiah there were professional bakers in Jerusalem from whom bread could be purchased (Nehemiah 12:38; Jeremiah 37:2), or it could be bought from male and female street vendors (M. *Hallah* 2:7). Incidentally, the Talmud mentioned that the wife of R. Joseph used to prepare flour and bake, even if it was a festival day, as if this were the common practice of the time. Bread was kept in a basket or cloth or sometimes placed in a smaller basket suspended from the ceiling, although this was then the usual method of storing meat and fish to keep them cool (*Pesahim* 112b).[5]

There were a number of different names for bread in the Talmud, probably indicating the size, shape, or material out of which the loaf was made, according to Samuel Krauss, although the exact identification of these names with the actual varieties of loaves enumerated in the Talmud is difficult. Whereas wheaten bread made of choice flour was eaten on the Sabbath, during the week breads baked from ordinary flour and from bran were widely consumed. The poorer sections of the population in Palestine ate a dark wheaten loaf called *cibar* bread, from the Latin term for black bread (*panis cibarius*), a loaf that was not very palatable or very easy to digest because it was made from coarse flour. In the Midrash there was mention of this bread, which was sold outside regular bakers' shops and which was darker than the seconds of barley flour (*Song of Songs Rabbah* 1:16). Among the Babylonian Jews there was a similar loaf called *gushkrah* bread, the Arabic word *hushkar* being derived from the Persian term for bran bread. Although there is evidence that throughout the Roman Empire fine wheat bread was eaten by the masters and that coarse *cibar* bread was reserved for the slaves, the rabbis from the time of the *Tannaim* taught that all sections of the population should eat the best bread. Daniel Sperber has suggested that another loaf known as *hardah* bread should be identified with the Roman barley loaf, *panis hordeaceus*. There was a third loaf referred to in the Talmud, where it was called *pat purni* (*Pesahim* 31b), which has again been thought to have been a bread of Roman origin being derived from the term for oven bread (*panis furnaceus*); this phrase has been translated in the Soncino edition of the Talmud as a large loaf because bread produced in a baker's oven tended to be larger than that baked in the oven of a private citizen.[6]

Also mentioned in rabbinic literature were Babylonian and Indian bread, the ancient equivalents of Iraqi bread, thin discs three times the size of ordinary pita bread,which are called *lahma dakika* in modern Hebrew; and of the present-day Indian loaves such as *parata* or *poori*, which have been described as a deep-fried, puffy bread. We know from illustrations on mosaics that the Graeco-Roman *quadroti* loaf with divisions in it was popular in Palestine, as it appeared on Jewish monuments and was later adopted by Christians for use as the host, the consecrated wafer of the eucharist ceremony; and there was also a loaf that resembles a squashed modern cottage loaf in shape. These cakes with multiple circles were known in Greek as *popana polyom-phala* and had an important place in Greek ritual. It is doubtful, however, whether the biblical word *pat* and the Aramaic term *pita* are directly connected with the present-day Greek *pita,* a flat bread of medieval Italian origin. This type of bread was brought from Italy by the Sephardim to Salonika in the sixteenth century, and hence the term *pita* passed into Judezmo (Ladino) and ultimately into modern Hebrew. We can see how even the types of bread relished by the Jews in Palestine were deeply influenced by Hellenistic and Roman cultural penetration, just as the foods consumed by the Babylonian Jews were influenced by ancient Mesopotamian culinary traditions and the outstanding example of Persian cookery.[7]

While the wealthy ate loaves of fine flour, particularly a white wheaten bread, and the poor ate coarser bread, even on the Sabbaths and festivals, the less privileged sections of the population enjoyed better bread at weddings and feasts. It is doubtful whether there was a special loaf of bread for the Sabbath in this period, although there has been a persistent tendency among historians to read a late medieval development back into a much earlier age. The affluent classes also relished beautifully baked small loaves and bread baked like a cake with ingredients consisting of oil, honey, milk, and eggs.[8]

During times of strong government in Judaea, as in the age of Herod, the king intervened when there was a famine and stripped his palace of gold and silver vessels, which were sold to buy grain in Egypt. According to Josephus, Herod distributed grain specially purchased from Egypt to those who could afford it, "but for those many that were not able, either by reason of old age, or any other infirmity, to provide food for themselves, he made this provision for them, that the bakers should make their bread ready for them." When Queen Helena of Adiabne visited Jerusalem during a famine she sent messengers to Alexandria to buy grain and imported dried figs from Cyprus. Likewise in Babylonia, whenever there was a serious shortage of food in any town, relief came to the stricken area through ships carrying wheat from other areas. Thus the famine in Pumbadita in R. Judah's time was in part relieved by ships bringing wheat from Parzina. During times of disturbance, as in early fourth-century Palestine, for example, a Rabbi Isaac declared that the verse in Genesis, "Thou shall eat grass (*esev*) of the field (Genesis 3:18), refers to present day generations when a man plucks from his field and eats it while it is still green and unripe (*esev*)." Saul Lieberman, by citing a parallel passage in the early Christian historian Eusebius, which stated that during famines people ate dried grass, showed that the passage we have just quoted from the Midrash was literally true. Many other examples of grass eating and the reliance on wild herbs and roots at times of shortage can be quoted from early modern Italian history.[9]

Other foods were used as substitutes for grain during times of drought and hardship in Palestine, and religious regulations were sometimes relaxed. During times of scarcity the poor sustained themselves on carobs, also known as St. John's bread, as they were to do again in the Middle Ages. In one talmudic passage it was claimed that Simeon b. Yohai and his son lived solely on a diet of carobs when they hid in a cave from the Romans for twelve years. In another rabbinic passage the question and answer were, "And why does he eat carobs? Only because he has no pressed dates available." There was also a rabbinic legend that King David caused such a catastrophic famine that the people were forced to eat bitter vetches, a leguminous plant normally used as fodder, another pointer to the food that was utilized during a famine in the talmudic age. Finally, we are told in the Talmud that the people of Jericho "made breaches in their gardens and orchards to permit the poor to eaten fallen fruit in famine years on Sabbaths and festivals" (*Pesahim* 56a).[10]

PALESTINIAN AND BABYLONIAN FOOD

Whereas Palestine belonged to the Mediterranean world with its dietary pattern of wheat, wine, and olive oil, the Babylonian climate, particularly in the south, was unsuited to the cultivation of the vine and the olive tree, their place being taken by the production of beer and sesame oil. In Babylonia passersby were allowed to consume wild dates, and the Palestinian sages envied the low cost of living of the Jews in Babylonia, blessed with a plentiful supply of grain. When first arriving in Babylonia, R. Ulla exclaimed in amazement, "A whole basket of dates for a zuz, and yet the Babylonians do not study the Torah!" R. Johanan attributed the absence of leprosy among the Babylonian Jews to their frequent bathing and their eating of beets and drinking of beer (*Ketubbot* 77b). Different kinds of oil were used by different Jewish communities. "What would the Babylonians do that have only sesame oil, what would the Medes do that have only nut oil, what would the Alexandrians do that have only radish oil" (*Tosefta Shabbat* 2:3). Because of the abundance of fish in the Babylonian rivers and canals, fish were also consumed on weekdays in Babylonia and unlike in Palestine were not reserved just for the Sabbaths and festivals. Beer was also commonly drunk in the southern portions of Babylonia, the finer quality being made from barley and being known as median beer, while another cheaper kind of beer was manufactured from the locally grown cascuta plant and from dates. According to R. J. Forbes, by the sixth century B.C.E. fermented date juice had succeeded in replacing beer as the most popular strong drink in Babylonia.[11]

The Palestinian Jews were contemptuous of the diet of their fellow Jews in Babylonia, particularly of the various dishes made from grain; they ridiculed their brethren in Babylonia, who ate porridge with bread, giving rise to a jibe about "the foolish Babylonians who eat bread with bread." R. Hisda claimed that he had once "inquired of the fastidious people of Huzal whether it was better to eat the porridge of wheat, with bread of wheat, and that of barley, with bread of barley, or the porridge of wheat with the bread of barley, and vice versa." We shall shortly see how the Palestinians were equally scathing about another dish made from grain called *kutah*, which was much beloved by the Babylonians; and there was also a gruel made from the flour of unripe grain, called *hasisa*, a word of Persian origin, that was dried in ovens. Moreover, it appears that when the Palestinian Jews prepared a porridge of grits, they made it in a distinctive fashion, seasoning it with oil and garlic (M. *Nedarim* 6:10; M. *Tevul Yom* 2:3); and it is probable that the Palestinian community consumed fewer grain dishes and larger amounts of vegetables, boiled beans, and lentils than the Babylonian Jews did (M. *Tevul Yom* 1:1, 1:2, 2:5; M. *Niddah* 9:7). Nonetheless, gruels such as *puls* and *alica* were popular in the Roman world, which deeply influenced Palestinian culinary trends. There were talmudic references to a food known as *helka*, a term used to describe individual grains split into two sections and probably eaten in the form of a porridge, for the word may have been related to the well-known dish of *alica* and *halica*, which was a porridge made of wheat.[12]

We have referred here to an ancient Persian dish known as *kateh* or *kashk*, which was called *kutah* in the Mishnah and the ingredients of which were described in the talmudic tractate *Pesahim* 42a in the following terms: "Our Rabbis taught: Three things were said of Babylonian *kutah:* it closes up the heart, on account of whey of milk; and it blinds the eyes, on account of the salt; and emaciates the body, on account of the stale crusts." It appears that while *kutah* was a much loved dish in Babylonia, the Palestinian Jews often despised it. We are told that "R. Johanan expectorated at [the mention of] Babylonian *kutah*. Said R. Joseph: Then we [Babylonians] should expectorate at R. Abba's fowl! Moreover, R. Gaza has related, I once paid a visit there [in Palestine] and prepared some Babylonian *kutah*, and all the invalids of the West [Palestine] asked me for it." Whereas *bamia kutah*, sweet and sour chicken and okra, was a meat dish that was much relished until recently among the Jews of Calcutta, some of whom were of Baghdadi descent, during the talmudic era it is clear that *kutah* was a milk dish; for when an oven was greased with fat, Raba b. Ahilai forbade the bread therein to be baked with *kutah* (*Pesahim* 30a). By the Middle Ages, the term *kashk* had two meanings among the Persians: the primary one, found in a ninth- or tenth-century epic, meant barley flour or a mixture of cracked wheat and barley (*kashk*); the other meant flesh or fowl cooked overnight (*kashak* or *kashba*). A tenth-century Arabic cookbook described two types of *kashk*, one that consisted of crushed wheat in water with a leavening agent and one that included sour milk, as does the recipe in a modern Persian cookbook. The latter dish seems close to the talmudic one outlined in *Pesahim*, which we have already mentioned, but the recipe is at least four hundred years earlier than the Arab source, while the Iranian meat porridge perhaps was the culinary ancestor of the dish known as *bamia kuta*. Through intermediaries in Central Asia, the Russians acquired a knowledge of the food known as *kashk* and cooked buckwheat grains in water, calling the resulting dish *kasha*, a term that passed into Yiddish, as this food became one of the staples of the diet of the East European Jews. Nor was this all. At the end of the Middle Ages the Persian dish of noodles called *lakshah* was diffused throughout the Balkans and Central Asia and so became known to the East European Jews, who adopted it as one of their basic foods, calling it *lokshen*.[13]

PULSE

Next in importance to bread and grain as a supplementary and complementary food in the talmudic age was pulse. We have seen how the letter of Aristeas in the second century B.C.E. attached a significant role to the cultivation of crops of pulse in Palestine. In the past leguminous crops were much more common in Palestine than in Babylonia; hence R. Judah's ruling that "the tenant farmers of Babylonia may change their crops from grain to pulse, not so those of Palestine" (*Bava Metzia* 107a). Further, there is passage in the Mishnah where R. Johanan b. Matthias, a Palestinian sage who was active in the years 120 to 140 C.E., said to his son that he should inform laborers that he would willingly engage them, provided they agreed to eat bread and pulse; and this no doubt was the diet of the agricultural laborer. So, too, archaeological evidence attests to the importance of pulse in the Palestinian diet. When the inhabitants quit a house in the village of Meiron in Galilee in the late fourth century c.e., they left nineteen storage jars whose principal contents were wheat, barley, king walnuts, and Egyptian beans (*ful* or *lubaya*). In the Jerusalem Talmud, we have a recipe for making a dish of beans: ". . . it is the way of Sepphoris [an important town in Galilee] people to prepare beans in that way, and they call it cress-dish [made by pouring vinegar into cold split beans and then warming them; this improves the beans]" (*Avodah Zarah* 5:3).[14]

Legumes were richer in proteins than cereals and were a cheap food chiefly eaten by the poor; but to be nutritionally effective they had to be eaten with grain in one form or another. In addition to lentils, the broad bean, and chick-peas that were already referred to in the Bible, other new legumes were introduced into household use in the talmudic age; among these were the cowpea called in the Mishnah the Egyptian bean, lupines, the grass peas, and vetch. According to the Talmud, lupines were cooked seven times to remove their bitter taste and were eaten as a dessert. The rabbis advised that a guest who had outstayed his welcome should be fed with legumes, while husbands had to provide their wives with four times as much wheat as legumes together with a supply of oil and dried figs. The relative quantities of wheat and legumes enumerated in the Mishnah (*Ketubbot* 5:8) must be a good indicator both of the relative amounts of each item of food stocked in the household storeroom and of their relative importance in the diet of that age. There is, however, another story in the Talmud that well illustrates the disdain of the upper class for legumes. A man from a wealthy family whose fortune had declined applied to R. Nehemia for maintenance. " 'What do your meals consist of' [the rabbi] asked him. 'Of fat meat and old wine,' the other replied. 'Will you consent [the rabbi asked him] to live with me on lentils.' The [other consented], lived with him on lentils and died" (*Ketubbot* 67b).[15]

VEGETABLES

According to the talmudic tractate *Berakhot,* the meal of the poor man often consisted of bread with salt (*Berakhot* 2b), a view that reiterated the dictum of the Mishnah that the student should be satisfied with bread and salt (M. *Avot* 6:4), but most families ate their bread with vegetables either as a sandwich or in the form of a stew. R. Huna declared that "no scholar should dwell in a town where vegetables are unobtainable" (*Eruvin* 55b), but other third-century rabbis in Babylonia drew a distinction between garlic and leek, which were regarded as necessities, and other vegetables such as the radish and beet, which, unless they were cooked properly, could be deadly. It appears that garlic and leeks together with onions were the three essential ingredients used by Babylonian cooks for flavoring food. Moreover, R. Hisda, who presided over the academy of Sura from 297 until 309 c.e., asserted that "when a scholar has but little bread, let him not eat vegetables, because it whets [the appetite]" (*Shabbat* 140b).[16]

Other rabbinic sources, however, testify to the importance of vegetables in the daily intake of Jewish laborers, a predilection that was to remain a characteristic of Jews in the Middle Ages. Rava declared: "One hundred zuz in land—salt and vegetables only." Again, there is the story of Roman clowns mocking Jews and asking a riddle as to why the camels were in mourning. To this the answer was, "These Jews now keep the Sabbatical year and they have no vegetables, so they are eating all the thistles and the camel is mourning." The Palestinian Rabbah b. Bar Hanah, an early third-century sage who recited more ancient traditions, proclaimed: "Eat onions (*bazel*) and dwell in the protection (*bezel*) of your house, and do not eat geese and fowls lest your heart pursue you. . . ," that is, do not develop a greedy appetite for expensive dishes. So, too, Ulla, another Palestinian rabbi who traveled to Babylonia, concurred with this advice, asserting that "in the West [Palestine] a proverb is current: He who eats the fat tail [of a sheep, *allitha*] must hide in the loft [*alitha*], but he who eats cress [*kakule*] may lie by the dunghill [*kikle* or place of assembly] of the town" (*Pesahim* 114a).[17]

Among the favorite vegetables of the poor were cabbages, turnips, colocasia, radishes, onions, and legumes such as lentils, the broad bean (*Vicia faba*), chick-peas, and the cowpea. The Talmud commended the cabbage for being "nourishing" (*Berakhot* 39a). This was repeated, but this time with a qualification:

> "Cabbage for sustenance and beet for healing". . . . "Woe to the house through which vegetables are always passing." Is that so? Did not Rava [299–352 c.e.] say to his attendant: if you see vegetables in the market, do not stop to ask me, What will you put round your bread. Abaye [fourth century] said: [it means, when they are cooked] without meat. Rava said: [It means, when they are taken] without wine (*Berakhot* 44b).

The stalks of cabbages were also relished (M. *Orlah* 2:7). The rabbinic saying, "Woe to the house where the turnip is common," clearly shows that it was a food consumed by the most deprived sections of the population. Both the beet and the colocasia plant were subjected to prolonged cooking to remove any bitter taste and to render them edible. In the ancient world the leaves of beet (*Beta vulgaris*) were chiefly eaten, although later its root was also consumed, but both the sugar beet and red beet were unknown. The tuber called colocasia, which was rich in starch, was introduced into Palestine from Egypt in the mishnaic period, and according to Goitein this vegetable played a role similar to the potato, even if it was less extensively used. Names such as Cicilian or Egyptian beans, Egyptian gourd and mustard, and muskmelon (*melafafon*), a name borrowed from the Greeks, give an indication of the foreign origin of many of these plants. The water-melon (*Citrullus vulgaris*) was another cheap food that was widely consumed in rabbinic times, just as in the early twentieth century, "the poorer inhabitants in the large cities of the East, as Damascus and Cairo, live[d] largely on bread and cucumbers and melons."[18]

During the winter months in particular, such wild herbs as mallow leaves and the rocket were gathered by the poor, while such garden vegetables as the artichoke (*Cynara scolymus*), ginger lily (*Arum palaestinum*), celery (Hebrew *karpas*), cress, and purslane were culti-vated and sometimes collected by the small Jewish farmers in addition to the vegetables enumerated in the Bible. Among the spices men-tioned in the Mishnah as being produced in Palestine were mustard, saffron, and fenugreek, out of which the Yemenite Jews have made a pungent sauce known as *hilbeh*. Similar spices were grown in Baby-lonia as well.[19]

The wealthier Jewish families in Palestine during the talmudic age lived in magnificent style, the details of which have been partly depicted in the Talmud and partly revealed only recently by excava-tions in Jerusalem. R. Johanan declared, "If a person is left a fortune by his parents and wishes to dissipate it, let him wear linen garments, especially of Roman linen, use glassware especially white glass, and engage workmen and not be with them, [especially to work with] oxen, which can cause much damage" (*Hullin* 84b). The excavations of Nahman Avigad in Jerusalem have uncovered, for example, rectan-gular tables of stone with a single leg used for holding drinking vessels, a wide range of glassware produced by ancient Jewish artisans, including many examples of the earliest phase of glassblowing, and many other household utensils. Members of affluent families dined on fish and meat daily with a cup or more of wine but also enjoyed a wider range of vegetables and fruit than their less-well-off brethren. Take these illustrations of this point. The Talmud proclaimed: "Our Rabbis taught: It once happened that the people of Upper Galilee bought for a poor member of a good family in Sepphoris a pound of meat every day" (*Ketubbot* 67b); and "once two disciples were sitting before Bar Kappara, and cabbage, Damascene plums and poultry were set before him" (*Berakhot* 39a) Again, it was related of the Emperor Antonius and R. Judah ha-Nasi "that lettuce, chate melon [*kishuim*, often

erroneously translated as cucumbers] and radish were not absent from
their tables either summer or winter" (*Avodah Zarah* 11a). On the
other hand, those of modest means enjoyed only those vegetables in
season. Incidentally, the rabbis regarded these chate melons as injurious to the body "as a sword" (*Berakhot* 57b).[20]

Vegetables were eaten fresh, dried, and preserved, or they were
cooked, stewed, and fried, but sometimes they were utilized to prepare
a soup. "R. Ashi said: When we were with R. Kahana, he told us that
over a broth of beet, in which not much flour is put, the blessing is 'who
createst the fruit of the ground,' but for a broth of turnip, in which
much flour is put, the blessing is 'who createst all kinds of food.' "
Further, "R. Hisda said: A broth of beet is beneficial for the heart and
good for the eyes, and needless to say for the bowels. Said Abaye: This
is only if it is left on the stove till it goes tuk, tuk," that is, until it is
brought to the boil (*Berakhot* 39a). In the modern age a dish of white
boiled turnips is eaten by Iraqi Jews on the Sabbath; possibly this dish
is descended from one of the recipes mentioned in the Talmud.
Glimpses of the practices concerning the cooking of vegetables in
Palestine in the talmudic age are provided in the Mishnah:

> If an onion [that was a Heave-offering] was put into [cooked] lentils
> [that were common produce] and the onion was entire, the lentils are
> permitted [to nonpriests], but if the onion was cut up [the matter is
> determined] by the principle of "that which gives a flavour." And with
> other cooked dishes, whether [the onion was] entire or cut-up, the
> matter is determined by the principle of "that which give a flavour." R.
> Judah permits pickled-fish [in which a Heave-offering onion has been
> cooked] since it is used only to take away the stench (M. *Terumot*
> 10:1).[21]

In *Hullin* 84a there was a passage attributed to R. Eleazar b. Azariah,
a sage who was active in Palestine in the years between 80 and 120 C.E.
"A man who had a *maneh* [a coin worth a hundred *zuz*] may buy for
his stew a *litra* of vegetables; if he has ten *maneh* he may buy for his
stew a *litra* of fish; if he has fifty *maneh* he may buy for his stew a *litra*
of meat; if he has a hundred *maneh* he may have a pot set on for him
every day. And [how often for] the others? From Sabbath eve to
Sabbath eve."

Nonetheless, although there was some evidence in the Talmud that
the poor often ate cooked vegetables together with bread, there was
other evidence that showed that in the humbler households housewives did not cook food daily. To prove the latter point, Louis Ginzberg
noted a rabbinic ruling promulgated in the Talmud that the ordinary
vessels of Gentiles were not regarded as having been used on any
particular day, as poor Gentiles, like poor Jews, did not enjoy cooked

food daily. It is interesting that in the eleventh century Rashi, in a reply to an enquiry, concluded that "in a country where rice is grown [even if] it is pre-cooked [in order to remove the husks] it is permissible [to use it for Passover] nevertheless, since the pots of non-Jews [used for the boiling] are not used on the same day [for cooking their meals]." This shows that conditions had barely changed so far as the preparation of food was concerned among the humbler families in the course of five hundred years.[22]

FRUITS

While the Bible enumerated only five fruits—the fig, the vine, the pomegranate, the olive, and the date palm (Deuteronomy 8:8)—the Mishnah in the tractate *Maaserot* also mentioned mulberries, peaches, pears, apples, pippins, medlars, quinces, the carob, and citron (M. *Maaserot* 1:2–4). Louis Rabinowitz pointed out that it was not until the talmudic age that olives were pickled for human consumption (M. *Terumot* 10:7), as prior to this period olives in their natural state were regarded as too bitter for human consumption and were utilized only for their oil. Recently, in the Philistine city of Ekron, no fewer than 102 installations for the processing of olive oil from the produce of Judaea have been discovered by archaeologists. These have been dated to the seventh century B.C.E., and it is surmised that they formed the plant of an oil-exporting syndicate. Daniel Sperber has suggested that the olive oil industry of Galilee collapsed after the Bar Kochba revolt (135 C.E.) but recovered swiftly by the end of the second century or the beginning of the next. So, too, the Jews of Galilee continued to export oil, causing Josephus to accuse John of Gischala (Gush-Halav) of making in one historian's words "excessive profits out of the sale of kosher oil to the Jews of Syria."[23]

Of all the fruit used to sustain the poorer classes in Palestine, figs were the most important, and there are many references in the Mishnah to fig-cake and dried figs (M. *Maaserot* 2:1–18, 3:1–2), while many of the vessels found by Yigael Yadin in Massada in the north storehouse bore such inscriptions as "crushed pressed figs," "pressed figs," and "dried figs." A laborer in Palestine would hire himself to assist in harvesting the figs "on condition that I and my family may eat of them" or "that my son may eat of them instead of my receiving a wage" (M. *Maaserot* 1:7). Further, R. Judah (mid-second century) stated: "It once happened that the house of Mamal and the house of Gurion in Rome were distributing dried figs to poor people, for these were years of drought. And the poor people of Kfar Shichin used to come in and eat figs after dark." Both Strabo and Pliny singled out the *caryotae* dates for special praise, saying that they were plentiful in Palestine, particularly in Jericho; and in Pliny's words, "Their outstanding property is the unctuous juice which they exude and an extremely sweet sort of wine-flavour like that of honey"; but the consumption of dates in Palestine never reached anywhere near the Babylonian level, where there was even a frequent dish of date porridge.[24]

By the time of the Second Temple, if not earlier, the citron (*etrog*) had reached Israel from its place of origin, which was either India or Southern Arabia, and it was then identified with "the fruit of goodly trees" mentioned in the Bible (Leviticus 23:40). Some suggested that the Jews acquired the citron during their exile in Babylonia; others such as Tolkowsky thought that the Hasmonaeans borrowed the citron from the Greek settlers in Judaea, who assiduously cultivated the fruit after it had been brought from India by Alexander. Moreover, it has been pointed out that the citrons were similar to cedar-cones in Babylonian libation ceremonies and fir-cones carried with a staff by the devotees of Bacchus and Dionysius. Under Greek or more wider Near Eastern influence the Hasmonaeans may have substituted the citron and palm branch for the cedar-cone and staff, symbols of the Tree of Life, which the king watered in a special ceremony. Whereas Pliny and earlier writers considered that the citron was inedible, among Jews the citron was, according to the Mishnah, savored by young children on the last day of the festival (M. *Sukkah* 4:7), perhaps in a ritual meant to symbolize a plentiful new year. Later, the Talmud reported that the citron was also pickled in vinegar or boiled to a pulp. Tolkowsky first assembled evidence from Hellenistic and Roman art and literature to show that the orange and lemon were known in the Roman world; it has been surmised that the talmudic references to the sweet citron and spherical citron may really have been describing oranges, which were known as "sweet lemons" during the Middle Ages (*Shabbat* 109b and *Sukkah* 36a). Although a method of preserving citrons was mentioned in Apicius' cookery book, a fourth- or fifth-century compilation based on a first-century original, and the citron's juice was used to strengthen vinegar, Roman cooks did not make much use of the citron.[25]

CHEESE

There were two clear references to cheese in the Bible and possibly a third one, but in the Talmud cheese was frequently mentioned as a foodstuff, which shows that this food must have been added to the diet of the Jewish people in this period. Cheese was exported from Syria to

Egypt during the Hellenistic age, and Syria also acted as a transit area for reexporting Greek cheese and other products into Egypt. R. Meir, a Palestinian sage who was active in the years 140–165 c.e., declared that Bithynian cheese made by Gentiles was forbidden to Jews (M. *Avodah Zarah* 2:4). The significance of this remark was that he was referring to Bithnyia, a Greek province in what is now part of northwest Turkey, where the pagan Greeks produced excellent cheese. At the time of the Second Temple the cheesemakers were important enough to constitute a special guild in Jerusalem, whose members were concentrated in the Tryopoeon Valley, Greek for the valley of cheesemakers. Is it possible that the Jewish cheesemakers were using the techniques of the Greeks, the renowned specialists in this trade in the ancient world? At a meeting allegedly held at the home of the sage Hananiah ben Gurion, a series of eighteen prohibitions were enacted forbidding Jews to buy the bread, wine and vinegar, oil or cheese of their heathen neighbors. Although the notable Jewish historian Graetz was of the opinion that this conference was called some four years before the destruction of the Second Temple in 70 c.e., an Israeli historian, Gedaliah Alon, has allegedly suggested that this meeting occurred at a later date, between 70 c.e. and the Bar Kochba revolt in 132 c.e., when nationalist fervor was rising. In a discussion with R. Ishmael quoted in the Mishnah, R. Joshua (possibly identifiable with R. Joshua ben Karha, who was active from 140–165 c.e.), extended the debate about the ban on the consumption of cheese produced by non-Jews. For this he adduced two reasons: first, milk was curdled with the rennet from the carcass of an animal that was not slaughtered in accordance with halachic requirements; and second, there was a risk of the milk being curdled with the rennet of calves sacrificed to idols (M. *Avodah Zarah* 2:5).[26]
. There were many references in the Talmud to the preparation of hard cheese, particularly in the Jerusalem Talmud. But according to Jean Bottéro, in ancient Mesopotamia they already made eighteen or twenty different varieties of cheese. Not surprisingly, cheese also figured among the items whose production was forbidden on the Sabbath. "One who milks, sets milk [for curdling], and makes cheese [the standard is] the size of a dried fig," is culpable, admonished the Talmud. Further, R. Nahman ben Gurea was told that the making of cheese was like building, meaning that the solidifying of the liquid was like constructing an edifice (*Shabbat* 95a). From the Mishnah it is clear that both plain and salted cheese were produced. On two occasions the Jerusalem Talmud remarked that cheese and water constituted a poor meal, but there were no doubt occasions when cheese was used as a substitute for the vegetable filling in bread. On the whole, milk was not an important feature of the Jewish diet in the talmudic age, and when

it was drunk, it would often be for some therapeutic purpose, as fresh goat's or cow's milk was supposed to have a special curative quality. So the Talmud related how after falling sick R. Judah ben Baba "took a goat and tied it to the legs of his bed, and he would suck warm, fresh, milk from it."[27]

4

SABBATH AND
FESTIVAL FOOD IN THE
TALMUDIC AGE

MEAT

Archaeological excavations in the City of David have revealed that
during the reigns of the kings of Israel and Judah red meat was widely
eaten, chiefly beef and lamb; but the evidence of food remains suggests
that during the period of the Second Temple the population preferred
to consume poultry and fish. What is so interesting about this conclusion is that it neatly ties in with the literary evidence analyzed by
Samuel Krauss. During the talmudic era meat was not really a daily
food of the Jews, however, and even the wealthier sections of the
population did not regard the eating of meat as of central importance,
although the Talmud was replete with cautionary tales of wealthy
young men feasting on meat and old wine daily (*Ketubbot* 67b and
Shabbat 119a). Moreover, St. Jerome in 392–393 c.e. stated that cattle
were scarce in Palestine, "where eating veal is regarded as a crime."
Whereas the chicken was not mentioned in the Bible, the Talmud
referred to various categories of domesticated poultry such as the hen,
goose, duck, and dove and other wild birds such as pheasants and
peacocks. City residents who were wealthy consumed large quantities
of poultry, unlike villagers, and according to Krauss the Jewish
population preferred to eat poultry rather than meat from cattle,
cooked fowl being one of the favorite dishes of the Palestinian Jews. It
soon became a custom to eat meat principally on the Sabbath, on
festivals, and on special family occasions when guests were invited.
The Mishnah stated that the four busiest times of the year for the
slaughtering of animals were the eve of the last day of Tabernacles, the
eve of the first day of Passover, the eve of the feast of Pentecost, and
the eve of the New Year. R. Jose added one more day, the eve of the Day

of Atonement in Galilee, where it was the custom to eat a rich, heavy meal prior to the fast (M. *Hullin* 5:3).[1]

Small goats and lambs were regarded as more choice than bigger animals, and the meat of a three-year-old calf was regarded as a particular delicacy, just as it was in the biblical age. Among the items discovered after excavating the center where the Essenes lived communally near the Dead Sea were pots containing the bones of sheep, goats, and a calf, the meat from which had been picked clean; once again, archaeology has vindicated the remarkable accuracy of the analysis of the talmudic literature by Krauss. Other portions of the animals that were relished were the kidneys, thighs, brains, and tongues, just as we shall see that the Spanish and oriental Jews valued these items in a later age. During the biblical age, the Israelites especially favored the fat tail of sheep and the shoulder, but even during the talmudic age the residents of towns were still very keen on animal fat, probably the fat tail of sheep. Meat was eaten after being roasted on a spit, fried, smoked, salted, and pickled. It was also made into sausages, and pieces of bread and meat were placed on skewers for the convenience of diners.[2]

With the destruction of the Second Temple in 70 c.e., "the number of recluses who would not eat meat or drink wine increased in Israel," we are told by the Talmud. Earlier, Jeremiah had praised the Rechabites, a group of ancient lineage who abstained from settled farming and wine, and some of the talmudic sages were proud to claim descent from them. Yitzhak Baer asserted that in the Second Temple period Judaism had a pronounced ascetic tendency, with perhaps thousands of adherents from among the Essenes and strange sects such as the Water Drinkers, but this is disputed by other historians, notably Ephraim Urbach, who declared that apart from Philo's writings Judaism lacked an essential attribute of Hellenistic philosophy, the antithesis between body and soul. R. Joshua questioned some of these ascetics after the destruction of the Temple:

> Why do you not eat meat or drink wine? They replied: Shall we eat flesh which used to be brought as an offering on the altar, now that the altar is in abeyance? Shall we drink wine which used to be poured as a libation on the altar, but is now no longer? He said to them: if that is so, we ought not to eat bread either, because meal offerings have ceased. They said: [You are right] we can manage with fruit. . . . But, he went on, we should not drink water, because we can no longer observe the ceremony of the pouring of water. To this they could find no answer, and he said to them . . . To mourn overmuch is also impossible, because we do not impose on the community a hardship which the majority cannot endure . . . [A man] may prepare a full-course banquet, but he should leave out an item or two. . . .

R. Akiba and R. Ishmael disputed the binding force of vegetarianism in Jewish law, the former stating that the right to eat meat had been granted by mishnaic law. The latter declared that "from the day the Temple was destroyed it would have been proper for us to refrain from eating meat and drinking wine; but we have not so ordained, because the Beth Din ought not to issue decrees that the people cannot abide by."[3]

Instead of imposing a general ban on Jews against eating meat, the later rabbinic authorities enforced the ban for a limited period of time: the first nine days of the month of *Av*. This was the date in the Jewish calendar commemorating the destruction of the two temples. According to the *Shulchan Aruch*, "Some authorities declare that we should not eat meat or drink wine during the entire week preceding the month of Av. Others say, from the beginning of the month of Av; while others say from the seventeenth day of Tammuz." Whereas the founder of the Karaite sect, Anan, who had fastidious aristocratic tastes, forbade the eating of all meat except for deer and all birds except pigeons, by the tenth century the Karaites had stopped eating meat altogether. Like the talmudic authorities, however, the Karaites found that such stringent regulations could not be imposed on their whole community, so that outside Jerusalem these anti-meat-eating regulations were suspended, and a few Karaite authorities even questioned the ban against eating meat in Jerusalem.[4]

FISH

There are many references in the ancient sources to the fishermen of Acre, a Mediterranean port, and Tiberias on the Sea of Galilee. An inscription from the second century has been found at Jaffa about a band of fishermen, and there are also early rabbinic references to the fishermen's guild of Tiberias. In the region of Tiberias, during the talmudic age pools were built where fish were bred. Incidentally, the fish-breeding industry has been revived in Israel today, particularly in Galilee, and there is an annual production of 7,000 tons of carp, mostly used for making gefilte fish. Strabo mentioned the Galilean city of Migdal Nunia (Tarichaea) as notable for its fish-salting industry and commerce. The fishermen salted the fish and brought their catch to market in baskets. The technique of salting fish practiced by the ancient world was similar to the modern Egyptian method of gutting fish and rubbing salt into their orifices; alternate layers of salt and fish were covered with mats and left to stand for three to five days, after which the fish were turned over for a similar period of time. During the process, the body fluids drained away, leaving the fish impregnated with salt, dry and hard. Before cooking the fish it was necessary to soak them thoroughly to rid them of the taste of preservative salt. The Talmud recounted a tradition that King Alexander Jannai (103–76 B.C.E.) of the Hasmonaean dynasty had possessed a city "where they used to take out sixty myriads of dishes of salted fish for the men cutting down fig-trees from one week-end to the next" (*Berakhot* 44a). The authenticity of this tale can be gauged by a parallel story from Egypt. Here in Thebes during the reign of Rameses, state workers were given a monthly allowance of 8.5 kilograms of fish. There was a fish gate and probably a fish market in Jerusalem, just as there were in other large cities such as Athens; so busy was the fish market at Acre that there was a popular saying, "Would you bring fish to Acre?" meaning the same as taking coal to Newcastle. However, Pelusium on the Nile Delta and Apamaea in Syria dominated the fish and *muries* (salt liquor) trade of the coastal town of Caesarea.[5]

In comparison with Palestine, there was an abundance of fish in Babylonia. When lakes or canals overflowed, such large quantities of fish were left behind that the surplus was salted for later consumption, even during a festival week; and Rav mentioned a teacher who tried to recruit pupils by advertising the attraction of frequent meals of fish. Because of the growing demand of the population for fish in Babylonia, fish were often bred in special ponds.[6]

Fish prized in the ancient Jewish world were the *colias*, identified with the tunny fish or the coly-mackerel, both of which were in the same family, and the *chalkis*, a small fish resembling a sardine. In Babylonia the choice of fish was limited to the *biz*, the *shabbut* (the *shibbuta* of the Talmud), the *bunni*, and the *chakar*, which, according to one English cookery writer, were closely related to the European barbel, roach, and tench; likewise, in the Sea of Galilee the bigger species of the carp family known as the *barbel* were to be found, and a fish named *musht* was found by the Arabs. Nonetheless, the ancient names for fish appear to be vague, and the *colias* or tunny fish was identified with the *shibbuta* in the gaonic period following the completion of the Talmud, although in one Syriac source the *shibbuta* was identified with the mullet. Fish were eaten pickled, boiled, broiled, and cooked in milk, mixed with eggs and fried, or enjoyed with an egg on top.[7]

Not only the upper classes but also wider sections of the population in the ancient world served fish sauces with hors d'oeuvres, used them as a relish with fish and eggs, or cooked their meat with the liquid. "Rav also said this, Adda the fisherman told me: Broil the fish with his brother [salt], plunge it into his father [water], eat it with his son [sauce], and drink after its father [water]" (*Moed Katan* 11a). The

Greeks and Romans used to liquefy small fish in a solution for pickling fish that filled large basins in their salteries. The liquid that was produced was known to the Romans as *liquamen* or *garum*, a word of Greek origin, while the residue that remained after the process of manufacture had been completed was designated as *allec*. However, Gaius Pliny stated that *allec* or *hallec* could also be made independently from small fish. What is astonishing is that all these sauces, *garum*, *allec*, and *muria*, which were so beloved by the Graeco-Roman world, were also an integral part of the Palestinian Jewish cuisine, as the same terms were employed by the Mishnah and the Talmud. Pliny mentioned the preparation of kosher *garum*, *garum castimonarium*, in his *Natural History*, while Avi Yonah, having pointed out that *oxygarum* was produced at Tarichaea and at Migdal Maliha on the Mediterranean, concluded that in the talmudic era probably a few big suppliers purchased the catches of these fisheries, from whence the finished product was exported to Greece, Italy, and Gaul. *Oxygarum* was a sauce of vinegar and *garum* to which boiled vegetable juices and spices were added, and *eleogarum* was a sauce of oil and *garum*. R. Hanina b. Gamaliel declared that the brine of *hallec* prepared by a professional manufacturer was permitted to be used by Jews (*Avodah Zarah* 34b). Cato recommended that *hallec* could be given to farm laborers as a relish, probably to be eaten with bread, after the oil squeezed from inferior olives had been used up. Today, in contrast, agricultural laborers dip their bread into olive oil of the first pressing and eat it with chopped garlic. So, too, it was a common practice among Jews in the talmudic age for bread to be dipped into brine, perhaps an indicator of their poverty (*Avodah Zarah* 40a). *Muria* was a very salty liquor held in low esteem by gourmets and was in character little more than a brine from the processing works for preserving cheese, meat, and fish.

> Abimi the son of R. Abbahu learned that *muries* of an expert is permitted . . . he however explained that only the first and second [extracts] from this fish [sauce] are permitted, but the third is forbidden, the reason being that these first and second [extracts] are quite fat and require no mixture of wine; after these, however, wine is put into it (*Avodah Zarah* 34b).[8]

Whereas some historians have drawn a distinction between the salted fish of the poor and the exotic spices and fish sauces of the affluent, it has been argued from the archaeological evidence of containers found in people's homes that the use of *garum* and other fish sauces was not confined to the upper classes in the ancient world but was quite general. Nonetheless, the more exquisite sauces such as mackerel sauce could be purchased only by the wealthy, while even the cheaper brines such as *muries*, when imported from Syria to Acre in Palestine could almost triple in price. From the Mishnah, we learn about the full range of fish dishes and brines that were then enjoyed by the Jews of Palestine. If a person took a vow to abstain from something, saying, "If I taste of fish or fishes, he is forbidden them, large or small, salted or unsalted, raw or cooked, but he is permitted pickled chopped fish and brine. If he vowed to abstain from small fish, he is forbidden pickled chopped fish, but he is permitted brine and fish-brine" (M. *Nedarim* 6:4).[9]

THE *KIDDUSH* ON WINE

The Friday-evening repast in Palestine during the talmudic age already contained three important elements: the blessings said on the wine and bread and the pure fish meal, all of which still survive in many Jewish households today. The sacred character of bread and wine were of ancient origin, as we are informed in the Bible that Melchizedek, the priest king of Salem, welcomed Abraham, who had been victorious in battle, offering him bread and wine, after which Melchizedek blessed Abraham. As part of the sacrificial cult, an animal was offered with bread and a libation of wine. The Church father Tertullian (155–225) listed the *cena pura*, the pure supper, among Jewish festivals and Sabbath ceremonies, and there have been many attempts by modern scholars to elucidate the meaning of this expression. Whereas we shall see that there has been some support for the theory that this expression meant the pure fish supper eaten at the inception of the Sabbath and festivals, Samuel Krauss identified the term with the loaves of fine wheat, the *panis candidus*, enjoyed by the Jews in the Roman Empire on a Friday night, just as the showbread in the Temple was made from the finest flour; but it is doubtful whether there was a special loaf for the Sabbath during this period, and not too much significance should be attached to the observation of Krauss. We shall now examine the reasons wine and fish figured so prominently in the Friday-evening meal and their underlying symbolism.[10]

In the ancient Near East wine was regarded as the divine fluid. The Greek god Dionysus represented not only fire but also wine and milk, all fluids that interestingly enough may still be used in the Jewish *Havdalah* ceremony, which marks the end of the Sabbath. Both Erwin Goodenough and Siegfried Stein have pointed out the parallels between the *Kiddush* ceremony and the blessings said by the Jews over a cup of wine and the practices of the pagan Greeks at symposia, who

sang a chant in honor of their wine god Bacchus before they partici-
pated in a banquet and sometimes sang a different refrain to Zeus and
other gods at the conclusion of the meal. According to Goodenough, at
the daily meal the head of the Greek household would dedicate a
portion of the food to the gods and would drink a little wine after
spilling a few drops on the floor, as a libation to the gods. There are
obvious parallels between the latter custom and the Jewish practice of
pouring out some wine from the cup in the *Havdalah* ceremony and
the spilling of wine from one of the four cups when reciting the ten
plagues during the *Seder* service at Passover; in both cases there are
strong taboos against drinking any of the wine that was poured out
because it originally represented the divine portion.[11]

Responding to the Greek influence in a creative fashion, the Jews
adapted the words of Psalm 104:1, 14, 15 into blessings for wine, "wine
to gladden men's hearts," even if these words were reformulated, and
for bread, "bringing bread out of the ground." Although the Talmud
attributed the invention of the *Kiddush* ceremony, which inaugurated
the Sabbath and festivals, and the *Havdalah* rite, the ceremony
marking the end of the Sabbath, to the Men of the Great Synagogue,
who flourished in Palestine between the sixth and fourth centuries
B.C.E., we cannot definitely trace the *Kiddush* back to a period earlier
than the first century B.C.E. Abraham Bloch has suggested that the
Kiddush ceremony was introduced into Judaism at this time either
slightly earlier than or at the same time as the blessing on the cup of
wine after the meal. However, if the closest disciple of Simon the Just,
one of the last survivors of the Men of the Great Synagogue, bore a
Greek name, Antigonos of Socho, it is possible that this creative
synthesis between Jewish and Greek ideologies had occurred in the
second century B.C.E. Moreover, the rules of the Dead Sea Scrolls sect,
which may have been framed at the end of the second century B.C.E.,
included blessings on bread and wine. Prior to the destruction of the
Temple in 70 C.E. there was a first-century controversy between the
rabbinic schools of Hillel and Shammai concerning the *Kiddush* that
appears to indicate that the ceremony had been established for at least
a century. Shammai asserted that "the blessing is first said over the
[sanctity of] the day and then of the wine, because it is on account of
the day that the wine is used, and [moreover] the day has already
become holy before the wine has been brought. The House of Hillel
says that a blessing is said over the wine first and then over the day,
because the wine provides the occasion for saying a benediction," a
view that has become the authoritative one (*Berakhot* 51b). Later, in
Babylonia in the third century C.E., it also became the custom to make
Kiddush in the synagogue at the end of the Friday-night service.
"Then according to Rav, why must he [the Reader] recite *Kiddush* at

home? In order to acquit his children and his household [of their duty].
And according to Samuel, why must he recite *Kiddush* in the synagogue? In order to acquit travellers of their obligation, for they eat,
drink, and sleep in the synagogue" (*Pesahim* 101a).[12]

It was argued by Erwin Goodenough that Philo (c. 30 B.C.E. to 40 C.E.),
the greatest philosopher of Hellenistic Judaism, held that God gave the
children of Israel Sophia (wisdom) and Logos (reason) and wine, oil,
and milk to drink from the well in the wilderness; and that the stream
was, in fact, a spiritual wine that induced a state of "sober drunken-
ness," thereby making the soul receptive to religious experience and
enthusiastic for the Almighty. There was an interesting passage in
Paul that partly echoed this sentiment when he stated that the
supernatural water drunk in the wilderness by the Israelites was Jesus
(1 Corinthians 10:3). Hence, when Hellenistic Jews imbibed wine and
ate bread at festive meals, the wine and bread symbolized various
universal philosophical and religious ideals. Arthur Darby Nock concluded that Goodenough was correct in asserting that Philo

> made emphatic and repeated use of the idea that manna as heavenly
> food could signify the nourishment of the soul . . . G[oodenough] may
> well be right enough in asserting . . . the idea of Dibelius . . . that
> Dicache 9f. points to the existence in Hellenistic Jewish table prayers
> of an association of bread with spiritual food and of bread and wine
> with life and immortality (for Dibelius the associations of the wine
> were eschatological).

The Didache, which was a second-century C.E. prayer recited by
Hellenistic Jewish Christians, also contained an interesting passage
referring to "the holy vine of thy servant David." Under the influence
of the pagan mystery cults, however, Christianity developed the
eucharist ceremony in the second century with its idea of eating and
drinking Jesus as a redeemer, an idea that was repugnant to Jews;
instead of the Jewish sequence of wine and bread partaken of on festive
occasions, the Christians in the eucharist ceremony reversed the order,
following the practice of the pagan cults.[13]

Nonetheless, we do not know for certain what symbolic meanings
the ritualistic drinking of wine by Jews had in the age of Hillel and
Shammai. Still, it has been argued by Erwin Goodenough that after the
failure of the Bar Kochba revolt against Rome, 132–135 C.E., the Jews
consciously adopted pagan symbols for their own ritual, particularly
from the third to the sixth century C.E. Grapes, cups, and vines, all
symbols associated with the Greek god Dionysus, started to appear in
synagogue scenes and on Jewish tombs. For instance, at the Chorazin
synagogue in Israel, there are scenes of vintners pressing grapes in a

series of Dionysiac loops, and the most important scene in the Dura Europos synagogue showed a great vine ascending to a heavenly throne with the twelve tribes of Israel, while Orpheus, the god of the underworld, figured predominantly in this painting; but as was pointed out by Nock, the pressing of grapes does not necessarily have a Dionysiac association, nor do birds on an amphora or masks. Nevertheless, in late antiquity Dionysus, the god of wine, was made to serve as a unifier of local pagan cults and as the redeemer of all mankind. Dionysus was both the wine god and the Lord of the souls, and both Jewish and Christian celebrants in their respective rituals of the *Kiddush* and the eucharist drank wine from a single cup to imbibe "enthusiasm" and the "medicine of immortality."[14]

Plutarch (c. 60–120 C.E.), a Greek writer, commenting on a synagogue service, declared:

> I suppose that their feast of the Sabbath is not without reference to Dionysus. For even now many call Bacchi "Sabbi." . . . And one would not be absurd in saying that the name was made with reference to a sort of excitement which grips those who celebrate the Dionysiac mysteries. And many themselves bear witness to the word when they honour the Sabbath, for they urge one another to drink and get drunk.

On the other hand, the fact that Tacitus had to refute the identification between the Roman god Liber (Dionysus) and the Jewish concept of God just shows how common the confusion was in the ancient world; and the whole notion could have arisen because of a complete lack of understanding by pagans rather than from any inclination by Jews to adopt pagan symbols. Jews may, however, have had syncretic ideas in mind when they borrowed the pagan gold-glass cups for their own ritual drinking; there was the ancient cult of Mamre at Hebron in a wine-growing area described by a Christian writer, when Jews among other offerings poured libations of wine into the well, while the site was also sacred to pagans and Christians; and at Smyrna in the third century C.E., Jews and pagans happily mingled at a civic celebration of a Dionysus festival, and there was a similar easy mixing of the population in Sepphoris, where a magnificent series of panels devoted to Dionysus has been uncovered.[15]

In the Midrash, an early commentary on the Bible, bread and wine were associated with the heavenly Torah, the Rock of the Wilderness, the Messiah, and the heavenly banquet in the next world. It was stated: " 'In the World to Come I shall prepare for you a great table, and idolaters will see it and be ashamed,' as it says, Thou preparest a table before me in the presence of mine enemies; thou hast anointed my head with oil; my cup runneth over. . . ." Again, it was claimed that for this reason the Holy One, blessed be he, will in the hereafter regale them in the Garden of Eden and prepare incense for them of all kinds of spices. . . . Because Israel exposed their souls to death in exile . . . and busied themselves with the Torah which is sweeter than honey, the Holy One . . . will therefore in the hereafter give them to drink of the wine that is preserved in its grapes since the six days of creation, and will let them bathe in rivers of milk.

Moreover, the Talmud asked:

What is meant by, And the child grew, and was weaned? The Holy One . . . will make a great banquet for the righteous on the day he manifests his love to the seed of Isaac. After they have eaten and drunk, the cup of Grace will be offered to our father Abraham, that he should recite Grace, but he will answer them, "I cannot say Grace, because Ishmael issued from me.". . . Then David will be asked: "Take it and say Grace." "I will say Grace, and it is fitting for me to say Grace," he will reply, as it is said, I will lift up the cup of salvation, and call upon the name of the Lord (*Pesahim* 119b).

Further, Goodenough pointed to an interesting third-century talmudic passage, in which it was stated by R. Jose, son of R. Hanina, that the cup used for grace after meals should be full to overflowing, for all who bless such a cup "will be privileged to inherit two worlds, this world and the next" (*Berakhot* 51a).[16]

On the other hand, critics of Goodenough assert that these pagan symbols were dead and devoid of meaning; but if the later example of the development of the messianic movement of Sabbatai Sevi (1626–1676) and hasidic mysticism after the Chmielnicki massacre in 1648 is remembered, the plausibility of Goodenough's thesis is apparent. The grape cluster appeared on Bar Kochba's coins, a symbol of the upright man and of messianic leadership. After Bar Kochba's defeat the Jewish people in Palestine were similarly affected by messianism and mystical longings, and these spiritual changes resulted in a new range of appropriate symbols. It is quite possible that the Christian eucharist ceremony developed out of the Jewish blessing on the wine and bread, but with a difference: the Jewish symbols were meant to represent not only the survival of the soul following death in a blessed afterlife in line with the Near Eastern Dionysiac and Orphic mysteries but also national regeneration. Bread was also offered in baskets as a sacrifice on Jewish monuments, and according to Goodenough this was a device for representing the sharing of a meal with the Lord and the hope of immortality; here Goodenough was exaggerating the mystical significance of bread in the Jewish tradition during the talmudic age, as it never attained the symbolic importance of fish and wine.[17]

FRIDAY NIGHT: THE PURE FISH SUPPER

Although it is clear that the fish course was one of the highlights of the Friday-evening meal, it is unlikely that the menu was restricted to fish. Our first reference to the big fish being eaten, presumably at the Friday-night dinner table, comes from the Mishnah. ". . . what was not put into hot water on the eve of the Sabbath may only be rinsed in hot water on the Sabbath, excepting old [alternative reading small] salted fish and tunny fish from Apamea [in Syria], for which rinsing is the completion of preparation" (M. *Shabbat* 22:2). Corroborative evidence for the importance of the fish course in the Friday-night meal is supplied by some obscure lines on the Sabbath from Persius Flaccus, a Roman satirist of the first century, which many scholars have interpreted as being a reference to the *cena pura*, or pure supper. "But when Herod's birthday is come, and the lamps put in greasy windows along with violets, emit their unctuous clouds of smoke; and when the tail of tunny floats curled round in a red dish, and the white jar bulging with wine, you move your lips in silence and turn pale at the circumcised Sabbath." What is so interesting about this passage is that the big fish is once again described as a tunny fish, just like the description in the Mishnah, while the Roman author also emphasized the drinking of wine on Friday night.[18]

These Palestinian and Italian culinary traditions, perhaps derived from Syria, were carried to Babylonia by Rav (160–247 C.E.), who was a disciple of R. Judah Ha-Nasi, the compiler of the Mishnah in Tiberias and of R. Hiyya in Sepphoris and who was himself the founder of the academy of Sura in Babylonia. "Wherewith does one show his delight therein [in the Sabbath]? R. Judah the son of R. Samuel b. Shilath said in Rav's name: with a dish of beets, large fish and heads of garlic. R. Hiyya ben Ashi said in Rav's name: Even a trifle, if it is prepared in honour of the Sabbath, is a delight. What is it [the trifle]? Said R. Papa [fourth century]: A pie of hash" (*Shabbat* 118b). Further, "Tanna debe Eliyahu [taught]: Though R. Akiba said, 'Treat your Sabbath like a weekday rather than be dependent on men,' yet one must prepare something trifling at home. What is it? Said R. Papa: Fish hash." Again, "R. Ashi said: I was standing before R. Huna, when he ate a fish pie [on Friday evening] which they had kept [on the stove for him]. . . . R. Nahman said: If it shrinks and is improved thereby, it is forbidden; if it shrinks and deteriorates, it is permitted. This is the general rule of the matter: whatever contains flour paste, shrinks and deteriorates, except a stew of turnips" (*Shabbat* 37b). However, eating too much fish hash was thought to be injurious to health and a cause of scurvy

(*Pesahim* 112b; *Yoma* 84a). We are told that Rava in Babylonia salted *shibbuta* for the Sabbath, and we have seen how this fish was identified with the tunny, the big fish, in the gaonic period. There was also the famous story in the Talmud of Joseph, who honored the Sabbath by investing his earnings in a great fish for the Sabbath meal, as a result of which he discovered a jewel of great worth (*Shabbat* 119a). So, too, there is a similar Indian folktale of a king who had a ring with a pearl that a fisherman found in the stomach of a fish and with which the talmudic story may be connected. What the rabbinic sources appear to be saying is that it was a meritorious act to eat a big fish for the Friday-night meal, but if this was not available a small fish or even fish hash could be substituted.[19]

Erwin Goodenough asserted that the pure fish meal served on Friday evening prefigured the messianic banquet that itself symbolized the hope of immortality, for which the Jews were ready to make a great financial sacrifice to secure a pearl of great worth. The fish was a sacred food in Syria and in Thracian mystery cults was being eaten daily in a ritual meal by priests in the temples of Atargatis. In the Syriac Apocalypse of Baruch, chapter 29, it was predicted that the two gigantic monsters, the behemoth and the big fish, leviathan, would be served as food "for the elect who survive in the days of the Messiah"; similar sentiments were contained in the Book of Enoch, where it was stated that both monsters would be given as food to the pious. According to Louis Ginzberg, the literature of the compilers of the Mishnah made no reference to the leviathan or the final messianic feast; but in the Talmud and the later midrashim the theme of the messianic banquet was highly developed. For instance, "R. Johanan says that at the time of the resurrection a banquet will be given by God to the righteous, at which the flesh of the leviathan will be served." A battle between an ox and a crocodile (the leviathan) on the banks of the Nile is depicted on the Beit Leontis mosaic, which is believed to date between the fifth and sixth centuries C.E. and is a motif that proclaims the beginning of the messianic era. Under Jewish influence similar scenes were represented in Christian art in the age of Justinian, the Byzantine emperor. Usually, in Christian funerary art a three-legged table with a fish was depicted, symbolizing the hope of immortality; likewise, Jewish gold-glass fragments have been found showing a table with a fish ready for eating, which scholars have connected with the pure fish supper. Scheftelowitz first suggested that although fish symbolism was pagan in origin, it was adopted by the Jews, who regarded the faithful as little fishes, who represented the Messiah by the symbol of the fish, and who utilized the fish as the symbol of immortality, and that Judaism later transmitted this symbolism to the Christians. The Hermetics, a Greek sect, ate a mystic meal consisting of vegetables devoted to the god of Life, which they regarded as "*coena pura*, one without flesh of animals." For different reasons the Babylonian Jews attached much importance to eating their pure fish supper with vegetables. The Babylonian sage Rava praised the good deeds of R. Huna, who "on the eve of every Sabbath [Friday] . . . would send a messenger to the market and any vegetables that the market gardeners had left over he bought up and had thrown into the river," as he was worried that the gardeners would have no incentive to provide an adequate supply in the future (*Taanit* 20b).[20]

On another level, fish was thought of as a symbol of fecundity, as Jacob gave his children a blessing that they should multiply like fishes. The rabbis encouraged marital relations, particularly on Friday night, unlike the author of the pre-Christian Book of Jubilees and sectarians such as the Karaites, who forbade sexual activity on the Sabbath. For this reason the Talmud recommended the eating of fish and garlic on Friday night because of their potential as an aphrodisiac.[21]

There is abundant evidence in the Talmud that fish and meat were eaten on the Sabbath. "The sons of R. Papa b. Abba asked R. Papa: We, for instance, who have meat and wine every day, how shall we mark a change?—If you are accustomed to [dine] early, postpone it; if you are accustomed to [dine] late, have it earlier, answered he" (*Shabbat* 119b). Nonetheless, the rabbinic literature also described a gigantic bird, the ziz, which was a delicacy to be served to the pious at the end of time, in addition to the behemoth and the wild ox, as a compensation for abstaining from unclean birds. Perhaps this was a good reason for Jews also to taste poultry or meat as part of their Friday night repast; Goodenough's sweeping views on the pure fish supper on Fridays should accordingly be qualified.[22]

The rabbis were divided as to whether the service marking the end of the Sabbath should start with the blessing on the light or on the spices, as the use of spices was originally optional. According to Jacob Lauterbach the Palestinian, Jews had a custom of placing aromatic herbs in the room when the family dined on the Sabbath. During the week, it was the custom at the end of a meal to strew aromatic herbs on a pan with live coals, causing a pleasant smell from the burning incense to waft into the faces of the diners, a custom borrowed from Hellenistic practice; but on the Sabbath this procedure could not be followed, and instead it became customary to arrange flowers, such as violets or better still roses, in the room where the family feasted, or fragrant plants such as the myrtle were placed on the table at the beginning of the meal. There was a famous talmudic story about R. Simeon b. Yohai and his son who, after thirteen years of hiding in a cave from the Romans, emerged and saw an old man on Friday afternoon carrying two bunches of myrtle "to honor the Sabbath"

(*Shabbat* 33b); the Essenes rubbed frankincense into the garments they wore on the Sabbath so that they should have a refreshing smell. At the end of the Sabbath, when in the talmudic age the second meal of the day was eaten, it became customary to emphasize the significance of the blessing recited over the spices, which were originally on the table, by burning them on coals in an incense burner (*matah* = shovel) to enhance the enjoyment of the meal, and from this the *Havdalah* ceremony originated. Similar customs were observed in the medieval Islamic world where, at the conclusion of a meal, it was customary to burn spices in a brazier to fumigate the room and to sprinkle guests and members of the family with rose water. On the one hand, the idea of having flowers and spices on the Sabbath was to enhance the beauty and aesthetic appreciation of the Sabbath day and as an aid to digestion. On the other hand, the myrtles and roses were meant to give steadfast Sabbath observers and participants of the *Havdalah* ceremony a foretaste of paradise. According to rabbinic sources, paradise was formed on the third day of Creation, and when the just man appeared at the gates of paradise eight myrtles were put into his hand and he was directed to a place with many rivers, surrounded by eight hundred kinds of roses and myrtles.[23]

WARM FOOD ON THE SABBATH

We have much information about the food eaten on the Sabbath in the talmudic age because of the wide-ranging discussion of the rules pertaining to the preparation of warm food for the Sabbath. We are first told in the Mishnah that

> flesh and onions and eggs may not be roasted unless there is time for them to be roasted the same day; nor may bread be put in the oven when darkness is falling, nor may cakes be put upon the coals unless there is time for their top surface to form into a crust. R. Eliezer, [who was active in the period 80–120 c.e.], says: Time for their bottom surface [only] to form into a crust (M. *Shabbat* 1:10).

The Talmud explained that such food had to be roasted before sunset and so long as the fire had taken hold of the greater part of the logs and the items of food were at least a third cooked, it was permissible to keep them on the spit and consume them on the Sabbath. In the Talmud's words, "That it may be roasted before sunset as the food of the son of Derusai," an enigmatic phrase that appears to mean if the food was a third cooked, while according to Rashi, Derusai was a robber who always ate in a hurry (*Shabbat* 20a).

The rabbis further decided that if the food was left in a pot on the stove on the Sabbath, the dish, if sufficiently cooked, was forbidden to be eaten in those cases where it had shrunk, thereby improving in quality; and among the foods it was forbidden to eat were mincemeat, cabbage, and beans, as these foods were said to have shrunk and improved in quality, although the ban on beans, an essential element in *cholent* or *hamin,* was later reversed. R. Nahman ruled, however, that if food shrank and deteriorated in quality, it was permissible to eat it. From this observation, a general rule was formulated that whatever contained flour paste shrank and deteriorated, except a turnip stew, which, though containing flour paste, shrank and improved, if the dish contained meat as well. When the family ate the dish with meat, the meat was cut into small pieces so that the fat pervaded the whole dish and prevented it from deteriorating, and there was thus a ban on eating it on the Sabbath. If visitors were invited for the Sabbath meals, however, the meat was cut into large pieces, and since the fat could not pervade the whole, the dish shrank and deteriorated, thus making it permissible to eat it (*Shabbat* 38a).

A number of interesting deductions may be made from these regulations. It became customary to eat fish pie on Friday night among the Babylonian and later Spanish and medieval Ashkenazic communities (*Shabbat* 37b). On the other hand, it was not permissible to eat mincemeat for lunch on the Sabbath. That is why it became customary among the North African, Syrian, Iraqi, and Spanish communities to eat mincemeat in various forms on Friday night, but even here certain communities, such as the Jews of Kurdistan, seemed to have ignored this ruling, as *kuba,* which contained mincemeat, formed part of their preparation for their local variant of *hamin,* called *mabote.* Taken together, the talmudic rules in the course of time permitted large chunks of meat to be slowly stewed with grain and with certain vegetables on the Sabbath, thereby assembling all the essential ingredients of *hamin* or *cholent.* Yet, according to the Mishnah, one must not place a pot inside or on top of an oven, an essential prerequisite for making *hamin;* but in certain conditions pots could be placed on top of a stove but not inside, which was again a forbidden act (*Shabbat* 38b). "When R. Jose went to Sepphoris . . . [in Galilee; he also found] shrunken eggs, and forbade them to them. Surely it means for that Sabbath?—No: for the following Sabbath. Now, this implies that shrunken eggs go on shrinking and are thereby improved? Yes" (*Shabbat* 38a). Later, among the *Sephardim* the decision was reversed and these eggs known as *haminados* continued to be slowly cooked in an oven for a long period of time for the Sabbath lunch.[24]

Nonetheless, the whole drift of the argument in the Mishnah and the Talmud, with its emphasis on keeping the Sabbath food warm by ensuring that it was covered and forbidding the cooking of food in an oven, points to the fact that in the early centuries of the common era the art of slow stewing was not practiced and that the dish of *hamin* had not quite evolved. According to the Mishnah, which had been completed by 200 c.e., one "may cover up hot food with clothes or produce such as corn or feathers or sawdust or hackled flax [that is, flax that has been combed]. R. Judah forbids fine hackled flax but permits coarse. They may cover up hot food with hides and may move them about, and with wool-shearings but these they may not move about" (M. *Shabbat* 4:1–2). When darkness was falling on the eve of the Sabbath, people were encouraged to "cover up what is to be kept hot" (M. *Shabbat* 2:7). Further, "If a double-stove had been heated with stubble or straw, cooked food may be set on it; but if with peat or wood, cooked food may not be set on it until it has been swept out or covered with ashes. The School of Shammai say: Hot water but not cooked food may be set thereon. And the School of Hillel say: Both hot water and cooked food" (M. *Shabbat* 3:1). "Rava [270–330 c.e.] also said: Why was it said that one must not put away food in a substance which adds heat, even by day? For fear lest he put it away in hot ashes containing a burning coal. Said Abaye to him, then let him put it away!—[That is forbidden] for fear lest he rake the coals" (*Shabbat* 34b). Shortly after the formulation of the Talmud, the *Geonim* reiterated that it was "not permitted to keep Sabbath dishes hot by putting them into ashes on Friday." All this points to the fact that sections of the Jewish population were ever seeking ingenious new ways of keeping the food for the Sabbath lunch really hot, and there is an interesting passage in the Talmud that illustrates this. "At first it was ruled: One who cooks [food] on the Sabbath unwittingly, he may eat [thereof], if deliberately, he may not eat; and the same applies to one who forgets. But when those who intentionally left it there grew numerous, and they pleaded, We had forgotten [it on the stove], they [the sages] retraced their steps and penalized him who forgot" (*Shabbat* 38a). Ancient classical and Christian authors appear to confirm that in the talmudic age Jews did not slowly stew their Sabbath food. The Roman satirist Juvenal (60–140 c.e.) ridiculed Jews for filling a large bucket with hay to keep the Sabbath food warm; and the Church father Ignatius warned Christians not to copy the Jews, by "eating things prepared the day before nor [by] using lukewarm drink."[25]

PASSOVER

On the fourteenth day of the month of *Nisan,* equivalent to March or April in the secular calendar, the Israelites slaughtered a year-old lamb or goat whose blood was smeared with a bunch of hyssop on the doorposts and lintels of their homes. At night each family consumed the Paschal lamb, which was roasted whole with *matzah* and bitter herbs (*merorim*). The *merorim* were wild plants that the Arabs still use to season their food. The ritual prescribed that those eating were to wear sandals, have their belts fastened, and were to hold sticks in their hands. Gedaliah Alon has argued that the highlight of the festival was the shared meal of Paschal lamb, to which the eating of unleavened bread and bitter herbs were mere adjuncts. Roland de Vaux contended that Passover was a springtime sacrifice of a young animal from the flock to secure the prosperity and fertility of the rest of the animals, while the smearing of blood on the doorposts was to give divine protection to the home and to ward off evil spirits. Similar practices have been observed among the bedouin in the south of Israel today. Added support for this last interpretation is derived from the strict injunction against breaking the bone of the Paschal sacrifice. Passover also had an important agricultural dimension, when the Israelites settled in their land after the Exodus from Egypt: it was the festival in which the new barley harvest was eaten for seven days in the form of unleavened bread without any impurities. In Leviticus 23:9–14 is mentioned the bringing of the first sheaf of the harvest to the Lord by means of the priest, after which people were allowed to eat "bread, and parched grain, and fresh ears." Naum Jasny has also pointed out that the leavening of bread was not common at the time of the Exodus from Egypt, from which suggestion it could be argued that *matzah* began to gain heightened symbolic significance in the talmudic age, when the consumption of leavened bread was more general. Coarsely ground barley bread known as *maza* remained the standard food of the Greeks, even in the second century c.e., according to Galen.[26]

We are fortunate to possess vivid descriptions of how the Samaritans and the Ethiopian Jews celebrated Passover in recent times, which can give us an insight into how Jews performed the Passover rituals before this was changed by rabbinic ordinance, after the destruction of the Temple. On the tenth of *Nisan*, the Samaritans selected the Paschal lambs or kids, which were males without blemish and one year old in accordance with the biblical prescription. At twilight on the fourteenth of *Nisan*, a ritual slaughterer selected from the Levites sacrificed the animals before the mass of the Samaritan people, who had gathered on Mount Gerizim for this purpose. Wooden staves were driven through the carcass of the sheep to assist with the roasting, without breaking any bones as directed in Exodus 12:9, after the stomach, kidneys, and fat had been removed and the blood had been drained by the application of salt. The men dipped their fingers in the Paschal blood and smeared some on their children's foreheads, while the lintels and doorposts of the homes where they were to stay during the Passover festival were similarly daubed with blood by using a branch of hyssop following the directions of Exodus 12:7. Other accounts suggest that both adults and children marked their foreheads and probably their arms and hands with blood. The right legs of the animals were burnt on an altar, after which they were given to the chief priest and his family. Ovens were dug out of the earth and lined with stones and then the Paschal sacrifices were lowered into the ovens, which were covered with earth and shrubs, and were left to roast for five hours. Each family was given a portion of the roasted sheep to eat with *matzah* and bitter herbs, but the men and women within the family ate separately. Whatever had been left was collected next morning and burnt on an altar. Zev Garber concluded that the Samaritan celebration of Passover followed the pre-Exilic practices of Judaism, as the Samaritans broke with the normative Jewish traditions in the fourth century B.C.E.[27]

Among the Ethiopian Jews, the first day of *Nisan* was observed as New Year's Day in accordance with Exodus 12:2, and on this sacred day the Falasha priests warned the people to prepare for the forth-coming festival. Four days prior to the festival the priests told the women to start housecleaning. Everything was removed from their thatched circular homes, which were thoroughly cleaned. All straw utensils, such as the circular table and baskets, were removed and replaced by new ones, while the housewives made new pottery for serving food, smashing or selling the old ones. For three days before Passover the Falashas refrained from eating leavened bread, subsisting on dried peas and beans. Like the Samaritans, they slaughtered the sheep at twilight, and the sheep's blood was sprinkled on the doorposts of the houses. The Falashas had a very strict concept of leaven (*hametz*), including any food to which water is added in this category. Therefore, all food, even their special *matzah* known as *keeta*, must be prepared just before the meal and all leftovers were thrown away. Milk was used for only one day, and dairy products such as cheese or butter, which were liable to ferment, were forbidden during Passover. On the Sabbath, when no cooking was possible, the Falashas ate toasted grains unmixed with water. *Keeta* was baked from flour kept especially dry and mixed with water drawn from a well, the significance being, as Jacob Lauterbach pointed out, that in ancient times wells were thought to be the abode of the deity.[28]

During the Second Temple period, it has been estimated that as many as 1,200,000 Jewish pilgrims flocked to the Temple for the Passover celebrations, particularly the sacrifice of Paschal lambs. Josephus related that 255,600 animals were sacrificed on the eve of Passover in the reign of Nero; the Mishnah also gave details of the repair of roads and the supply of water to wayfarers along the pilgrims' routes to the capital. It has been argued that with the destruction of the Temple in 70 c.e. the *Seder* service was completely revised by R. Gamaliel II, the patriarch at the end of the first century and the opening decades of the second century c.e., who deemphasized reenactment and stressed the importance of instruction of *Haggadah;* and further that without the Temple the eating of the Paschal lamb lapsed as a constituent part of the service. R. Gamaliel was in favor of the practice of eating helmeted kids, that is, a kid roasted whole with its head and shanks placed with its entrails, but he was overruled by the sages. In the Mishnah it was stated that in "a place where they [the people] are accustomed to eat roasted meat on the nights of Passover—they eat [it]" (M. *Pesahim* 4:4). Gedaliah Alon, on the basis of several other passages in the Mishnah, suggested that the practice of eating roasted lamb on the eve of Passover continued after the destruction of the Temple, adducing further evidence from a Haggadah text from the Cairo Geniza to show that the practice continued as late as the tenth or eleventh century. Not only was the question about roasted meat still there among the child's questions, but there was a special blessing to the Lord, "who did command our ancestors to eat unleavened bread, bitter herbs and meat roasted on the fire. . . ." Moreover, after the compilation of the Mishnah in the *Tosefta Yom Tov* there was a passage that related that "Todos of Rome directed the Romans [the Jewish community in Rome] to take lambs on the nights of Passover and they prepared them roasted whole." Such practices spread outside the ranks of the Jews in the Mediterranean area, for a spit-roasted suckling lamb is still the traditional Easter dish in Rome and throughout Greece. True that all sacrifices for the eve of Passover had stopped by the middle of the second century, yet Baruch Bokser is not correct in attempting to downgrade the importance of the dish of roasted lamb for Passover, which long continued among the Jews in the Mediterranean area as a substitute for the original sacrifice and as a tradition subtly influenced their Christian neighbors.[29]

A number of writers have drawn attention to the fact that during the talmudic age, after the destruction of the Temple, the rabbis responded to the loss of the Paschal sacrificial cult by remodeling the *Seder* on the pattern of a Greek or Roman banquet or symposium. This influence was twofold, including both the dining arrangements and the actual courses and order of the meal. Athenaeus, a writer who lived in Rome at the end of the second century and the beginning of the third century c.e., quoted various Greek texts to stress the importance of pouring water over the hands before and after meals, while it has been suggested by Siegfried Stein that the prayer recited on the washing of hands, *netilat yedayim,* incorporated the Greek expression, to which the usual Jewish words of blessing were added. Athenaeus remarked

that ". . . Philyllius in Augê, has 'over the hands,' thus: 'At last the
ladies have finished their dinner; it's high time to take away the tables,
then sweep up the floor, and after that give "water over the hands" to
all, and some perfume' " (Athenaeus IX 408e).[30]

In biblical times only royalty and the aristocracy used to recline
while eating. Amos, a prophet of the eighth century B.C.E., denounced
those "that lie in beds of ivory and stretch themselves upon their
couches . . ." and "That drink wine in bowls. . . ," perhaps referring to
something such as the Greek mixing bowl, in which wine and water
were mixed, as this was how wine was drunk in the talmudic age
(Amos 6:4, 6). In the course of the seventh century C.E. the Greeks
adopted the oriental custom of reclining at banquets instead of sitting
upright as at Homeric feasts. Both the Greeks and Romans dined on
sloping couches, each with three reclining places (*triclinia*), grouped
around a table in sets of three. By the time of the empire, Roman
matrons possessed sufficient status to demand a place beside their
husbands on the couches, and slaves were permitted this privilege on
holidays. Similarly, in Palestine, where the values of the Roman world
prevailed, the Mishnah decreed that "even the poorest man in Israel
must not eat [on the eve of Passover] until he reclines" (M. *Pesahim*
10:1); and the Jerusalem Talmud made reclining obligatory for the
ordinary housewife. During times when the individual was in
mourning for a near relative, the couches were turned upside down
and the mourner sat on the upturned couch. In contrast, in Babylonia,
where perhaps under Persian influence women had a lower status, it
was taught that "a woman in her husband's [house] need not recline,
but if she is a woman of importance she must recline. A son in his
father's [house] must recline" (*Pesahim* 108a).[31]

We shall now analyze the *Seder* service on the one hand, and the
aristocratic Greek symposium and Roman banquet on the other,
carefully noting the points of congruence and contrast in the two
ceremonies. Whereas the Greeks started with the washing of the hands
and proceeded to pour a libation of wine to the gods onto the floor, the
Seder service reversed the order, opening with the *Kiddush*, the
sanctification recited over the first cup of wine. Siegfried Stein noted
the resemblances between the *Kiddush* and the *Hallel* on the one hand
and the Greek paeans to the gods on the other, quoting Athenaeus:
"Every gathering among the ancients to celebrate a Symposium
acknowledged the god as the cause for it and made use of chaplets
appropriate to the gods as well as hymns and songs." What is the
procedure for the reclining on ordinary occasions, the Talmud asked.

The guests enter and sit on stools and chairs till they are assembled.
When water is brought, each one washes one hand. When wine is

brought, each one says a blessing for himself. When they go up [on the couches] and recline, and water is brought to them, although each of them has already washed one hand, he now again washes both hands. When wine is brought to them, although each of them has said a blessing for himself, one now says a blessing on behalf of all. (*Berakhot* 43a).

It was customary to wash only one hand in Egypt, the right hand, as the other hand was used for unclean purposes. This washing of the hands corresponded to the first washing of the hands in the *Seder* service, without a blessing being recited; and the two occasions when the hands were washed at the *Seder* seem to follow the etiquette of Greek and Roman diners as much as the rule adduced by the Talmud in *Pesahim* 115a that the hands were washed whenever food was dipped into liquid.[32]

Some scholars have argued that in the talmudic age the hors d'oeuvres and the main dish were eaten first at the *Seder*, after which the child asked the Four Questions and the *Haggadah* was recited. One Friday night, "Rabbah b. R. Huna visited the *Resh Galutha* [the Exilarch, the head of Babylonian Jewry]. When a tray [with food] was placed before him, he spread a cloth and sanctified [the day]. It was taught likewise. And they both agree that one must not bring the table unless one has recited *Kiddush*; but if it was brought, a cloth is spread [over it] and *Kiddush* is recited" (*Pesahim* 100b). Further, it was stated that for the *Seder*, "R. Simi b. Ashi said: Unleavened bread [must be set] before each person [of the company], bitter herbs before each person, and *haroseth* before each person, but we remove the table only from him who recites the *Haggadah*. R. Huna said: All these too [are set only] before him who recites the *Haggadah*. And the law is as R. Huna" (*Pesahim* 115b). In Palestine, where couches were in vogue, three couches with places for nine persons were arranged around a table with three wooden legs and with a round tabletop some twenty inches in diameter usually made of soft limestone but occasionally of hard reddish Jerusalem stone. In size these tables, corresponded to a modern coffee table. Because of their stone tops, it is unlikely that these tables were pushed under the couches when not in use or hung by a ring on the wall. Nahman Avigad also found rectangular stone tables about the height of a modern table and with a thick central leg in recent excavations in Jerusalem. These tables, which originated in the Hellenistic East—although the fashion spread to Rome—were used to hold drinking vessels and were placed between groups of diners reclining around the smaller tables. In Babylonia food was served on trays (Aramaic *taka* from the Assyrian *tuku* shield), probably in a similar fashion to the later Islamic world, where food was placed on a round copper tray (Arabic *siniyya*) between two and three feet in diameter, which was put onto a stool about fifteen inches high. By this means it was possible for as many as twelve persons to sit around this tray. When the Talmud mentioned the tables were brought in at the beginning of a meal and removed at the end of the repast, it was probably referring to the Babylonian practice of eating from such metal trays.[33]

Other similarities between the *Seder* and the Roman banquets were the wine taken before, in the middle, and after a meal, which was equivalent to the four cups of wine prescribed on the night of the *Seder*. Various manuscripts of the Talmud cited by Rabbi Menachem Kasher showed that the tractate *Pesahim,* page 118, originally mentioned a fifth cup, although modern texts refer only to four cups. In the *Tosefta Pesahim* 10:4 it was asserted that on Passover a man should make his wife and children happy by giving them wine to drink, as "wine gladdens the human heart" (Psalm 104:15). The Greeks were moved by similar ideas; for instance, Astydamus declared that "he revealed to mortals that cure for sorrow, the vine, mother of wine." A favorite symposium game among Greek diners was *kottabos,* the flicking of wine from a cup at a target, and it is possible that the ancient ceremony of flicking wine from cups when chanting the ten plagues at the *Seder* was a Judaic adaptation of this custom. Among the Romans the hors d'oeuvre called *gustatio* often consisted of eggs, giving rise to the phrase *ab uvo usque ad mala* from the Roman practice of beginning a dinner with eggs and ending with fruit, but the preliminaries to a meal also included vegetables such as lettuce and nuts. Among the Ashkenazim eggs continued to play a prominent role at the *Seder,* for it was customary to start the meal by dipping a hard-boiled egg into salt water, and in a similar fashion in medieval Europe some Christian communities distributed special painted eggs at Easter. Athenaeus referred to lettuce seven times in his *Deipnosophists,* and bread eaten with lettuce figured in the Graeco-Roman menu, just as the Jews ate *matzah,* unleavened bread, with lettuce in the form of a sandwich at Passover. Even the Greeks occasionally attached great symbolic importance to unleavened bread, for when brides and children were introduced into their husband's or their father's phratry, or brotherhood, unleavened bread was offered at the shrine of Delphi. According to Stein, Athenaeus described dishes similar to *haroseth,* and the Roman cookery writer Apicius mentioned sweet dishes with similar characteristics to the Sephardic version of this paste. What is certain is that in the medieval Islamic world sauces [sals] made of ground walnuts and almonds mixed with vinegar or lemon were common and were probably survivals of Graeco-Roman cuisine. Even the name *hullake,* a mixture of date juice and nuts, the equivalent of *haroseth* among the Syrian and Iraqi Jews, was probably derived from *hallec*, the Roman fish sauce. Heracleides asserted that nuts should be served first at a dinner, instead of for dessert, as this aided the digestion. Solomon Zeitlin has pointed out how the dipping of blood on the lintels and doorposts and perhaps daubing individuals too after the Paschal sacrifice became transformed into the two dippings of the vegetable into salt water and the bitter herbs into the *haroseth* in the rabbinic ceremony.[34]

After eating the hors d'oeuvres and drinking the first cup of wine the diners in wealthy Jewish homes in Palestine would leave their chairs in the antechamber and repair to the dining room, the *triclinium*. In the *Ethics of the Fathers*, R. Jacob referred to these Roman dining practices, exclaiming: "This world is like a vestibule before the World to Come. Prepare thyself in the vestibule that thou mayest enter into the reclining hall" (M. *Avot* 4:16). Now the main course, the *mensae primae*, of the Roman dinner was eaten, which consisted chiefly of roasted and boiled meat, poultry, or some delicacies. A Greek poem by Philoxenus dated to shortly before 391 B.C.E. stated that ". . . the slave sets before us . . . meats of kid and lamb, boiled and roasted and the sweetest morsel of . . . entrails . . . as the gods love." So, too, there is an interesting parallel passage in *Tosefta Pesahim* 10:5 in which it was related that "the shammash [waiter] minces the entrails and puts them [as a kind of appetizer] before the guests. . . ." As recounted in the Mishnah, the father originally answered the child when the child asked one of the Four Questions, ". . . on all other nights we eat meat roasted, steamed, or boiled, this night only roasted" (M. *Pesahim* 10:4). After the destruction of the Second Temple, this question was eventually dropped. The main course at Roman banquets was taken with wine and corresponded to the second cup of wine drunk at the *Seder* service. The Mishnah further said that two cooked dishes were eaten at the *Seder* table to differentiate this night from ordinary weekday meals, as poor households would normally eat one cooked dish at a meal. The Talmud asked, "What are the two dishes? Said R. Huna: Beet and rice. Hezekiah said: Even a fish and the egg on it. R. Joseph said: Two kinds of meat are necessary, one in memory of the Passover-offering and the second in memory of the *haggigah* [the festival sacrifice brought on the first day of a festival]" (*Pesahim* 114b).[35]

The second course, *mensae secundae*, consisted of fruit or other kinds of sweets. Rav and Samuel in Babylonia used to eat mushrooms and pigeons for dessert, but Samuel declared that they must not be eaten after the Paschal meat on Passover, and R. Johanan added parched corn, dates, and nuts to this list. Guests could, however, continue to eat sponge cakes, honey cakes, and a rich *matzah* known as *iskeritin*, for their dessert provided they ate a piece of *matzah* at the end of the meal. The rabbis recommended that children play games with nuts at Passover, while the Roman author Lucian mentioned playing with nuts on the festival of Saturnalia, although these games were not confined to children. The serious drinking started after the meal and included the third and fourth cups, and maybe the fifth cup favored by so many rabbinic commentators, which became Elijah's cup. The directions in the Mishnah for the *Seder* ended with the comment, "After eating from the Passover offering, they do not end with *afiqomon*" (M. *Pesahim* 10:8). The expression *afiqomon* came from the Greek word *epikomios,* which was a term that covered the revelry common after a banquet, which was forbidden to the participants at the *Seder.* The curbing of the amount of wine consumed at the *Seder,* the rabbinic insistence on diluting the wine with water, and the eating of lettuce, which was a well-known antiaphrodisiac, were all meant to ensure that the *Seder* did not degenerate into the licentiousness of a Greek or a Roman banquet, as described by Clement of Alexandria:

> The wild celebration ends up as a drunken stupor, with everyone freely confiding the troubles of his love affairs. And as for all-night drinking parties, they go hand-in-hand with the holiday celebration, and, in their wine-drinking promoted drunkenness and promiscuity. . . . The exciting rhythm of flutes and harps, choruses and dances, Egyptian castanets and other entertainments get out of control and become indecent and burlesque. . . .

Further, "Even among the ancient Greeks, there was a song called the *skolion* which they used to sing after the manner of the Hebrew psalm at drinking parties and over their after-dinner cups." The *Seder,* through its literary texts and through its preservation of ancient dining arrangements associated with the symposium, remained a vehicle for teaching each succeeding generation the miracle of the redemption from Egypt and gave the Jewish people fresh hope of national salvation.[36]

SPECIAL FOODS

According to Samuel Krauss, the Jews in the talmudic age were conversant with a form of noodle, a point confirmed and clarified in recent research by Charles Perry, who attributed the invention of pasta to the Greeks. The Aramaic term *itriyah,* from which the Hebrew word for noodles was borrowed, was derived from the Greek word *itrion,* while the Greeks had a completely different term, *laganon*. Both the latter foods were originally unleavened, thin, flat cakes of dough eaten with oil and honey. In the Jerusalem Talmud it was asked whether "boiled dough satisfies the religious requirements of unleavened bread," from which evidence Perry inferred that the dough had come to be boiled in the Byzantine Empire by the fifth century c.e. and that it was now consumed in the form of noodles. Nonetheless, during the same period in the Babylonian world there was a dish called *rihata* made from boiled flour and honey, from which the Arabic word for noodles, *rishta*, which means string, was derived, but the oldest Arabic references to this term were from the thirteenth century. Hence the talmudic term *rihata* (*Berakhot* 37b) predated the Arabic word by almost a millennium. According to the Talmud, in the *rihata* of agricultural laborers there was a large quantity of flour, while townspeople tended to use a greater amount of honey in this food. It is thus questionable that noodles were invented exclusively in Greece and more likely that similar dishes were concocted in the Near East as well.[37]

A dish that was prepared in a fashion akin to *rihata* was *habiz*, which consisted of pounded grain and honey boiled in a pot; sometimes crumbs of bread were broken up and added to the *habiz*. According to Professor Maxime Rodinson, there was a medieval Arab dish called *habis*, which was a delicacy made from syrup or oil and of sweetened sesame but having the consistency of a jelly of starch. It is almost certain that this medieval dish was a later version of the food first mentioned in the Talmud. However, *habis* was one of a number of foods the Arabs had taken over from the Persians, just as the Babylonians had earlier been deeply influenced by Persian cuisine.[38]

The Mishnah referred to Syrian cakes shaped in figures, cakes made of spongy dough or perhaps crackers, honey cakes, and paste balls (M. *Hallah* 1:4), while the sages said that Syrian cakes shaped in figures must not be made on Passover (*Pesahim* 37a). Accordingly, it is quite possible that many Lebanese pastries were not only of medieval origin but also stemmed from the ancient world. In the Midrash to Psalms, there was already an allusion to a pastry, the *kadaif*, then made of pounded wheat, a delicacy that later became well known in the medieval Islamic world. A medieval Arab poet described *kadaif*:

> When in my friends the pang of hunger grows,
> I have *kadaif*, like soft folios;
> As flow of lambent honey brimming white
> So amid other dainties it is bright,
> And, having drunk of almond-essence deep,
> with oil it glitters, wherein it doth seep.

Also mentioned in the Talmud were thick biscuit rings known as *Kaak* (*Berakhot* 38a and 42a), which are still popular today with Jews whose ancestors hailed from Syria and Iraq. According to the Midrash, honey cakes were made from fine flour kneaded with butter and honey, while there were also references to another type of flat honey cake or waffle. Despite the contentions of Krauss, it is doubtful whether the Romans and Palestinian Jews knew how to make a modern pancake, combining butter, milk, eggs, and flour. Yet another type of dessert was *ashishim*, cakes made of ground roast lentils impregnated with honey (*Nedarim* 40a). The Talmud also alluded to a pudding that was probably made from minced meat mixed with spices and wine (*Pesahim* 56a and *Ketubbot* 65a). R. Jose reminisced with pardonable exaggeration that "I saw Sepphoris in its prosperity, and it contained a hundred and eight thousand markets for pudding dealers." Finally, there are also references in the Talmud to *troknin* (*Berakhot* 37b), which has been identified with the Latin word *tracta* or *tractum*, variously described as a flat, fried cake or a layered arrangement in a pastry; and to *ludit*, gladiator's food of wheat and beans.[39]

5

TRADITIONAL JEWISH FOOD IN THE MIDDLE AGES

ITALY, GERMANY, AND FRANCE

In many essentials, the Jewish food of Italy was similar to that of France and Germany, although a separate cuisine tended to develop in the latter two countries. In particular, the economy of northern Italy was closely intermeshed with that of northern Europe, and Italian recipes flowed with commerce into Germany, Austria, and central Europe for many centuries. Unlike that of Max Weinreich, recent scholarship has suggested that the cradle of the Yiddish language was not in the Rhineland but in southern Germany, Austria, and Czechoslovakia; and in these last three regions the cuisine of the Yiddish-speaking Jews also evolved, a cuisine with a mixture of Italian, southern German, Austrian, and Slavic elements. Geographically, only a small Austrian triangle separated Italy from eastern Europe. We would commend the hypothesis of the author of an article in the *Universal Jewish Encyclopedia* who suggested that "the Jewish food habit grew during the Italian period and was carried eastward" into Europe. Italian recipes traveled in this direction in waves over the centuries; during the early Middle Ages there came pies, tortes, possibly flat cakes (*floden*), *khremslekh* (vermicelli), and sauces that were later followed by brawn and marzipan.[1]

Meat pies were first mentioned by Rabbi Nathan ben Yehiel of Rome (1035–1106) in his lexicon to the Talmud, the *Aruch*, published in 1101; afterward the dish was introduced into Germany, Austria, and France. It was a popular dish among Jews from all three countries, frequently referred to by Rabbi Isaac ben Moses of Vienna, the Or Zarua (1180–1260), and in the writings of the French Tosafists, the French commentators on the Talmud of the twelfth and thirteenth

79

centuries, who also mentioned fish pies. The Romance word *pastata*, a food of dough filled with meat that was derived from the medieval Latin term *pasta* (dough), entered the Yiddish language, having been adopted by the French Jews, who called it *pastide;* both the food and the medieval name for it were taken over by German Jews. Pies were filled with a variety of different kinds of meat, including udder, in contradistinction to the flat cakes filled with cheese or fruit that were often *milchic.* Thus, rabbinic authorities were reluctant to authorize the baking of pies and flat cakes, *floden,* together with bread because the odor from the meat pie could penetrate the bread, thereby rendering it, in Jewish law, unfit to eat. Rabbi Meir of Rothenburg (1215–1295) forbade the baking of bread with cheese or meat pies, but if these articles were baked together he did not prohibit the eating of such bread or cheese; and some earlier rabbinic authorities used to cover the different articles if they were baked together in the same oven so as to avoid contamination. Medieval pies were either baked at home in the more affluent households or taken to the baker's oven, but if need be they could be cooked on the hearth. During the Middle Ages, they were often prepared in a thick whole-wheat and rye pastry made without the addition of fat, as the pies were served for more than one meal and only part of the crust was removed at each sitting. If, however, the pies were to be kept for a shorter period of time, they were made with a wheaten flour.[2]

Rabbinic sources frequently mentioned a related flat cake, *floden,* consisting of two layers of dough with a filling of cheese and that was likewise possibly of Italian origin. This was first mentioned in a tenth-century source in a discussion between Rabbi Judah ben Meir Ha-Kohen, otherwise known as Rabbi Leontin, and Rabbi Eleazar ben Gilo. Patti Shosteck has suggested that *floden* may be similar to the Italian lasagna dishes, which go back to at least the fourteenth century, but it is more likely that they are directly descended from the pizza recipes or those for *torta col formaggio,* cheesecake. The German word *Fladen,* a flat cake, clearly stemmed from the medieval Latin term *flado,* or *fladonis,* while the eleventh-century French word was *fladon,* which became contracted into *flaon* by the twelfth century; hence the modern French and English pastry, the flan. If the food was not of Italian origin, it probably flourished first in the Rhineland, and we should recall that Rabbi Leontin was active in Mainz. *Floden* were made with cheese fried in butter with apples and prunes and were sometimes filled with raisins. Another cake with sugar that had come to Germany from Italy was *Torte,* a fancy cake or tart. Although the earliest German source mentioning the word dates from 1418, in Jewish sources there was a reference two hundred years earlier in the work of Rabbi Samson Bar Zedek, a pupil of the Maharam, Rabbi Meir of Rothenburg. So, too, the thirteenth-century English rabbi Elijah of London declared that fruit tarts (*tortes*) could be eaten even if they were made by Gentiles. The German word *Torte* was derived from the Italian word *torta*, meaning a cake or pie, which in turn stemmed from the medieval Latin term *tortum*.[3]

Pasta may have been invented somewhere in the East Roman Empire and was then adopted in the Byzantine parts of Italy between the sixth and eleventh centuries; noodles were also a dish indigenous to Persia, China, and Central Asia, where they could have originated as well. Between 1260 and 1290 a cookery book appeared in Italy that included recipes for making vermicelli, *tortelli*, and *tortelletti*, the first published references to pasta. During the same century, ravioli had already become well established. In the next century Kalonymos ben Kalonymos (1286–1328), an Italian-Jewish satirist, included macaroni and *tortelli* among twenty-seven Purim dishes. At some stage during the Middle Ages in Italy, dough was boiled in a pot instead of being baked or fried to make real pasta; but even in the fifteenth century one cleric was denouncing citizens of Florence for eating their pasta fried with garlic, while the sixteenth-century culinary writer Christoforo Messisbugo still gave recipes for fried macaroni with honey, butter, cream cheese, and cinnamon.[4]

Among others, Jewish merchants and rabbinic families brought *grimseli*, the ancestor of vermicelli, to Germany from Italy. According to a report in the *Or Zarua*, in the twelfth century Rabbi Judah ben Kalonymos had the custom of eating *grimseli* (*khremzlekh*), probably in a dish of strips of baked dough doused in honey, after *Kiddush* on Friday evening, in order to be able to recite the traditional blessing on cakes, the *mezonot*. He was one among a number of rabbinic families in the Rhineland who had emigrated from Italy. Also, Rabbi Eleazar ben Judah ben Kalonymos, the Rokeach from Worms in the thirteenth century, had the custom of eating *verimselish* on a Friday night, a custom still maintained by Rabbi Isserlein in the fifteenth century, if the eve of Passover coincided with a Friday night. All these Hebrew and later Yiddish variants, namely *grimseli*, *verimselish*, and *vermslish* were derived from the Italian word *vermicelli*, which came from the diminutive form of the Latin term for a worm, *vermis*, and were in turn related to the old French expression *vermesiel*, for which the Tosafists used similar words. From an examination of these medieval rabbinic texts, it appears that these strips of dough were baked in an oven, but other rabbinic texts show that they were sometimes cooked in pots, although it was not until the sixteenth century that Rabbi Joseph Hahn of Frankfurt mentioned the alternatives of baking or cooking. True that Charles Perry has demonstrated that noodles reached Germany from the Slav countries all the way from Persia by the sixteenth

century, and in the sixteenth century the distinguished Polish Rabbi
Isserles (c. 1525–1572) described *verimselish* (vermicelli) as being the
same food as *lokshen* (noodles); yet the suspicion must remain that
pasta dishes also reached Austria and Germany from Italy and Spain
much earlier than the sixteenth century, as four centuries seems a long
time for noodles to travel so short a distance between Italy and central
Europe. Moreover, if pasta had reached England by the thirteenth
century, as new evidence suggests, it is possible that R. Judah ben
Kalonymos was eating real pasta in the twelfth century.[5]

Italy may have obtained ravioli from Persia or Central Asia, as
similar types of food are scattered throughout the region; like vermicelli they came to Europe via Byzantium. Maimonides had already
traced the origins of cooked doughs to Persia and the Near East. Ravioli
are pasta envelopes of egg-noodle dough and were well established in
Italy at an early date, particularly in Genoa. *Tortelli* and *tortelletti* are
ring-shaped envelopes of dough, the origin of which goes back to at
least the twelfth century in Italy, while *crespelli* are ribbons of dough
fried in oil whose usage was restricted by a sumptuary law in Bologna
in 1294. *Cappelletti* are cap-shaped envelopes of dough, sometimes
served in sauce and sometimes in soup, but they appear to be of more
recent origin than the other pasta dough, as one of the earliest
examples was to be found in Ferrara as late as 1529.[6]

Like the Italian food vermicelli which was the ancestor of both
khremzlekh and, in part, of noodles if the contribution of *lokshen* is
also taken into account, *kreplekh* became differentiated into two
distinctive foods among the East European Jews; it was both a fritter
and a dumpling in soup. In medieval Latin we encounter the words
crispa, crespa, and *crispus* in the thirteenth century, meaning a
pastry, from which the English word *crisp* is derived and with which
some important French and German food terms are connected. Rabbenu Tam in France in the twelfth century referred to *krepish*, from
the medieval French term *crespe*, a word that is related to the modern
French term *crêpe*, a pancake, as soft dough that was wrapped around
a bird's stomach and intestines and roasted. Moreover, the German
word *Krapfen*, meaning a fritter or doughnut, to which the Yiddish
word *kreplekh* seems the closest related, appears to be dependent on
the original French culinary terminology. Rabbi Moses of Evreux, a
pupil of Rabbi Meir of Rothenburg described *kreplinsh* as a dough that
was fried in oil, something like the Italian crespelli. Earlier, Rabbi Isaac
ben Moses of Vienna, the Or Zarua (1180–1260), mentioned that in the
Slav lands they served *kreplekh* with whey. Later *kreplekh* were
cooked, baked, and fried and stuffed with meat, cheese, or fruit. The
Ménagier de Paris, a cookbook compiled in 1392 or a year later, has a
selection of fritters, pancakes, and rissoles (*risollez* are mentioned

already by Rabbi Elijah of London), while an edition of the *Viandier* from the first half of the fifteenth century supplied a recipe for pancakes (*crespe*) rolled around sticks of cheese and heated to become crisp, much like *kreplekh*.[7]

In the thirteenth century Rabbi Meir of Rothenburg referred to dumplings, but it is unlikely that the custom of serving meat-filled *kreplekh* with soup originated in Germany, as the Germans already had a dumpling in soup of their own. This was known as the *Knödel*, from which the Yiddish term *kneydlekh* is derived by way of the Czech word *knedliky*. Further, the Italian food *cappelletti*, to which the *kreplekh* in soup seems most akin, was not much known before the sixteenth century, leading to the conclusion that the Yiddish version must have followed a century or two later.[8]

Another confection from Italy that the Jews readily adopted was marzipan, which was made with ground almonds, sugar, and honey and scented with rose water. The European name of the confection— Italian *marzapana* and German *Marzipan*—was a direct borrowing of the Arabic term *mautaban*, which was itself taken from the Arabic word for white, *uataba*. Although the use of marzipan among the aristocracy and royal courts cannot be documented before the twelfth century in Europe, it was known centuries earlier in the Islamic world, where sugar sculptures were common in North Africa by the eleventh century. From Venice, this sweet confection traveled from its place of origin in the Middle East to Germany by means of such ports of entry as Lübeck and Königsberg and on to Poland. Among Jews the first reference we have to marzipan was from Italy, where a gift of six tarts of marzipan was made by Lazzaro da Volterra to one of the Medici in 1492. By the sixteenth century marzipan was eaten by the Jews of Poland, as there was a reference to it in the rabbinic work *Emek Beracha*. Between the fifteenth and seventeenth centuries statues of sugar became *de rigueur* in Italy and in southern French cities for grand-ducal weddings and were featured at royal feasts in England, where they were known as "subtleties"; thenceforth, the use of these marzipan statues spread to ever-widening ranks of society. When Haham Azulai visited the chief rabbi of Amsterdam in 1778 on Purim, he saw a replica of the palace of Ahasuerus and a table laden with fruit, cheeses, and pickles, all made with sugar and perhaps with almonds.[9]

Although the Italian Jews developed a unique cuisine, it is difficult to trace the historical evolution of the individual dishes, but many of them appear to be of considerable antiquity. In Italy certain vegetables, such as beet and eggplant (the aubergine), were little consumed except among Jews; in North Africa among Jews we find a similar predilection for vegetables, a cheap and nutritious source of food, which was neglected by the bulk of the population but utilized by the Jews, many of whom were poor. In Rome, the earliest Jewish community in western Europe, there was one outstanding dish, known as *carciofi alla giudia*, young, tender artichokes deep-fried in oil. During the Middle Ages, the artichoke was eaten in Europe only in Muslim Spain and Sicily, from where its cultivation spread to Italy; the dish became especially prized among the Jews of Rome but probably not before the fifteenth century. Further, the suggestion that the Jews brought pizza to Italy from the Middle East, since pizza resembles pita, the Middle Eastern flat bread that they were accustomed to eat, has little to commend it. Pita was adopted by the Spanish-Jewish immigrants to Turkey in the sixteenth century or even later, but the pizza dish was established in Naples in the early Middle Ages and perhaps was enjoyed by the inhabitants of Pompeii. In Pitigliano, a small town near Florence, there was a delectable dish of veal and chicken of considerable age known as *chazarello*, little pig, a precursor of kosher bacon from the United States.[10]

According to Kalonymos ben Kalonymos (1286–1328), during the fourteenth century on Purim Italian Jews feasted on a wide variety of meat dishes, poultry, and game, including a highly seasoned stew (ragout), sheep, the gazelle, the roe deer, the dove, the turtledove, goose, capon, swan, duck, pheasant, partridge, moorhen, quail, and the paunch of a stuffed fowl. Among the pasta dishes mentioned by this writer were macaroni, *tortelli*, and *tortelletti*, the last two being ring-shaped envelopes of pasta of different sizes stuffed with meat and spices, especially nutmeg. Italian Jews in this period also enjoyed fritters, hearthcakes (*focaccia*), *mostacciuoli* (hard little cakes of flour and honey, sometimes containing raisins), and pies.[11]

According to a distinguished Jewish doctor Amatus Lusitanus (1511–1568), the Italian Jews were accustomed to eat goose, duck, smoked beef, vegetables, and much salted cheese; they were also keen on meat pies, just as the French and German Jews were, baked meat, peas, beans, and lentils. The doctor advised his Jewish patient to eat white bread that was light and well kneaded and covered with caraway seed, although the patient should try to avoid eating *matzah*. The doctor recommended that his patient should desist from eating the cold meats so popular among Jews, such as strongly salted meat, goose, and duck, and likewise he was to refrain from consuming quail and turtledoves. He could eat chicken, goat meat, calf, and mutton. He should no longer eat salted cheese and foods prepared from it and mixed with *matzah* meal to make macaroons. Fish taken from sandy or stony water beds were recommended, but preferably they were to be cooked in water or broiled, not fried in oil. Vegetables that were approved were chicory, spinach, golden cabbage, lettuce, and parsley, but lentils and beans were to be expressly avoided. Fruits allowed were grapes, well-ripened figs, raisins, almonds, pistachio nuts, and melons. Again, soft-boiled eggs were acceptable but hard-boiled or fried eggs were not. It is interesting that the varieties of meat and poultry consumed by Italian Jews between the fourteenth and sixteenth centuries according to the descriptions of Kalonymos ben Kalonymos and Lusitanus remained the same, while a number of dishes stayed popular throughout these three centuries. In many respects this diet was similar to that of the medieval French and German Jews, apart from the pasta dishes, although it differed significantly from that of the Jews of the Middle East.[12]

In northern Europe during the Middle Ages, the French Jews were renowned for their love of food and of extravagant dishes. In a letter ascribed to one of Maimonides' followers and probably dating from the thirteenth century, the French Jews were reprimanded for their interest in choice dishes. They study the Talmud, declared this stern critic, "with their stomachs full of meat, vegetables and wine!" So, too, they were mocked because they "perceive God only when eating beef pickled with vinegar and garlic called in their language 'sala' (sualce, sauce)." Both in France and in Germany the medieval Jews ate roast meat, salt beef, and a variety of poultry, while Rabbi Meir of Rothenburg (1215–1293) mentioned that coarse bread was specially baked for the fattening of geese. Rashi (1040–1105) described a pot roast as meat cooked in its own fat and juices with a seasoning of onions. So entrenched did the use of garlic become in Askenazic cooking that a fifteenth-century Karaite scholar in Turkey poured scorn on Ashkenazic students "who eat their dishes prepared with garlic which ascends to their brains"; at the beginning of the eighteenth century the publicist J. G. Schudt in Germany referred to the Jews' immoderate use of garlic. Since the medieval Spanish Jews flavored their meat dishes with garlic and it remained an essential ingredient in Middle Eastern cooking, however, the alleged distinction drawn by H. J. Zimmels between Askenazim and Sephardim in their use of garlic is untenable. To return to the medieval French Jews, Rashi, who cultivated vineyards in northern France for a living, was no exception to this craving for gourmet living. "On one occasion," declared his disciple Rabbi Shemaiah, "I saw brought to him on a cone-shaped vessel meat or spiced meat, or eggs fried in honey." The French medieval rabbinic commentators, the Tosafists, mentioned twenty different types of cake eaten by their Jewish contemporaries, including a sponge cake fried in oil, a cake made with flour fermented in grape skins, a gateau (*galton*), and a cake made from a mixture of sugar, almonds, spices, and flour. Eggs and nuts were commonly fried with honey, while items served for dessert included baked apples, dates pounded and mixed with sesame, cinnamon sticks, and biscuits in the shape of birds and trees. Other special French foods partaken of by Jews were dishes of pounded wheat (*trijes* from old French *tragiées*) and *treille*, a food of flour mixed with wine and various kinds of wafers. To complete the meal on a festive occasion there would sometimes be pieces of hailstone *gelda* (from Latin *gelida*, cold) floating in a goblet of wine to keep it cool. East European Jewish cuisine drew in part on a heritage from medieval France, which added flair and piquancy to its dishes.[13]

The Greeks and Romans cooked a flat pancake in a round pan, the cake being called in Latin a *placenta*. The English and German terms for a pancake are connected with the medieval Latin word *panna*, meaning frying pan, which stemmed from the Latin terms *patella* and *patina*. The original heavy, unfoldable pancakes were made from flour mixed with water and oil. The medieval Latin term for a pancake was *frixum ex ovis*, something fried with eggs, and the presumption is that the Jews imitated their Gentile neighbors and also made their pancakes with eggs, although certain medieval recipes demanded only the whites of eggs. In Jewish sources pancakes were first mentioned in the twelfth century in Germany. Omelettes were sometimes filled with raisins, fish, or minced meat, but the earliest Jewish references to these practices are much later and were made by Rabbi Abraham Danzig (died 1820), who spoke of pancakes prepared with egg and cheese. Rashi mentioned a type of pancake that was baked in the well of the oven, a method that was still followed in central and east Europe until recently. Just as important in medieval Jewish cuisine were the *oublies* and *oblâtes*, which were a variant of the communion wafer and which were purchased in France from non-Jewish waferers who tempted buyers with free samples. The *oublies* had a close affinity with the waffle, which was made with a special waffling iron well described by Isaiah Horowitz of Prague (died 1628), and the waffle itself was first mentioned by Rabbi Israel Isserlein in Austria in the fifteenth century. He referred to a non-Jew presenting a basketful of waffles (*hol-hipe*, Middle High German) to the father of the bride, who distributed them without qualms to his Jewish guests. According to William Woys Weaver, waffles were eaten in medieval Germany only during times of festivity or at Lent. Originally, waffles were no more than slices of buttered bread tightly placed between hot iron molds, but later yeast and baking soda were added to the recipe.[14]

In contrast, many of the medieval German Jews favored an ascetic regimen as far as food was concerned. Judah Asheri, the son of a famous German rabbi who migrated to Spain with his father early in the fourteenth century, asked in his ethical will:

> Why, forsooth, were ye brought into this world? Not to eat and drink and wear fine linen and embroideries, but for the service of God. . . .

> Food to a man is like oil to a lamp; if it have much it shines, if little it
> is quenched . . . be diligently on your guard against over-feeding. More
> heinous than homicide is suicide. Gross eating is as dangerous to the
> body as a sword, besides that it bars one from occupation with the Law
> of God and the reverence due to him.

Eleazar of Mainz, a learned layman who died in 1357, wrote in his
testament, "Now, my sons and daughters, eat and drink only what is
necessary, as our good parents did, refraining from heavy meals, and
holding the gross liver in detestation. The regular adoption of such
economy in food leads to economy in expenditure generally, with a
consequent reluctance to pursue after wealth, but the acquisition of a
contented spirit, simplicity in diet, and many good results." Later
there were similar ascetic groups in eastern Europe.

> In 1700, 31 families were advancing from Poland. . . . They were
> heading for the Promised Land. . . . These Jews lived like hermits,
> taking cold baths daily, did not sleep in beds, and slept only one or two
> hours during the night, devoting the rest of their leisure to the study of
> the Talmud. Throughout the week they ate only bread and oil—and
> that only after stars appeared in heaven.

Against this frugal regime advocated by Jews steeped in the German
rabbinic and east European traditions is the comment in the will of a
Provencal or Spanish layman of the fourteenth or fifteenth century,
characterized by Solomon Schechter as a convivial person who enjoyed his dinner and glass of wine. He reminded his children of the
regulations he had imposed on himself as an example for them to
follow.

> Again, that I shall take three meals every Sabbath, consisting of bread
> or fruit in order to subdue my appetites, and to restrain myself from
> enjoying in this world more than is necessary for the maintenance of
> my body, I must not eat at one meal more than one course of meat, or
> more than two courses altogether; nor must I drink more than two
> cups of wine at one meal . . . except on Sabbath, Festivals, Hanukkah,
> New Moon, and at religious banquets.

It is pertinent to add at this point that we shall be exploring the food of
the Spanish Jews in a later chapter.[15]

In her survey entitled *Food in History*, Reay Tannahill pointed out
that in fourteenth-century western Europe the diet of the poor among
the general population consisted of dark bread made from rye or
barley, something from the stockpot, with some cheese or a bowl of
curds. In the early Middle Ages the staple articles of diet in Germany

were meat, soup, fish, bread, vegetables, and fruit for dessert. In the eighteenth century the chief foods of the bulk of the German population were meat, sausages, cabbages, lentils, rye bread, and beer together with a bowl of broth at almost every meal. During the week, bread was the principal item of food of the French Jews, but they also depended on a monotonous diet of coarse soups, gruels, cheese, and vegetables such as cabbages, onions, and leeks for their daily fare; the diet of the German Jews must have been similar to this, although we know that they consumed a considerable quantity of pulse as well. Rashi mentioned bread made from secondary flour, old French, *seondier,* the equivalent of the Roman *panis cibarius,* a dark wheaten loaf, while later central and eastern European rabbinic authorities described bread made from rye and dark bread, coarse loaves that the bulk of the Jewish population ate. Among the everyday food relished by the poorer Jews were gruels (*muos,* related to *muesli, Papp,* and *Kleister*) made from various types of grain, sometimes with beans and lentils added, and soups with pieces of bread thrown in or in which pieces of *matzah* were crumbled; or these Jews drank vegetable soup cooked with goose fat or butter. Vegetable soup is already mentioned in a thirteenth-century responsum by Rabbi Meir of Rothenburg, while his pupil Rabbi Moses Parnes referred to mush by the name *Brie.* This name was also utilized by Rabbi Jacob Ben Moses Molin, the Maharil (1355–1427), when he described a soup with crumbled *matzah* as *matzah brie* soup. Eugen Weber has shown how the French peasants in traditional society subsisted on soup on a daily basis, hence the English word *supper,* but his research has wider implications by suggesting the crucial importance of this item of diet in northern Europe both for Jews and for Gentiles. Further, we know that in fifteenth-century Austria, during the week Jews nourished themselves on a diet of milk, butter, black bread, eggs, cheese, soup, vegetables, sauerkraut, rice, and herring.[16]

During the Middle Ages, cheese and milk products gradually gained recognition as subsidiary items of diet among Jews in northern Europe. However, the evidence for this is fragmentary and contradictory. Among the medieval peasantry in England, "white" meat became a minor supplement to the diet and similarly among the Jews of northern Europe cheese and dairy products were no more than this. Cheese never attained the key role it acquired among the Dutch in the seventeenth century. On the other hand, there was scarcely a mention of such products in the voluminous commentaries by Rashi in northern France in the eleventh century, so we should not exaggerate the significance of this item; a century or two later the Tosafists attached more importance to cheese and dairy products. Again, cattle were fewer in southern Europe, with the consequence that milk production was lower, and in Rome in the seventeenth and eighteenth centuries the consumption of cheese and milk products was accordingly small. Much the same conclusion can be drawn for the rest of southern Europe. Yet Eliahu of Pisaro, traveling by ship in the Mediterranean in 1563, noted that Jewish passengers purchased "Jewish cheese" on the island of Zante and bread and food in Corfu, although not too much should be made of this isolated incident. Conclusive evidence of the growing significance of dairy products in the medieval northern European diet may be deduced from the emergence of the concepts of *milchic* (dairy) and *fleyshic* (of meat), which Weinreich asserts were Yiddish words with German components that cannot be translated into Hebrew; in contrast, in the Jewish communities in the medieval Islamic world, the kitchen was not divided into separate meat and milk sections because so few dairy products apart from cheese were utilized.[17]

Rashi recommended that the poor should not differentiate between the Sabbath and weekday meals if they would thereby become dependent on charity. Although his successors the Tosafists cited an anonymous midrash to prove it was customary to alternate daily meals of fish, fowl, beef or veal, and vegetables, it is doubtful whether persons other than members of the Jewish elite, even in France, could live on such a luxurious diet. To the European peasants, white bread, chicken, and wine were luxuries, and to what degree the ordinary medieval Jews consumed fish, meat, and white bread other than on the Sabbath and festivals is a difficult question we shall explore later.[18]

THE JEWS IN THE ISLAMIC WORLD

Meshullam ben R. Menahem, an Italian Jew who traveled to Egypt and Palestine in 1481, commented adversely on the table manners of the Egyptians. "They sit on the ground or the carpet or a linen box without a cover. They put neither a cloth nor knife nor salt on the table, they all eat out of one vessel, both servant and master, they eat with their fingers, and most are always squatting. . . ." In Jerusalem the manners of the inhabitants appeared to be just as uncouth to this Renaissance traveler. "The Muslims also the Jews of this place are pigs at their eating. They all eat out of one vessel with their fingers, without a napkin, just as the Cairenes do, but their clothes are clean." When Jacob Sapir visited Egypt in 1858, he still found Jews eating food with their hands, but we should remember that in the 1920s there were orphanages in eastern Europe where the children ate with spoons and did not know how to use a knife and fork. Although Meshullam ben

R. Menahem was granted lavish hospitality in a Jewish household in Jerusalem, "he could not eat and enjoy their dishes, for they are different to our people's and strange to a healthy man. . . ," an observation that shows the marked difference between the Italian-Jewish cuisine and that of the Jews in the Arab lands in the Middle Ages.[19]

All the fifteenth-century Italian-Jewish travelers to Palestine were agreed that the country was fertile but that the Jewish community was on the whole poverty-stricken, apart from a few wealthy merchants, as employment was scarce, and that the Jewish population was decimated from time to time by plague and the onslaughts of famine. Despite the cheapness of food when the harvests were successful, the purchasing power of the bulk of the Jewish community was weak, and their diet was predominantly vegetarian. Meshullam remarked that

> the land flows with milk and honey although it is hilly and ruined and desolate, and everything is cheap; its fruits are choice and very good. There is a Karob honey . . . also date honey, and the honey of bees, and wheat and barley and pomegranates and all kinds of fruits good and fine; and they have good olive oil, but they only eat sesame oil, which is very fine.

Obadiah of Bertinoro, writing in 1488, declared that

> most of Jerusalem is desolate and in ruins; needless to say that the city has no wall. The population, I am told, numbers some 4,000 householders, but of the Jews, only seventy householders of the poorest class remain, without a source of livelihood. There is scarcely a soul with enough to eat and one who has bread for a year is considered rich. For every man there are seven aged and forsaken widows of the Ashkenazic, Sephardic, and many other communities.

Further, he mentioned that there was a dreadful famine prevalent when he came to Jerusalem. "Many Jews died of hunger, they had been seen a day or two before asking for bread, which nobody could give them, and the next day they were found dead in their houses. Many lived on grass. . . ." One German rabbi in Jerusalem, who was renowned for his humility, "for six months tasted no bread between Sabbath and Sabbath, his food consisting of raw turnips and the remains of St. John's bread, which is very plentiful here, after the sugar has been taken out of it . . . " A traveler who visited Safed in 1495 reported that "the holy community number some 300 householders, and most of the Jews keep shops with spices, cheese, oil, legumes and fruit," a good indication of the diet of the local Jewish population; he added that "food is cheap . . ." Rabbi Levi ben Habib described the meager diet of the Jerusalem scholars in the early sixteenth century. "Not only do the scholars of Jerusalem not eat delicacies, but they eat bitterness and woe, and whoever is fortunate enough to be able to afford to buy the head or intestines of a sheep or goat, or even fowl, for the Sabbath and festivals accounts himself as having gone forth from the house of bondage to freedom and as having sat in the seat of the almighty."[20]

Until recently in the Middle East bread was the chief food, and both Hebrew and Arabic have words to signify "that which is taken together with bread." In medieval Fustat in Egypt, large rations of bread were supplied to the Jewish poor, consisting of "flat rations of bread that were eaten fresh" on the Sabbath and a hard kind of biscuit that was distributed twice a week. Whereas in Yemen in the earlier part of this century, Jewish women rose early in the morning to grind corn and to bake bread, so that many households had freshly baked bread with each meal, in medieval Egypt, Jewish women utilized the services of a miller to grind the grain or called on a baker to bake their bread. Again, in contrast with western Europe, where until after the Black Death all classes ate bread of barley, rye, or mixed flour, the majority of people in the Middle East during the Middle Ages principally consumed various varieties of wheat bread, including a white loaf of fine flour. Maimonides expressed a dislike of barley bread and *matzah*, having a preference for bread baked of unrefined ground wheat flour with plenty of salt added. Loaves of barley or carobs, otherwise known as St. John's bread, were foods reserved for the very poor; barley as in talmudic times was utilized as animal fodder. If people had means, they stored a supply of wheat in big clay jars to last their household for one year. The reasons for this were agricultural disasters, particularly a low Nile, famine, the breakdown of public order, the speculations of grain merchants, all of which caused rapid fluctuations in the price of grain, and the Geniza letters showed a constant preoccupation with grain scarcity. In medieval Egypt, bread eaten with onions or such other substitute vegetables as garlic, thyme, or radishes formed the major part of the diet of laborers and the poor. A seventeenth-century European traveler remarked that when the Egyptian poor mixed vegetables with bread they called the resultant dish *tabikh*, cooking in Arabic. During the Middle Ages, the thick *mulukhiya* (garden mallow) vegetable soup, the daily fare of the Egyptian peasant, was also popular with the urban lower classes, and *mulukhiya* was widely known as "the Jewish vegetable." Eggplants, which have been dubbed the "poor man's meat" were much consumed in the Geniza period. Another popular vegetable was the colocasia plant, which had thick starchy roots, fulfilling a role similar to that of the potato. In a letter sent from Palestine to an immigrant in Fustat in Egypt, the immigrant was asked to return to "eat onions in Jerusalem instead of chicken in Egypt," a remark that underscores the pervasiveness of the poor man's fare in Palestine and the higher standard of living in Egypt.[21]

In medieval Cairo the fruit and fish markets did a bigger volume of business than the meat markets, as the lower classes consumed fish and fruit in greater quantities than meat. Similarly, in medieval Iraq the chief foods of the poor were coarse bread, or rice bread and vegetables, fish cakes, and dates. A medieval Spanish visitor reported that fish and pickles were one of the most common foods in Cairo, while the Geniza records reveal a glass jar with minced fish pickles being sent as a present and salted tuna being dispatched to an even more distant place. Cheese was utilized in smaller quantities, rarely on the European scale. Among the cheeses eaten were salted cheese, a cheese made of buttermilk and curds, and a cheese mixed with herbs, while the Jews also imported cheese from Sicily and Greece for the wealthier members of the community. In Egypt dates were the most important fruit, followed by figs, and sycamore figs were also popular among the poor. During times of scarcity, dates replaced wheat as the basic food, other substitutes for wheat being bread of barley, durra, or millet. Maimonides recommended date honey on bread as nutritious food for a poor scholar, unless he preferred almonds and raisins, a combination that became famous in later Yiddish folklore. Egypt imported a vast range of fruit, including almonds, hazelnuts, pistachios, peaches, and prunes from Palestine, Syria, and Iraq. So, too, in medieval Iraq, dates, pears, peaches, figs, pomegranates, and watermelons were considered products that only the poor could eat. According to Salo Baron, Jewish farmers in medieval France introduced the cultivation of the watermelon into Europe, an indication of the Jewish partiality for this fruit, while both Rashi and Obadiah of Bertinoro mentioned the Jewish consumption of chestnuts, another of the choice foods of the poor in medieval Europe. The Crusaders introduced the Ashkelon onion into France, however, where it was known as the *scallion*, hence the English word *shallot*. In the eleventh century the markets of Jerusalem and Old Cairo sold great quantities of bananas, a fruit that was then unknown in the West.[22]

Wherever there were centers of Jewish population within the Roman Empire in the Mediterranean, the cultivation of the citron was encouraged for religious reasons; Erich Isaac has pointed out that these early centers of Jewish population in the Diaspora coincide with the areas of citrus production in the Mediterranean today, areas such as Spain, Sicily, Calabria in Italy, the Nile Delta, the Levant, and certain parts of North Africa, particularly the area between Menkes and Fez. Hence he reached the conclusion "that it is the antiquity of citrus culture, originally introduced in these regions by Jews, for whom the cultivation of other citrus species was a by-product of citron cultivation which explains the persistence of this horticultural speciality." Citron trees in these areas from the tenth century c.e. onward served as grafting stock for other varieties of citrus, especially the orange. So, too, Samuel Tolkowsky had suggested earlier that if after the barbarian invasions destroyed the Roman Empire, "the culture of citrus continued to maintain itself in some corners of Italy and Spain or on the islands situated near the coasts of the countries, it is probably to the activities of Jews that we are in the main indebted for this survival." During the Middle Ages, Jews in Egypt ate a special variety of bitter orange, and the production of lemon juice was also important, but by the thirteenth century citrons, oranges, and lemons were widely grown in Palestine, although not as yet in southern Europe. Through contacts with the Levant and Egypt, Italians imported the food habits of the Islamic world, and apothecaries shops in the fourteenth century started to stock orange and citron juice. A century earlier, the Italian Rabbi Judah ben Benjamin of Viterbo gave permission for the preparation of lemon juice on the Sabbath, as the object was to provide "seasoning of food . . ." Further, Jewish peddlers in England in the eighteenth century specialized in the sale of oranges and lemons, only later being supplanted by the Irish after the Irish famine in the 1840s led to a mass migration so that the intimate association of the Jews with the citrus trade stretched across centuries. Again, at the beginning of the eighteenth century, Volckamer referred to oranges and lemons sold in the shops of Italian Jewish traders, who had settled in Germany, and of Italian merchants, who set up stands at fairs for the sale of citrus.[23]

From the Middle Ages until the latter part of the nineteenth century, Jewish merchants journeyed between northern and eastern Europe on the one hand and southern Europe on the other to purchase citrons and palm branches for sale to their coreligionists, who wished to utilize these ritual articles during the festival of Tabernacles. In the fourteenth century Florence had a flourishing export trade in citrus, probably with Jewish merchants who traveled from Germany and Austria to acquire citrons for the annual religious requirements of their communities. We know that in 1389 Albert III of Austria gave three Jewish messengers permission to proceed to Trieste to acquire Italian citrons for Tabernacles, besides granting them exemption from customs duties and tolls. Moreover, the distinguished fifteenth-century Austrian Rabbi Israel Isserlein thought the citrons that came from Apulia in southern Italy were superior to those of Rome on account of their "finer taste and fragrance." In addition to traveling to Italy at the beginning of the seventeenth century some sixteen German-Jewish merchants visited Spain annually to purchase the essential prerequisites for celebrating the festival of Tabernacles. According to J. B. Farrarius in 1646:

> Numerous Jewish merchants . . . from Poland, Germany and Mantua . . . arrive annually towards the beginning of . . . August on that part of the Ligurian coast which is called San Remo in order to buy in good time citron apples and palm branches . . . on the island of Corcyra (Corfu) the wealthiest Jews take care to buy up at very high prices those citrons which excel in point of smoothness and freedom from blemishes . . . they pack these apples into small boxes . . . and send them to their friends in Italy . . . and other countries as presents. . . .

When King Roger of Sicily sent Jews to Corfu in the twelfth century to develop sericulture they also started growing citrons on the island. Corfu had a large share of the market for citrons in the northern Jewish communities until the anti-Jewish riots on the island at the end of the 1880s. Thereafter, pro-Zionist rabbis and leaders diverted much of the citron trade to Palestine.[24]

When Obadiah of Bertinoro settled in Jerusalem he was amazed by the covered market with its merchants' bazaar, the spice bazaar, the vegetable market, and the one in which cooked food and bread were sold. In the medieval world the Middle East was much more sophisticated than the West in its culinary habits; among the medieval Muslims, Jews already had an enviable reputation for their cooking. A well-known saying advised people to "sleep in a Christian bed and enjoy Jewish food." Like their Muslim neighbors, the Jewish middle class in medieval Egypt bought cooked food in the bazaar for their evening meal, and possibly the merchants resorted to the butcher shop for lunch, as was common in traditional society in Aleppo. They purchased *harisa*, minced meat and wheat fried in fat, *jahish*, a mixture of groats cooked with meat and dates, certain other cooked meat dishes, and numerous appetizers and relishes. They also purchased cakes, pastries, and sweetmeats in the bazaar, including fritters made of unleavened dough, honey, and almonds (*zalabia*), and the *kadaif*, of which the ingredients were also flour and almonds together with rose water. While honey was used in the preparation of sweetmeats, it is noteworthy that with fine white flour and melted butter it was made into a thick paste or cake known as *asida*. This cake was presented as a gift on special occasions, such as childbirth, and was similar to the honey cake of the medieval German Jews, which was likewise bestowed as a gift on auspicious occasions. Not only were Jewish sugar makers prominent in medieval Egypt but some operated large industrial establishments and were among the wealthiest persons in the Jewish community. Jews were frequently vendors of fried seeds and almonds, while chewing gum was almost as popular among medieval Jews as among their modern American counterparts.[25]

In a startling passage a Karaite author from Jerusalem in the latter half of the tenth century denounced the Jews of Cairo for their infringement of the dietary laws. If the propagandist undertones of the passage are discounted, it provides a clear insight into the behavior of the medieval Egyptian Jews, who mixed easily with their neighbors and bought much of their cooked food from non-Jews, despite rabbinical prohibitions. "How can I help worrying when some Jewish notables and many of their congregation send messengers to the Gentile market-place to buy their bread and their boiled and salted provisions. . . . Yet they eat them publicly in the judgement place, as well as privately in their homes, without fear of the Lord." Others

> buy . . . from the Gentiles all kinds of sweetmeats made with Gentile lard and sugar and prepared in their pots and vessels which have been contaminated by unclean food? How can I keep silent when many of them eat meat from carcasses skinned by Gentiles? . . . Even the meat slaughtered by the Jews is cut up with the same knife used to cut up meat slaughtered by the Gentile, and the same butchering block used to cut up the flesh of the animal slaughtered by the Jew is used also for the animal slaughtered by the Gentile. . . . How can I refrain from sighing when I know some Jews send a sheep or kid to the Gentile cook to have it roasted?

From our knowledge of the Aleppo Jewish community of the early twentieth century, we know that some Jewish traders lunched at butcher shops that were mostly operated by Muslims but at which the meat had nonetheless been ritually slaughtered by Jews. Hence these Jewish merchants felt free to eat a piece of lamb broiled over the charcoal fire, and we would surmise that conditions in medieval Egypt were similar.[26]

6

SABBATH AND FESTIVAL FOOD IN THE MIDDLE AGES

FRIDAY EVENING

Since the talmudic age, it was the custom among Jewish families to include fish in their meal on a Friday night. In medieval France, Jews ate herring, salmon, tunny, and carp, while in Germany they subsisted mainly on such freshwater fish as the barbel, trout, tench, and pike, a fish that used to be served in the Middle Ages with sharp sauces of mustard, horseradish, or saffron. In fifteenth-century Spain, Jewish merchants traded in salted cod, sardines, and herring, giving a good indication of the food consumed by their coreligionists. In France fish was more expensive than meat, a point alluded to by the Tosafists, who observed that in the talmudic age the reverse was the case. Perhaps this also explains why Rabbenu Tam held against the German author-ities that the *barbuta* was a kosher fish, a controversy that was revived in the eighteenth century and in more recent times. Whereas L. Low identified the *barbuta* with the sturgeon, Dr. Levinger has argued that the *barbuta*, which Judah the Pious declared was forbidden to those who wished to taste the messianic meal of the leviathan, was in fact turbot, the *Rhombus maximus*. Further, Dr. Levinger maintained that the permissive authorities, including certain French rabbis, confused the identity of the *barbuta* with the *barbue*, the French for brill, the *Rhombus Leavis*, a fish closely related to the turbot, but whose kosher status was indisputable. Turbot was, however, recognized as kosher in the Hague until the Second World War and in Britain throughout the nineteenth century and then until 1954, when there was an incident at a kosher banquet.[1]

During the Middle Ages, French Jews used to eat small fish fried in the fat of their entrails and flour on a Friday night, and fish were also served in a jelly or with different sauces, as can be seen in the recipes contained in the fourteenth-century cookery treatise, the *Viandier* of Taillevent. Fish in medieval France were also prepared by placing them on a grill above twigs in order to grill them. We shall provide evidence in a later chapter to show that German Jews could already try various kinds of gefilte fish. Fish were also eaten dried, smoked, salted, or pickled during the Middle Ages. Not only did an early medieval responsum in the *Sefer Hadinim* show that Jewish merchants traded in salted fish, but Rabbi Isaac of Vienna, the Or Zarua, mentioned that Austria imported salted fish from Hungary. Meir of Rothenburg (1215–1293) was asked whether or not Jews could eat fish smoked by a Gentile. He held that smoking and salting of fish were methods of preserving fish and not of cooking them. Hence, a Jew could eat such a fish, but not fish cooked by a Gentile.[2]

Despite this latter prohibition, there are numerous examples in rabbinic literature that prove these rules were not always strictly observed. The Tosafist Eliezer of Metz ate herring baked by a non-Jew on the Sabbath. The Polish Rabbi Solomon ben Yehiel Luria (1510–1573) remarked that he would

> disclose the perverse nature of the German Jews. A Jew of wealth and power is not censured for drinking wine prepared by Gentiles or for eating fish prepared by them. . . . But while they condone these serious transgressions of the law they attach an undeserving and exaggerated importance to trifles. To study the Talmud or to partake of food with head uncovered is regarded by them as an act of apostasy.

Nonetheless, this departure from orthodox practice was not confined to German Jewry, but Luria's contemporary Rabbi Isserles reprimanded his fellow Polish Jews, "some [of whom] also had no scruples about eating fish prepared by Gentiles and bread baked by non-Jewish bakers." What is interesting about both comments is that they were not referring to isolated examples of lax conduct, but seemed to be highlighting certain general trends.[3]

There was great competition between Jewish and Christian customers in medieval Europe in their purchase of fish. During the Middle Ages, the Church imposed many fasts, quite apart from the forty days of Lent, so that half the days in the year were meatless. Equally, there was a heavy demand for fish by Jews on Fridays, resulting in a shortage of supplies. Cities such as Nuremberg, Metz, Munich, and Strasbourg passed laws that compelled Jews to buy their fish on Friday afternoon, after Christian customers had made their purchases. In some towns such as Nuremberg, Regensburg, and Wurzburg, Jews were forbidden to purchase any fish during Lent so as not to compete with Christian customers. Menachem Mendel Krochmal (1600–1661), the Moravian chief rabbi, agreed that a Jewish community council could order its members not to purchase fish for two months, when non-Jewish fishmongers started to overcharge the Jewish public. On the other hand, certain Jewish communities, such as those of Spain, maintained their own fish markets, while in Amsterdam there was a guild of Jewish fish merchants. There were both Jewish fishermen and dealers in salted fish and herrings in sixteenth-century Turkey; the Jewish fishermen of Salonika migrated to Palestine with boats in the 1940s, forming the nucleus of the future Israeli fishing industry.[4]

According to the Maharil (1355–1427), many Jews kept the table-cloth spread throughout the whole of the Sabbath. During the summer months, the houses in Germany were sometimes infested with flies, and although people were supposed to sup only in front of the Sabbath candles, Rabbi Meir of Rothenburg permitted them to dine in the more salubrious surroundings of their courtyard; but he was adamant that the Jews of one German locality should store wine for making *Kiddush* for use in periods of shortage and should not use beer as a substitute. From the writings of Rabbi Israel Isserlein (1390–1460) and his pupils, we have a detailed knowledge of how Austrian-Jewish families dined on Friday evening, but the conditions prevailing then must be equally applicable several centuries earlier. In Austria Rabbi Isserlein declared that Jews stored their wine in cellars, selecting the best wine for the Sabbath. Rabbi Isserlein shopped for the fish in the market himself and he used to prepare the fish for the Friday evening meal. On one occasion, Rabbi Isserlein recounted that he ate herrings and onions on a Friday evening and the Sabbath, instead of a more choice fish; this was probably due to the numerous restrictions placed on Jews in many towns when they tried to buy fish, as first preference was given to the Christian inhabitants.[5]

If the medieval Jews were fortunate enough to start their Friday-evening meal with a fish course, they followed it by eating a piece of meat pie. After singing table songs with his family and pupils, Rabbi Isserlein used to distribute a slice of meat pie (*pastide*) to each of his students; according to the Maharil, the two layers of dough between which the meat lay were meant to be a reminder of the two pieces of manna that the Israelites collected in the wilderness on Friday. Joseph Yuspa Hahn, who died in Frankfurt in 1637, recounted a delightful story of a Jewish child captured by robbers who was released from captivity by Jews on their hearing his pitiful cries for a slice of pie on a Friday night. By the time of Rabbi Abraham Danzig, who died in Vilna in 1820, however, there were only a few places in eastern Europe, where they baked pies in commemoration of the manna. So, too, according to Joseph Karo (1488–1575), the medieval Spanish Jews enjoyed eating meat pies known as *empanada* on the Sabbath, presumably on Friday evenings. Among the modern Sephardic communities of Turkey and the Balkans of Spanish descent, there was a custom of consuming *pasteles,* small round cakes filled with meat and made from a flaky dough for the Friday-night meal, no doubt a custom ultimately derived from the original medieval practice. From the writings of a sixteenth-century Marrano doctor we know that "the Jews and especially the Jewish workmen are accustomed [in the Mediterranean area] to celebrate the [Sabbath] eve by rest and abundant food."[6]

The feasting of the Jews on the Sabbath deeply influenced the Muslims among whom they lived and the Christian communities of the Middle East. Among the wealthy Muslim families in modern central Asia a festive meal of mutton and rice was served on Friday evening at the end of the Muslim Sabbath, a clear echo of the Jewish Friday evening repast; and there was a perennial battle in the early Church between those who wished to continue to feast on the Sabbath like the Eastern Christians and those who desired to substitute Sunday as the day of rest, by transforming the Jewish Sabbath into a gloomy fast day like the Church of Rome.[7]

At the end of the fifteenth century, Obadiah of Bertinoro stayed in Alexandria in Egypt for the Sabbath and related that

> on a Friday all go to bathe, and on their return the women bring them wine, of which they drink copiously; word is then brought that the supper is ready, and it is eaten in the daytime, before evening. Then they all come to the synagogue, cleanly and neatly dressed. . . . On their return home they repeat Kiddush, eat only a piece of bread the size of an olive, and recite grace after meals.[8]

His description of how Jews in the medieval world ate their principal Sabbath meal is a famous and much-quoted passage. He incidentally mentioned that the Jews in Cairo cooked at home only for the Sabbath:

> The following is the custom in all Arabian countries. They sit in a circle on a carpet, the cup-bearer standing near them near a small cloth which is spread on this carpet; all kinds of fruit which are in season are then brought and laid on the cloth. The host now takes a glass of wine, pronounces the . . . (Kiddush), and empties the cup completely. The cup-bearer then takes it from the host, and hands it successively to the whole company, always refilled, and each one empties it, then the host takes two or three pieces of fruit, eats some and drinks a second glass. Whoever sits next also takes some fruit, and the cup-bearer fills a second glass for him. . . . Then a second kind of fruit is partaken of, another glass is filled, and this is continued until

each one has emptied six or seven glasses. Sometimes they even drink when they smell flowers which are provided for the occasion. . . . The wine is unusually strong, and this is especially the case in Jerusalem, where it is drunk unmixed. After all have drunk to their heart's content, a large dish of meat is brought, each one stretches forth his hand, and eats quickly, for they are not very big eaters. Rabbi Moses brought us confectionery, fresh ginger, dates, raisins, almonds, and confectionery of coriander seeds; a glass of wine is drunk with each kind. Then followed raisin wine, which was very good, then malmsey wine from Candia, and again native wine. I drank with them and was exhilarated.

So, too, Meshullam ben R. Menahem, commenting on the eating habits of the Egyptian Jews, added that "when they want to show honour to anybody they bring raisin wine a thousand times stronger than malmsey. You have to drink twice before they give you anything to eat except fruit. Finally you have to drink to all those who are sitting round . . . and you have two hours before you come to the meal." Israel Cohen, in his travel book published in 1925, mentioned that Sephardic households in the Far East served an abundance of fruit on the Sabbath, including oriental fruit such as the pawpaw and the pomelo, while even today Yemenite Jews serve a trayful of fruit and beans (*gelea*) at the Sabbath meal.[9]

We owe to Captain James Riley, a shipwrecked American, a wonderfully vivid description of how the Jews in the town of Saffy in Morocco entertained him at their Friday-night dinner in 1815. Before partaking of the meal, his hosts

brought forward a cup in the form of a tankard, and some white bread, in which some green herbs had been chopped up, and mixed with it before baking: they all arose at once and formed a circle around the supper dish, consisting of boiled fowls, which was set on the floor . . . all took their seats around the dish as near as they could get, on their legs and on the floor, having first washed their hands: some vigorously seized the boiled fowls, which they soon carved by pulling them to pieces, and then passed these pieces around the company. Their bread was made of barley-meal; this they dipped in the dish, after each bite, and called it a sop: the gravy in which they dipped their bread was the liquor in which the fowls had been boiled, mixed with vinegar.

CHOLENT AND HAMIN

Even from the time of the Mishnah, the earliest codification of Jewish Oral Law, which was reduced to a final form at the beginning of the third century C.E., it was the custom in Jewish homes to eat warm food on the Sabbath in order to enhance one's delight: ". . . food may be covered [concealed] to retain its heat" (M. *Shabbat* 2:7). The Hebrew phrase for this was *"toemnin et hahamin"*; hence the Sephardic term for the Sabbath food of *hamin*. In a garbled form, the early Church father Ignatius understood this when he warned Christians not to keep the Sabbath in the Jewish manner, by "eating things prepared the day before, nor [by] using lukewarm drink . . ." According to an account in Baladhuri, an Arab historian who died in 892 C.E., the Jews prepared a special Sabbath dish known as *harisa,* the forerunner of *cholent,* a semolina dough stuffed with meat and spices and saturated with fat that was slowly cooked for the Caliph Mu'awiya (661–680); the Yemenite Jews still prepare the dish under the same name for their Sabbath lunch. Nonetheless, it makes better sense to attribute Baladhuri's tale to a date a century or two later to coincide with the rise of the schismatic Karaite sect.[10]

During the early Middle Ages, starting with Anan in the eighth century, there was a sharp controversy between the rabbis and the Jewish sectarians, the Karaites, as to the correctness of having lights burning on the Sabbath and as to the enjoyment of warm food on that day. Qirquisani, discussing the division of opinion among the Karaites in the tenth century, declared that "some of them do not allow keeping food hot until the approach of the Sabbath, but let it get cold before the Sabbath comes in; they assert that if it is left hot some (internal) changes, expansion and contraction take place in it during the Sabbath . . ." It is likely that the clash of opinion between the rabbis and the Karaite apologists in the Middle Ages led to a renewed emphasis on serving hot food on the Sabbath and to the further evolution of the Sephardic dish of *hamin,* from the Hebrew for hot, and its Ashkenazic equivalent known as *cholent.* Both the *Geonim* and a later fourteenth-century Spanish rabbi known as Abudarham held that anyone who refrained from eating hot food on the Sabbath was drifting close to heresy.[11]

If the Sabbath dish was of European origin, how are we to explain its spread throughout the length and breadth of the Middle East from Kurdistan to Persia and Syria and to Morocco in North Africa in its Sephardic form of *hamin?* Kurdistan spans the Zagros mountains in Asia and because of its harsh terrain was an isolated area with a very ancient Jewish community, yet a special Sabbath dish is to be found there known as *mabote.* This food was made from ground wheat, chick-peas, meat, *kuba* (flat cakes of ground wheat or rice stuffed with fried meat), cow's intestines, and stuffed chicken. Both the Yemenite and Kurdistani recipes for *hamin* appear to follow the talmudic formula, which permitted the warming of meat and flour during the

Sabbath. So, too, in Shiraz in Persia the Jews ate a dish for their Sabbath lunch called *khalebibi*, the ingredients of which were beef, turnips, leek, cabbage, beans, lentils, and rice, which were precooked and then kept heated all night until eaten. This dish was in many respects reminiscent of European *cholent*.[12]

Both *cholent* and *hamin* were widely diffused throughout the Jewish centers in Europe and the Mediterranean; but it is unlikely that a medieval European dish would have been adopted by Jews in the Middle Eastern communities, for the flow of innovations in Jewish cuisine was in the opposite direction. Like noodles, *hamin* probably entered Europe through Spain or Italy, having originated among the rabbinic Jews of Byzantium, Iraq, Egypt, or Persia, who ate warm food on the Sabbath to differentiate themselves from the Jewish sectarians. Reduced to essentials, the ingredients of *hamin* and *cholent* were the same—meat, grain, and pulse; and these were precisely the only victuals the rabbinic codes permitted housewives to place in their ovens before the Sabbath so that their cooking could commence and the food could then be kept warm until eaten at the Sabbath lunch.

Unlike the Sabbath dish in whose cooking the Jews lingered, the regular *harisa* eaten by the medieval Muslim population in the Middle East was prepared rapidly and just as quickly consumed. The result was that the ingredients were not given the chance to permeate the dish thoroughly and impart to it an exquisite taste. Within the course of a few centuries, the recipe for making the ordinary kind of *harisa* spread from the Middle East into North Africa, and it is mentioned in an Arabic cookery book from this area in the thirteenth century. Among the Spanish-speaking Jews of Tangiers, the Sabbath dish until recent times was still called in local dialect by its ancient name of *horisa* and was a simple dish without meat and consisting of crushed wheat, to which red pepper was added. When the bakers' assistants in Morocco brought back pots of *s'hina* on the Sabbath, they cried *"âlârîsa,"* as this was the only equivalent term known to the Arabs for the Jews' Sabbath food.[13]

However, through the splendid researches of Lucie Bolens on the cuisine of medieval Andalusia, based on an examination of the recipes in Spanish cookbooks in Arabic, we now know that *harisa* was made in thirteenth-century Spain with pounded wheat cooked with meat and fat. This *harisa* recipe not only had certain resemblances to the modern Spanish *olla podrida* dish but was also closely related to the medieval European dish of *frumenty*, from the French for wheat, *froment. Frumenty* was a dish of hulled, boiled wheat slowly cooked in almond milk and thickened with egg yolks, which was served with slices of venison simmered for a long time in water; here we have the probable west European ancestor of *cholent*, although not the only one. The medieval egg sauces eventually evolved into the *haminados,* the hard-boiled eggs of the Sephardic Sabbath dish. Moreover, Lucie Bolens also mentioned another important thirteenth-century Spanish Sabbath dish consisting of a chicken stuffed with minced meat, meatballs, and kneaded dough, all garnished with the yolks of eggs and well cooked under the hot ashes at home or in a great oven. In certain respects this recipe resembles the Sabbath dish of the Iraqi Jews today, who stuff a chicken by removing its entire skin, after which they fill it with a mixture of rice, chopped chicken meat, herbs, and spices, making a dish known as *tebit* or *tanouri.* So, too, Maxime Rodinson has shown that this dish was of medieval origin by citing the thirteenth-century Syrian cookery book known as the *Kitab al Wusla,* in which there were four recipes for utilizing the skin of a chicken this way.[14]

In medieval Spain, particularly in the South, the word used to describe Sabbath food, possibly from the eleventh century onward, was *adafina* and not *harisa.* Malvina W. Liebman claimed, however, that the recipe for *adafina* was to be found in a tenth-century text, but she failed to cite the actual source for this statement. In Old Spanish *adafina* denoted a special food or porridge consumed by the Jews. The word was borrowed from the Arabic root *d-f-n,* meaning to hide, conceal, or bury, the equivalent of the Hebrew expression *taman,* which was used in the phrase we have previously quoted from the Mishnah. It probably referred to an ancient mode of stewing food in an underground oven or in a pot buried in cinders. Among the Jews of Algeria and Tunisia the Sabbath food was known as *dfina,* a word alluding to the embers in which the dish was cooked.[15]

According to Richard Ford, an early nineteenth-century writer,

> The national cookery of Spain is Oriental; and the ruling principle of its preparation is stewing; for, from a scarcity of fuel, roasting is almost unknown; their notion of which is putting meat into a pan, setting it in hot ashes, and then covering the lid with burning embers. The pot, or *olla,* has accordingly become a synonym for the dinner of the Spaniards. . . . Wherever meats are bad and thin, the sauce is very important; it is based in Spain on oil, garlic, saffron, and red peppers. In hot countries, where beasts are lean, oil supplies the place of fat, as garlic does the want of flavour, while a stimulating condiment excites or curries up the coats of a languid stomach.

To further impart the best flavor to the dish, the pot should be made of earthenware, but the *olla* was only well prepared in Andalusia, where there was incidentally a heavy Jewish settlement, and not so well in the rest of Spain; there it was ". . . a poor affair, made of dry beef, or rather cow, boiled with *garbanzos* or chick-peas, and a few sausages."[16]

We have some knowledge of the way *adafina* was prepared in the sixteenth century from the records of the Inquisition in the Canary Islands. "Ana Goncales deposes that when she was in the service of Ana de Belmonte, she saw that her mistress cooked mutton with oil and onions, which she understands is the Jewish dish *adafina.*" Another servant called Fatima distinguished between the Jewish and Christian methods of cooking. ". . . my [Jewish] master told me to fry a little onion in oil in the pot, and then throw in the chick-peas (*garbancos*) and then add a little water, after which I wash the meat and throw it in . . . Before this I had another master, but he only ate stews such as the Christians eat, putting in the meat and bacon and then the turnips, chick-peas and cabbages." It has been pointed out that because of the shortage of fresh water in Spain, vegetables were rarely boiled, but more often were sautéed in oil.[17]

True that the famous Spanish stews known as the *olla podrida* (literally meaning rotten pot) from Castile and its equivalent in Galicia known as *pote gallego* had certain similarities to *adafina,* and some culinary experts believe that the Jewish dish was the ancestor of the Spanish *cocido,* in which the eggs in the *hamin* (the *haminados*) were replaced by pork and lard, but it is more likely that the *cocido* was an innovation of the Muslim invaders of Spain and that what the Jews contributed to Spanish cooking was the refinement of the dish by the all-night slow stewing process. Although the recipes for *adafina* and *harisa* are distinctive, it is possible that the idea of preparing a Sabbath stew, which was borrowed from the Jews of North Africa, may have triggered the invention of an alternative type of stew among the Jews in Southern Spain, who adapted the dish to local ingredients and culinary traditions.[18]

In the interior of Morocco the Sabbath dish was known as *s'hina* from the Arabic *shn,* to heat, which was the equivalent of the Ashkenazic term *cholent.* In medieval Andalusia the word designated a gruel of flour and was borrowed by Old Spanish (*zahinas*) from Arabic to describe a "kind of thin porridge." In Morocco the ingredients of *s'hina* at the beginning of this century were eggs, potatoes, rice, chick-peas, and sometimes meat and saffron; stripped of such accretions as rice and potatoes, the dish originally had a flour base and was akin to the Middle Eastern Sabbath stew of *harisa.* In 1815 Captain Riley, an American sailor who was shipwrecked in Morocco, declared that

their [the Jews'] principal and standing Sunday dinner, is called *skanah* [*s'hina*]; it is made of [chick-]peas baked in an oven for nearly twenty-four hours, with a quantity of Beeves [oxen's] marrow-bones (having little meat on them) broken to pieces over them; it is a very luscious and fattening dish, and by no means a bad one: this, with a

few vegetables, and sometimes a plum-pudding, a good bread, and
Jews brandy distilled from figs and aniseed, and bittered with wormwood, makes up the repast of the Jews who call themselves rich. The
poor can only afford *skanah* and barley-bread on their Sunday, and
live the rest of the week, as they can.

Whereas the main course was an indigenous Moroccan or oriental
creation, the pudding probably owed something to the influence of
European Jewish merchants. Thus *s'hina* resembled *harisa* in having
a base of some form of cereal, wheat, or rice but differed from *adafina*,
which was composed of chick-peas and onions sautéed in oil with meat
added.[19]

It is possible, given the antiquity of the word *s'hina*, that the idea of
cholent reached France from Jews living in the Christian part of Spain
in the twelfth century or earlier, as Muslim parts of the country were
absorbed in the Christian reconquest. Even the French *pot-au-feu* may
have been borrowed from Spain. Max Grunbaum believed that the
term *cholent* was derived from the Old Spanish word *escalentar* (kept
warm), whereas Krauss linked it to the Spanish word *escallento*
(warm). Whatever the original Spanish word, it was probably derived
from the Latin present participle *calentem*, meaning that which is
warm, just as Weinreich traced the origin of the word *cholent* to the
same source. Spanish cuisine also knew of warmed-up dishes, such as
gazpacho caliente, and this is an interesting parallel as far as the
origin of the word *cholent* is concerned.[20]

Among the Ashkenazim the first reference to the Sabbath stew,
cholent, was by Rabbi Isaac of Vienna (1180–1250), the Or Zarua, who
reported what he had witnessed in his teacher's home at the end of the
twelfth century in France.

> I saw in the house of my teacher Rabbi Judah bar Isaac [who died in
> 1224] that sometimes their *cholent* which was concealed [in a pot] was
> cooling and on the Sabbath close to the time of eating the food the
> servants lit the fire close to the pots, so that they should be well-
> heated. Sometimes they would remove them and put them near to the
> fire . . . and the opinion was to allow this. . . .

Some French Jews went further and sent their servants to obtain bread
baked by Gentiles on the Sabbath. Moreover, the Maharil, Jacob ben
Moses of Molin (c. 1360–1427), a German rabbi, described how pots
and pans were left lying near the fire on a Friday night for a wedding
feast, and the Gentile attendant fell asleep, allowing the fire to go out
and later rekindling it when he awoke, thereby heating the food.
Although certain authorities, such as the French sage Rabbenu Tam,

approved of such actions in emergencies, when ovens were too small to cope with the demands of a large assembly of wedding guests, the Maharil looked askance at this practice. He also mentioned that the *hasidim,* the medieval pietists, refrained from partaking of food that was kept warm on the Sabbath. Both the German and Spanish rabbis opposed the permissive rulings of some of their French colleagues, who allowed their servants to warm their houses on the Sabbath by heating the oven, a practice that could have an important bearing on warming cooked food. Both Rabbi Solomon ben Adret of Barcelona (1235–1310) and Rabbi Meir of Rothenburg hid the keys from their maids on the Sabbath to prevent this.[21]

Like the *harisa* dish, the French *cholent,* from the Old French *chauld* or *chaud,* meaning warm or hot, may have been an adaptation of a non-Jewish peasant stew, in this case a concoction from Alsace or Languedoc known as *cassoulet.* In the Languedoc region of southern France there was a peasant dish of pork and sausages and white beans, based perhaps on a Spanish model that had crossed the barrier of the Pyrenees and that itself owed much to the example of Arab cooking. This dish even more closely resembled the *cholent* available later in Hungary, where the beans slowly simmered in goose fat. From Languedoc the *cassoulet* dish penetrated into Alsace-Lorraine, but all the while knowledge of the slow stewing process was being acquired by the Jews in southern France and in the Rhineland. Mordechai Kosover, analyzing the changing terms used for the ingredients of *cholent,* concluded that the special European preparation of the dish had originated in France, from whence it was introduced into Germany, and from there it was diffused among the Slav countries.[22]

Nonetheless, because of the permissive attitude of the French rabbis of the twelfth century and their readiness to have dishes reheated on the Sabbath by servants, it is unlikely that the slow twenty-four-hour stewing process evolved there. It is more probable that it came to fruition in southern Germany, where the rabbis decreed that the ovens should be sealed with clay. Added to this, the *kugel* was a southern German and Austrian pudding that the Jews in these areas used as a dessert course to supplement the *cholent* dish. In southern Germany and Austria and the neighboring Slav lands the *cholent* was left in a warm oven in the bakery or communal oven (*schalantus*) over the Sabbath, where it would be collected by servant girls or young Jewish boys for the Sabbath lunch, as was the case in fifteenth-century Austria and almost certainly in the fourteenth century as well. Sometimes the dishes of the hidden warmed food, called *hatmanah hamin* in the Maharil's phrase, were wrapped in rags and coverings so that the food retained its warmth. If food was to be kept heated, it should not

be placed near the stove in the winter house on the Sabbath, asserted
the Maharil and other sages, but the dishes could be left on wooden
boards on the stove in the winter house.[23]

Joseph Karo (1488–1575), author of the *Shulchan Aruch,* entreated
Jews to eat meat and delicacies and to drink wine on the Sabbath.
During the medieval period, two meals were eaten daily by the Jews,
one in the morning and the other in the evening, but as the Talmud
decreed that Jews were to partake of three meals on the Sabbath, some
Ashkenazim in the Middle Ages divided the Sabbath morning meal
into two. The Maharil mentioned that in the Rhineland during the
summer it was customary to eat hard-boiled eggs for the third Sabbath
meal. The third meal, late in the afternoon, became popular only later
when the Kabbalah endowed it with mystical appeal.[24]

A NOTE ON THE CONSUMPTION
OF MEAT

The great French historian Fernand Braudel has argued that European
civilization, unlike the rest of the world, was distinctively carnivorous;
that there was a great increase in meat consumption in Europe,
particularly between 1350 and 1550; that meat consumption remained high in Europe until the seventeenth century, when there was
a resurgence in the production of vegetable foods that lasted until the
mid-nineteenth century, after which meat consumption again acceler-
ated because of the rising import of meat from America.[25]

Although this subject has as yet been little explored, there is no
doubt that the Jewish household in medieval Europe ate huge
amounts of meat and followed these general trends. It was during the
peak period of meat consumption in Europe that ritual slaughterers
became professionalized and that women were disqualified from
killing animals except in Italy. Originally, all Jews could slaughter
animals provided they were well versed in the requirements of ritual
law, but now the slaughterer became a communal official, combining
this function with that of an examiner of the lungs of the dead animal
to ascertain whether or not it was healthy. In the fourteenth century
Rabbi Asher ben Yehiel of Toledo wrote: "In the olden days butchers
could slaughter their own animals . . . but nowadays in the entire
Diaspora it is customary not to trust butchers, but to appoint reputable
men in charge of slaughtering and the post mortem examination. . . .
[We still allow] private individuals to slaughter at home for their
personal use . . ."[26]

We have some fragmentary evidence of heavy meat consumption

among Jews in medieval Europe in which they followed national
trends. In 1308 the Jewish community at Frankfurt on Oder concluded
an agreement with the city council allowing 10 Jewish butchers to
slaughter up to 2,500 oxen per year. In 1485 the city council of Cracow
allowed the 1,400 Jews in their midst to maintain 4 butcher shops for
their needs, but from a contemporary source we know that despite this
limitation on their numbers there were 27 Jewish butchers in this city.
In the town of Lvov (Lemberg) 8 Jewish butchers were allowed in 1608,
but there may have been 70 Jewish butchers in 1610. Obviously, the
large number of Jewish butchers is an indication of the heavy meat
consumption among Jews. Braudel also mentioned that in Rome
cheap butchers' shops sold buffalo meat to unfortunates and Jews.
Baruch, the doctor of the ruler of Saxony, in 1464 received certain
payments in kind including 30 bushels of wheat, 1 cask of wine, 6
quarts of beer, 20 ewes, and 1 ox per year, together with free accom-
modation. A medieval count from Barcelona rewarded his Jewish
official Eleazar with 2 pounds of meat each day from the Jewish
slaughterhouse at Saragossa, the first of a series of such gifts. According to the Or Zarua, cantors were entitled to receive gifts of special
cuts of beef at weddings, on Purim, and on Simhat Torah.[27]

Despite the fact that Jews frequently ate chicken in the talmudic age,
it disappeared from the menus of the European Jews during the Dark
Ages and was not consumed regularly during the Middle Ages, when it
was customary to eat meat pie on Friday nights. The German rabbi
Yair Chaim Bacharach (1639–1702) in an aside mentioned that "the
taste of fowl does not awaken the joy of the festival as does the taste of
beef." With the revival of European cuisine in the twelfth and thirteenth centuries, the Tosafists recommended that chicken be served
on festivals, and in 1326 there is a reference to Jewish butchers and
dealers in fowl in Cologne. The Or Zarua stated that at the completion
of a tractate of the Talmud or at weddings a whole chicken would be
served to a guest in order to honor him, while *hatanim* on Simhat
Torah in Saxony and elsewhere arranged a feast for their communities
consisting of fowl. But what was remarkable about the fare of medieval
European Jewry was the great variety of poultry and game that graced
their tables, including the barnacle goose, a species of wild goose that
some more simpleminded members of the community believed was a
vegetable product. Yet the suspicion must linger that the Friday-night
fare of chicken did not become popular among European Jewry until
the sixteenth or seventeenth century, when, according to Rabbi Bacharach's evidence, "many householder . . . raise[d] roosters and chickens
during the summer season." Moreover, in fifteenth-century Austria
Rabbi Joseph Bar Moses declared that because of the shortage of meat,
poultry was consumed on Friday night.[28]

In contrast to northern Europe, the Jews of medieval Egypt ate little
meat. Even the household of a ritual slaughterer tasted meat only twice
a week, that is, on Friday evening and on the Sabbath. A Kurdish Jew
once explained: "We eat meat only on the Sabbath, not on weekdays
when we work. Meat makes [men] lazy." The Roman legions introduced the chicken into Europe from the Near East, but whereas the
chicken was a scrawny and neglected bird in Europe during the Dark
Ages, it continued to thrive in Egypt. Maimonides (1135–1204) favor-
ably recited the testimony of his teacher Abu Merwan Ibn Zohar, who
regarded fowl and chicken soup as beneficial for the feeble-bodied.
Among Jews in medieval Egypt chicken was eaten on weekends,
holidays, and when someone was sick. The family of one medieval
clerk hankered after a hen cooked in lemon sauce and spices for the
Sabbath, a dish that is still regarded with delight. On festivals meat
was consumed, mutton being generally preferred to beef throughout
the Middle East, while the fat tail of sheep was regarded as a choice
item. Ishak al-Isra'ili, the renowned ninth-century physician known in
the West as Isaacus, was opposed to eating beef, a meat that was dry
and that he suspected was a source of thick and murky blood. Apart
from chicken, Maimonides recommended the meat of the kid, calf, and
lamb. Another holiday food in medieval Egypt was *burayq*, which was
perhaps the dish of eggplants known as *buran*.[29]

Animals that were imperfectly slain (*nevelah*) or that had certain
blemishes, such as adhesions on their lungs (*trefah*), and the hindquarters of cattle that had not had their veins removed were sold to
non-Jewish meat dealers. It has been estimated that the hindquarters
represented as much as half the weight of a dressed carcass. During the
Middle Ages, certain practices that had been permitted by the Talmud
when deciding whether or not meat was *trefah* were prohibited.
Outside Germany, the papal states, and the province of Castile in Spain
the restrictions on the Jewish meat trade were not rigidly enforced in
areas of dense Jewish settlement in Europe. More important than
ecclesiastical pressures against Christians buying meat that had been
slaughtered for Jewish consumption was the opposition of the Christian butchers' guilds, particularly in Germany, that resented Jewish
competition. In Mainz Rabbi Eliezer could not find non-Jewish customers for half a carcass, compelling him to throw the meat into the
garbage. Gradually, the severity of the regulations in the German
towns increased in the fourteenth and fifteenth centuries until the
Christian butchers eliminated the competition of their Jewish rivals by
obtaining a monopoly of the animals that were supplied to Jewish
slaughterers in many towns. In numerous German cities Jews were
assigned to special meat stands from which Christians were forbidden

to buy, although the meat vendors were often Christians working under the supervision of the Jewish ritual slaughterers. For instance, in Regensburg in 1420 Jews were compelled to purchase all their meat from one Christian butcher, while in Landshut in 1344 the Jewish butcher was forced to purchase all his cattle through Christians. When the German Jews lost control of their slaughterhouses in many places, the rabbinical rulings as to the *kashrut* of meat became much stricter.[30]

Elsewhere, the rabbinical authorities either tried to make the appropriate concessions to Christians and Muslims so as not to offend their sensibilities and to encourage them to continue buying meat that was surplus to Jewish requirements or had to relax the rules as to the *kashrut* of meat. In medieval France some non-Jewish butchers insisted on piercing the heart of the animal immediately after the ritual slaughterer had killed it, as the Gentiles would not buy meat that had been slaughtered by a Jew because they claimed its meat was too red in color. Rashi pleaded with his master, Rabbi Isaac HaLevi of Worms, to permit this practice; otherwise French Jews would be unable to eat meat. Karo (1488–1575) remarked that "you should know the reason why the Rabbis in Castile permitted animals with adhesions [on their lungs] . . . was as follows: the non-Jews in their country were very scrupulous not to eat the meat of animals slaughtered by Jews. Because of this animals which had become *trefah* meant a complete loss to Jews. If the Jews had employed the stricter practice a considerable financial loss would have ensued." So, too, in Egypt in the sixteenth century Rabbi David ben Solomon ibn Zimra stated that "should we undertake now to refrain from slaughtering when the animal is turned eastward [as was the Muslim practice] the Mohammedans would note the fact and henceforth refuse to eat of our meat. The earlier rabbinical authorities raised no question against the casual compliance with this Mohammedan ordinance, and the practice in Egypt has been in consonance with their opinion."[31]

Some upper-class Italian Jews during the Renaissance seemed to have enjoyed hunting, and among other instances it was recorded in January 1471 that Bonaventura da Volterra sent his friend Lorenzo the Magnificent a buck and two fawns after an excellent day in the field. Most rabbis totally condemned hunting, however, the Or Zarua stating that Jews who went hunting with dogs would not receive a portion of the leviathan and the behemoth in the feast awarded to the righteous in the world to come; and Rabbi Ezekiel Landau of Prague in the eighteenth century prohibited hunting, partly because of unnecessary cruelty to animals and partly because of the danger to human life in the chase.[32]

FESTIVALS

We move now to a discussion of the food customs associated with the
Jewish festivals during the Middle Ages. In the talmudic age it was
sometimes the custom to eat a hen for the New Year, but the *Geonim*,
particularly Natronai Gaon, influenced by the example of the Persians,
substituted the head of a sheep, the symbolic equivalent of the boar's
head consumed annually at Christmas during the Middle Ages. So, too,
in medieval Egypt it was the custom of Jews to eat the head of a sheep
on the New Year to symbolize a fresh beginning, while among the Jews
of Morocco, a sheep's or goat's head was displayed on the table. In the
ancient Jewish communities of Avignon and Comtat Venaissin in
Provençe and also in Italy, freshly planted grains of corn and sometimes beans were placed on a plate on the table for the New Year, being
discarded some ten days later. This was an adaptation of the pagan
tradition of sowing grain in earthenware containers, known as Gardens
of Adonis, that were displayed at the annual memorial ceremonies for
the god, after which the receptacles were cast into the sea or into
running water; however, it is not clear whether or not the Jews carried
this tradition with them from Babylonia or acquired it locally. There
may also be some connection between the plates of sprouting beans
and the bean in the Twelfth Night cake that was the forerunner of the
Christmas cake.[33]

On the New Year in France in the twelfth century "the custom was
[for the Jews] to eat red apples; in Provence they ate white grapes,
white figs, and a calf's head, or any new food easily digestible and tasty
as an omen of good luck to all Israel." An Italian illustration from the
1470s showed the master of the house saying a blessing on the new
fruit, which included pomegranates and white grapes. Rabbi Jacob
Molin, the Maharil, in the fourteenth century mentioned the custom of
eating an apple dipped in honey during the evening meal as a long-
established one based on Nehemiah 8:10. He also stated following the
Babylonian tradition that the head of a ram was consumed during the
meal to recall the sacrifice of Isaac, a point also made by Rabbi Meir of
Rothenburg in the thirteenth century. In central Europe in the seventeenth century the head of a lamb was still being served on the New
Year, according to Isaiah Horowitz. On the eve of Yom Kippur during
the fourteenth century, the adult members of the house partook of a
certain kind of cucumber or melon, the *Erd Epel*, to dampen their
sexual drive before commencing the fast.[34]

Both the Romans and the ancient Persians ate sweet dishes on their
New Year, believing this to be a good omen, while the Romans
presented gifts and gold coins to one another. In fifteenth-century

Austria, where the Ashkenazic traditions were consolidated, the Jews were accustomed to eating bread dipped in honey, the head of a ram, certain kinds of fish, carrots, cucumber, and a number of different kinds of fruit. In the late medieval period a favorite Ashkenazic dish for the New Year was carrot (*mern*) *tzimmes,* as it was thought to be auspicious to consume this food because the Yiddish word *mern* had the additional meaning of increase; the slices of carrot glistened like valuable gold coins. Yet, although there was an interesting parallel between this late medieval Ashkenazic tradition and the ancient Roman one, it was unlikely that there was a direct historical link. Likewise, the eating of fish on this occasion was a hopeful sign of the future fertility and prosperity of the Jewish people, while the apple was a secret allusion to the Garden of Eden in Kabbalistic literature.[35]

In the Talmud it was laid down that the *sukkah* should be decorated with "branches of fig trees on which there are figs, vines with grapes, palm branches with dates, and wheat with ears . . ." (*Sukkah* 13b). It was also stated that pomegranates and phials of wine as well as embroidery could be used to embellish the *sukkah,* while later authorities added various kinds of nuts. Both Maimonides and Karo supported these rulings. Archaeologists have recovered pale-blue and ivory glass bottles from the first century c.e. that were specially made for the festival of Sukkot and were intended to be filled with water from the Pool of Siloam—the place of Water-Drawing. These vessels were decorated with grape clusters and pomegranates, which we recall from a previous chapter were potent symbols of the belief in resurrection and were accordingly buried in Jewish graves. In the Middle Ages the Provençal scholar David bar Levi of Narbonne declared that "in some places in Aragon they make a *sukkah* in the courtyard of the synagogue and the entire congregation makes kiddush there and then they leave and go home and eat. This is surely . . . an error of theirs." In medieval Germany it was the custom of Jews to eat cabbages (in German, *Kohl*) on Hoshannah Rabbah because an important prayer was said on that day with the words *kol mevasar,* meaning "a voice announcing."[36]

During the Middle Ages, the European communities, especially those in northern Europe, adapted the ritual of the *Seder* to suit their own needs. While retaining many of the features of the *Seder* in the talmudic age, the European communities subtly jettisoned some of the customs of the Graeco-Roman and the eastern Mediterranean worlds: the carrying in and out of small tables was discarded; the Paschal lamb was no longer eaten; in central and eastern Europe horseradish replaced the other bitter herbs; eggs gained a new significance under Christian influence; and new distinctions arose between the Ashkenazim and the Sephardim over the consumption of beans during Passover.[37]

In the course of the Middle Ages there was one major change in the order of the *Seder* service: the Four Questions and the *Haggadah* recital were disposed of before the sumptuous Passover meal instead of after it, as was the case in the talmudic age. During Maimonides' lifetime it was the custom to dip a vegetable into the *haroset* (the Passover sauce) and to remove a special small table on which were arranged the bitter herbs, a vegetable, the *matzah*, the *haroset*, and the substitute for the Paschal lamb and the festival sacrifice from before the reader of the *Haggadah* while he was reciting the Four Questions. When he had finished with the questions the small table was returned, but this practice became superfluous in western Europe where there was one large table around which the whole family with their friends were gathered. Both Joseph Karo and the Polish rabbi Isserles ruled that all the special Passover foods should be displayed on a plate placed on the table near the master of the house.[38]

Interestingly enough, the oldest *Seder* plate in the Israel Museum is a ceramic fifteenth-century plate from Spain colored brown, blue, and yellow. According to *Haggadah* illustrations, *matzah* was distributed to congregants in a synagogue, and the plate may have been used for this purpose, as the *Haggadah* illustrations do not show plates of such a size on the table for the home *Seder* in Spain. There is still extant a beautiful porcelain *Seder* plate made in Prussia in 1770. *Seder* plates with indented compartments were not manufactured before the nineteenth century, however, the earliest being of pewter from the Austro-Hungarian Empire. A fine example of such a plate from Carlsbad in Czechoslovakia was adapted from a plate originally made for serving oysters. In the mid-nineteenth century nearly all the *Seder* plates in central Europe were made of bronze and pewter, while in Italy they were mostly of silver and in England of painted ceramic. Whereas the Italian plates showed tables laden with food and crystal decanters, the east European tables were depicted with but a single bottle of wine and scarcely any food. We can now understand how the *Seder* plates became essential requisites for the European tables once the small oriental tables could no longer be carried in and out of the dining room.[39]

The custom of dividing the *matzah* at the beginning of the *Seder* service was first found in the *Machzor Vitry* in the eleventh century. During the Middle Ages, the *matzot* that were prepared only for Passover were an inch thick and were frequently decorated with figures of doves, fish, and animals; one *matzah* in an Italian manuscript from the fourteenth century showed a flowered border in which there was a four-legged animal with a human face with Egyptian characteristics. While Maimonides permitted bakers to make *matzot* with designs, he prohibited ordinary householders from doing so in case individuals made these designs without a mold. In the end the use of molds was forbidden, and perforations were made in the dough with a sharp-toothed comb called a *redel*.[40]

We have seen how the custom of eating a Paschal lamb survived among the Jews into the medieval period, particularly in Egypt, but elsewhere the custom tended to die out, as it was felt that it was wrong to imitate the sacrifices of Temple times. On the other hand, the ram's head at the New Year was permitted because this custom was not originally associated with a Temple cult. Until recently in Morocco, however, sheep's tripe of liver, heart, lungs, stomach, and intestines, which was cooked in oil with garlic, saffron, paprika, and pepper, was eaten as the main dish at the *Seder*—a vestige of the ancient practice. A suckling lamb roasted on a spit is the traditional Easter fare in Rome, while in Greece it was the custom to roast the lamb on a fire of vine branches; both practices seem to indicate a Jewish origin, and we will recall the story about Todos of Rome in the ancient world, who directed that lambs should be roasted whole for Passover. Among the medieval European rabbis there was a controversy as to what objects should be substituted for the Passover sacrifices, some saying two types of boiled meat; Rabbi Alfasi from Morocco declared that a bone and some broth were suitable but not a bone and an egg, while others said it did not matter. Both Joseph Karo and Rabbi Isserles agreed that a shank bone and an egg should be used as the substitute for the two sacrifices.[41]

As we have seen, the Romans often started their meal with an egg, and there was a reference in Martial that shows that the Romans were well acquainted with roasting eggs. Further, the Talmud asked, "What are the two dishes [representing the two sacrifices]?—Said R. Huna: Beet and rice . . . Hezekiah said: Even a fish and the egg on it. R. Joseph said: Two kinds of meat are necessary, one in memory of the Passover offering and the second in memory of the *haggigah* [the burnt offering brought to the Temple on festivals]. Rabina said: Even a bone and [its] broth" (*Pesahim* 114b). It is thus possible that the Christian pasche egg had its origins in Jewish practice at Passover, which in turn was a custom borrowed from the Romans and subsequently elaborated. The practice of using a roasted egg to represent the *haggigah*, however, became fixed only in the medieval period. So, too, in the talmudic age the lentil and not the egg was the symbolic food of the mourner. Hence the widespread use of the egg during the *Seder* ceremony may have been a symbiotic adaptation to the Christian civilization of Europe during the Middle Ages. The Jewish practice of displaying a roasted egg on the Passover plate and eating hard-boiled eggs with salt water may have been borrowed from the Romans but may have been a creative response to the challenge of medieval Christianity at Easter; at any rate, the colored eggs much loved by the eastern European Jews at

Passover were acquired from their Christian neighbors. The egg took
on the meaning of resurrection among Jews similar to that of the
Christian Easter egg, both in the sense of "spiritual rebirth" after the
slavery of Egypt and for good fortune in everyday life, as well as being
a symbol of mourning for the destruction of the Temple.[42]

On the other hand, the ban on the consumption of legumes during
Passover by the Ashkenazim may have arisen because of a pagan
association. The prohibition was first mentioned by Rabbi Asher ben
Saul of Lunel in early thirteenth century Provençe, who asserted that
it was customary not to eat legumes on Passover because they were
subject to fermentation, a viewpoint contrary to that of the Talmud.
Provençe was precisely the area of France where the pagan cult of the
dying god who was reborn persisted and where there was a ritual
ceremony of growing corn or beans on a plate during the other Jewish
New Year. Another Provençal authority, Rabbi Manoach of Narbonne,
rejected the prohibition as the grounds for the ban, namely that
legumes, such as lentils, were associated with death and mourning
were insufficient, but to broaden his argument other legumes, such as
beans, represented birth and resurrection; it is possible that the rabbis
of medieval Provençe wanted no confusion between Passover customs
and dying and reborn gods, be they pagan or Christian. Many leading
medieval Ashkenazic authorities, such as Mordechai ben Hillel and
Rabbi Jacob ben Asher, refused to accept the validity of the prohibition, as it appeared to lack a sound halachic basis.[43]

A proverb common to England, Spain, and Italy held that "a Jew will
spend all on his Pasches, a Barbarian [Turk] on his nuptials, and the
Christian on his quarrels and law suits." The Mishnah enumerated five
vegetables that could be utilized as the bitter herb for the *Seder*
service, all of which should have leaves. Rabbi Alexander Suslin of
Frankfurt, who died in 1394, was the first authority to permit the use
of horseradish, where lettuce was not available, although this vegetable was primarily a fleshy root that did not strictly conform with the
halachic requirement of eating leaves. The medieval German rabbinic
authorities appear to have identified horseradish incorrectly, *Merre-
tich* in German with *merirta*, the Aramaic form of *maror*, the Hebrew
for bitter. An illustration from Spain of 1320–1330 showed a wealthy
member of the community distributing *haroset* and *matzah* to poor
householders, just as the poor were later provided for on Passover in
eastern Europe. Rabbi Elijah of London, a medieval sage, suggested
that all the fruits mentioned in the Song of Songs should be used as
ingredients of *haroset*, including "apples, dates, figs, pomegranates
and nuts, crushed together with almonds and moistened in vinegar."
He also mentioned the use of valerian or nard when making *haroset*,
and interestingly this was a seasoning much favored by the Romans.[44]

In Germany the medieval Jewish pietists refrained from eating fowl on Passover during the first part of the festival in case there were still some grains of corn left inside the meat. A twelfth-century rabbi from the Rhineland, Eliezer ben Joel Ha-Levi, remarked on a distinction between the Ashkenazic and Sephardic communities in their celebration of Passover: "And in responsa I saw that even these days it is the custom in Spain and in Babylon that the cantor on Passover conducts the *Seder* in the synagogue for the benefit of the ignorant who are unskilled in reciting the *Haggadah.*" During the sixteenth century, in the Venetian ghetto at the end of Passover, Gentile porters who carried bread into the Jewish quarter were pelted with mud and stones and beaten with brushes, but no other examples of this unique custom have come to light.[45]

Among the medieval Ashkenazic communities, the day on which the little boy entered the Jewish elementary school, the *heder,* was marked by an important ceremony. In some communities the school started on the new moon in the month of *Nisan*; elsewhere, the school commenced on Shavuot, the festival of the giving of the Torah. In eastern Europe honey cake (*honig lekech*), to which gingerbread was closely related, was offered to guests at engagement ceremonies and on many festive occasions, but its popularity among Ashkenazim can be traced back to twelfth- and thirteenth-century sources. Among the earliest references to honey cakes are those of Simcha of Vitry, a French sage who lived in the twelfth century and was the author of the *Machzor Vitry*, and the German rabbi Eleazar Judah ben Kalonymos (1160–1238), known as Eleazar Rokeach. According to the latter, "It is the custom of our ancestors that the education of the children is commenced on Pentecost, since on that day the Torah was given. The child is covered lest he see a dog on the day that he is introduced to the holy letters." On the appointed day the child was placed on his teacher's lap and a slate was brought in on which the Hebrew alphabet had been written both forward and backward. The teacher then read out the letters of the alphabet and some exhortations from the slate, which the child repeated, after which honey was smeared on the letters on the slate that the child licked off with his tongue. Following this, a cake kneaded with honey was produced bearing inscriptions from the prophets and the psalms. Next, a cooked egg was brought to the attention of the child with inscriptions on its shell including the verse, "How sweet are Thy words unto my palate! Yea, sweeter than honey to my mouth!" Once again, we can appreciate how eggs gained a completely new symbolic significance in Jewish ritual during the Middle Ages. Originally, the names of angels were inscribed on the honey cakes and amulets were attached to them, but later this practice was discarded. According to the account in the *Machzor Vitry*:

They wash him [the child] and dress him in clean garments, and they knead him three cakes of fine wheat in honey. . . . And they boil him three eggs and bring him apples and other kinds of fruit, and seek a worthy sage to conduct him to the school house. He covers him with his prayer-shawl and brings him to the synagogue, where they feed him with the loaves of honey and eggs and fruit; and they read him the letters. After that they cover the board with honey and tell him to lick it off. Then they lead him back to his mother.[46]

Cake letters of the alphabet and noodle letters were first prepared for children in the Roman primary schools to encourage learning, and these gentler educational methods were espoused by teachers in the Middle Ages, after which they were copied by Jewish teachers. So, too, in England special hornbook molds for baking Latin letters of ginger-bread were popular from the fourteenth to the nineteenth centuries.[47]

Gingerbread and the related honey cake was the sweet festive loaf of central Europe. In Germany the first references to *Lebkuchen*, ginger-bread, dated from 1320, although Jewish sources mentioned honey cake two centuries earlier. In the *Leket Yosher* it was stated that Rabbi Isserlein would not eat *lezelt* without washing his hands, unless the gingerbread was baked with spices. A similar spelling, *Lezelt* for gingerbread, occurred in the writings of Nicholas Von Basel in the fourteenth century, and the word *Lebzelt* is the Austrian and Swiss variation of the spelling of the German term *Lebkuchen*. Although the Yiddish word for honey cake, *lekech*, was thought to be related to the German term *Lebkuchen*, Samuel Krauss pointed out that the Yiddish word was more likely derived from the German word *lecke*, lick.[48]

By the sixteenth century the custom of consuming a honey cake and an egg at the ceremony marking a child's initiation into the world of Jewish learning was disappearing in southern Germany. However, in the early seventeenth-century work the *Brentspeigel* (Burning Mirror) of Moses Henochs of Prague, it was related that the new pupil was given wafers dipped in honey by his parents before attending the *heder* for the first time; Rabbi Jacob Emden (1697–1776) of Altona in northern Germany mentioned that after his first lesson in school he received a gift of honey cake and a peeled egg, after which the ap-propriate verses were recited. Elsewhere, in eastern Europe the cere-mony of *Alef-Vayzn*, showing the first letter of the Hebrew alphabet, *aleph*, to a child became firmly established. Nevertheless, in the late nineteenth century here too in eastern Europe it was by now rare to find cakes inscribed for a child's first lesson, although the practice of smearing alphabet slates with honey remained popular, and the children eagerly ate alphabet letters and almonds (a substitute for eggs) engraved with Hebrew letters or coins, and sweets were show-ered on the child to attract him to learning. Honey and the brains and hearts of animals were thought to stimulate a child's memory, whereas east European Jews believed that the eating and absorption of the end pieces of bread and cake baked from dough remnants could impede the memory and the learning process. With the decline of the traditional *heder* and the lesser significance attached to learning by rote, a ceremony that in the Middle Ages overshadowed the *bar mitzvah* in importance faded from memory in the late nineteenth and the twentieth centuries.[49]

We know from a responsum of Rabbi Meir of Rothenburg in the thirteenth century that large quantities of cake were consumed on the Sabbath and festivals, particularly by the children, as there was a query addressed to him as to whether or not the erasure of the writing on them was permissible on a feast day. According to the testimony of Kalonymos ben Kalonymos, the Jews in Provençe at the beginning of the fourteenth century used to eat a specially prepared honey cake in the shape of a ladder on Shavuot. Later in Germany the cake was made with seven rungs, symbolizing the seven spheres rent by the Almighty when He descended to give the Law. So, too, the earlier thirteenth-century Provençal philosopher Jacob ben Abba Mari Antoli asserted that it was customary for Jews to partake of milk and honey on Shavuot, as these foods were compared with the sustenance derived from the Torah. Among the Christian community, during Lent honey cakes shaped like ladders were consumed, and no doubt the Shavuot cake was modeled on a Christian example, even if the Jews' neighbors ate their cake a month or two earlier.[50]

In central and eastern Europe dairy foods replaced the honey cake of Provence on Shavuot, partly because there was an abundance of milk at this time of the year and partly because dairy dishes were the standard festive food at Whitsun in several parts of Germany, and the Scots celebrated the festival of Beltane on May 1, when many dairy dishes were consumed. By the early fourteenth century, according to the evidence of the Maharil, Jews used to bake meat pies and flat cakes (*floden*) for festival meals, while Rabbi Isserlein in fifteenth-century Austria permitted poor Jews to bake *floden* on festivals for later payment. On Shavuot, which was the supreme dairy festival, Jews from the time of the Maharil used to bake a big *floden*, probably with raisins, known as Sinai cake, and on this festival Rabbi Israel Isserlein used to partake of a piece of *floden* and eat fish fried in butter. In Poland, according to Rabbi Isserles (1525–1572), for Shavuot the *floden* was kneaded with milk, as were the biscuits (*kichelech*); in Germany it was the custom to eat cheese *floden* on the New Year, while on Sukkot they ate a *floden* with layers of fruit and dough symbolic of the harvested crops. During the seventeenth century in Germany, the Jews baked a cake with seven peaks for Shavuot.[51]

In the fourteenth century the Maharil mentioned that it was the custom to eat a honey cake on Purim, and a century later we have evidence that the Austrian Jews ate *kreplekh* on Purim and *kremzlekh* on holidays such as Passover. Hayyim Schauss, following Moritz Steinschneider, assumed that the German Jews had borrowed the custom of eating *kreplekh* on Purim from their Gentile neighbors, who celebrated Shrove Tuesday, which occurred at the same time of the year, by consuming pancakes that were similar. Schauss further pointed out that the beating and noise made on Purim in the synagogue when Haman's name was mentioned was originally connected with an attempt to frighten evil spirits at this time of the year, when winter changed into spring. Hence the custom of eating *kreplekh*, boiled dumplings stuffed with meat that had been chopped and "beaten." Although the custom of eating cheese dishes on Hanukkah can be traced to the story of Judith, an Israelite heroine in the Apocrypha who gave the enemy general Holofernes milk to drink before assassinating him, this practice of eating cheese delicacies did not become popular until the Middle Ages, when it was referred to with approval by Rabbi Nissim ben Reuben in the fourteenth century. Kalonymos ben Kalonymos (1287–1377) also stated that special cakes were eaten on Hanukkah, and he wrote a poem for the festival extolling the merits of eating pancakes that were fried in oil. Throughout Europe and the Middle East, Jews ate these pancakes to commemorate the miracle of the lights that burned for eight days in the Temple, although there was a supply of oil sufficient for only one day.[52]

7

THE FOOD OF THE SEPHARDIM

THE SPANISH JEWS: WEEKDAY FOOD

In this chapter we shall examine the food of the Western Sephardim, the Jews from Spain and Portugal. It has been estimated by Salo Baron that in 1490 c.e. there were 250,000 Jews in Spain and 80,000 in Portugal. After their expulsion from Spain in 1492 the Jews, numbering some 50,000 persons, settled principally in the Turkish Empire, North Africa, Holland, Italy, and America, and many sought temporary refuge in Portugal, taking their cuisine with them. The recipes of the Sephardim in Turkey bore the closest affinities to the cuisine of the southern Spanish provinces of Andalusia and Valencia and the Balearic Islands. We shall try to analyze the cuisine of the Spanish Jews in the Turkish Empire to ascertain which Spanish food styles they retained and which culinary elements they adopted and absorbed from the Turks and the Arabs. Our task is made the more difficult by the fact that the basic research in this field has been undertaken only recently and by Spain's Islamic heritage, so that it is hard to disentangle new adaptations from long-standing food patterns. Again, it is not always easy to distinguish between the food of Spain and Portugal; for instance, Lady Montefiore's *The Jewish Manual,* first published in 1846, is in small part a melange of Portuguese and Spanish dishes obscured by idiosyncratic spelling. A *chejado* turns out to be the Portuguese word *queijadas,* meaning an egg-thickened tart often filled with cheese and ground almonds; *impanada* is the Spanish word *empanada,* a term used to describe fish in a pastry crust; *prenesas* were fried pancakes, but this is an obscure term, as the Spanish Jews commonly called these fritters *bulemas.* From time to time Lady Montefiore mentioned *chorizo,* a Spanish-style sausage, made with meat, paprika, black pepper, and garlic, as an ingredient in several recipes. Nor was the process of cultural exchange flowing merely in one

121

direction. Spanish cookery books have references to Jewish dishes, some of which must be authentic, such as trout prepared in the Jewish way (*Truchas a la Judia*). Here the trout is first fried with garlic, then cooked in sauce and served very cold, a typical Sabbath dish.[1]

Like the Jews in medieval Egypt, the Western Sephardim and the Ashkenazim in Jerusalem at the end of the nineteenth century still bought large quantities of foodstuffs for the winter season, as it was then difficult to gain access to the important food and vegetable markets in the Old City. In every house in Jerusalem there was a small storeroom where each family would keep the essential foods that were purchased in advance for the times of scarcity in the winter season. Among the items kept in bulk in Sephardic households were rice, flour, lentils, beans, olives, and cheese. Similarly, Itta Yellin has recorded that her parents, who were Ashkenazim, lived in Jerusalem in 1881–1882, outside the walled city, in a house that had two cellars, where stocks of charcoal, wine, spirits, olives, and sesame oil were laid in for one year, while large supplies of wheat packed in wooden crates were stored in the house itself. At the end of the summer housewives also collected a large supply of eggs that were packed in slaked lime in large earthenware jars for the winter season. So, too, in Turkey Sephardic housewives would put a string through tomatoes, peppers, and okra when they were in season and hang them up to dry for a few days in the summer for use in winter. Recalling his childhood in Salonika, when it was part of the Turkish Empire, Leon Sciaky wrote:

> Autumn brings the usual hustle and bustle of preserving and jam-making. In the large kitchen the copper kettles simmer gayly and the house is fragrant with the smells of fruits. Basketfuls of luscious apricots, yellow quinces, and juicy oranges are transformed into *dulces*, to be placed for days in the sunshine of the *chardak* [Turkish for hut] before they are stored in the deep recesses of cupboards. Everyone is busy as the ripe tomatoes are turned into paste for the winter.

Further, "Even Bisnona Miriam and Tia Garcia come to help make noodles and *fideos*, the tiny bits of rich dough that will go into the soups of the months to come."[2]

During the summer season, when the markets were full of fruit, housewives in Jerusalem would prepare cherry and marmalade jams and all kinds of sweet things. In the winter Sephardic housewives made preserves from the peel of quinces, apricots, and lemons. Quince preserve, a Sephardic speciality called in Ladino *dulce de bimberio*, is still made in Portugal and Spain, where it is known as *dulce de membrillo*. It was almost certainly taken by Spanish Jews on their travels to the Middle East. According to Jane Grigson, as quince paste was known in Portugal as *marmelada*, the Portuguese were probably the inventors of marmalade. The word *marmelada* may be traced through Greek and Latin to the ancient Semitic Assyrian and Babylonian word for quince, *marmahu*. In Scotland there was a vital change when marmalade, now made with orange peel, was no longer served as a dessert at dinner but became an essential item at the breakfast table. Having said all this, the practice of serving sweet preserved fruits as a snack was something that was indigenous to the Middle East from ancient times, and the Arabs, according to C. Anne Wilson, introduced the recipe for quince cooked with sugar into Portugal and hence Spain. Further, the Mozarbic word *malmâlo* was the ancestor of the Portuguese word for quince, *marmilo*.[3]

During the grape harvest, most families in Jerusalem would buy a large quantity of special red grapes and white grapes for the preparation of wine. Among the Sephardim, two professional wine makers would call at a house by appointment, bringing basins with them that they filled with grapes. After carefully washing their feet with soap and water, they stepped into the basins and trod the grapes. Having collected the juice, they strained it and poured it into earthenware jugs to which slices of apple were added to encourage fermentation. The jars were then sealed but opened in about a month when the wine was ready for consumption. In the Ashkenazic Pines household, in nineteenth-century Jerusalem, the family made four or five different kinds of wine and brandy.[4]

In the 1880s in Jerusalem, women would come with sieves to neighbors' houses to sift the wheat and to separate little stones from the grain, after which it was taken to a mill to be ground into flour. When the flour was collected, it was divided into three grades: the finest flour was used for baking *hallot* and biscuits, the coarse flour was used for cooking, while the medium flour was allocated for making ordinary bread. Yakov Yehoshua, reminiscing about his childhood at the beginning of the century, described how his mother would muster all her strength on a Thursday night and prepare the dough in a kneading bowl for baking bread. After she had completed the kneading, she covered the dough with a thick blanket until the following day. On Friday she would be up before sunrise, separating a piece of dough and rolling it with her hands into the shape of a loaf, after which flour was scattered on it and it was placed on a board before being baked in an oven. At that time in Jerusalem there were a few bakeries, but many Sephardic householders preferred to bake their own bread. The homemade bread was a little dry because it was baked only twice a week, that is, on Mondays and Fridays. Bread was expensive and pieces of dry bread were not thrown away but kept in a pot, after which they were soaked in water and white oil, and pepper and cheese were added. Then, by frying portions of this mixture, the resourceful Sephardic mothers made a tasty kind of pudding known as *boyos de pan*. This concoction is similar to the famous Spanish dish called *migas*, which literally means crumbs and the origin of which is medieval. Interestingly enough, it was formerly served in Spain, often in the household of impecunious army officers when their financial resources were at a low ebb. Sephardic parents ensured that every dish was eaten with a decent portion of bread, and various later sociological surveys have shown that in the land of Israel oriental Jews, particularly those hailing from Kurdistan and Iran, were much larger consumers of bread than were Ashkenazim.[5]

During the week, the Sephardim in Jerusalem drank soup and ate mainly beans, peas, lentils, noodles, and pieces of fila pastry. When a Spanish journalist visited Istanbul in the 1960s, he was amazed to find the Sephardim still loyally drinking typically Spanish soups of chickpeas and white beans. These soups have been described as vegetable stews, which were ravenously consumed by the peasantry in the autumn, winter, and spring rather than in the summer. The beans and other legumes were always eaten with a plateful of rice, which was the staple food among the Sephardim of Jerusalem. So, too, rice was eaten daily in Spain, where it was prepared in a large variety of ways. The Spanish word for rice, *arroz*, can be traced to the Arabic, and the popularity of rice among the Spaniards, which deeply influenced the Sephardim, is in itself a legacy of the Muslim invasion of Spain. Winter vegetables included beans, peas, and spinach. The importance of beans as an ingredient in a large variety of Sephardic dishes, including *hamin*, may be gauged by the fact that the Spanish word for beans and Jewess is one and the same, *judia*, although it has also been argued that this similarity is a coincidence. In fact, all the family were mobilized on a Thursday evening in Jerusalem to clean the vegetables for the Sabbath.[6]

During the summer, lettuce salads were popular with the addition of a small side plate of tomatoes mixed with cucumber and parsley and small pieces of hot pepper. If the children behaved cheekily or uttered unkind words, their lips were smeared with hot pepper as a punishment. Tomatoes and cucumbers were available for the salad only when they were in season. Unlike the Ashkenazim, the Sephardim made little use of onions and garlic, but the Sephardic mothers would sometimes try to persuade their children to eat them on the grounds that these vegetables brought a glow to the cheeks of the Ashkenazic *yeshivah* students. The Sephardim, however, had freely eaten garlic and onions in Spain, where they were known as "the country people's cure," as they were the food of the masses. When the Sephardim settled in Turkey, they imbibed the feelings of aversion of the Muslims for these plants, particularly for garlic, which has a strong odor and was supposed to be invested with the power of expelling evil spirits and healing, something that was at once beneficial and terrifying. Large quantities of olives were cleaned, and small children were used to pound them with stones while sitting outside in the courtyards of their homes in Jerusalem. The Sephardic women used to pickle aubergines and small lemons in oil and vinegar together with hot spices. Both adults and children could not consume a dish without the benefit of one of these pickles. The pasta dishes were principally prepared in the summer, when there was an abundance of eggs, while to give the pasta different shapes the Sephardic women would dip their fingers in oil. People would also buy tasty lunchtime snacks from stands in the streets of Jerusalem, snacks such as noodles with cheese, *borekas* filled with salted cheese, or spinach with hard-boiled eggs. The Sephardim were well acquainted with pasta before their expulsion from Spain, as the Arabs had introduced different varieties of pasta into Spain in the eleventh century.[7]

The Sephardic inhabitants of the Old City supplied milk only to pregnant women and sick persons. Goat's milk was given without boiling as a medicine to persons suffering from malaria. If neighbors saw milk outside a house, they asked the occupants, "Who has fallen sick?" So valuable was milk that the Sephardim mixed ground almonds with boiling water as a substitute, almond milk being a well-known medieval European food with its source in Arab or Persian cuisine. Arab peasants from the villages surrounding Jerusalem sold *laban*, or sour milk, in the city. Soft cheese was kept by the Sephardim in tins of salt water to preserve it. The poor ate *ricotta*, a Middle-Eastern dish consisting of the leftovers of cheese, scrambled eggs, and chopped tomatoes, to which pepper was added; it was also a dish much beloved by children. Boiled eggs were the lot of Europeans or were given to sick persons or weakly babies, but the Sephardic children preferred an omelette in which they could dip bread.[8]

Unlike the Ashkenazim, the Sephardim avoided eating herring, which was a very nutritious fish, and they had a preference for a fish called *gratto* and for small sardines, the latter no doubt being an eating habit acquired during their sojourn in Spain and Portugal. Yakov Yehoshua recalled that his father would sometimes eat for lunch two or three small sardines mixed with oil and lemon together with salad, tomatoes, and red peppers. Fresh fish was a rare and expensive food in Jerusalem, particularly in the winter. Salted cod was sold in the grocery shops, and the Sephardic women would keep it soaking in water from Thursday night until Friday morning to rid it of its salty taste. It was then soaked in tomato juice and graced the table on both the Sabbath and on weekdays. Another fish that was available in Jerusalem was *bouri* (gray mullet), which was caught by fishermen in Jaffa and prepared in a jelly with nuts; in the summer it was served with oil and lemon. Fish was also used as a folk cure to help persons suffering from shock who had been overwhelmed by having sad tidings related to them.[9]

In the 1870s meat was a rare commodity in Jerusalem. It was eaten only on the Sabbath and festivals, although this was not the case a few decades later. For most of the nineteenth century, only the Sephardim were allowed by Muslim authorities in Jerusalem to slaughter animals, until an Ashkenazic boycott broke the Sephardic monopoly of the kosher meat trade in 1870. Prior to this the Sephardic butcher shops admitted only Sephardic customers in the morning and only after they had been served choice portions of meat were the Ashkenazim allowed to make their purchases.[10]

In Jerusalem and in Smyrna chicken remained a luxury item rarely consumed, unlike the situation prevailing among the Jews in medieval Egypt. Beef, however, was regularly eaten; almost every limb of the animals was exploited by the Sephardic mothers. Between Purim and Passover in both Jerusalem and Turkey the meat of goats and lambs was in season. It was a time when ribs of tender lambs were roasted and joyfully eaten while drinking a glass of red wine; the salivary and liver glands of sheep were also regarded as delicacies. At this time of the year the leftovers of meat were so plentiful in the butcher shops that they were often used for family parties. The Sephardim enjoyed meat soup, stuffed intestines, brains served with lemon, chopped meat, and the vast quantities of bones that were sold with the meat. Traditional Moroccan-Jewish cooking also exploited all the different portions of an animal. At the turn of the century, workers and craftsmen used to eat meat at least once a day in Jerusalem. When they came home from work they would go to the butcher shop and buy at a cheap price the lungs, liver, and legs of the animal for the evening meal. Heavy meat dishes were eaten in winter, but in summer different meat dishes would be served, often with fried dumplings. At midday or in the evening the vendors of kosher meat set up their stands in the streets of Jerusalem, selling cuts of meat roasted on coal and the thin legs of cattle, with beans. Similarly, in Aleppo some Jewish merchants used to frequent Muslim butcher shops at lunchtime, when they would buy a piece of kosher lamb that had been broiled over a charcoal fire. In the Turkish town of Smyrna, between the wars, Monday and Thursday were the days when the kosher meat was slaughtered. The meat eaten was chiefly beef and veal, as mutton was regarded as too greasy, but not every Jewish household served a meat course daily.[11]

A whole series of popular beliefs developed around the eating of the different portions of an animal. It was thought that if a person ate a limb or an organ of an animal, the corresponding part of the human body would be strengthened, but an exception was made for the heart, brain, and liver. For instance, if a man had weak legs, he was given the legs of a fine animal in the form of a soup. The oriental Jews in Jerusalem, particularly the Persians, believed that if the heart of a prematurely born animal was eaten it was a remedy that could cure people overcome by desperate attacks of fear. For a man whose sexual powers were waning, it was thought to be a helpful remedy if he swallowed five grams of the powdered testicles of an ox with a glass of old wine every day, a cure still followed in Spain today. If someone was ill for many days, the Sephardim used a remedy known as *mumia*. This was a small piece of decayed flesh, preferably from a mummy, which was pounded into a powder, which the patient drank. It is interesting to note that the patient had to take great care not to smell any garlic or onions. According to Rabbi David ben Zimra (c. 1479–1573), the swallowing of a piece of *mumia* was permissible, as the flesh of the embalmed body had reverted to dust.[12]

According to Rabbi Solomon ben Adret of Barcelona (1235–1310), the diet of the medieval Spanish Jews consisted of meat—even if the latter was not a daily food—fish, bread, cheese, eggs, and soup. Like the Jews of eastern Europe and like most of the population in preindustrial Europe, the Spanish Jews frequently added saffron to their food to enhance its flavor, but Rabbi Adret was wary of buying it from shops, as he complained that the saffron was often adulterated with wine or flour. Later, in traditional society among the Sephardim in the eastern Mediterranean, the principal daily foods were bread, vegetables, beans, rice, and perhaps cheese. J. C. Hobhouse reported in 1813 that "the lower servants, or porters of the factories [in Smyrna], are Jews, who, notwithstanding their laborious employ-ments, live chiefly on bread and dried olives . . ." Later, Yakov Yehoshua wrote about a man who went on journey from Jerusalem to Jaffa equipped with flat bread, onions, olives, and cheese, which seem to have been the common foods of the poor. This is corroborated by a Judeo-Spanish folktale of a wealthy woman who gave a beggar some bread and *kaskaval* cheese, the latter being a Turkish word derived from the Italian *caciocavallo*. So popular was this cheese among the Jews of the Near East that the Greeks called it *casheri*, that is, kosher cheese.[13]

Andrés Bernáldez, a chaplain to one of the Spanish inquisitors, complained that "they never lose their Jewish way of eating, preparing their meat dishes with onions and garlic and cooking them in oil, which they use in place of lard, so that they will not have to eat pork fat;

and oil with meat is something which gives the breath a very bad odour; and their houses and their doorways smell very bad because of this way of cooking . . ." Moreover, the liberal Spanish historian Salvador de Madariaga concluded that the Spanish practice of generously using olive oil for cooking was a Jewish custom that the Spaniards had unconsciously imbibed. Much of the interest of the passage quoted from Bernáldez lies in the fact that it refutes the notion that the abundant use of garlic and onions was restricted in the Middle Ages to Ashkenazic cooking, although Madariaga may have erred in minimizing the partial contribution of the Moors to the spread of the custom in Spain of using olive oil as the cooking medium. [14]

In 1650 Moshe Porges wrote an account of life in Palestine, mentioning that sesame seeds were crushed to make an oil for cooking "which is pretty good, cheap, and is much better than goose fat or butter." In the mid-eighteenth century Alexander Russell asserted that the poorer class of Syrian Jews in Aleppo lived "chiefly on bread, pulse herbs, and roots, dressed with . . . oil of sesamum [sesame], which is seldom eaten by other inhabitants." So, too, Lane remarked that the Egyptian Jews in the nineteenth century made an immoderate use of sesame oil in their cooking, while the late-Victorian writer Lucy Garnett criticized this characteristic of the cuisine of the Spanish Jews living in the Turkish Empire when she stated that "sesame oil enters largely into the composition of the majority of the Jewish dishes, and consequently renders them quite unpalatable to Gentiles generally. This oil is also used for making pastry, which also has the drawback of being exceedingly heavy and indigestible." [15]

The Sephardim did not make special desserts, but at the end of the meal they would eat grapes, dried figs, and dates. Here they followed Spanish practice, as the only special dessert that was utilized in Spain was flan (crème caramel), and this was reserved for party occasions. Incidentally, as early as the late fifteenth and sixteenth centuries Jews played an important role as retailers and wholesalers of almonds, chestnuts, raisins, and other dried foods in the Ottoman Empire, which gives an indication of the significance of these foods in the Jewish diet. The Sephardic children became acquainted with fruit soup after the communal kitchens were opened for the pioneers who came flocking to Palestine from eastern Europe, but the Sephardic mothers did not know how to cook and boil apricots and peaches. As a treat, mothers would cut the soft part out of a chunk of bread and then pour oil, salt, and sugar into the scooped-out section, after which they would stuff the soft part of the bread into the crust. The children were accustomed to eating this food in the evening in the courtyard with a tomato, after they had returned from the Talmud Torah. [16]

THE SPANISH JEWS: SABBATH AND FESTIVAL FOOD

On Fridays in Jerusalem at the turn of the century, the Sephardim ate no meat in order to create a distinction between the ordinary food eaten during the week and the choice dishes reserved for the Sabbath. On Thursday night dairy or *pareve* food was invariably served, and Yakov Yehoshua recalled that on Friday itself his family ate a plate of beans with rice and lentils. In the winter, when the days were short, certain Sephardic families refrained from eating lunch to bestow more honor on the Sabbath meals. We shall discover that through the Jewish law codes these eating patterns were common not only among the Jews of Spanish origin but throughout the Ashkenazic and oriental Jewish communities as well. One family in prewar Smyrna would eat light, milky dishes for Friday lunch such as cheese *pasteles* (Spanish pastry) and *borekas* (Turkish *borek*), a pastry with a filling. *Borekas* were first encountered in Judezmo (Ladino) texts in the eighteenth century and were a food acquired relatively late by the Spanish-Jewish migrants in the Ottoman Empire. However, Mahmut Shirwani had already mentioned a sweet confection called *Sheker bourek* in his fifteenth-century additions to an earlier Turkish cookery book, so that this provided evidence that the Sephardim were slow to absorb Turkish mores.[17]

A rabbinic decision made several centuries ago in Turkey specified that employers were to pay their staff on Thursday night or Friday morning at the latest to enable them to purchase food for their families for the Sabbath. On the island of Rhodes poor Jews visited the households of the wealthier members of the community on Friday morning, carrying pots and bottles while they begged for food. When the containers were filled with beans, some form of meat, oil, and other food, they returned to their homes to celebrate the Sabbath. In addition, the synagogue distributed bread to the poor, an ancient practice that is still continued in certain congregations in Israel. The grandfather of Viviane Alchech Miner made wine for the Sabbath in September and October, when sweet grapes were available, for which purpose he used a hand-operated wine press. Raisins were reserved for making *arak* or *raki*, a pungent, syrupy liquor popular in the eastern Mediterranean. In some households the Sephardic women were accustomed to lighting the wicks of oil lamps known as *lampara*, instead of kindling Sabbath candles.[18]

Special fish dishes were prepared for Friday evening, in particular fish with lemon sauce known as *pescado con huevo y limon*; other special sauces with which fish were served were *tomat* (tomato) and

Avram-mila, a sauce made with green plums. The latter was eaten because there was a tradition that Abraham sat under a plum tree following his circumcision. Not only were the lemon-sauce fish recipes reminiscent of Spanish cooking, particularly medieval Catalan cuisine, but the Spanish-born rabbi David ben Zimra (c. 1479–1573) already mentioned the preparation of large quantities of lemon juice in barrels in Egypt for export, some of which was diluted with water and much of which was used to season food. Barbara Kirshenblatt-Gimblett has pointed out how the combination of egg-lemon sauces with fish forcemeat balls and fish was a distinctive trait of the cuisine of the Sephardim from the Iberian peninsula, many of whom settled in Turkey. Further, Rudolf Grewe drew attention to the fact that in medieval Catalonia under Arab influence the juices of bitter orange, lemon, pomegranate, and unripe grapes (*verjus*) were used in cooking, while the sauces were thickened with raw egg yolks. We should also recall that the Portuguese Marranos in London in the mid-sixteenth century were enamored of fried fish; a Ladino ballad from Yugoslavia even has a woman present her lover with "wine and a meal of fried fish and lemon." Fish dishes similar to those mentioned here were also served on festival evenings.[19]

Traditionally, a meat course would follow. Sometimes Sephardic families would eat *pasteles*, a dish of medieval Spanish origin, consisting of small meat pies, or *migina*, the equivalent of strudel, a single-layered cake filled with meat, probably a variant of the Spanish dish known as *migas;* both these Sephardic dishes were reminiscent of the fare served by the Ashkenazim in the Middle Ages on Friday night, while Joseph Karo (1488–1575), the Spanish-born compiler of the *Shulchan Aruch*, mentioned the consumption of *empanada*, pie, on the Sabbath. During the winter in Turkey, the pies were filled with chopped meat or cheese, but at other times of the year the filling in the pies consisted of a purée of pumpkin, eggplant, and spinach mixed with cheese.[20]

Other dishes gracing the table at the start of the Sabbath were *fijon* (Spanish *frijol*), or kidney beans fried with onions, and *baniza de spinica*, or spinach pastry. In prewar Smyrna the poorer Jewish families would eat *porotas*, that is, white beans plus pieces of meat or *yaprakes finos*, vine leaves stuffed with rice and ground beef. The wealthier families in Smyrna, however, ate steak on Friday night. Rabbi Moshe Israel, the chief rabbi of Rhodes between 1714 and 1726, wrote a responsum in favor of eating *yaprakes* after some pietists argued that vine leaves could not be cleaned sufficiently to detect all the insects and that the food should be forbidden. Although the consumption of stuffed vine leaves may be traced to the courts of the Sasanian kings in Iran (208–632 C.E.) and later to Ottoman sultans, there is a controversy as to whether or not stuffed vegetables were first popularized by the Turks or by the Greeks, but it seems likely that this innovation should be attributed to the Persians. As far as the Sephardim are concerned, the responsum mentioned here seems to indicate that vine leaves and *borekas* were a relatively new eighteenth-century addition to their menu. Warm *pita* bread filled with kidney beans was a favorite treat of the children in Salonika on a Friday night, but *pita* was a southeastern Judezmo term, and the expression for it was acquired by the Spanish Jews in the area around Salonika. *Pita* was derived from the Greek word *pitta* but ultimately from the Italian *pizza*. The Sephardim concluded their Friday-evening meal by eating hazelnuts, almonds, and dried fruit with the addition of the seeds of roasted pumpkins, known as *pepida*.[21]

During the winter, on the Sabbath morning after prayers, a *hamin* consisting of meat, white beans, rice, and potatoes together with *koklas,* or dumplings similar to the east European *kneidlach,* would be eaten by the Jews in Jerusalem. According to Yakov Yehoshua, however, different kinds of *hamin* were consumed depending on whether it was winter or summer. Among the types of *hamin* dishes listed by him were a *hamin* consisting of intestines filled with rice and meat, rice mixed with pieces of meat found in the belly of a cow, *hamin* made with little pumpkins, *hamin* prepared with beans and the foot of cattle, *hamin* of wheat (*hamin di trigo*), and *hamin* made with spinach or vine leaves. In the autumn, on *Shabbat Berashit,* a special *hamin* with seven layers was prepared corresponding to the seven days of the creation of the world, and between each layer were pockets of rice. For the New Year of Trees at the end of winter there was a *hamin* consisting of grits or grains, which were coarsely ground, and the foot of cattle. In particular, the legs of bulky animals were valued for their special taste and were put into the *hamin* for the winter months, especially for *Shabbat Bshalach.* The Sabbath meals always included *haminados,* the eggs cooked with the hamin, which had a special taste; there was a popular saying that ten Jews could live off one of these eggs. Following the Spanish example, fresh, uncooked fruit was the universal dessert, and a glass of arak was also drunk with this meal.[22]

According to Elie Eliachar, during the summer dishes other than *hamin* were eaten by the Sephardim in Jerusalem. *Desayuno* means breakfast in Spanish and is a term used to describe light meals usually reserved for Sabbath mornings in summer, for festivals, and for Friday lunch. A large variety of appetizing pastry dishes were served, including *bulemas,* or fila dough coils filled with cheese, spinach, or eggs, *filas,* or layers of thin dough wrapped around courgettes, aubergines, and cheese, *borekas,* or a flaky dough filled with cheese and shaped like a crescent. All these pastries were carried to the neighbor hood baker on a *tafsin*, a great copper tray, for baking and were later collected by the family. Alternatively, these pastries were heated on a stove on top of a metal sheet that covered the flame, a practice that is permitted in rabbinic law as the food is not liquid. A summer food borrowed from the Turks was *sutlatch* (*sut* is milk in Turkish), a tasty dish of milk and ground rice boiled into a gruel sprinkled with cinnamon that was eaten frozen. It was served after morning prayers on the Sabbath and similarly on the festival of Shavuot. In prewar Smyrna, after they had returned from the synagogue on the Sabbath, one family used to eat *fritadas*, a Spanish omelette made with spinach, leeks, or tomatoes and *ensaimadas*, a Majorcan bun the size of a small plate and consisting of a light, flaky dough twisted into the shape of a turban and sprinkled with sugar, which is believed to be of Moorish origin. Savory pastries of pie dough, flaky pastry, or fila, a paper-thin pastry, all of them containing a cheese or vegetable filling, are common in the Middle East; the *sanbusak*, a pastry of Iraqi and ultimately Persian origin, was mentioned in a poem recited at a banquet of the Caliph Mustaki at Baghdad as early as the tenth century, a fact that seems to indicate that these pastries were part of the court cuisine of the Abbasid caliphs and their later Ottoman successors. Among the other items displayed on the table for the Sabbath meal were ring-shaped rolls known as *roskitas di gueve* (Spanish *rosca*) and *bizcochos*, biscuits. We would, therefore, conclude that the consumption of light refreshments, *desayuno*, was a Spanish-Jewish practice but that when the Sephardim migrated to various parts of the Ottoman Empire they adopted a number of indigenous foods, particularly savory pastries such as *borek*, which we have seen were of Turkish origin.[23]

In Venice the *Libro Novo*, a cookery book dedicated to the Este family, who befriended Spanish-Jewish refugees, was published in 1549. Among other items it contained a recipe for making *albondigas*, a meat dish of Jewish style consisting of chopped veal, oily herbs, raisins, and yolks of hard-boiled eggs. The large meatball was cooked in a soup with herbs, nutmeg, and saffron, after which it was cut into slices and was sometimes served on slices of bread. This Spanish recipe was no doubt supplied by the Sephardic refugees in Italy, as *albondigas* has remained a favorite food of the Sephardim on the Sabbath and festivals. Modern Spanish cookery books include recipes for balls of chopped fish and meat, both of them known as *albondigas*, and it is interesting that Lady Montefiore in her cookbook published in 1846 supplied similar recipes for both fish and meat, perhaps relying on Sephardic recipes; indeed, her fish forcemeat recipe has certain resemblances to that for the Ashkenazic dish of gefilte fish. The medieval Arabs, however, had a tradition of utilizing the tougher parts of meat by chopping them up and preparing meatballs from them, so that the Spanish dish of *albondigas* (Arabic *bunduga*) may have been introduced into Spain by the Moors. Noteworthy in this respect is the fact that the Moroccan Jews regularly served a traditional dish of meatballs on Friday night, while the recipe also was featured in a medieval cookbook from North Africa during the time of the Almohades.[24]

In Jerusalem after the Sabbath breakfast, the grown-ups would study while the children returned to the synagogue, where they were examined on their Hebrew studies of the previous week. At noon sweets and drinks would be distributed. In the summer there would be sherbet, a fizzy drink made with a sweet-sour powder, and *dulce,* a sweet preserve or jam. According to the *Jewish Encyclopedia,* the idea of giving gifts of *dulce,* "a confection wrapped in paper bearing a picture of the 'magen David' " on festivals was the adoption of a Spanish custom that had been given a Jewish form.[25]

Unlike the Ashkenazim, who made a single blessing on a special food when celebrating the New Year, the Sephardim pronounced seven such blessings, and this practice was common both to those reared in the Spanish tradition and those from oriental communities. In the evening, prior to the meal the family gathered for the ceremony that opened when an apple was sometimes dipped into honey in a fashion similar to that of the Ashkenazim; in Bulgaria they utilized a baked apple for this purpose while reciting a prayer in Hebrew and Ladino with the words, "Send us again a fruitful year and sweet from beginning to end." In Turkey a special apple compote called *mansanada* was prepared for this blessing. The family then recited other prayers before eating other kinds of food. When partaking of dates, they declared, "May we date the new year that is beginning as one of happiness and blessing, and peace for all men." Next the family said that "in the coming year may we be rich and replete" with acts of piety "as this pomegranate is rich and replete with seeds." Now a pumpkin was eaten as the family declared that if enemies reproached them the Lord would protect them. When consuming leek, which is called *karti* in Hebrew, the family expressed the hope that their enemies would be cut off, making a pun on the Hebrew words for leek and to be cut off. As a beetroot was eaten, the family prayed that their enemies would vanish; likewise there was a pun on the Aramaic word *salka,* meaning Swiss-chard and the Hebrew word for disappearing. Much of this ceremony was a means of ensuring the consolidation of in-group Jewish solidarity against the threats of external enemies.[26]

Some families would arrange for the head of a sheep to be displayed on their table, in which case they would pray to be the "head" and not the tail, which meant that they would move forward into good health for the year. If, instead, they had a fish on the table, a blessing on fruitfulness was recited over the fish. Certain Sephardic communities would not place fish on the table because the Hebrew word for fish reminded them of the word for anxiety. It was the custom of the Spanish Jews to dip their bread into sugar on the New Year. On the island of Rhodes they ate *fijones*, or black-eyed peas, *rubiya* in Hebrew. During the day on Rosh Hashanah, the Sephardim ate a delicacy known as *moussaka*, consisting of alternate layers of aubergines and minced meat and onions. Although both the Greeks and the Turks claim to have invented this dish, the name is an Arabic one, and its probable source is an ancient concoction known as *maghmuma*.[27]

At first, in medieval Spain the institution of the Ashkenazic *Kapparot* ceremony on the eve of the Day of Atonement was opposed, but later the custom became popular among the Sephardic communities in the Turkish Empire. At the turn of the century, after sunset the leading ritual slaughterer in Jerusalem would go on his rounds accompanied by his attendant, who carried a lantern. The father in each family would pass a live chicken over the heads of each individual while reciting the *Kapparot* prayers, and among the Sephardim the slaughterer would sacrifice the bird, catching its blood in a metal basin filled with sand. Similarly, on the island of Rhodes, the slaughterer killed a cock for males and a hen for females and smeared a little blood from the chickens on the forehead of the person on whose behalf the bird had been slain. Among the Sephardim in Jerusalem at the turn of the century chicken was a great luxury eaten only on the eve of Yom Kippur and after the fast; chicken soup was reserved for the sick and for pregnant women. In medieval Germany, at this time of the year the Jews distributed fowls among the poor or gave the poor gifts of money instead, and until the Second World War the Jews on the island of Rhodes adhered to similar practices with the addition of gifts of bread for the poor as a possible substitute. At the end of the fast in Jerusalem, everyone received a small piece of bread dipped in olive oil, while before the actual meal to break the fast a special drink, the *pepitada*, made of ground melon seeds, was handed to every member of the family. Immediately after this meal, a start was made on the building of the *sukkah*. In Rhodes, during the festival of Tabernacles fruit and sesame-seed biscuits known as *bizcochos* were suspended from the roof of the *sukkah*.[28]

Although the Sephardim were in general allowed to eat rice, beans, and peas, the staple items of diet in the Mediterranean during the eight days of Passover, the Spanish Jews usually refrained from eating rice in case some small pieces of another grain became mixed with the rice. There was a custom of Salonika Jewry, however, whereby the eating of rice and potatoes was permitted during Passover provided they were served hot enough to burn the tongue. Rabbi Haim Palagi of nineteenth-century Smyrna declared that if rice was first roasted and then placed in boiling water, its use was permitted during Passover, the source of this custom being a talmudic injunction; nonetheless, this practice was forbidden by the *Shulchan Aruch.* In earlier times the Sephardim did not sell their *hametz,* their leaven food, to Gentiles as the Ashkenazim did prior to the festival. At the *Seder* the Sephardim recited the whole of the *Haggadah* in both Hebrew and Ladino. When the Rev. P. Beaton visited Smyrna in the mid-nineteenth century, he "saw preserved passover bread, which was not round and thin, as in Germany, but square, made up of thick rolls and pierced with holes. Cakes of the finest flour, kneaded with wine, are baked as fancy bread for passover." Among the archives of the Bevis Marks synagogue was a recipe for *haroset* from 1726, the ingredients of which were raisins, almonds, cinnamon, pistachios, dates, ginger, hazelnuts, walnuts, apples, pears, and figs. Meat pies made from *matzah, migina,* and jellied fish, *pikhtee,* were popular main-course dishes during Passover. As an accompaniment to the main dish, the Sephardim often served *matzah* noodles, *sodra,* meaning deaf, instead of rice and potatoes, together with a beetroot salad. Dairy foods that delighted the Sephardim were leek patty, *prasa fuchi,* spinach pie, *mina de spina, bulemas,* and *matzah mogados.* In the evening a dish of fava beans cooked in a chicken or meat broth was well received by the Sephardim. In Israel the Sephardim had a custom of encouraging their unmarried daughters to remove the roasted egg from the *Seder* plate and eat it behind the door, as the egg represented marriage and children.[29]

At the end of Passover, the children would pick a few stalks of wheat, barley, or grass and tie them together before handing them to the head of the family. In Jerusalem the father or grandfather would tap each member of the family on the back with the sheaf, wishing everyone *"santak khadra,"* symbolizing the hope for a green and productive year. In other countries where the Sephardim settled, the heads of the family threw grass, money, or wrapped sweets on the floor for the children to collect in a ceremony known as *Prasa-in-agna-levadura.* In the past, on the last day of Passover in Jerusalem the Arabs sent their Sephardic friends a copper bowl packed with bread, goats' butter, and honey, while in return the Jews gave them presents of *matzot* and jam. So, too, a meal was eaten at the termination of the festival that consisted of pickled and salted fish, including smoked herring and raw salted mackerel, *liquierda.* It has been suggested that the ceremony practiced by the Jerusalem Sephardim at the end of Passover was borrowed from the Moors, as there were no parallel ceremonies to be found among the Arabs of the eastern Mediterranean; it is obvious that there are connections between the rites observed by the Sephardim with their emphasis on ripening grain and fish as an additional fertility symbol and the *Mimouna* festival celebrated by Moroccan Jews at this time of the year. Further, there was a link between the gift-exchange network among Jews and Arabs at this time of the year that operated in Jerusalem and the similar exchange system in Morocco. There were even more interesting parallels in fifteenth-century Spain in the town of Huete, where Jews and Christians exchanged gifts of food at the end of the Passover festival, and the Jews reciprocated by sending gifts at Christmas. For instance, a woman "sent to them [the Jews] lambs and other things for the Festival of Unleavened Bread and they in turn brought her of the same bread for that season and she ate of it . . ." Further, "Sometimes from my house we sent presents to some Jews at the close of festivals . . . [of] cheese and eggs and lettuce." Some persons kept a piece of *matzah* because of the belief that it could stop a storm. Passengers would put a piece of *matzah* in their pocket as a good-luck charm before embarking on a journey on a ship.[30]

It was the custom of the Spanish Jews to eat cheese-filled pastries during Shavuot, but unlike the Askenazim they did consume meat meals during the festival as well. For this festival a special bread was baked called *El Monte,* with reference to Mount Sinai, on which the Five Books of Moses were given. Many Spanish-Jewish communities baked *hallot* in different forms, including bread shaped to resemble the seven heavens, *siete sielos,* a book, *livro,* stairs, *skalera,* a bird, *pashariko,* or a lamp, *lampara.* The Sephardim also baked cakes shaped to look like the tablets of Law, which they called Sinai cakes. The icing for these cakes was white to represent the purity of the Law or the cloud at Mount Sinai. During the all-night learning session the men were supplied with Turkish coffee and *bizcochos.* Among some sections of the Sephardim, on Shavuot the Book of Ruth was read by the children, who were rewarded with a gift of sweets as a reminder of the sweetness of the *Torah.* So, too, it was a practice among the Ashkenazim in the Middle Ages to initiate pupils for entrance into the *heder* on Shavuot by offering them sweet foods, while the custom seems to have survived in a modified form among the Spanish Jews.[31]

Turning now to the minor festivals, on Hanukkah the Spanish Jews in Turkey used to make fritters known as *bimuelos,* which were fried in oil and dipped in honey or sprinkled with cinnamon and sugar, but sometimes the *bimuelos* were made on a griddle and were flat like a pancake. These pastries were known in sixteenth-century Judezmo as *bunywelo,* derived from the Spanish word for doughnut or fritter, *bunuelo* (from Celtic *buna*). The word was already found in manuscripts in thirteenth-century Spain, but *bunuelos* were later regarded with disdain as they were associated with Moors and perhaps Jews because the fritters were made with olive oil. Interestingly, *bunuelos de viento* (puffs of wind), or very light doughnuts, were munched in

Spain on All Saints Day, the first day of November, which is close
enough in the calendar to Hanukkah, and it is clear from where the
Jewish custom arose. For the Sabbath of Hanukkah clothing was
brought to the synagogue in Rhodes, where it was distributed on the
sixth day of the festival. In Jerusalem children would go with their
teachers to houses in order to collect food and sweets. Then a picnic,
known as the *Miranda,* was organized, a borrowing of a Spanish
custom where these out-of-door festivities were called the *Merender.* In
Turkey, on the last day of Hanukkah, relatives and friends took food to
another family's house and a meal was prepared; at its conclusion
children were given gifts of money. On the evening of the New Year of
Trees, Tu be-Shvat, the family would gather around a table on which
the fruits of the land were displayed. During the day, each child would
be given a bag of fruit, peanuts, almonds, raisins, sweets, carobs, and
habechuches, a type of peanut. On Lag ba-Omer, the thirty-third day of
the Omer, the whole community in Jerusalem visited the tomb of
Simon the Just. As a treat, the children were given toffee-apples, sour
anbar, a variety of sweet, nougat, and fine-colored threads of toffee
known as "girl's hair." Arab vendors of drinks walked around the
crowd gathered under olive trees, selling iced *soos* (Arabic), a beverage
made from licorice wood, and other drinks, such as fruit juice and
lemonade.[32]

On Purim in Jerusalem in the past, groups of musicians would sing
outside houses, accompanied by the music of mandolins, a harp,
violin, drums, and cymbals. Groups of mummers strolled in the street,
dancing and miming all day. On Rhodes, plates of sweets and baked
food traditionally exchanged between relatives and friends on Purim
were delivered by children, who received gifts of money as a reward. In
Jerusalem in the past, the Sephardic head of the community distributed money to the needy and gifts in sealed envelopes to Turkish
officials, both Christian and Muslim. Among certain groups of Spanish
Jews, the traditional foods associated with Purim were *foulares.* A
circle of pastry dough was formed with a hard-boiled egg at its center;
strips of dough were then woven across the egg from this base, after
which the *foulares* were baked. Although the *foulares* elsewhere were
shaped either to symbolize Haman's ear or foot, on Rhodes they were
clearly made to resemble Haman's ear. In Turkey on Purim they
formed *shamlias,* or Haman's ears, *orejas de Haman,* out of strips of
dough that were bent into the shape of an ear and then fried. Many
other tasty morsels were also prepared in Turkey on Purim, including
a honey pastry dipped in syrup, *pinonate,* honey-nut fila triangles,
trigona, honey-nut pastry, *travados,* called *pestinos* in Andalusia, and
a pastry made of fila leaves, chopped walnuts, cinnamon, oil, and
sesame seeds and known as *baklavah à la Emilie* and *kadaif.* In the

early years of the century most Balkan pastry shops offered only *baklavah* (Turkish from the Arabic word *baqlawa*) and *kadaif*, which were of Arab origin or even pre-Arab in the case of *kadaif*, and other syruped pastries, but the honey pastries of the Sephardim may have been of medieval Spanish origin, even if local fila pastry was used. Another medieval Spanish food consumed on Purim and Shavuot were *roskas*, hard, round rolls or cakes.[33]

Turkish coffee was brewed in an urn and offered to visitors at all times of the day and night. The guests were always offered coffee with a *dulce*, or preserve. There were two kinds of sweets: one was a thick white syrup containing sugar, egg white, lemon juice, and sometimes chopped nuts and was known as *sharope*; the other was a thick fruit confection made of quince, oranges, lemons, dates, or sour cherries. These *dulces* of preserved fruit were of ancient Middle Eastern origin, but many European medieval merchants, such as the famous merchant of the Italian town of Prato in the fourteenth century (Francesco Di Marco Datini), had developed a taste for them. No doubt, the Spanish Jews in Turkey and other parts of the Middle East quickly acquired a liking for them, particularly as they had been accustomed to quince jam in Spain since medieval times. In Turkey visitors were expected to take only a teaspoonful or two of the preserves, which were served in bowls on silver trays that were an essential part of a bride's dowry. After taking some of the preserve, the guest would place the used fork or spoon in the receptacle that had been provided and would take a drink of water. Only then would the coffee be offered to guests.[34]

The Sephardic mothers were skilled at baking their own cakes, pastries, and biscuits; many of the recipes were based on traditional recipes brought from Spain: for instance, *pan de España*, a medieval sponge cake that was eaten at circumcisions, the almond cakes on Passover, and pastries such as those made with ground almonds and sugar and known as *mogados* and *maronchinos*, which are still popular in Portugal today and which were introduced by the Moors. Many of these pastries have a lozenge shape, thereby indicating their Arab origin, as these diamond-shaped almond cakes were called *loz* in Arabic. Nut crescents, which were called *mustachudos* by the Sephardim and which were made from ground walnuts and orange rind, were also a Spanish dish known as *mostachon andaluz*. Another cake that was much liked by the Sephardim was *tish pishti* (Turkish, *tez pisti*), which was often eaten on the New Year.[35]

All the Sephardic ceremonies to accompany the stages in a life cycle were marked by elaborate meals. According to Max Grunwald, the Sephardim used to eat stuffed tomatoes, *Frankis entschidas*, vine leaves stuffed with meat, *nugada*, and stuffed paprika, *papras entschidas*, at a circumcision, *Bar Mitzvah*, or anniversary to commemorate a death. In Turkey, at a circumcision the guests would sit on sofas, eat sweets, and drink wine. There was also a ceremony for naming a girl, known as *fada* (Spanish for fate, destiny, or luck). On Rhodes, Friday was considered the most auspicious day for marriages, and after the wedding the guests accompanied the newly married couple home, where they would be entertained and plied with Jordan almonds, *baklavah*, and sweets made of almond paste. For weddings in Jerusalem they also prepared almond cakes as well as marmalade, apricot, and almond confections and almond sweets colored white and pink. On the occasion of the anniversary of a death, family and friends would gather and observe the *Meldado*. The men would hold a service, study a section of the Mishnah, and listen to a discourse from their rabbi, thereby increasing the solidarity of all the participants. After this, Turkish coffee was served with biscuits, *bizcochos*, and a sesame confection, while in Rhodes the participants at a *Meldado* were supplied with hard-boiled eggs, sweet rolls, olives, and arak. When a period of mourning commenced for a close relative, which lasted for a year, the mourner refrained from drinking his coffee with a *dulce*. At the end of the year, a neighbor brought the mourner some *dulce* for him to consume with his coffee, thereby marking his reintegration into the normal, humdrum world.[36]

Having surveyed the Sabbath and festival food of the Spanish Jews, we can now appreciate how both pastries with lemon peel, pine nuts, almonds, honeyed syrups, and the *bunuelos* were carried to Turkey and Palestine with the Sephardim after the expulsion of 1492. Other Spanish recipes still utilized by the Jews were the lemon and other sauces with which meat and fish were eaten, while in Smyrna a stew of haricot beans seasoned with oil and fried onions called *Avas* (Castilian Spanish, *havas*) was much enjoyed by poor families. In Turkey the Spanish Jews adopted the filo, or strudel pastry dough, stretched thin layers of dough, that the Turks invented for their pastries in the fifteenth century; later, the Sephardim borrowed the recipes for *borekas* and the *yaprakes finos*, which as we have seen may have been of Persian origin. Cooked aubergines mashed with bread crumbs and cheese in a dish known as *Almodrote de Berendjeda* were a favorite food for the Sabbath breakfast, *desayuno*, and may be the vestiges of a dish that has all but vanished from the modern Spanish kitchen, as aubergine recipes were mentioned in medieval Spanish-Arab cookery books. Charles Perry has suggested that the Muslim invaders of Spain may have introduced two aubergine recipes, one with meat and the other without it. Only among the Sephardim and the Andalusians was there a dish of olives mixed with pieces of orange. Pita bread was also heartily espoused by the Spanish Jews in the region around Salonika, but this type of bread may have been borrowed from the Italian Jews.

Just as the Italian Jews diffused the use of pita bread throughout the Balkans, so Sephardic merchants and their families may have been intermediaries in spreading the technique of making strudel dough throughout the Balkans and central Europe, from where it reached Poland, as the Sephardim had already become acquainted with puff pastry in medieval Spain.[37]

THE FOOD OF THE DUTCH AND PORTUGUESE JEWS

In this short section we shall explore the food of the Portuguese Jews, who settled mainly in Holland. Among the Portuguese Jews there were no special conditions concerning the food eaten on Friday nights, apart from the custom of partaking of a fish dish. In Holland a dairy or fish meal was served at the Sabbath breakfast, the *desayuno*. On the New Year, the Portuguese Jews recited the usual blessings over the apple and honey for a sweet year but did not recite the additional blessings over the head of a sheep or fish and various fruits and vegetables, as was the practice of the Spanish and oriental Jews. During the eighteenth century, on the feast of Tabernacles the Portuguese Jews used to consume a veal meat pie made with apples that was called *patel mitapuhim*. As the name of the dish resembles a Dutch specialty, namely a meat pie that was prepared with veal ragout, it has been suggested that the dish was of Dutch rather than of Portuguese origin. On Passover the Portuguese Jews in Holland in the mid-eighteenth century ate an unnamed delicacy made of the yolk of eggs, honey, and cinnamon that had a very sharp taste, possibly akin to the Portuguese dish of *ovos molos*. On Shavuot the Portuguese Jews used to eat a cake filled with preserves of lemon peel that was known in Portuguese as *tarte sucade* and in Dutch as *sucade-koek*. Again, this recipe was of Dutch origin, although the preserves of lemon peel were an Italian novelty. Whereas the Portuguese Jews ate dairy food on the evening of Shavuot, they were not adverse to eating meat meals during the day. On Hanukkah the Portuguese Jews used to eat waffles, a batter of flour, milk, and eggs baked between waffle irons, a Dutch specialty. After supplying a recipe for making Haman's fritters, Lady Montefiore in *The Jewish Manual* (1846) turned her attention to making "waflers." The Portuguese Jews celebrated Purim by eating a round pastry made with sugar, milk, and pieces of lemon-peel preserve or *sucade*, the only Portuguese ingredient of which was the sweet syrup the Jews called *calder*, from the Portuguese *calda*. To Portuguese Jews this meant tasting a Dutch-style cake known as a *bolus*, from the Portuguese term for cake, *bolo*. No doubt, Lady Montefiore referred to a cake with certain resemblances to this under the name of *bola d'Hispaniola*, while declaring that the *bola* should be formed with pieces of dough with layers of sliced orange and lemon peel between them.[38]

Barbara Kirshenblatt-Gimblett has recently pointed out affinities between certain recipes in *The Jewish Manual* (1846) of Lady Montefiore and Portuguese cuisine. The *sopa d'ora* of Lady Montefiore, which consisted of pieces of toast mixed with sugar, water, and yolks of eggs, resembled the Portuguese *sopa dourada*. Instead of the Spanish term *dulce*, Lady Montefiore used the Portuguese word *doce*. *Escobeche*, mentioned by Lady Montefiore, was marinated meat or fish and was similar to the Portuguese or Spanish dish called *escabeche*, which the Arabs brought to Spain. Her *chejados* were the Portuguese *queijados*, a variety of tarts with egg-thickened fillings that were sometimes prepared with cheese or blanched almonds. Among Lady Montefiore's recipes were *bola d'amor, bola Toliedo, bola d'Hispaniola*, and plain *bola*, which as we have seen bore similarities to the Dutch cake known as a *bolus*, which was first mentioned in a volume on Jewish law by D. Pardo, published in Amsterdam in 1689.[39]

In the mid-nineteenth century Henry Mayhew wrote that in London

> the cakes, known as "boolers" [*bolas*]—a mixture of egg, flour, and candied orange and lemon peel, cut very thin and with a slight colouring from saffron or something similar—are now principally, and used to be sold exclusively by the [Dutch] Jewish boys. Almond cakes (little rounded cakes of crushed almonds) are at present vended by the Jew boys, and their sponge biscuits are in demand. All these dainties are bought by the street lads o[f]the Jews pastry-cooks. The difference in these cakes, in their sweetmeats, and their elder wine, is that there is a dash of spice about them not ordinarily met with. It is the same with the fried fish, a little spice or pepper being blended with the oil. In the street-sale of pickles the Jews have also the monopoly; these, however, are seldom hawked, but generally sold from windows and door-steads.

Among the Dutch recipes included in Lady Montefiore's manual were waffles, butter cake (*boterkoek*), fish stewed in the Dutch fashion, Dutch *fricandelle*, which was another fish recipe, Dutch toast, and possibly pancakes.[40]

Other Sephardic food terms referred to by Lady Montefiore were *amnastich*—chicken stuffed with forcemeat and stewed in gravy and rice; *descaides*, which were chicken livers thickened with egg yolks served on toast; *macrotes*, thin, long slices of French-roll dough fried in oil and dipped in sugar and lemon essence, and *prenesas*. However, as yet the country of origin of these recipes has not been determined.

Stuffed monkeys were a half cake and half biscuit stuffed with candied peel, their name being derived from a shortened corruption of Monick-[endan], the famous London Dutch-Jewish patissiers. What is clear is that the Dutch Jews contributed well-seasoned fish fried in oil, *bolas*, waffles, butter cake, and stuffed monkey to the Anglo-Jewish cuisine. Whereas the Spanish Jews in the Turkish Empire preserved many of the culinary traditions for centuries, the Portuguese Jews seemed to have been much more influenced by the example of Dutch cooking during their stay in Holland.[41]

THE SEPHARDIM AND THE INTRODUCTION OF NEW FOODS

The role of the Sephardim in the exploration and settlement of South America and the West Indies was crucial in introducing new popular foods to the European markets—a process that has been called "the Columbian Exchange." Of critical significance was the Jewish contribution to development of the international sugar industry. Sugarcane originated in India, where its product was called *sarkara* in Sanskrit; hence the Persian and Arabic terms that passed into the European languages. By the eleventh century rabbinic commentators such as Rashi referred to sugar as *sukra*. Already in medieval Egypt sugar production was the major industry, and certain wealthy Jewish families owned a large portion of this industry, including huge plants for the manufacture of sugar. In 1532 the Portuguese Marranos transplanted the cultivation of the sugarcane from Madeira to Brazil. Although Jews had some importance as sugar planters in Brazil, their main function was the setting up of the first sugar mills and acting as sugar brokers. By conducting a clandestine trade as early as 1620, the Marranos circumvented the Portuguese trading restrictions and organized the export of some 50,000 chests of sugar to Amsterdam, thus laying the foundations for the sugar-refining industry of Amsterdam, where sugar was refined and exported all over Europe. By 1656 Jewish entrepreneurs, such as the Del Pinas and Isaac Mocado, established sugar refineries in Amsterdam; others such as Abraham Davega and the Pereiras followed their example shortly afterward.[42]

Jewish refugees who fled from Brazil to the West Indian islands owned by the more tolerant Dutch, French, and English regimes established sugar plantations and introduced the techniques for drying and crystallizing the cane juices that had been extracted. By the 1640s they helped the Dutch to build new sugar industries in Barbados and Jamaica, while a later influx of Jewish merchants stabilized the economy of the islands, which developed on the successful cultivation of sugar. Benjamin d'Acosta introduced the sugarcane and its refining to the French island of Martinique in 1655 and settled some 900 Jews there. So, too, by 1730 more than a quarter of the four hundred plantations in the Dutch colony of Suriname, the most prosperous of their colonies, were owned by Jews.[43]

Moreover, chocolate making became an important Jewish industry in Amsterdam in the 1660s, when Venezuelan *cacao* was imported into Holland, and the Jews laid the foundation for the famous Dutch chocolate industry. The Sephardim spread the secrets of chocolate making into France, particularly into Bayonne and Bordeaux, while by the eighteenth century there were Jewish chocolate makers in England. Further, the Jews of the Levant had a predilection for drinking coffee, and nowhere more so than in Egypt, where it was known as the "Jews' Drink." Not surprisingly, the Jews played an active role in spreading the habit of drinking coffee into western Europe. In 1650, ". . . Jacob, a Jew opened a Coffee House in the Parish of St. Peter in the East, Oxon; and there it was by some, who delighted in noveltie, drank," wrote Anthony Wood. This was the first reference to the use of coffee in England, while there was a further reference by Wood to Cirques Jobson, a Jew born near Mount Lebanon, who also ran a coffeehouse at Oxford and who may be identical to the person called Jacob but who may have been someone else. In the second half of the seventeenth century a number of Levantines, particularly Armenians, started opening coffee shops in Paris, but some such as Joseph, a Levantine, and Etienne of Aleppo may have been Jewish. In our century Jews transferred the typical Viennese coffeehouse to the streets of many cities, including London and New York.[44]

Luis de Torres, a linguist with Columbus' expedition in 1492, discovered the valuable substitute for wheat known as maize, the cultivation of which spread rapidly in southern Europe. *Mamaliga,* a maize porridge, was not only the daily food of the peasant in certain parts of Romania but was also beloved by the Jews who migrated from there. Although the role of Sephardim in the diffusion of the potato has never been discussed, it is quite possible that some Marranos were involved in the discovery of the potato in the Peruvian highlands and in its subsequent distribution in Europe, particularly the Sephardim of Hamburg, who may have transplanted the potato into Germany. What is certain is the Sephardim of Safed in early Ottoman Palestine imported the yam, the sweet potato, into the Middle East.[45]

8

EVERYDAY FOOD OF CENTRAL AND EASTERN EUROPEAN JEWS

INTRODUCTION

Our knowledge of the diet of the poorer Jews in traditional society in central and eastern Europe is considerable. The main components of the diet from the sixteenth until the eighteenth centuries were black bread, followed by gruels and cheap vegetables, and herrings. Olearius in the 1630s declared that the Russians' daily food consisted of "groats, beets, cucumbers, and fresh or salt fish," and much the same could be said of the daily diet of the Jewish population. In the late eighteenth century 40 percent of the arable land in Russia was sown with rye, and a century later the percentage was only slightly lower. Although in Poland, too, the chief item in the diet was black bread, the Polish Jews also made bread from millet, rice, buckwheat, and peas in the seventeenth century. Rabbi Moses Isserles (1525–1572) wrote from Poland to a former German pupil who was seeking an appointment there that "you will indeed be better off in this country even though you will have to subsist on dry bread; at least you will have peace of mind." Similarly, the Poznan elders in 1642 issued an appeal to feed Jewish wanderers from Germany "with bread and food." According to Adam Jarzembski, who wrote a satirical work in 1643, the Polish Jews subsisted on carrots, cucumbers, and radishes, living most frugally. Fernand Braudel has drawn attention to the importance of coarse soups and gruels in the traditional European diet. So, too, an anonymous Jewish writer reminiscing about his childhood in Prague in the seventeenth century recalled that "I was full of ulcers, and the meals I ate were very unwholesome, for it is the custom in Prague to eat at the

145

midday meal peas and millet with a little butter, which proved very injurious." He later complained of another household, where he had been supplied with "coarse village bread, which caused me severe headaches and stomach trouble."[1]

Likewise the philosopher Solomon Maimon (1754–1800), a person of Lithuanian origin, mentioned his grandfather's house in a village near the town of Mir, where "the principal food consisted of a poor kind of corn-bread [almost certainly black bread made of rye] mixed with bran, articles made of meal and milk, and of the produce of the garden, seldom of flesh meat." In his youth Solomon Maimon was a tutor to the family of a poor farmer, not far from his home. This family, he declared, lived in

> a hovel without a chimney, but with merely a small opening in the roof for the exit of the smoke, an opening which was carefully closed as soon as the fire was allowed to go out, so that the heat might not escape. The windows were narrow strips of pine laid crosswise over each other, and covered with paper. This apartment served at once for sitting, drinking, eating, study and sleep. Think of this room intensely heated, and the smoke, as is generally the case in winter, driven back by wind and rain until the whole place is filled with its suffocation. Here hung a foul washing and other dirty bits of clothing on poles laid across the room in order to kill the vermin with the smoke. There hang sausages to dry, while their fat keeps constantly trickling down on the heads of the people below. Yonder stands tubs with sour cabbage and red beets, which form the principal food of the Lithuanians. In a corner the water is kept for daily use, with the dirty water alongside. In the room the bread is kneaded, cooking and baking are done, the cow is milked, and all sorts of operations are carried on.[2]

The descriptions of the living conditions of the Jews in eastern Europe depicted in nineteenth-century memoirs were almost equally gloomy, but from the mid-nineteenth century onward potatoes were mentioned as a new staple item in the diet as the reliance on grain decreased. Chaim Aronson (1825–1888), whose father was a teacher of young pupils in Serednik, a small town between the Prussian border and Kovno, recalled how his family lived in dire poverty in a hut that had formerly served as a *sukkah*. "In that hut, twelve boys and girls crowded together around the table by the window all day long, learning to read their prayers. At the side of the wooden plank which served as a table, my father kept a barrel filled with potatoes and vegetables. At noon time, when the children went to have their meal, the plank was covered with a white cloth and bowls and spoons for our meal." At one point Aronson's meals consisted of potatoes baked in their jackets with cooked groats. Ephraim Zunser (1840–1913), later famous as a composer and singer of folk songs, taught a farmer's family the rudiments of Hebrew in the town of Bobruisk in the province of Minsk. Here he used to eat "a bit of bread, baked from oats and barley, with a little groats, to which a few drops of oil were added . . . Throughout the week not a morsel of meat came into the house, and the week days were 'passed away' with this bread-of-misery and the 'soup' in which even the Jewish impressors could not find a groat." Israel Kasovich (1859–1929) related how his father tried to sell whisky illegally to the peasants who could not afford to buy it until the living conditions improved in the spring. During this period, his family could not afford even black bread and had to subsist on potatoes and some black gruel. In the spring his mother plucked some nettles, chopped them, and after cooking them served them to her family as their meal.[3]

R. E. F. Smith and D. Christian, in their history of Russian food, again and again emphasize that despite the fact that peas were common, in general pulses did not play a significant role in the diet. Nonetheless, in times of famine and in particular in the mid-nineteenth century, when there was a switch from a dependence on grain to the much wider cultivation of the potato, the use of peas and beans could be crucial. In the winter and spring of 1868 there was a serious shortage of grain in the northwestern provinces of Russia and Lithuania because of a bad harvest. Fuenn, a famous exponent of enlightenment within Lithuanian orthodoxy, pleaded in his newspaper with the rabbinic authorities to allow pulses to be eaten during Passover, although this was usually forbidden by the Ashkenazic rabbinic authorities. "This will make it possible for poor households to meet their dietary needs on the festival with legumes, which are much cheaper than wheat and potatoes. The poor will be forced to buy only a minimum of wheat for the required *matsah.*" He also pointed out that when there had been a famine in Brest-Litovsk earlier in the nineteenth century, Rabbi Meir Padua issued a proclamation permitting the consumption of pulses during Passover, while the rabbi also suggested that the prominent men of his town should eat peas and beans so as not to put the poor to shame. The rabbis of Vilna proclaimed in 1868 that

> in a gathering to discuss the sad state of the poor and the needy of our city, who, because of the great rise in the price of wheat, are swollen with hunger . . . and also since there is not enough to go around for all who are in need, in this year of catastrophe when even potatoes have risen very high in price . . . we have seen fit to be lenient this year to the people of our community and to permit the eating of beans . . . peas. . . . We have also permitted the buying of millet for Passover. . . .

In Kovno Rabbi Isaac Elchanan Spektor and Rabbi Israel Salanter issued similar proclamations, but elsewhere conservative rabbis such as Rabbi Traub of Kaidany condemned the use of pulses during Passover and asserted that the poor of his town preferred to eat cheap subsidized potatoes rather than millet and legumes. In 1869 Rabbi Spektor wrote to Rabbi Salanter:"My family as well as the most prominent Jews of Kovno will eat peas on Passover, and I implore you, Rabbi Israel, to do likewise, so that the poor whose mainstay this food is will not suffer the embarrassment of regarding themselves as transgressors." Incidentally, during a cholera epidemic on Yom Kippur in 1848 Rabbi Salanter stood at the reader's desk and partook of cake and wine, as he believed that fasting would weaken the resistance of the congregation to the disease.[4]

THE BASIC INGREDIENTS OF THE DAILY DIET

Bread and Bagels

Of all items in the daily diet of the Jews, bread was the most significant. In eastern Europe at the time of the First World War the daily loaf was baked in most Jewish homes, although bakers provided bread in Lithuania for the non-Jewish peasant farmers, who brought their produce to the market. There were bakeries at the turn of the century, especially in large towns such as Warsaw, where the employees could work for twenty-two hours at a time; but all the mixing, kneading, and baking were still done manually in an unhygienic fashion, the sweat dripping off the workers into the dough. All the Jews, like their Gentile neighbors, chiefly ate bread made from a coarse rye flour that had been ground only once, and sometimes the skin of the grain was utilized as well. This oval-shaped loaf was known as *Rozover* bread and was brought by Russian Jewish immigrants to Britain and the United States, where it remained popular until the Second World War. If the grains of rye were ground more than once, a semiwhite loaf was produced. To make black bread, however, the coarse rye flour was mixed in a wooden bowl with warm salt water, after which the bowl was covered with a tablecloth and the dough was left to ferment from the warmth overnight. The next morning the dough was kneaded and left in a warm place for another four or five hours to enable it to rise. During the summer, some housewives collected grass that grew near the lakes in Lithuania, placing it under the loaves of black bread to give them a nice fragrance and to prevent them from sticking to the oven.[5]

Although Hirsh Abramowicz suggested in his memoirs that these loaves weighed fifteen or twenty-five pounds, this figure seems somewhat exaggerated, and several informants have suggested a more realistic figure of three to five pounds. Many Jewish housewives in Lithuania tended to coat their everyday loaves of black bread with a mixture of flour to lighten their appearance, whereas non-Jewish housewives gave their loaves such a special treatment only on feast days. The black bread was particularly bitter and sour due to the lactic acid it contained, but this acid was an important dietary supplement, while the heaviness of the bread made it slow to digest and an ideal food for persons engaged in onerous manual labor. The Jewish working class in Lithuania used to eat black bread with sour milk, claiming that this combination of food gave them the strength for their physical exertions.[6]

Jews sometimes enjoyed a meal of very sour pickled cucumbers with bread, a food preference that distinguished them from their Lithuanian neighbors, who had no special liking for pickles. Describing the sweated Jewish labor of New York in 1890, Jacob Riis wrote: "A comely young woman is eating her dinner of dry bread and green pickles. . . . Pickles are a favourite food in Jewtown. They are filling, and keep the children from crying with hunger." Thus the consumption of bread in bulk remained a characteristic of the Jewish immigrants from eastern Europe, while their predilection for pickles can be explained as a means for making this very stodgy diet digestible.[7]

According to Abraham Ain at the beginning of the century, the small town or *shtetl* of Swislocz in the district of Grodno possessed eleven bakers, two of whom baked only black bread and four both black and white bread, rolls, and *hallah*, while the rest of the bakers sold cakes and pastries. So, too, when musing, Sholom Aleichem's Tevye the milkman complained of having to "rupture" himself "on a pot of thin gruel, a loaf of barley bread . . ." Likewise, Shmarya Levin, writing about the same *shtetl* of Swislocz a few decades earlier, declared that a family of raft-binders adorned their table with *hallah* made of wheat only on festivals but not on the Sabbath; another family with slightly higher aspirations graced their table with wheaten loaves on the Sabbath. Mainès Sperber (born 1905) asserted that in his birthplace, "when they baked the plaited *challah* for the Sabbath, they ate only as much of it as was necessary to justify the prescribed blessings. The rest was saved for the week, in case anyone fell ill." Lesley Chamberlain has remarked that even in recent decades white bread was still regarded as something exotic and foreign in Russia, with the result that it was hardly sold in rural areas. Nonetheless, in Lithuania between the two world wars the younger generation of Jews in the towns had a marked preference for white bread; Polish immigrants in the United States rhapsodized about eating white bread and meat every day just like millionaires. In the United States the bakers' shops mirrored the earlier conditions in the home country at first, so that Louis Wirth reported that in the 1920s the Chicago bakeries had their shelves lined with rye bread, poppy-seed bread, and pumpernickel, described as a sweet, dark bread.[8]

Another everyday food was the bagel. The Yiddish word *bagel* was first mentioned in the ordinances of the Cracow community in 1610, which stated that they could be sent as gifts to women about to give birth and to midwives. So, too, in Bessarabia pregnant Jewish women wore buns around their necks as food amulets. A bagel has been described as a doughnut with rigor mortis, although in eastern Europe there were also egg bagels, which were made of dough similar to that of *hallah*, so that they did not rapidly become as hard as bone when slightly stale. The bagel was a ringlike roll of south German or Austrian origin, as the term *bagel* is said to be derived from the German word *Bügel*, either meaning a bow-shaped piece of metal or wood or *Steigbügel*, meaning a stirrup; hence the round shape of the bagel with a hole in its center. Bagels were related to another widespread European food known as pretzels in Germany, *pletzels* in Poland, *bretzeln* in parts of Austria, and *bracciatelli* in Italy. *Bretzeln* were served by Jews at circumcisions as their shape was supposed to offer protection against evil spirits. Various hypotheses have been advanced as to the origin of the bagel. Evelyn Rose has suggested that bagels may be descended from the boiled bread (*pain échaudé*) of the fifteenth-century French bakers, but bagels were of German origin and the French connection is doubtful. Further, the Italian Jews had pastry rings known as *ciambelle*, which closely resembled bagels and were utilized on Sukkot. *Bracciatelli*, which were little *ciambelle*, were hung around sticks by street vendors in Italy for sale at Easter, just as bagels were sold in a similar fashion by street vendors in eastern Europe. Indeed, one food historian has asserted that Bartolomeo Scappi, an Italian culinary expert, in 1570 described rings of dough, *ciambellette*, which were similar to bagels and were their immediate ancestor; but an examination of such recipes in Renaissance cookbooks proves that the baking and boiling of doughnuts was unknown to Italian cuisine. Although Herman Pollack has linked the word *bretzel* to *Brett*, meaning a board or plank, as it was a flat kind of roll, most food historians would trace the etymology of the word *pretzel* to the medieval Latin word *bracchium*, meaning the forearm, and the Italian word *bracciatélla*, meaning small armful, as the pretzel was supposed to look like a closed arm.[9]

The first written reference to pretzels was made by Isidore of Seville (c. 560–636 c.e.), who called them by their Latin name of *bracchium*.

William Woys Weaver has pointed out that "most ring-like traditional breads may be related in some way—regardless of size." By the late Middle Ages pretzels had evolved into three varieties: beer pretzels, boiled in lye before baking and sprinkled with salt or sometimes caraway seed; egg pretzels, made with sweet dough or ground almonds (note the parallel with egg bagels and certain kinds of Italian doughnuts from the sixteenth century); and soft pretzels from south Germany, which were thick dough rings somewhat resembling bagels in shape. Today in Cracow in Poland a species of braided bagel covered with poppy seeds is still made that is probably related to the early seventeenth-century bagel mentioned earlier. According to Weaver, bagels, *ciambelle,* and doughnuts were all descendants of the medieval pretzel; in some cases their recipes were like those of the medieval pretzel, in which dough was both boiled and baked.[10]

Yehuda Zlotnik (Elzet), an early student of east European Jewish folklore, who was born in 1887, classified bagels as a commonplace food. In one *shtetl,* Gdalye, who was also a shoemaker, baked bagels and flat rolls (*pletzels*) on Tuesday, Wednesday, and Thursday that his wife sold in the market; many other small towns also appear to have had bagel and *pletzel* sellers. On Friday Jewish housewives did their own baking, and there was usually enough bread for the household until Tuesday. In his memoirs Shmarya Levin (1867–1935), writing about the poor children who attended *heder* in White Russia in the 1870s, mentioned that they used to bring some dry bread, a tail of salt herring, and a bagel for lunch. If the bread had butter or was smeared with chicken fat, this meant that either the bread or the bagel had badly deteriorated. Since the Second World War, shops selling bagels have multiplied in the United States, and in complete contrast with eastern Europe, where a plain bagel was regarded as a treat by children, bagels are now eaten with a thick coating of cream cheese and smoked salmon, particularly on Sunday mornings. In a structural analysis Stanley Regelson suggested that the eating by American Jews of smoked salmon, a bloodlike fish that bore a resemblance to ham, and cheese subtly challenged the dietary laws: a forbidden food appeared to be relished, while meat and milk foods appeared to be enjoyed together.[11]

The Potato

During the nineteenth century, the potato became the staple food of eastern European Jews, somewhat replacing the use of gruels and pulses. The potato was often eaten by Jewish families in different forms two or three times a day. Without the potato, there would have been no phenomenal Jewish population explosion in eastern Europe, as the rate of increase of the Jews was twice as fast as that of their Gentile neighbors; the increasing population depended on the potato for their survival, as it was a cheap and easily obtainable food. In 1825 the Jewish population of Russian Poland numbered 1.6 million, but by the census of 1897 their numbers had increased to 5 million. The Jewish dependence on the potato as a cheap food can be compared with that of only one other people—the Irish. Potatoes were discovered in the highlands of the Andes in the sixteenth century, but the European peasantry, apart from the Irish, were reluctant to adopt it, despising its qualities as a food and fearing that it caused leprosy, typhoid fever, and cholera. Potatoes could grow in two or three months, instead of the ten months it took grain to ripen, while the yield of the potato was twice that of grain. The potato, because it is rich in starch, has a high carbohydrate and calorie content; it also contains a rich assortment of the more important mineral elements as well as a sufficient quantity of ascorbic acid, the antiscurvy vitamin C. Nonetheless, the potato was deficient in certain essential vitamins that were present in milk, and we shall see that milk was an important feature in the diet of the Jews of Poland and Lithuania.[12]

Not until the bad harvests of 1839 and 1840 did the cultivation of the potato spread rapidly in Russia, so that by the 1860s the potato crop was well established, and by 1900 Russia had become one of the world's leading producers. The main areas of the production of the crop were in the Baltic and the western provinces of Russia, where there were large Jewish concentrations of population in Lithuania, White Russia, and in the adjoining areas of Poland. By 1861 the consumption of the potato was dominant in the peasant diets in the Vilna region of Lithuania, and it was just as widely consumed by Jews living in the area. Redcliffe Salaman suggested that the potato was almost the sole food of the masses in Poland before the Second World War, but more correctly it has been described as "the second staple food of the Polish diet," after grain. By the beginning of this century poor persons in the Moscow region consumed an average of 200 kg of barley and rye, 150 kg of potatoes, 80 kg of *sauerkraut* and cucumbers per annum, and no meat, and although there was some consumption of meat on the Sabbath and festivals among poor Jews, this gives us a rough indication of the relative amounts of vegetables, particularly potatoes, and cereals consumed by impoverished Jewish families in eastern Europe. Poor Jews in Lithuania, whose families consisted of six to seven persons, tried to store three to four tons of potatoes in their cellar for the winter. In addition, Jewish families would stockpile a few puds of carrots, cabbages, beetroots, onions, and other vegetables, one pud being the equivalent of forty Russian pounds. Jews in Lithuania often planted a crop of potatoes in their gardens or in a plot of land near their home; or they would make payments in cash and kind to peasants or give them manure from their own cows and goats for use as a fertilizer in return for which the peasants would lease a strip of land to the Jews for two years. The Jews would utilize this land to grow crops of potatoes and cereals with hired labor.[13]

We can see how the increased cultivation of the potato in the 1840s, 1850s, and 1860s was much appreciated by the Jews, who rapidly developed a taste for the vegetable. A yearbook of the aristocracy issued in 1842 exclaimed, "Let us look into the terrible habitations of the Jews in towns . . . and we will then be convinced that the clothes of all members of the family are, for the greatest part, merely filthy rags, and their daily food—some onions, bread and potatoes." Similarly a Russian statistician commented in 1863 that in the province of Grodno in Lithuania, "the bulk of the Jews there are poor . . . In most cities a pound of bread, a herring and a few onions represent the daily fare of an entire family. Even in the Ukraine where conditions were better most of the Jews lived in squalor, their food consisting of bread and vegetables." It is doubtful whether the omission of the potato as a staple of the Jewish diet in Grodno in the 1860s is correct, as by the twentieth century the district was known in Russia as the "Grodno potato"; and we have already seen that in the 1860s potatoes were popular in the nearby provinces of Vilna and Kovne, while in Kaidany in the Kovne region during the famine of 1868 the Jewish poor expressed the view that "they did not want to eat millet [on Passover]. Therefore, potatoes were sold to them (the poor) at a lower price than millet." Mendele Mokher Sforim described a tailor's workshop, where the master placed a bowl of potatoes in their jackets on the table for the workers and apprentices at lunch:

> . . . it is well worth the price of a ticket to see how skilfully the potatoes are peeled, tossed into the mouth and swallowed. Masterfully! Such craftsmen at potato eating as our tailor boys are hard to find in the world. They have become proficient in it through the years and have developed a great dexterity at it, because potatoes are their food, if you please, daily.

Rebecca Berg, in her memoir of a Lithuanian childhood, showed that Mendele's social reportage was accurate, as she drew a portrait of a shoemaker's workshop where the apprentice and many children would breakfast on potatoes in their jackets, which they would clutch with their nightclothes.[14]

As has been remarked by many writers, potatoes were eaten daily in eastern Europe, sometimes two or three times a day, and they were prepared in a variety of ways, including cooking them with onions and pepper: they were baked in their jackets and cooked in their skins, merely being washed and cooked; often the potatoes were scraped and cooked, as the Lithuanian Jews did not want to waste the skins of the potatoes, but in this way the best part of the potatoes were reserved for human consumption; they were, when baked or cooked in their jackets and eaten together with raw shredded onions, regarded as a choice food; they were grated and made into pancakes (*latkes*), but this dish was not universal. Moreover, potatoes were mashed with chicken fat; they were plainly boiled; they were eaten together with cabbage, carrots, and other vegetables; as a treat, particularly on Fridays and the Sabbath, they were served in the form of a potato pudding. As potatoes did not have a pronounced taste, they were eaten frequently with onions to make them more palatable and interesting. A favorite in this respect was a dish known as "empty fish," a concoction of sliced peeled potatoes, fried onions, and fat, but in summer the dish was eaten with a little butter and sour or sweet cream. When neighbors had cooperated in doing some chore, such as plucking feathers for bedding, they regaled each other with folk stories and sang songs and consumed some *sauerkraut* or a dish of "empty fish," a term synonymous with that of supper and perhaps derived from the Russian phrase "empty soup," meaning cabbage soup without seasoning. Already, a sixteenth-century account of the Jews of Prague mentioned that "they feed continually upon onions and garlic. . . ," so that their predilection for these vegetables was well established in central and eastern Europe. More recently Yuri Suhl remarked that ". . . the main stand-by for flavouring and trimming was the onion. There was no limit to its use and versatility and there was no meal without it. Sliced, browned or cooked it was there."[15]

Again, in Lithuania they grated potatoes and added flour made from buckwheat (*kasha*) or rye to make buns that were given to children to quiet their hunger. In the more prosperous households, the buns were avidly eaten hot with sour cream or a little butter. Again and again, we shall note how milk, sour cream, and cream were used to supplement dishes of potato, grain, and flour, particularly among the more affluent sections of the population, to make up for the vitamin deficiency in a diet often dominated by potatoes. A much-prized dish of the Polish peasant farmers in the summer was potatoes smothered in sour milk, and this dish was also popular among Jews, although in recipe books the dish has been upgraded to potatoes with sour cream. When the potato buns were supplied with little caps and smeared with poppy seed, they were known as gypsies. So, too, the gypsies were sometimes cut into sections and doused in sour cream or butter before being placed in the oven again. Potato pancakes (*latkes*) were made with grated potatoes fried in poppy-seed oil or fat. Among the poorer families, the grated potato flour was eked out by the addition of rye. *Teygekhts* were another food prepared by grating potatoes, adding flour and onions, and placing the resulting mixture in a pan in the oven to produce a type of baked pudding. In the winter big dumplings (*kneidlech*) were made from potato dough and were often filled with oatmeal, chopped onions, and goose or chicken fat; smaller, more digestible dumplings were made from mashed potatoes that were placed in a bowl of warm milk. From the Middle Ages dumplings were popular in German cuisine, and the Yiddish *kneidl* was almost certainly derived from the south German *Knödel*, meaning a dumpling, but in a Western Slavic environment.[16]

In the town of Swislocz in the Grodno province of Lithuania, on every weekday Jews used to make a thick soup of barley or groats known as *krupnik*, the name of the soup being taken from the Russian word for grains prepared for cooking, *krupa*. In the winter, when meat was cheap, the more comfortable households in the town used to augment the soup of barley and buckwheat (*kasha*) groats with a slice of lamb or veal, but it was always served with the inevitable potato. *Krupnik* was a soup beloved by the poor Jews in Lithuania, Poland, and the Russian provinces of Volin, where it was known as *kolish*. During the Middle Ages, *kashk* was an Iranian dish of barley and later wheat, but when this food penetrated central Asia it was adopted by the Russians in the form of buckwheat (*kasha*), a crop better suited to the Russian soil. Like the Persians and the Arabs, the Russians sometimes served this dish with meat and sometimes with milk or sour milk, as did the Jews in eastern Europe, according to Elzet. Since the mid-nineteenth century the use of buckwheat has sharply declined among the Jews, as *kasha* was supplanted by the potato, though in the past it had been so frequently consumed that there was a saying among the Russians that "buckwheat gruel is our mother—and rye bread is our father." We shall see that there were other dishes in addition to *kasha* that were related to the Iranian food term *kashk* and the Arabic variant *kishk*, which the east European Jews shared with their brethren in the Middle East. *Farfel*, a type of noodle that was made from a mixture of barley, buckwheat, peas, and beans in Lithuania, was made into a soup with milk during the summer, when the inevitable potato was added. According to Kosover, the term *farfel* may be connected with the German word *würfel*, meaning a cube, as *farfel* were crumbs of dough that were cooked in soup.[17]

Sours

In addition to black bread and potatoes, a third basic article in the diet of the Lithuanian and Polish Jews was sours, a general term that embraced beetroots (*borscht*), cabbage (*sauerkraut*), and sorrel (*schav*). There was a long-established tradition among the Russian workers for meals in winter to contain some element of acidity to counterbalance the dull taste of the black bread, gruel, and potatoes, and this was regarded as more important than a helping of meat; it was a food preference that the Lithuanian Jews in particular acquired from their neighbors. In other societies people digested their heavy starch diet with the assistance of sauces, chili peppers, olive oil, or sugar-based products. During the winter, cabbage soup, sometimes with chunks of meat but more often with potatoes, was served; if sours were not available in this form, *borscht*, a soup made from beetroots and *rosl*, a brine that housewives prepared themselves by leaving beets to ferment in water close to the oven, graced the table instead. The Yiddish word *rosl* was derived from the fifteenth-century Polish term *rosol* in its meaning of a salt solution for preserving food. It was carried northeastward into Lithuania and White Russia, where the Jews in the sixteenth and seventeenth centuries narrowed the term to mean a brinelike liquid of beets. We would conjecture that the popularity of *borscht* among Jews must date from this period. In western Poland there was only a limited diffusion of this soup; according to I. J. Singer, the Polish Jews in Lodz sneered at the Litvak migrants, calling them "Lithuanian onion heads . . . *Borscht* with herring." Even in Lithuania beetroots were used less than cabbages in the winter, when the principal foods were often cabbages eaten with baked potatoes or bread, whereas in the Ukraine beetroots were used far more extensively.[18]

In the spring the Lithuanian Jews prepared sorrel (*schav*) soup made from sorrel leaves with a few drops of lemon juice, to which thin sour cream or sour milk was added. Kim Chernin remembered this soup "served cold, with sour cream, chopped egg, and onion, large chunks of dry black bread." Chaim Grade has described how earlier in the century the landlords of small boarding houses in Lithuania, between the fasts of the Seventeenth of Tammuz and Tisha B'Av, reserved their "butter, cheese and sour cream for the summer visitors while they and their families made do with black bread soaked in sorrel soup thickened with a bit of milk." In the ancient world people living in the Roman Republic utilized only the leaves of the beetroot. So, too, in the summer the Lithuanian Jews used to cook the green, leafy parts of the beetroots with sorrel grass in a mixture of *kvas* to make a soup known as *botvinya*, in which pieces of fish floated. *Kvas* was an acidy beer made by Jewish housewives, who used to ferment grains of rye in water for a couple of days, although this beer was also widely bottled in breweries. In some households in Lithuania, families used to consume cold *borscht* with sour cream and hot boiled potatoes during the summer as an alternative to *schav*.[19]

Originally in medieval Germany men pickled meat and fish to preserve them for the winter. At the same time, the Slavs developed new techniques for preserving *sauerkraut,* beets, and beans, which spread westward during the Middle Ages into Germany and which became a task allotted annually to women. With the onset of the cold weather, Jewish women in eastern Europe would prepare a stock of provisions for the winter by pickling cabbages, beetroots, and cucumbers. Often as many as six women were hired by a family for this purpose, or friends rendered their assistance on a voluntary basis. The cabbages were sliced into thin strips, particular attention was paid to cutting out wormy bits of cabbage, and caraway seeds were scattered among these pieces of cabbage, which were pressed down into a wooden barrel filled with salt water. Between the layers of cabbage, some apples, carrots, and beetroots were placed, each layer being pressed down tightly into the barrel by a special instrument. All the barrels were covered and weighed down with a heavy stone, the cabbages being examined daily to ensure that the vegetables were covered with brine, and they were also poked with a stick to release nauseous gases. The barrels were coated with honey, and the cabbages and other vegetables were left to ferment for five or six days in a cellar or sometimes, in poorer households, in the outhouse. The cabbage cores, the *katchelkihs,* were prized as a dainty morsel, and according to Shmarya Levin the poor children in *heder* used to eat these cabbage cores with bread as a second breakfast. Here we should also mention stuffed cabbages, *holoptsches,* which were related to the Turkish and Greek stuffed vegetables.[20]

The Herring

It has been estimated that in 1904 British steam trawlers caught herring worth £1,870,000, while the Dutch catch was valued at £575,000 and the German at £220,000. By 1913 the British exported cured and salt herrings worth £5.5 million, of which Russia and Germany took the bulk of the exports, but half the pickled herrings sent to Germany from Britain were reexported to Russia. According to A. M. Samuel, "Germany and Russia were our best export markets, these countries taking pickled, but very few smoked herrings, while Italy and Greece took them smoked and salted but not pickled. . . ."[21]

Because of the significance of herring in the daily diet of the east European Jews, Jewish traders were deeply involved in the import of British herrings into eastern Europe. One of the biggest importers of British herrings into Russia before the First World War was the Finkelstein family, whose total imports from Britain then reached 108,000 barrels. "Many Jewish firms for importing herrings into

Libau—made Libau on the Baltic—by 1913 on the eve of this first
World War—the greatest port for the import of British cured herrings in
the world. It reached 613,000 barrels—with about 1,000 herrings in
each barrel," wrote Harry Finkelstein in his memoirs. Further, "Libau
could not afford to buy [Dutch] matjes [smoked schmaltz herrings]—
and stuck to the hard cure variety. Baltasound [in the Shetland Isles]
herrings contained more fat than the usual hard cure—so it was a very
good substitute for the matjes—it was also strong in the belly and fair
in size." In 1912 Harry Finkelstein joined the great German Jewish
firm of Leo Dinesman. He helped in buying 90,000 barrels of herrings,
including 50,000 barrels from England, 25,000 from Scotland, and
15,000 barrels from Dutch, German, and Norwegian cure.

> Most of the herrings were sold and railed to Poland and South West
> Russia—until . . . Odessa. Only 5,000 barrels were sold in East Prussia.
> These herrings were examined by Jewish Commission agents from
> Russia who lived in Konigsberg. These agents had their clients in
> Poland and Russia and bought these herrings on instructions from
> their clients. . . . It is characteristic that the White Russian city of
> Grodno and its surroundings were great buyers of Dutch herrings—all
> other districts of West Poland, West Ukraine including Odessa pre-
> ferred British quality. I remember one Jewish buyer in Warsaw—who
> took on the eve of Jewish New Year—3,000 barrels . . . [from Great
> Yarmouth].

A lady from Cork recalled that her father, Solomon Birkhahn, traveled
to the Shetland Islands at the turn of the century to buy the herring
catch for export to a brother in Russia. In Austrian Poland, Galicia,
herrings were imported from Holland prior to World War I, and pickled
herrings, rollmops, were already sold in small jars all over Galicia.
Even between the two World Wars three-quarters of the fish consumed
in Poland, chiefly salted herring, was still imported.[22]

Chaim Bermant declared with pardonable exaggeration that in
eastern Europe, "on Sunday, one had pickled herring; on Monday,
soused herring; on Tuesday, smoked herring; on Wednesday, baked
herring; on Thursday, herring fried in oatmeal (delicious!); and on
Friday, one had herrings in sour cream . . ." Apart from sours, which
included pickled cucumbers, herring was regarded as the only other
appetizer in the daily fare of the east European Jews, and this explains
the ingenuity with which it was utilized in so many recipes. According
to Edouard de Pomiane, writing in the 1920s, Polish Jews consumed
one herring a day. The simplest method of preparing the salted herring
was to soak them in water for a couple of hours, after which they were
dressed with oil and in addition sometimes with vinegar and eaten with
bread. Another dish combined herrings with their roe and apples,

although this took longer to prepare because the flavor of the herring and apple had to mingle overnight. According to Mark Zborowski and Herzog, a common dish in eastern Europe consisted of potatoes and herrings, and if the family was too poor to afford herring, the potatoes were cooked with salt, pepper, and onions to give them the flavor of fish; hence the dish known as "empty fish." One informant stated that poor women came to his aunt in Vilna, who sold herrings, with saucepans to collect the brine (*rosl*) for making soup. In one shoemaker's household in Lithuania the mistress would prepare roast herring for the master for breakfast and would pour water over the herring before serving it, the resulting soup being distributed among her children and some apprentices.[23]

Milk, Fruit, and Vegetables

In northern Russia milk was plentiful in the towns during the summer but was difficult to obtain in the winter because of the shortage of cattle fodder, and even in summer milk was scarce in rural areas. Was this generalization true, however, for the Jewish population? Shmarya Levin recalled that his poor classmates in *heder* in the 1870s did not drink milk. "Milk was either for the very little ones, or else to be sold. Of dairy food they knew only sour milk and an occasional piece of soft food cheese. An egg was a rare luxury." Nonetheless, goats were commonly kept in Jewish households in eastern Europe, although, according to one outside observer in 1842, the possession of a goat was a sign of plenty. Chaim Aronson (1825–1888) came from a penurious family, yet his father still managed to keep a goat that supplied the family with milk daily, even if the goat led a wretched existence in the autumn and winter. In his memoirs Israel Kasovich (1859–1929) related that his father leased a dairy from a Lithuanian nobleman with a herd of cows, which enabled him to sell butter and cheese to Jews in nearby towns. The dairy also provided the family with "buttermilk, and once in a while also a bit of butter and a tiny morsel of cheese." Later Kasovich, after becoming seriously ill as a teenager when the family fortune was at a low ebb, was nursed by his mother. "She knew goat's milk was good for the heart [following the talmudic medical tradition], and of the goats she now had two, so she gave me several glasses of milk a day. To be sure, the milk had a peculiar odour, but mother insisted that I drink it, and every time I took a glass of milk, she would say 'Good health.'" One informant, whose family lived in Lithuania in the early decades of this century, remembered that they owned a cow that provided milk and cheese. The parents of Chaim Weizmann (1874–1952) lived in Motel, a *shtetl* in the province of Minsk, and were among the better-off families in the community possessing "some acres of land, chickens, two cows, a vegetable garden, a few fruit trees. So we had a supply of milk, and sometimes butter. . . ."[24]

Goats were called the national Jewish cattle in the Lithuanian towns, and whoever possessed a pregnant cow or goat could hope for a supply of milk at the height of the winter. For this reason, we would doubt that milk was drunk only by the most prosperous families in the opening decades of this century, and we would surmise that the wider strata below this level would also have a patchy supply of milk. Even the poorest Jewish families sometimes benefited from the voluntary work of charitable women such as Kasovich's aunt in south Russia, who provided "needy sick persons with milk and fresh butter from her cow . . ."; in Otvosk in the province of Warsaw tall Libe, the dairy-women supplied dozens of needy persons or widows with milk for themselves or for their sickly children. In the small towns in eastern Europe there were Jewish-owned dairies with a small number of cows, and milkmen and women delivered fresh milk to customers daily, the unsold milk being made into butter or cheese. As a young boy, Isaac Bashevis Singer assisted Reb Asher, the dairyman, a man with a "comfortable income," in delivering milk in Warsaw and bought milk, butter, cream, sour milk, and cheese in his shop.[25]

The potato, although a staple item in the diet of the Jews of eastern Europe, was deficient in two important vitamins, namely vitamin A and vitamin D. Whereas lack of vitamin A caused night blindness and skin diseases, a shortage of vitamin D caused a weakening of the bones and a disease known as rickets. That is why milk was an essential element in the diet of these Jewish communities, and so many recipes, particularly for potatoes, contained milk ingredients in one form or another; but milk remained a rarity in the cuisine of the North African Jews or the ancient Spanish-Jewish community in Jerusalem because potatoes were eaten less frequently. Milk possessed vitamins A and D, and where Jews in Lithuania consumed potatoes in vast quantities without being able to afford a sufficient amount of milk, they were afflicted with the "English disease," presumably meaning rickets.[26]

In Romania and Galicia poor persons ate *mamalige* or *kulesha,* a maize porridge that was cooked until hard and eaten with milk or cheese. Maize was introduced into the Balkans in eighteenth century from America and filled as crucial a role in the daily diet of the mass of the population as did the potato in the other parts of eastern Europe. I. J. Singer's grandfather, a rabbi who lived in comfortable circum-stances in Bilgoray, a town in the province of Lublin in Poland, usually had a breakfast of bread with butter and groats with milk. Lunch in Lithuania was a snack eaten at three o'clock that could consist of bread with cheese or *podsmitanya,* a mixture of sour milk and sour cream.

Sometimes poor families in Lithuania made pancakes out of the dough that was used to bake black rye bread. They added some sweet flour to this dough and ate these pancakes with sour cream or melted butter, while the wealthier families made these pancakes of wheat. When Tevye the Dairyman invited a guest home for supper, he asked his wife to make *borscht.* "If not, I'll take *knishes* or *kreplach,* puddings or dumplings. *Blintzes* with cheese will suit me too." The guest could not recall "when he had eaten such a dairy supper, such perfect *knishes,* such *vertutin."* The latter consisted of cheese or cooked cherries rolled in dough. *Blintzes* were pocket pastries descended from Ukrainian *blinchiki* and were related to the Russian *blini,* while *knishes* were a similar type of pastry from Russia; ultimately all these foods may have been of Persian, central Asian, or perhaps Arab origin. In the Carpathian mountains of Romania, kosher dairies made two kinds of white cheese, one a thin kind without fat processed from cow's milk; the other contained more fat and was a mixture of sheep and cow's milk. Isaac Bashevis Singer, recalling his childhood in Warsaw, declared that the winter of 1917 was one long fast in which his family survived on frozen potatoes and farmer's cheese.[27]

As soon as winter came the peasants refused to bring their produce to the market in the towns for sale, and the price of potatoes, beets, cabbages, and other essential commodities rose steeply. Abraham Cahan spoke of the large vegetable market in Vilna, where "with spring, loads of carrots, cabbages, green peas, berries, most important of all, cucumbers from the peasant gardens of surrounding villages" were brought for sale. As we have already mentioned, many Jewish families grew potatoes on plots of land, while others cultivated vegetable gardens where they planted radishes and spring onions. Although tomatoes were introduced into Europe from Mexico in the sixteenth century, they were rarely cultivated until a hundred years later. Tomatoes were not considered kosher by many Jews in eastern Europe, as they were thought to contain blood and were also suspect because they were thought to be an aphrodisiac. When Kim Chernin's mother first tasted a tomato on immigrating to the United States her apprehensions caused her to vomit. It took considerable time in the United States for the children of immigrants to become acculturated and to enjoy the taste of lettuce and tomatoes; and to the last Jacob Marateck, an immigrant from Poland, despised "green salads as grass for the cows."[28]

One informant whose family lived in a small Lithuanian town asserted that his family ate fruit only in season. While oranges and grapes were never on sale, apples, pears, and cherries were available in season. But Chaim Nachman Bialik, when visiting the city of Kovno in 1932, was impressed by the sight of bananas and oranges. In an orchard in the Ukraine described by Sholom Aleichem there were "apples and pears and cherries, plums and gooseberries and currants, peaches, raspberries, rough cherries, blackberries"; this region of Russia was famous for the variety and abundance of its fruit. On the other hand, Kim Chernin claimed that only peasants in villages had ready access to pears and apples and that her great-grandfather, after traveling through the countryside, used to bring home fruit for the Sabbath to the town of Chasnick. In the *shtetl* of Sniatyn in Galicia there was a fruit merchant who imported melons and grapes from Hungary and Romania and dates, figs, oranges, and pineapples from farther afield, while he exported apples, pears, and plums, which were plentiful locally. Other Jews in the same *shtetl* bought up the crops of local orchards in advance, exporting the best fruit, storing other unripe fruit in special cellars for Passover, and selling the inferior-quality fruit to a local jam factory; elsewhere there were similar business activities, and the wives of tailors trapped by seasonal unemployment sold fruit from orchards managed by their husbands. Just as vegetables were carefully pickled and stored for the winter, so housewives in eastern Europe preserved some of the glut of the summer fruit crop and kept a supply for the lean winter days. Chaim Grade remembered how women in Lithuania filled large and small jars with preserved fruit, such as sugared cherries, and strings of dried apples and pears for making compote. Deborah Kreitman, in an autobiographical novel, described how her grandmother was adamant that the cherries, gooseberries, black currants, plums, and raspberries were not to be touched, for they were utilized in the making of jam, preserves, gooseberry tarts, and fruit juice, the latter an essential remedy in time of illness.[29]

THE DIFFERENT CLASSES OF THE POOR

The Talmud Student

Many writers in their memoirs have commented on the unenviable fortune of the young *yeshivah* students who had to board with various families during the week for their daily sustenance, a system that often resulted in their starving for certain days in the week or for longer periods. Young and inexperienced youths from small towns had to find families who would provide them with lunch and supper for one day a week; often, particularly when they had first started studying, they found themselves in the position of Aronson (1825–1888), who could find families for only four out of the six weekdays. Breakfast was eaten in Aronson's *yeshivah*. On Mondays and Thursdays two *yeshivah* students visited the grocery stores in Vilna and charitable women provided them with rye, wheat, corn, salt, and butter, which were mixed in a big copper pot and served as gruel for every student for breakfast. Each student had to find his own bread, begging for it if necessary. On one occasion Aronson went for two days with nothing to eat because he could not secure families' home at which to eat. On the Sabbath the meals for students were provided by members of a sacred fraternity, the *Gemilat Hasadim* Society. In the 1840s the students at the famous *yeshivah* of Mir breakfasted on bread and water, while for lunch they drank *krupnik* soup, grits cooked in water. In the late nineteenth century the students of the *yeshivah* of Volozhin had to be content with "bread and tea for breakfast and supper, bread and some warm dish for luncheon, and meat once a week—on the Sabbath." In the 1890s conditions were so bad at the Ramayles Synagogue *yeshivah* that the students went on strike, claiming that they were not receiving enough bread. In 1898 Z. Scharfstein wrote that in Kovno starving *yeshivah* students no older than ten or twelve years of age were roaming the streets in pairs begging for food and alms. Chaim Grade wrote of an impecunious peddler who gave his guest, a *yeshivah* student, chopped radishes and chicken fat or chicken fat on bread sprinkled with salt for lunch on the Sabbath; the final Sabbath meal consisted of hard-boiled eggs, but he stuffed the lad's pockets with apples as a treat—details obviously distilled from memory.[30]

Nonetheless, conditions could vary for the same *yeshivah* student over a period of time, and sometimes an excellent and varied diet was provided. Israel Kasovich (1859–1929) attended a *yeshivah* in the town of Kurenitz, where the poor families treated him well, but in the wealthier families he was ordered to sit at a corner of the table. Hannah, the bagel seller, gave him a glass of milk and two large bagels for breakfast, while for dinner he was regaled with wheat bread, herring, rice soup, and some meat, the sort of fare he had tasted only at weddings. In his twelfth year he enrolled at a *yeshivah* in Minsk, where breakfast was a slice of rye bread. "The mad scramble of students during the distribution of bread was simply intolerable; and I, as the smallest of the lot and somewhat bashful withal, would get the poorest portion." Further, "For the two days on which I had no free board, I would buy two pounds of cheese, and occasionally also a pickled cucumber, and when I had a strong craving for potatoes, I would buy a couple and bake them in the oven of the synagogue and feast like a lord." During the very cold winter "the poor died of cold and hunger. . . ," and when his uncle was away, he ate only dry bread on his boardless days. In addition, the beadle in the synagogue gave him white bread, herring, and soup. He was then sent to the only *yeshivah* in Zaslov, where two families competed to supply him with meals. "To be sure, the board was nothing much—almost every day, the same small potatoes, the same coarse black bread, a little beet, cabbage or groat soup, sometimes prepared with a dash of milk, and sometimes with a bit of fat." It is interesting how this passage confirms the characteristics of the standard Lithuanian Jewish fare. During his stay at Volozhin in the 1890s while studying at the *yeshivah*, Harry Finkelstein lived in a house where for thirty rubles per month he was provided "with three meals daily—mostly eggs—butter and cheese—cucumbers and fruits. On Sabbath—chicken and *kugel* was [sic] served."[31]

Peddlers

In Bohemia and Moravia, modern Czechoslovakia, peddlers in the late eighteenth century carried kosher provisions for their week's journey through the countryside. These provisions usually consisted of a jar of dough crumbs and a packet of ground coffee. If possible, Jewish peddlers in modern Poland would take a kosher milk pot and utensils with them for their week's travels, and they would eat dairy food at a peasant's table. An itinerant tailor wandered around Gentile homes during the week in Piaski in the province of Bialystok, subsisting on herring and a piece of bread. He was often paid in kind by the peasants with beans, chick-peas, and potatoes. In the late nineteenth century peddlers in Atlanta, Georgia, who were of east European origin carried cooked vegetables and hard-boiled eggs if they were away from home for a few days. Israel Solomons related how until 1830 there were inns on all the main roads in England, where Jewish peddlers, many of German origin, could keep their cooking utensils locked in a cupboard so as to comply with the laws of *kashrut:*

> And when a Jew used the utensils, he saw to the cleaning of them and before putting them away . . . wrote with chalk in the bottom of the utensil his name, [the] day of the [Jewish] month and year together with the portion of the Law read on the Sabbath of that week—all in Hebrew . . . Some of the hotels were in the centre of populated districts, and the pedlars . . . would congregate of a Friday evening at these hotels and stay over the Sabbath . . . They generally formed a club and one of their number, licensed by a rabbi to slaughter animals, was paid by the club for one day's loss of profit . . . to get to the hotel on Friday early enough to kill [an] animal or poultry [or to] purchase fish . . . cook or superintend it [so] that it should be quite kosher.

Surely these must have been long-standing practices of Continental Jewry that were transplanted to England.[32]

REGIONAL VARIATIONS

Not only did the Polish Jews share many basic foods, such as bread, cabbage, raw onions, herring, tea, and fruit during the summer, with their coreligionists in Lithuania, but the Jews in both regions used oil and goose fat as a cooking medium, giving their food a distinctive flavor and distinguishing their dishes from those of their neighbors, who favored lard and butter. In the same way, the descendants of the Spanish Jews in Turkey cooked with sesame oil, giving their dishes a unique taste and separating their cuisine from that of their Muslim neighbors. So, too, the Polish and Lithuanian Jews both made use of sours to render palatable their boring and bulky carbohydrate diet. Again, in both regions there were class differences in diet, as evidenced by the following song:

> Aleph—The rich man eats fruit preserves,
> Beyz—The poor man gnaws bones.
> Giml—The rich man eats geese.
> Daled—The poor man eats poverty.
> Zayen—The rich man eats buttered buns.
> Ches—The poor man has sicknesses.
> Mem—The rich man drinks whisky,
> Nun—The poor man is sober.

As early as the 1830s and 1840s the rich Jews in Poland frequently ate meat, although it was not always kosher, as well as fish and asparagus and other expensive vegetables. Nonetheless, the cuisines of the Polish and Lithuanian Jews differed in one important feature, namely, the abundant use of sugar in many recipes in Poland.[33]

Marvin Herzog has argued that the area in which gefilte fish was prepared with sugar in Poland coincided both with the domain in which Hasidism was dominant and in which a special Yiddish dialect was spoken; elsewhere, as in Lithuania, the gefilte fish was prepared with pepper, the vernacular was distinctive, and Hasidism failed to flourish. Many of the other variations in the preparation of food in Poland and Lithuania, such as the different methods of making *farfel*, were of marginal significance compared with the use of sugar. Diane and David Roskies posed an additional question: did the variations in the preparation of gefilte fish, with or without sugar, come before or after the rise of Hasidism?[34]

We would put forward the hypothesis that sugar was a relatively rare ingredient in the food in eastern Europe during the eighteenth century. Rabbinical literature in this period defined the different types of sugar, while earlier in the seventeenth century Rabbi David Halevi of Lvov doubted whether crystal bars of sugar could be utilized on Passover because they might have been contaminated with *hometz*. Sidney Mintz estimated that some 245,000 tons of sugar reached consumers throughout the world in 1800. One expert has asserted that ". . . sugar cane (and sugar beet) produce larger quantities of utilizable calories per land unit in a given time than any other cultivated plant in their respective climatic zones." Further, it has been estimated that while an acre of good subtropical land will produce more than eight million calories of sugar, it would take more than four acres of land in Europe to produce potatoes with a similar yield in calories and between eight and nine acres if sown with wheat. Sugar was so much cheaper to produce than even the potato and had a higher yield in calories that it was inevitably adopted as a sweetener by the mass of the Jewish population in Poland in the latter half of the nineteenth century, just as its use was vigorously espoused by the west European working class.[35]

In the early nineteenth century the Polish gentry in Volhynia and Podolia developed plantations of sugar beet on modern capitalist lines. The Jewish entrepreneur Hermann Epstein built a sugar refinery in Poland in 1838 that by 1852 was the largest in the land. Israel Brodsky (1823–1889) was a pioneer of the sugarbeet industry in south Russia, and he and his sons Lazar (1848–1904) and Leon (1851–1923) opened numerous refineries, rapidly becoming the largest sugar manufacturers in Russia. By 1914, 86 sugar refineries in Russia were Jewish owned, and when Jewish-run companies are added to this total, it appears that two-thirds of the sugar industry was in Jewish hands. Apart from the Ukraine, sugar beet was grown extensively in the areas of fertile loess soil in the south of Poland. More important, vital segments of the wholesale sugar trade and the retail distribution network through peddlers were controlled by Jews. One informant declared that his grandfather, who was a Polish peasant farmer, exchanged some of his produce with Jewish peddlers for sugar and boiled sweets for the children; such examples can be multiplied. By 1860 total world production of sucrose, that is, both cane and beet sugar, had reached 1.37 million tons, but it then leaped to six million tons by 1890. We would suggest that sugar became an important feature in the diet of the Polish Jews and the Gentiles only in the second half of the nineteenth century, but particularly in the last two decades; and that sugar-based recipes that were part of Polish-Jewish cuisine were relatively new innovations.[36]

Sugar was extensively utilized in Polish-Jewish cuisine as a seasoning in soup, and fish were similarly flavored with onions and sugar. Jewish-style carp was eaten with almonds, raisins, onions, and then sprinkled with salt, pepper, and sugar. Vegetables, such as cabbages, carrots, and turnips, were cut into small pieces, moistened with goose fat, and coated with a white sauce consisting of flour mixed with vinegar and sugar. Even *hallah* for the Sabbath was often prepared with sugar.[37]

We can now answer the Roskies' question about the making of gefilte fish with sugar and positively declare that the rise of the hasidic movement in Volhynia and Podolia from 1730 until the 1770s antedated the cultivation of sugar in those provinces. Possibly the taste for locally produced sugar, which was acquired at an early date by the hasidic pioneers, may have meant that they eagerly promoted the consumption of sugar among their followers when they spread throughout Poland in the first half of the nineteenth century and that sugar became associated with the joy and sweetness of religious celebration. But it is equally plausible that the Jewish domination of the sugar industry in Poland between 1850 and 1914 meant that the Jews created an active network of promoters of the consumption of sugar and that their first converts were their fellow Jews, whether or not they were *hasidim*. Moreover, if it can be shown that gefilte fish without sugar was consumed in Volhynia and Podolia, provinces that were the original seat of the hasidic movement, then there would be a measure of proof that the flavoring of gefilte fish with sugar had nothing to do with hasidic ideals and practices but was more closely related to the commercial promotion of the consumption of sugar in the second half of the nineteenth century, as sugar among other things was used in many different kinds of Polish-Jewish fish recipes. Sugar was an attractive, cheap ingredient and an excellent source of energy; it offered Polish Jews an alternative method of digesting food to the sours that were a traditional feature of the diet of the east European Jews.

THE CONSUMPTION OF MEAT

Here we wish to focus briefly on two questions. Were there any variations in the consumption of meat among Jews in Poland and Lithuania? Have we any knowledge of the actual quantity of meat consumption per head in Jewish households in eastern Europe? We would at once admit that our knowledge is fragmentary and that the existing research has concentrated on the evils of the notorious meat tax, known as the *korobka* in Russian, from the German word *Korb*, meaning a basket. In the Duchy of Warsaw a kosher meat tax was instituted in 1809, the proceeds of which were earmarked for the state treasury, while there was also a similar tax to finance the requirements of the Jewish community. Kosher meat in the region was twice the price of meat eaten by the rest of the population and almost prohibitive in price for the Jewish poor. After the Polish uprising of 1863 the kosher meat tax was abolished and the state no longer mulcted the Jewish community, but there was still a meat tax to raise revenue for Jewish communal purposes. In Galicia in Austrian Poland at the beginning of the nineteenth century kosher meat was so expensive that it was claimed that beef was seldom eaten by the poorer Jews; more generally the *korobka* was attacked as a direct tax that the wealthy Jews had to pay on behalf of their poorer brethren. In 1839 the Russian government instituted the meat-tax regulations that were modified in 1844 and were applied to the whole of the Pale of Settlement with the exception of Russian Poland. The tax was allocated for the payment of government tax quotas by the Jewish community, for the liquidation of communal debts, the maintenance of Jewish schools, the promotion of Jewish agricultural enterprise, and the support of communal charities, while the collection of the tax was left to tax lessees assisted by state officials.[38]

Nonetheless, it is possible that after the abolition of the meat tax in Russian Poland in 1863, the incidence of the surcharges on kosher meat was lighter than in the rest of Russia and Lithuania and that consequently the consumption of meat per head was significantly higher among Jews in the larger towns in Russian Poland than in Lithuania and Galicia. Israel Joshua Singer (1893–1944), describing the situation in Lodz in the 1880s in a novel, asserted that Lithuanian Jews lived on a meager diet of bread and herring together with *borscht* and that they "couldn't understand Polish Jews, who thought nothing of eating meat daily. They stared in disbelief when local housewives roasted a goose for the Sabbath and baked trays of biscuits. They wondered how Polish Jews could go to a restaurant to drink beer or whisky, munch chick-peas, order chopped liver. They gaped when grown women went into a confectionery for a bar of chocolate. . . ." Such a description would probably make better sense of the social scene some twenty years later, while the remark about daily meals of meat enjoyed by some sections of Polish Jewry appears to be an achievable aspiration. In his memoirs Isaac Bashevis Singer claimed that his father, who was a rabbi in Warsaw, was constantly amazed by the size of the cooking pots, "veritable caldrons," utilized by the Jews, as Singer's father's family cooked a pound of meat in a modest-sized vessel. When a young girl came to ask his father a question about *kashrut,* as a quantity of milk had fallen on some meat, she incidentally mentioned that she had been cooking ten pounds of meat and one chicken in a pot.[39]

Turning to the consumption of meat in Jewish families, in the Grand Duchy of Warsaw at the beginning of the nineteenth century it was estimated that the average weekly consumption of meat was one pound, or .45 kilograms, in a Jewish household. In poor Jewish families in the Ukraine in 1736, the average household contained 4.5 persons, but if for the nineteenth century a slightly higher multiplier of five to six persons per household seems a reasonable conjecture, the average consumption of meat would be 2.66 ounces or 166.66 grams. Isaac Bashevis Singer assumed that the consumption of meat among Jewish families in small towns in Poland was likewise a pound of meat per week at the beginning of the twentieth century. If this assumption was correct then it would appear that in the small *shtetlech* in Poland the consumption of meat in poor Jewish households had remained unchanged for more than a century. Nonetheless, this assumption appears to be wrong, as poor families in the Duchy of Warsaw and Galicia hardly consumed any meat in the early part of the nineteenth century. We would argue that there was, in fact, a small rise in the consumption of meat among poor individuals in the course of a century, which was even higher than our figures seem to indicate, for by the mid-nineteenth century, with the spread of the *Haskalah* spirit many Jews, particularly those in south Russia and the wealthy elite in Warsaw, ceased to eat kosher food, an example later followed by nonobservant affluent Jews in Vilna; yet despite this, huge surpluses on the kosher meat tax continued to accumulate in the state bank from the 1880s, showing that there was no decline in consumption.[40]

Moreover, a considerable quantity of meat and poultry was slaughtered without the paying of any taxes. The *hasidim* from the time of the *Maggid* of Mezritsh in the mid-eighteenth century insisted on *shochetim* using polished knives to perform the functions of ritual slaughter properly, thereby differentiating the form of *shechitah* practiced by *hasidim* from that of other Orthodox Jews. The hasidic slaughterers circumvented the laws of 1789 and 1810, which permitted them to reside only in cities, by visiting villages or by slaughtering in private homes, thus avoiding payment of the meat taxes. They also slaughtered not only for the families of rebbes but also for the large contingents of *hasidim*, who came to their masters' courts for the Sabbath and festivals. In Galicia if the tax lessees opposed the control of the *hasidim* in matters of *shechitah*, the rabbis responded by organizing boycotts of the tax lessees and proclaimed anonymous and highly effective bans on the consumption of meat. Rebecca Berg's father in Lithuania in the 1880s bought up produce from peasant farmers cheaply just as the market was closing, after which he rode over the border into Latvia, where he exchanged the produce for kosher meat, on which no tax was paid. She well recalled one occasion when her father smuggled half a dozen calves' feet for jelly, *fisnosgis*, a Sabbath delight, a lung, a liver, and a side of meat for a widow who peddled pieces of meat from door to door. The *shtetl* of Yanesok, where the Berg family lived, was terrorized by the Jewish official appointed by the tsar, the *dershednik,* whose business it was to collect the meat tax and to try to stamp out the smuggling of kosher meat across the border; such evasion of the payment of the meat tax was probably common in other Lithuanian towns, particularly in border areas. Abraham Ain declared that in Swislocz at the beginning of the century the permit for slaughtering poultry was a few kopeks, but for permission to kill a cow or an ox a certain tax was payable, while an additional tax was levied on the meat, apart from the lung, liver, head, and legs of the animal; hence the popularity of these items.[41]

By way of comparison we would cite the evidence of Zosa Szajkowski, who concluded that in the 1840s Parisian Jews consumed 50 kilos of meat per person throughout the year or an average of 961 grams of meat per person for a week. Thus the meat consumption of Parisian Jews, although it was inferior to that of French Gentiles, was almost five times the level of consumption attained by the east European Jews throughout the nineteenth century, apart from those living in large towns such as Warsaw. In the last decades of the nineteenth century, however, Jews in eastern Europe appreciated that if they immigrated to the United States they would be able to eat meat on almost a daily basis, and they quickly learned that fat meat was cheaper than lean. So, too, in Argentina families in Jewish rural settlements often ate ample portions of meat for both lunch and dinner on a daily basis.[42]

9

SABBATH AND FESTIVAL FOOD OF CENTRAL AND EASTERN EUROPEAN JEWS

THE SABBATH: PREPARATION

In eastern Europe Jews went to the market on Thursday to buy meat, chicken, and sometimes fish for the Sabbath. According to De Pomiane, however, many persons purchased their fish in the Polish town of Cracow on a Friday morning, a point confirmed by Joachim Schoenfeld, who stated that in the town of Sniatyn in Galicia carp arrived in tanks by train from Romania on a Friday morning and that cheaper fish were bought by Jewish customers from the local Gentile fishermen, who peddled their fish around the houses on the same morning. In the *shtetl* of Lopantin in eastern Galicia the servants of the local squire poached some carp with golden striped scales from his lake and hid them in their boots, exchanging them with the Jews for brandy steeped in wormwood or for a glass of rum. In the Cracow fish market there were expensive pike for sale, and large carp swam around in huge fish tanks, but for the Jews who were not affluent, carp halves were sold. Although the common carp was domesticated in southern China in prehistoric times, it has been suggested that Jewish traders along the silk routes assisted in the dissemination of the carp throughout southern and eastern Europe. The Sephardim in Salonika seasoned carp with walnut and wine sauce. Nonetheless, the really poor Jews in eastern Europe were offered cheap river fish, such as roach, tench, and chub, for the Sabbath, or even a piece of salted herring. Among the

171

German Jews similar fish were consumed on the Sabbath with the addition of the delectable barbel and trout.[1]

Chickens and geese were purchased on a Thursday, after which they were immediately slaughtered by a *shochet* so that if some defect was later discovered they were taken to a rabbi to decide whether or not they were kosher. If he rejected their suitability, they were sold to someone outside the Jewish community. When the east European Jews emigrated to the United States, they retained many of these shopping practices. In the immigrant community of Chicago in the 1920s, Jewish housewives purchased carp, pike, and herrings on a Thursday, while in the butcher shops serving meat and sausages, *shochetim* killed fresh poultry for the Sabbath at a customer's behest.[2]

On Thursday evening in eastern Europe, the women kneaded the dough for the Sabbath loaves and rose early on Friday morning to bake them. In Galicia housewives did a massive amount of baking on Friday, not only preparing the loaves of *hallah*, biscuits (*kichlech*), *knishes*, and sponge and honey cakes for the Sabbath, but baking the ordinary black bread on cabbage leaves for the week as well. In some parts of pre-First World War Poland and Lithuania the loaves of braided *hallah*, the butter, egg, and fruit cakes, and the gingerbread were baked on Thursday, particularly in winter when there was little time to complete the Sabbath preparation on a Friday. Rabbis in small towns in Lithuania made an important contribution to their earnings by selling yeast to women on Fridays for baking purposes. Among the poorer families, the housewives were careful not to waste the supply of wood for heating the oven and baked all the bread for the week as well as the *hallot*. Before placing the loaves in the oven, the housewife broke off a piece of dough and threw it into the fire while reciting a traditional blessing, as a reminder of the commandment to set aside the first of the dough as a gift to the priest. After this some additional dough was rolled flat and cut into strips of *lokshen* (noodles) for the Friday-evening meal. Between the world wars, in the larger towns in Lithuania, women bought their braided *hallot* and cakes from bakeries.[3]

There were universal Sabbath rules among both the Ashkenazim and the Sephardim for distributing food to the poor on a Friday and for inviting Sabbath guests. In Germany in the eighteenth century, the poor gathered at the gates of the ghetto to obtain funds for celebrating the Sabbath. As the transient population increased steadily in eighteenth-century Germany, guests were chosen by lot for people's homes, but because these duties were regarded as burdensome they were often neglected. In pre-Second World War Poland some families used to distribute food, including bread, meat, and sometimes boiled fish, to the respectable poor in their hometowns. Elsewhere in eastern

Europe beggars often made the rounds of regular houses for some money or food. In Jerusalem at the beginning of the century, women kept watch in the market on Wednesday and Thursday to see who had failed to appear for their regular Sabbath shopping, and when this had been ascertained, parcels of eggs, beans, flour, rice, and *hallah* were prepared and delivered anonymously to their recipients.[4]

The *Shulchan Aruch: Orach Hayim,* compiled by Joseph Karo (1488–1575), a Sephardic rabbi, stated that it was meritorious to desist from having a set meal of the kind that one was accustomed to on weekdays on a Friday before the onset of the Sabbath; virtuous persons fasted on the eve of the Sabbath, so that according to the *Mishnah Berurah* of the Hafetz Hayim (1838–1933), they would have an increased appetite for the Sabbath. So, too, Rabbi Joel Sirkes (1561–1640), a Polish Ashkenazic rabbi, praised Jews who ate light meals in the afternoon preceding a Sabbath or festival to heighten their enjoyment of their subsequent feasting. Accordingly, the custom of eating light meals on a Friday was widely observed. In the childhood home of Bella Chagall in eastern Europe in Vitebsk, no cooked lunch was provided on a Friday, but everyone was given a large pastry stuffed with fried onions, which was called a *tsibulnik,* to eat. In Lithuania it was a custom to cook dried peas on a Friday morning and to consume them with a drink made from beetroots. In the household of I. J. Singer's grandparents, the water carrier was treated to a loaf baked from the final scrapings of dough called *wyskrobek,* while the young Singer was given little breads to nibble as compensation. On the other hand, in Swislocz in the province of Grodno the daily *krupnik* was prepared with stuffed gut, *kishke,* on a Friday and was eaten with fresh rolls.[5]

HALLAH

Dovid Katz has put forward a fruitful hypothesis that the Yiddish language and culture originated in southern Germany and beyond, not in the Rhineland. The centers of Yiddish culture were the towns of Regensburg, Rothenburg, and Nuremberg in southern Germany and in other places in Austria and Bohemia inhabited by Jews. Food was an essential part of Yiddish culture, and the hypothesis of Katz assists us in understanding how the rabbinic and culinary traditions of southern Germany, Austria, and Bohemia were all part of one unified tradition that was transplanted to Poland. These customs were particularly important as regards the adoption of a special loaf for the Sabbath, *hallah,* the serving of carp in a sauce on a Friday night, and the special cooking techniques for making *cholent* for the Sabbath lunch. We should also recall that the crucial Jewish food term, *pareve*, food that was considered neither meat nor milk, was derived from the medieval Czech word *párové*, meaning a pair, or even from a similar Polish word.[6]

In the East, oriental Jews still retained the traditional round shape of bread for the Sabbath loaf, the *hallah*. Israel Cohen in his *Journal of a Jewish Traveller* remarked, "The Sabbath table presented the traditional genial appearance except that the 'loaves' were large, flat, blistered pancakes, though tasting unmistakably like bread. I was told that the Sabbath bread of this shape was baked in the homes of all orthodox Eastern Jews. . . ." In Salonika before the Second World War the Spanish Jews baked *hallot* from fine flour; these were hollow, coated with egg, and had poppy seed scattered over them. They were often round but sometimes rectangular in shape. Among the Spanish Jews in Bosnia, which was part of Yugoslavia, it was the custom to bake *Pan d'Espagna*, a sponge cake consisting of egg white, flour, and sugar for the Friday-night repast; elsewhere among the Sephardim small loaves of bread called *pitikas*, almost certainly round in shape, were distributed among the poor on a Friday. The Jews of Kurdistan baked only plain loaves of bread that were sprinkled with sesame seed; nor did the Jewish community of Shiraz in Iran make a special loaf for the Sabbath. Because of the widespread distribution of the custom of baking fresh loaves of bread on a Friday among disparate Jewish communities, it is quite possible that this was a tradition that had its roots in the talmudic era (*Taanit* 24b and 25a); strangely this custom was ignored by medieval rabbinic commentators and was revived by the Austrian author of *Leket Yosher* and by Rabbi Moses Isserles in Poland only in the sixteenth century, suggesting a possible lax observance of this custom in the Middle Ages. At the end of the Middle Ages, however, it was clear that not merely fresh bread was baked for the Sabbath, but in western and eastern Europe loaves with special characteristics were baked.[7]

Within the borders of Germany the Jews baked a long, braided loaf of bread for the Sabbath called *Berches*, or *Barches*, which had the taste of sour dough. So, too, the use of this name spread to Hungary, where the Sabbath loaf was known as *barhes*, and as far west as Alsace. According to Samuel Krauss, the loaf took its shape from two interlocked arms, the name being derived from the medieval Latin word for arms, *bracellus*, and the Old High German *brezitella*, *brezita*, *bergita*, and hence the term *Berches*. The latter word was also connected with the terms *pretzel* and *bretzel*, medieval foods familiar to us from chapter 8. More speculatively, it has been asserted that the word *Berches* was related to the name of the German goddess *Berchta*, for whom German women baked braided loaves made to resemble plaits of hair and that there had been a time when the German women had sacrificed their hair to the goddess of fertility. Nonetheless, although leading folklorists in the past had shown that the *Berchta* cult had no ceremony with plaited braid, the hypothesis was revived in a new form; it was proposed that as Jewish women had already cut off their hair or kept it covered on marriage, they could offer only a portion of dough, the *hallah*, and then the plaited loaves as a sacrifice, but this modified form of the hypothesis was dismissed by Krauss as an absurdity. In the western part of Germany the Sabbath bread was known by the name of *Taatscher* or *Datscher*, names that Samuel Krauss proposed were linked to the French word *torte* and the Italian *torta* but that were ultimately derived from the Latin word *tortus*, meaning twisted.[8]

Nonetheless, recent scholarship has suggested that the etymological pedigree advanced by Krauss for the western Yiddish terms for the Sabbath bread, *berches* or *datscher*, is fanciful; these words were the equivalent of the eastern Yiddish word *hallah*. If this is the case the medieval Jewish origin of the special plaited Sabbath loaves is unlikely. It has been asserted that the most plausible explanation for the term *berches* is the folk one that states that it is derived from the Hebrew word *birkat* (blessing) in the phrase, "The blessing of the Lord, it maketh rich" (Proverbs 10:22), a phrase that was engraved on the knives used to cut the Sabbath bread. What makes this explanation the more convincing is that it also makes sense of the alternative western Yiddish term *datscher*, which appears to be derived from the Hebrew word *taasher* (maketh rich) in the same phrase. One of the earliest references to the word *berches* was contained in the writings of Rabbi Kirchan, who lived at the end of the seventeenth century, again hinting at the relatively late adoption of plaited *hallot* for the Sabbath.[9]

The first reference to the word *hallah* in its meaning of Sabbath loaf is in the *Leket Yosher* of Rabbi Joseph Bar Moses, a late fifteenth-century work by a pupil of the renowned Austrian Rabbi Isserlein. He recalled that

> on every Sabbath eve they made for him [Isserlein] three fine *hallot* kneaded with eggs, oil and a little water. The middle [sized] *hallah* he put at night in the middle of the table-cloth, and under the *hallah* was a big loaf which was complete, although it was black, and . . . a small roll of fine flour. And in the morning he put the big *hallah* and the big loaf on the table as at night and for the third meal he took the small *hallah* and a complete bread.

However, the sixteenth-century Polish Rabbi Isserles, following the same tradition, referred to the Sabbath bread that was baked on a

Friday under the name of *lachamim* (loaves of bread), while a similar designation was used in the early nineteenth century by the author of the *Kitzur Shulchan Aruch*, the shortened version of the authoritative code of Jewish law. In contrast, the original Sephardic code of Karo was silent. Moreover, Zechariah Mendel, the Baer Hetev, a seventeenth-century luminary from Cracow, stipulated that the Polish Jews should not "eat the bread of Gentiles on the Sabbath and should eat *hallot* on the Sabbath." We would suggest that this new term for the Sabbath bread originally coined in Austria was now becoming important in Poland.[10]

With the migration of the German Jews eastward the use of plaited loaves for the Sabbath bread spread slowly, first into Poland and then into Lithuania. *Hallah* in Poland was often prepared with sugar and had a sweet taste, but this was a mid- or late-nineteenth-century innovation, while the *berches* were made with no sugar or almost no sugar. Despite assertions to the contrary, braided *hallot*, known as *kitkes*, as well as ordinary *hallot* were common in Lithuania in the period between the two world wars. Earlier, however, the term *kitke* was reserved to describe twisted *hallot* only baked in the small towns of Lithuania for the festivals of Tabernacles, Shavuot, and Purim, whereas plain *hallot* were baked for the Sabbath; even in Poland in the nineteenth century Jews often baked plain *hallot*. If *berches* was a medieval term, we would have expected it to have passed into Eastern Yiddish, instead of which the word *hallah* and a variety of other terms were used to describe the Sabbath bread. Again, there are indications in the rabbinic sources of Jews in medieval Spain and England preferring to eat hot non-Jewish bread on the Sabbath rather than stale Jewish baked bread, evidence that as yet a special Sabbath loaf had not evolved. Hasidic rabbis following Kabbalistic practice introduced the use of twelve loaves of bread on the Sabbath into the Ukraine and Galicia in the eighteenth century, yet another indication of relatively new and incomplete adoption of braided *hallot* in the sixteenth and seventeenth centuries, as other types of *hallot* were easily accepted. In origin the braided Sabbath loaf was, however, the special Sunday bread of the German Gentiles.[11]

FISH

The Friday-night fish course traditional in Jewish homes since the talmudic era encouraged Jews to evolve interesting recipes and culinary techniques that often passed into the national tradition of the country in which the Jews happened to be residing. Moreover, the

Hafetz Hayyim ruled that it was meritorious to eat fish at each of the three Sabbath meals. Heinrich Heine (1796–1856) recalled "the carp in brown raisin sauce which my aunt prepared so edifyingly on Friday evenings . . ." in her home in Germany. The first reference to a Jewish-style carp dish was in the *Rieder-Sachsisches Koch-Buch* published in Altona and Lubeck in 1758, but the recipe was for carp cooked in a thick sauce whose principal ingredient was beer, although sliced onions and spices were added; similar recipes appeared in the *Neues Hannoverisches Kochbuch* under the title *Judenbrühe zu Karpfen* (Jewish broth for carp) and in *Colner Kochinn* (1806).[12]

To find another recipe for carp in a brown sauce, we must again turn to the *Neues Hannoverisches Kochbuch,* where there is a recipe for brown carp without any reference to a Jewish connection. The anonymous author declared that after cutting the carp into slices, it was well cooked in a sauce made from brown flour, vinegar, lemon, sugar, and pounded spice. Later variants of this recipe surfaced in Jewish cookery books as an authentic Jewish dish. Joan Nathan published the sweet-and-sour carp recipe of her grandmother, who lived in Bavaria. The carp was served every Friday night and on the New Year because of the messianic symbolism of the fish. The ingredients included vinegar, sliced lemon, half a cup of raisins, brown sugar, peppercorns, and *Lebkuchen* (gingerbread). However, a recipe for carp in brown butter in Rebecca Wolf's cookbook published in Berlin in 1875 omitted raisins and sugar from the list of ingredients. The Polish-Jewish-style carp dish was a sweetened version of this recipe and was obviously modeled on the older German dish. Alexandre Weill, an Alsatian Jew, in his memoirs mentioned the Friday-evening course of fish in a Jewish-style sauce as a recipe that had become part of German national cuisine. Accordingly, it is uncertain whether both German carp dishes were of Jewish origin or whether the dish of carp in brown sauce was in the course of time confused with the eighteenth-century dish of carp cooked in beer and given an undeserved Jewish attribution.[13]

Although the culinary expert in the *Universal Jewish Encyclopaedia* doubted the antiquity of gefilte fish, it was indisputably of medieval origin and probably older still. Undoubtedly the dish of chopped fish mentioned in the Babylonian Talmud was the ancestor of gefilte fish (*Shabbat* 118b). Nonetheless, the earliest recipe for stuffed pike (*gefeulten Hechden*) appeared in a manuscript written in Würzburg in southern Germany in about 1350 that instructed readers to scoop out the innards of the fish, chop the flesh, add salt, pepper, caraway seeds, and sometimes egg, and bake the resulting concoction in an oven. A recipe in a later German cookery book entitled *Von Speisen* that was published in 1531 recommended that a pike be divided into four pieces; the first quarter was to be roasted; the second quarter was to be boiled with wine and spices; the third quarter was to be stuffed (gefült), while the remaining quarter was to be baked. Then the fish was to be reassembled and strewn with parsley and was finally served with small bowls of salt or vinegar. Similar recipes were quoted in other sixteenth-century cookery manuals. So, too, the Maharil (1360–1427), the medieval rabbinic authority, who lived in the Rhineland communities of Mainz and Worms, ruled that vinegar could be added to a fish hash on the Sabbath. Here was perhaps a glimpse of the direct ancestor of gefilte fish or possibly of chopped herring, which were taken by German Jews on their migration eastward to Poland and Lithuania. Moreover, W. H. Hohberg, a non-Jewish German author, also included a recipe for stuffed pike (gefüllter Hecht) in the cookery book in Volume 3 of his Georgica Curiosa, published in 1715. Likewise Rebecca Wolf in her Jewish cookery book published in Berlin in 1875 supplied a recipe for gefilte fish made from pike that was cooked rather than baked.[14]

When the gefilte fish recipe was imported into Poland from Germany in the seventeenth century, if not earlier, however, carp was substituted for pike as the fish most utilized. Carp was introduced into France and Germany only in the fifteenth and sixteenth centuries through Italy and Turkey, countries connected with the silk trade and ultimately with China; the breeding of carp spread slowly into Poland, where Jews in their management of farms sometimes controlled fish ponds. According to Ignacy Schipper, Jews bred new species of fish in Polish waters, which they obtained from the Black, Azov, and Caspian Seas and from the Don River, becoming outstanding pisiculturalists. Carp became associated with Jewish culinary art because the breeding of this fish was diffused throughout Turkey, the Balkans, and eastern and central Europe by Jewish traders.[15]

One of the earliest recipes for gefilte fish made from carp was in a volume entitled Le Cuisinier Roial et Bourgeois by Massialot, which was published in Paris in 1698. The author suggested that the fish was cleaned and the skin filled with the flesh from the carp and an eel, to which should be added fine herbs, salt, pepper, cloves, nutmeg, thyme, butter, and mushrooms. The skin of the stuffed carp was stitched or tied together and the fish was then left to cook in an oven in a sauce of brown butter, white wine, and clear broth; it was served with mushrooms, capers, and slices of lemon. In Alsace today there is still a special gefilte fish cooked in white wine, carpe farcie à l'alsacienne, which must be descended from this recipe. In 1722 Massialot brought out a new and enlarged edition of his cookery book, containing additional recipes for stuffed pike and chopped carp, which were popularized in a German translation in 1739, this being the first

German translation of a French cookery book. Jewish cooks in Germany and Poland adapted the medieval and later recipes for stuffed or gefilte pike and carp to the needs of the kosher kitchen; although the fish was prepared with salt and pepper, in eastern Europe it was still often baked in an oven following the traditional method rather than poached on a stove. Originally, gefilte fish was a forcemeat made from chopped freshwater fish and *matzah* crumbs that were stuffed into slices of carp; today a variety of sea fish are used, a recipe departing further from the sophisticated French original.[16]

Gefilte fish was popular with the bulk of east European Jewry because the recipe enabled families with slender resources to stretch the quantity of fish available to provide for the whole family. The recipe also neatly dovetailed into the rabbinic doctrine of *borer* by enabling pious Jews to eat fish already picked off the bone without infringing any Sabbath regulations relating to prohibited categories of work.[17]

Nonetheless, Jewish cooks often prepared gefilte fish as plain fish balls without encasing it in a skin. Again, they followed the practice of cooks since at least the sixteenth century, if not earlier. A recipe that appeared in a German cookery treatise in 1566, but that repeated earlier recipes, suggested that the fish should be chopped, mixed with salt and butter and good spice, and made in a bowl with *Lebkucken*, the resulting patties being known as *Kuchlin von Fischen* (fish cakes). In Rebecca Wolf's 1875 German volume there was a recipe for fish balls, *Fisch-Bouletten*, the ingredients of which consisted of chopped fish, the crumbs of a roll, greens, eggs, salt, and pepper. Similarly, Esther Levy's cookery book, which was published in the United States in 1871, also contained a recipe for stewed fish balls; the latter volume was said to disclose a "strong German influence."[18]

In chapter 8 we adduced reasons for supposing that sweetened fish in Poland, particularly gefilte fish with sugar, was a mid-nineteenth-century innovation. Many Jewish fish recipes in Poland were made with onions and sugar, giving them a bland taste, even the classic dish of Jewish-style carp, according to critics such as De Pomiane. This latter dish was prepared with slices of carp, chopped almonds and raisins, and garnished with puréed onions and its cooking liquid, which turned into a jelly when left to cool. Whereas abroad sweetened fish was known as "Polish fish," within Poland fish prepared in this fashion was called "Jewish Fish." Among the Jewish recipes enumerated by Marja Ochorowicz-Montatowa in her volume on Polish cooking at the turn of the century were aspic of carp Jewish style, which featured prominently on the menus in pre-Second World War Polish-Jewish restaurants, stuffed pike and stuffed perch Jewish style (gefilte fish), and smothered carp Jewish style.[19]

We would suggest that the Lithuanian gefilte fish prepared with pepper and served with horseradish was older than the Polish sweet-ened version, as the Russians made similar fish balls with pepper and onions that were eaten with horseradish sauce. Both gefilte fish and horseradish sauce were foods of probable late medieval origin with a widespread distribution in central and eastern Europe. It appears that the western Yiddish term *kreyn* is closely related to the south German word for horseradish, *Kren,* which in turn is said to be derived from the Czech word *kren.* By the sixteenth century the Germans regularly utilized horseradish as a sauce when eating fish and meat, although horseradish had sometimes been employed to enliven proceedings at the *Seder* table in Germany since the fourteenth century. What is uncertain is whether the Jews adopted the habit of eating gefilte fish with horseradish from the time of their medieval sojourn in southern Germany and took it with them on their journey to Lithuania and whether these habits were merely reinforced in Russia, where there were similar foods; or whether the consumption of gefilte fish with horseradish sauce was a unique combination of foods acquired afresh in Russia by the Jews. To this writer the most plausible hypothesis is that the Jews acquired gefilte fish in a German environment and that the custom of eating it with horseradish was picked up in a western Slavic environment or in a peripheral German area penetrated by the foods of the Slavs.[20]

English Jewry had a classic dish of cold fried fish that was adopted by its Gentile neighbors. Israel Zangwill extolled its virtues, declaring that "with the audacity of true culinary genius, Jewish fried fish is always served cold. The skin is a beautiful brown, the substance firm and succulent. . . . Fried fish binds Anglo-Jewry more than all the lip-professions of unity." The Portuguese Marranos in England in the first half of the sixteenth century not only greatly relished fried fish but it is quite possible that the Sephardim introduced the use of olive oil in the frying of fish, as at that time the Portuguese Christians disliked olive oil as a cooking medium. The Sephardic recipe was popularized by the Dutch Jews in England, who were of Spanish and Portuguese descent. It was only after their arrival in England, chiefly after the 1880s, that the Polish and Lithuanian Jews copied this Sephardic recipe for cold fried fish from the Dutch and German Jews.[21]

Oil in which the Jews fried fish did not solidify when cold and thus even in this condition the fried fish tended to retain its taste, unlike fish fried in lard, which was an ingredient forbidden to Jews. That was why cold fried fish was praised by gourmets and recommended by non-Jewish cookery experts. Again, this was a recipe that can be traced back at least to the eighteenth century, as it was included in the revised edition of Hannah Glasse's *The Art of Cookery Made Plain and Easy* (1781):

Take either cod, salmon, or any large fish, cut off the head, wash it clean, and cut it in slices as crimp'd cod is, dry it very well in a cloth; then flour it, and dip it in yolks of eggs, and fry it in a great deal of oil, till it is of a fine brown, and well done, take it out and lay it to drain, till it is very dry and cold. Whitings, mackarel, and flat fish are done whole. . . . Frying fish in common oil is not so expensive with care; for present use a little does; and if the cook is careful not to burn the oil, or black it, it will fry them two or three times.

So, too, the recipe was admired by Thomas Jefferson (1743–1826), and according to his granddaughter, the beloved dish was akin to the recipe printed by Soyer in *A Shilling Cookery for the People* (1855). Soyer declared that "in some Jewish families they dip the fish first in flour, and then in egg, and fry in oil. This plan is superior to that fried in fat or dripping, but more expensive . . . and being generally eaten cold, it saves them a good deal of cooking." The well-known Victorian cookery writer Eliza Acton in her *Modern Cooking for Private Families* (1887) gave a similar recipe and continued: ". . . when it [the fried fish] is perfectly cold, dish and garnish it with light foliage. The Jews have cold fried fish much served at their repasts. Fillets of sole, plaice, brill, small turbots, or other fish, may be fried as above. . . ." All fried fish in Britain is now made with olive oil or cheap vegetable oils in imitation of Jewish practice; and incidentally some have staked a claim for Joseph Malin, one of many Jewish fishmongers, as the inventor of the classic English dish of fish and chips in 1865. According to Paul Barker, around 1870 in Lancashire, the Jewish fried-fish trade joined up with the Irish potato shop, which sold both potatoes and chips, to create this national dish. The honorary Wasp Sholom Aleichem, despite his denigration of London, commended the hot fried fish that was tasted there in a compatriot's home in the East End; it was prepared in an oven, perhaps a continuation of practice emanating from the *Heim*. It is interesting to note how the cold fish dishes for the Sabbath were added to the national culinary repertoire in Germany, Poland, and England.[22]

THE FRIDAY-EVENING REPAST

According to Rabbi Joseph Bar Moses, the disciple of Isserlein (c. 1390–1460), as meat was scarce in fifteenth-century Austria, poultry was consumed on a Friday night; we have also seen the allusions to this situation in the writings of the German Rabbi Yair Chaim Bacharach (1639–1702). Throughout central and eastern Europe the partaking of meat pie, *pastide*, at the Friday evening meal fell into desuetude in the modern period, and the custom of eating meat pies was hardly alluded to by Rabbi Solomon Ganzfried (1804–1886), the author of the *Kitzur Shulchan Aruch*, who mentioned that "in some places the custom prevails to make pies for the Sabbath eve in commemoration of the manna. . . ."[23]

Heine recalled the carp in brown sauce that he had relished at the Friday-evening repast in Frankfurt, the soup in which dumplings floated, and the stewed mutton eaten with garlic and horseradish. Sholom Aleichem (1859–1916), who was born in the Ukraine, described a Friday-night dinner in winter as consisting of spicy fish with horseradish, fat chicken soup with noodles, and pot roast with potatoes and prunes. Hayyim Schauss, who hailed from the *shtetl* of Geruv in Lithuania, asserted that in eastern Europe the Friday-evening meal included gefilte fish, noodle soup, stewed carrots (*tzimmes*), and poultry. In his memoirs Abraham Cahan corroborated this description by writing about a Friday night in Vilna when his family did not have their regular meal of gefilte fish, noodles, meat, and hot *tzimmes* with a cold dessert, but only the regular braided loaf of *hallah* and baked herring. The reason for this was the community was saving the money to buy substitutes to do military service. To these items other writers would add stewed parsnip (*pasternak*), which happened to be a favorite of my grandfather, stuffed derma (*kishkele*), stewed meat or chicken or both these items. Because of the European meat shortage between the sixteenth century and the middle of the nineteenth century, the custom of serving meat pies on a Friday night was for the most part discarded, the meat being replaced by poultry; but toward the end of the nineteenth century European meat consumption rose again, with the consequence that both meat and chicken were served in some east European homes on a Friday night.[24]

Even if its place in the meal had changed, the chicken soup with noodles consumed on a Friday evening seems to have replaced the medieval dish of *kremslekh* (eastern Yiddish for *vermicelli*) or *grimslekh* (western Yiddish) eaten after *Kiddush;* but Mordecai Kosover's identification of the east European noodles (*lokshen*) with the medieval German dish of *kremslekh* appears to need clarification. The Romans prepared a dish of fried strips of dough served with honey or garum, the ubiquitous fish sauce, which was the ancestor of the medieval dish known to the Jews. The Yiddish word *lokshen* (noodles) is derived from the Persian word for noodles, *lakshah*, meaning to slide, and was not a culinary descendant of the medieval dish of *kremslekh*. Already an Arabic cookery book from the tenth century described how the dough was rolled "with a rolling pin and cut with a knife into strips," much as the east European Jews were later to prepare noodles. Although Max Grunwald pointed out the Persian origin of the Yiddish word in 1928,

Charles Perry has recently shown that noodles had not been incorporated into German cookery before the sixteenth century, but the fact that pasta reached Spain and Italy in the eleventh and twelfth centuries and even England by the thirteenth century makes Perry's conclusion about German cuisine somewhat dubious. *Lokshen* reached the Slav lands through central Asia and was adopted in Poland, as the Yiddish word appears to be closely related to the Polish term *lokszyn* and the Ukrainian *lokschyna*. There was, however, an interim dish of boiled dough (*vermiculos*) in western Europe mentioned by Platina, Bartolomeo Sacchi, in his *De Honesta Voluptate* (1450) that required cooking for one hour, giving the pasta a different consistency. Likewise, Rabbi Eleazar Rokeach of Worms (c. 1160–1238) had stated that *vermicelli* were cooked in a pot, unlike the ancient Roman dish. Thus Jews from the medieval German lands cooked a primitive form of pasta. When they migrated to Poland and other parts of eastern Europe in the sixteenth century, this predisposed them to adopting the similar dish of *lokshen* from their Slav neighbors. That was why the pasta dish was so quickly appropriated and the word *lokshen* can be found in the writings of Rabbi Moses Isserles in sixteenth-century Poland, although in Germany noodles were called *frimzls* (western Yiddish), a word derived from the medieval term.[25]

The Friday-night festive meal ushered in a new week by laying stress on the symbols of fertility, increase, and prosperity by the consumption of fish, carrots, and choice wine and fat meat. So, too, the east European Jews chose the same symbolic foods to grace their table on the eve of the New Year to inaugurate a fresh year in a propitious way. The Hafetz Hayim was of the opinion that fish represented the leviathan that the righteous would eat in the world to come or when the Messiah came. This midrashic tale was still invested with great significance and was taught to *heder* boys not only in Poland, as both Shmarya Levin and I. J. Singer confirmed in their memoirs, but in England as well. Nonetheless, it is likely that the great fish symbolism and its messianic undertones assumed their greatest importance at the New Year and at Shavuot rather than at the humdrum Friday-evening repast.

THE SABBATH LUNCH: *SCHALET* AND *CHOLENT*

It was universal to eat *schalet* (*shalet*) or *cholent* on the Sabbath in eastern and central Europe, although it varied in both name and form in the different parts of Europe. In Germany and Holland the special

hot dish for the Sabbath lunch was known as *schalet* (western Yiddish), and a similar term, *schulet,* was used in Bohemia (Czechoslovakia), whereas in Poland it was called *cholent* (eastern Yiddish); the
latter name preserved the designation by which the dish had been
known since the thirteenth century, when first mentioned by Rabbi
Isaac of Vienna (1180–1250), the author of *Or Zarua,* who regarded
himself as a citizen of Bohemia. Here again, in the use of the word
cholent we would stress the continuity between the Polish and the
Austrian and Bohemian rabbinic traditions. The word *schalet* first
appeared in a Yiddish manuscript at the beginning of the fifteenth
century and later in a commentary on the prayer book by Rabbi
Naphtali Hertz printed in Tubingen in Germany in 1560.[26]

The disciples of Rabbi Israel Isserlein (1390–1460) described how
Jews in fifteenth-century Austria brought *cholent* to the bakery on a
Friday afternoon, where it was slowly cooked in an oven until collected
by a maid or a child for the midday meal on the Sabbath. Thus was
initiated a pattern of communal living followed by Jews in western and
eastern Europe until the present century. In the Middle Ages in
western Europe, if people had bread to bake or pies to cook they took
them to the local baker, as no one apart from the largest households
possessed their own ovens. Rabbi Isaac of Vienna, the *Or Zarua,* a
major thirteenth-century authority, permitted the placing of a pot of
food in the coals of an oven sealed with clay before the Sabbath. Here
he was followed by Rabbi Isserles, the *Rema,* the eminent sixteenth-
century Polish authority and the modern *Mishnah Berura.* So, too,
depicting the life of the early German-Jewish settlers in Chicago in the
1840s, Mayer Klein declared that "the families had all brought with
them their old-country piety, and also their *Shabboth* lamps with six
or seven arms, filled with stearic oil, [and] made cotton wicks by
hand . . . of course, [they] had to have a fire woman, *Shabboth goye,*
whenever a light or fire was needed on the Sabbath. They had a
congregational oven to which all who belonged brought their pots and
kettles on Friday afternoon. The oven was heated, the pots placed in,
and the oven doors sealed with clay in order to retain their heat, and
kept closed until Saturday noon, when they came to get them. The
coffee for the Sabbath morning was kept hot on ashes on top of this
oven. At one time I was honoured with an invitation by an acquain-
tance of mine to participate in eating a genuine *Shabboth Kugel*
(pudding)." Here we have a clear example of the rabbinic practice of
sealing the oven doors with clay when cooking *cholent.* According to
the *Kitzur Shulchan Aruch,* "It is desirable that the door of the oven
which is closed with clay should be opened by a non-Jew, or, if a
non-Jew is not present a child should do it, but in the absence of either

it may be done by anyone in a way somewhat different than would be done on ordinary days" (72:20).[27]

However, much cooking in the Early Modern period was cleverly done on the hearth. According to the seventeenth-century German Rabbi Yehiel Mikhel Epstein, "The pots with the hot food [*cholent*] were placed on Friday afternoon on the fire-place and covered with hot ashes mixed with live coals. The ashes kept the food warm till the Sabbath noon meal." Popular pressure in Poland appears to have resulted in a modification of the talmudic practice, as prescribed in the tractate *Shabbat* 34b. Writing of conditions in England in 1738, Abraham Mears declared that "the Jews suffer their Christian servants to kindle fire, by which they warm themselves, and let their victuals and their chocolate, coffee and tea be heated." It is difficult to decide whether this was an aberrant west European practice or one with wider significance akin to that prevailing in the tolerant and easygoing conditions in France in the thirteenth century that was observed by the *Or Zarua* when visiting one of his teachers. Moreover, in certain villages in Alsace at the turn of the century each family possessed an iron furnace lined with bricks, a *Stobche*, which slowly burned charcoal and on which was a metal sheet for keeping the coffee hot for breakfast and the *schalet* warm for lunch.[28]

Although many Ashkenazic communities had the custom of taking *cholent* and the customary pudding, the *kugel*, to a baker on a Friday and collecting it for the Sabbath lunch, there were significant variations in these arrangements between the different communities. In the townlet of Sommerhausen in southern Germany, at eleven o'clock on a Saturday morning the young men and women of the village would gather to collect their parents' pots and exchange harmless banter, while in pre-Second World War Vilna the married women would assemble at the bakery, where they would gossip and criticize the conduct of one another's families, thereby reinforcing the dominant communal social values.[29]

In the immigrant eastern European community living in London's East End at the beginning of the century, the *cholent* and *kugel* were placed in a copper saucepan imported from Russia, over which a white cloth was tied. This was carried by young boys on a Friday afternoon to a bakery, where they were given a metal token with a number, a tag with the same number being attached to the saucepan. After the Sabbath morning service, the young boys would queue for their families' *cholent*, which was extracted from the oven by the baker with a long wooden paddle. "What memories the picture of Grodzinski's baker shop in Fieldgate Street brought back," wrote a Mr. Press to the *Jewish Chronicle*. "As a child I remember my mother and others taking their flour and baking things to bake large cakes and *kichels* at the bakehouse which Mr Grodzinski let them use for a few pence. . . . We had only small gas ovens which could never be used for the baking tins which everybody had in those days because of their large families."[30]

In Holland in the early part of this century the *schalet* pots were stone vessels filled on Friday afternoon with soup, *kugel*, meat, and vegetables, each layer being separated from the next by a plate. "The urns were entrusted to a Christian baker, who kept them in his oven, and they were taken out on a Saturday morning and six or eight such urns were suspended from long poles and carried by bakers' delivery boys to the homes of their owners, where they were usually placed in a bed or some such place to retain their heat." So, too, in eastern Europe an old sack or a worn greatcoat was used to cover the remnants of the Friday-evening repast to keep them warm for the Sabbath. In Germany on a Friday the *schalet* or sliced fruit dumplings (*Schnitzel-Kloese*) were placed on occasions in a hay box (*Kochkiste*) to cook overnight, instead of being taken to the communal bakery.[31]

We can now understand how different social and age groups in various Jewish communities were involved in the transport of the raw and cooked *cholent* and *kugel* dishes, thereby intensifying communal ties; sometimes the social ritual was akin to that of a youth club or a marriage bureau; sometimes the function of this social process was to act as an arbiter of communal values; sometimes, as in Holland and the North African communities, the process entangled Jews and their Christian and Muslim neighbors in a web of reciprocal relationships. Whereas in the Jewish communities in Syria and Morocco the Sabbath food was taken to a Muslim baker to be heated, in southern Germany, Poland, Lithuania, and the immigrant community in England there was a distinctive tradition in which families brought the dishes to a Jewish baker and the communities tended to be more self-sufficient.[32]

In southern Germany in the village of Sommerhausen on the Main, on a Friday afternoon every family brought its pots filled with *Gesetzte* soup and mostly smoked meat to the baker, who placed them in his oven. Across the border the *Gesetztisup* of Alsace Lorraine was a soup of split peas, white beans, sausages, or meat; doubtless the *schalet* of the southern German communities must have been similar to that of the neighboring French Jews. According to George Lang in his book on Hungarian food, the closer the Jews were to Vienna, the fewer beans and the more barley were added to the *solet*, while in Vienna they utilized only barley with goose legs and peas.[33]

In the eastern part of Germany and Austria, *schalet* was made with a fat piece of meat, a marrow bone, white beans, barley, and the stuffed neck of a goose; other vegetables such as turnips, cabbages, and leeks were utilized too. Max Grunwald attributed the use of a leek to the belief in German folklore that it possessed aphrodisiacal qualities and hence was conducive to marital relations on the Sabbath. Heine rhapsodized about a Sabbath meal he had enjoyed in Frankfurt, dwelling on the delights of *schalet,* dumplings, and goose giblets; he composed a warm eulogy extolling the virtues of *schalet* but which contained ironic undertones:

> *Schalet,* ray of light immortal!
> *Schalet,* daughter of Elysium. . .
> For this *Schalet* is the very
> Food of heaven, which, on Sinai,
> God himself instructed Moses
> In the secret of preparing.

In his poem Heine compared *schalet* with "ambrosia," the food of the Greek gods, and concluded that *schalet* was the greater delicacy. Moritz Saphir (1795–1858), who had likewise abandoned Judaism, also commended the virtues of *schalet,* reminding one of the affection felt by the Marranos in Spain for their Sabbath dishes.[34]

A rabbi's wife in pre-Second World War Poland claimed that there were over three hundred recipes for *cholent,* but when asked by the cookery connoisseur De Pomiane for details she had great difficulty remembering even forty of these recipes; yet even so this is a good indication of the range and variation of the *cholent* recipes. In Poland and other parts of eastern Europe the *cholent* consisted of meat, beans, and potatoes cooked with fat until they turned brown and glistened like dates. In the small Lithuanian *shtetl* of Pumpian, Don Gussow recalled that his mother usually made chicken and noodle soup for the Sabbath, but they were a poor family and *cholent* was served only once a month or once every two to three weeks. There was no assistance from Gentile helpers in keeping the food warm as the Sabbath *goy* was unknown in these small towns. Meir Lanksy, who grew up in poverty in an immigrant family on the East Side in New York, declared that depending on the fluctuating family income there would sometimes be a hunk of beef for the Sabbath *cholent,* sometimes a scraggy piece of meat, and on occasions no meat at all. A stuffed chicken neck (*helzel*) was sometimes added to the *cholent,* and it was invariably eaten with a pudding that was placed in the cholent pot and slowly cooked with it for eighteen hours.[35]

Rabbi Joseph Yuspa Hahn (1570–1637), who ended his career in Frankfurt, referred to *matzah schalent, vermicelles schalent,* by which he meant a noodle *cholent* and a *Weck Schalent,* a baked pudding in a round form. All were different types of pudding cooked with the *cholent* and that became known to the Polish Jews under the general name of *kugel*, a Yiddish word derived from the German for ball or sphere. The *Weck Schalent* was the prototype of the *kugel*, *Weck* being the northern and western German dialect word for bread roll; the *Schalet-Kugel* in the 1870s was still made from softened rolls, flour, fat, raisins, some eggs, ground almonds, grated lemon peel, pepper and salt, and syrup. The Polish version was similarly prepared, apart from the absence of syrup or sugar, raisins, and the ground almonds, but all these latter ingredients appeared in a recipe for a sweet *kugel* that was of doubtful authenticity. In southern Germany the *Schalet or Apfelbuwele* (little apple boy), utilized for dessert at the Sabbath, was dough filled with apples, raisins, and cinnamon and rolled to form a number of layers, after which the pastry was twisted into the shape of a circle and baked in a pot. Apple pies, *Apfelkuchen* or *Pasteten*, had been popular in Germany since at least the seventeenth century, after the consumption of meat pies declined; it is easy to see how the German Jews borrowed and adapted this dish from their neighbors, perhaps even developing it out of the medieval Sabbath dish of fried apple and egg. Possibly the apple *Schalet* was the culinary ancestor of the apple charlotte. Further, in a town in Wuerttemburg a *matzah* apple *Schalet* recipe was popular on Passover.[36]

The Polish *kugels*, which were similar to the German *Schalet* recipes, included the traditional *kugel* made with flour and bread crumbs, a *matzah kugel*, a bread *kugel*, a *lokshen* (noodle) *kugel*, a potato *kugel*, and a bread-and-apple *kugel* with the cake and apples arranged in alternate layers. On special occasions in Poland, such as the Sabbath following Passover, a rice *kugel* was prepared, an adoption of German practice, as rice puddings were used as symbols of fertility from the fourteenth century in Germany. According to De Pomiane, the chief characteristic of the *kugel* was the blending of the fat and flour without the addition of water, while elsewhere it has been pointed out that the traditional seventeenth-century boiled pudding was unsweetened. It is interesting to note how the Jewish cuisine of Poland and Lithuania combined the apple pies of southern Germany with some of the puddings of western Germany, such as the *Weck Schalent*, showing how in the course of centuries Jews from both parts of Germany migrated eastward. These puddings stemmed from the Middle Ages, if not earlier; a *matzah cholent* was reported from Austria in the fifteenth century, but the heyday of the German and English puddings seems to have been the seventeenth century, when the Jewish versions in eastern Europe began to proliferate. Despite Mordechai Kosover's suggestion, little was owed to French culinary influence, as the French chefs themselves borrowed English recipes for puddings; and it is doubtful whether the *kugel* was as ancient as the *cholent* dish of which it became an inseparable part.[37]

In fact, the Yiddish term *kugel* was an abbreviation of the original name of *Kugelhopf* and *Gugelhupf*, which were yeast breads found in southwest Germany, Alsace, and Austria and which were baked by housewives on a Sunday when the baker was not working. Once again the recipes of southern Germany had a predominant influence on Polish-Jewish cuisine. Traditionally, these yeast breads were baked in a round form, and raisins were a common ingredient just as in the Jewish *kugel*, while the German version had less-rich ingredients than the Austrian did and was adopted by the Jews for the Sabbath lunch. At some point the shortened Yiddish term *kugel* was substituted in Poland for the German name *Schalet-Kugel*. Hohberg's original German recipe published in 1715 included pieces of roll, eggs, sugar, almonds, and rose water and was more akin to the version the Jews adopted, as it was made without yeast, unlike the Austrian *Gugelhupf*, and was more suitable for the lengthy slow stewing process of *Schalet*.[38]

In Galicia, Austrian Poland, on the Sabbath the Jews partook of a *Galitsyaner Schalet*, consisting of chopped eggs and onions. Rabbi Baruch Bar Isaac of Worms, in a work published in 1202, mentioned that people used to peel onions and that it was a custom on the Sabbath to eat them raw with salt; perhaps this explains the origins of the Galician dish. In the medieval Rhineland communities raw onions and hard-boiled eggs were eaten separately on the Sabbath, but at some point in the Early Modern period when geese and then chickens were more frequently used these ingredients were combined with liver to make the well-known east European dish of chopped liver. In Bohemia from the Middle Ages Jews had crammed geese and Humbold's *Kochbuch* (1581) mentioned the liver of a goose force-fed by Jews that weighed over three pounds that could also be mashed into a purée; no doubt the Jews had similar recipes. The Jews in the Rhineland community of Alsace specialized in the breeding of fat geese, the livers of which they chopped up into a paste and out of which Jean-Pierre Close, the chef of one of Louis XIV's commanders in seventeenth-century France, developed *pâté de foie gras*.[39]

According to one memoir, a Sabbath lunch in Russia consisted of such appetizers as peeled radishes, cucumber, and chopped liver with onions. For the main course a calves' feet jelly (*p'tscha*), *kasha*, soup, and *kugel* were served. Apart from the absence of the main *cholent* dish, the accuracy of this account is confirmed by Mendele Sforim, who described the Sabbath lunch with the following dishes: fish, radishes, *p'tscha*, liver, onions, and eggs. A similar list of dishes was supplied by

Sholom Aleichem, who mentioned radishes, onions, *p'tscha,* and *kugel,* while Mordecai Spector stated that chopped chicken was eaten with onions, and many writers claimed that radishes and onions were consumed with *shmaltz,* chicken or goose fat. When visitors arrived or there was a sudden emergency, neighbors sent dishes for the Sabbath, including different varieties of *kugel.* So tasty was *kugel* considered that a nobleman in the town of Serednik used to dine every Sabbath with the richest Jew in town to savor its delights.[40]

Let us concentrate our attention on calves'-feet jelly, or brawn, which was an interesting medieval dish that was probably adopted by the Jews in Germany, where it was called *Kalbfuss Gallerte.* In eastern Europe the dish was known under a variety of names such as *gallerte foos, cholodnyetz, fisnogen,* and *drelies.* During the Middle Ages in western Europe this meat jelly was called *gele* or *gelatina,* and in Platina's fifteenth-century Italian cookery treatise it was made from sheep's feet, vinegar, white wine, and salt. Lady Montefiore, whose husband's family hailed from the Italian port of Livorno, in her Jewish manual (1846) presented a recipe for calves'-feet jelly, which resembled that of Platina and which contained sugar, lemon juice, white wine, whites of egg, two calves' feet, and lemon peel. This aspic may have been indigenous to western Europe, and the dish was probably invented by the Italians, as in the fourteenth century the non-Jewish merchant of Prato eagerly devoured jellies of pork and veal; from Italy the dish spread into southern Germany and eastern Europe.[41]

A NOTE ON THE FESTIVAL FOOD

On holiday occasions throughout Italy and Germany loaves were baked by Christians in special shapes, such as doves, fish, and Easter eggs; no doubt these baking practices spread into eastern Europe, where the peasantry added decorative symbols to wedding loaves in Poland and Lithuania and similar practices were followed by the Jews for the designs embossed on the New Year *hallah.* At the evening meal on the New Year it was customary to enjoy a plate of glazed carrots, *mern tzimmes,* with the carrots neatly cut into slices and browned in sugar and fat so as to resemble coins. At the same time, a prayer was recited entreating the Almighty to increase the rewards for one's merits. Max Weinreich has rightly pointed out that although the custom of eating sweetened carrots originated in a Gentile milieu, it was adopted by the Jews. The Yiddish word *tzimmes* was derived from the German word *Zummus,* meaning a compote or spicy vegetable concoction. Nonetheless, we know that the *Ménager de Paris,* written about 1392 or 1393, referred to carrots as an expensive novelty sold by the handful for a silver penny, which is an indication that the dish with carrots must have evolved a century or two later in Germany. According to Rabbi David Oppenheim, who died in Prague in 1736, and Rabbi Abraham Danzig, who studied in Prague and died in Vilna in 1820, it was a custom among Jews to partake of a dish of turnips or carrots during the New Year. The German word for turnip, *Rube,* was punned with the Hebrew term for increase, *ribbuy,* just as the Yiddish word for carrots, *mern,* was punned with the Yiddish verb, *mern,* meaning to multiply. In Jewish folklore carrots were associated with gold, a symbol of good fortune, and were regarded as a token of prosperity for the forthcoming year. Because the custom of eating sweetened carrots was unknown among the Polish peasantry, it was likely that this practice was originally acquired by the Jews in Germany in the late Middle Ages and carried by them into Poland.[42]

Jews, who operated small dairy farms in Lithuania, used to leave the farms in the hands of non-Jewish neighbors and travel to nearby cities for the High Holidays. So, too, it was the custom in Swislocz for many of these boorish rural types, *yishuvniks,* to bring cakes and sweetmeats to the synagogue on the eve of the Day of Atonement to distribute to fellow congregants before the fast. No one refused these gifts, for by tasting them one was already fulfilling one of the worst destinies that could be allotted, namely that of becoming a beggar.[43]

We shall recall that at the start of the winter, cabbages were pickled in barrels. Hence it was customary to eat sweet-and-sour cabbage stuffed with minced meat in Poland and Russia, particularly on Tabernacles. The dish was known as *holoptsches,* but also as *holipce* and *geluptzes,* all variants of the word for little pigeon in Russian, and in addition called by the distinctive name *praakes.* Asher Barash recounted how the *hasidim* in Galicia on the Day of the Rejoicing of the Law "went from house to house to taste of the pottage of sweet cabbage cooked with fat and raisins and, especially, the stuffed cabbage fried in honey. In houses where there was wine, they drank wine; where there was beer, they drank beer; and in the houses of the poor they contented themselves with a little spirits—pure or diluted with water." Yehuda Elzet also suggested that the dish was designed for *Simchat Torah* and speculated that the cabbage was chosen as an antiaphrodisiac. On the other hand, an informant from Lithuania declared that *golubtsy* was relished throughout the winter months. His mother soaked the cabbage in water to soften it and stuffed it with meat and pieces of black bread, adding spices and fat. Doubtless these dishes were related to the stuffed vine leaves and vegetables of the Middle East, known as *dolmeh* to the Persians, *dolmathes* to the Greeks, and *mahshi* to the Arabs, and were probably descended from ancient Persian court cuisine.

While it has been claimed that the Tartars introduced stuffed cabbage into northern Russia in the fourteenth century, it was already a well-established dish in Hungary prior to the Turkish invasion of the sixteenth century.[44]

During the Middle Ages, the Jews in the Rhineland provinces developed specialist skills in the breeding and fattening of geese to provide food, and above all, fat for essential cooking purposes in the winter months, especially the Hanukkah and Purim pastries. Goose fat was particularly important as a cooking medium in northern and eastern Europe, as the modern substitutes, margarine and vegetable oil, were not available until the present century, while non-Jews depended on the pig for lard. Traditionally, the Jews ate a goose at Hanukkah and the Christians a goose at Christmas, but during the last couple of hundred years a turkey has been substituted for the goose at Christmas, and the goose has disappeared from the Hanukkah table. A responsa of the famous thirteenth-century sage Rabbi Meir of Rothenburg mentioned coarse bread baked especially for the fattening of geese. Hanz Wilhelm Kirchof wrote in 1562 that "they say that the Jews have good and fat geese . . , and further they love the liver of the goose"; and earlier the Maharil, the fourteenth-century rabbinic authority from the Rhineland town of Worms, referred to the well-browned and roasted bits of goose skin, the *gribenes* or *grieven* from the German word *Griebe* for the remains of melted fat, which were regarded as a great delicacy. The Taz, Rabbi David Halevi (c. 1586–1667), claimed that those whom the community wished to honor were given pieces of fried goose cracklings and for long afterward they were regarded as a special treat, so much so that individuals kept their own jars of *grieven*. Rabbi Isserles, the great sixteenth-century rabbinic authority, took a lenient view as regards the forced feeding of geese, but certain pious persons refrained from eating or breeding such geese because of the unnecessary suffering inflicted. A volume published in Paris in 1881 praised the arcane and exclusive knowledge of the Jews of Metz and Strasbourg in the fattening of geese; we have seen how the recipe for *pâté de foie gras* developed from the goose livers provided by the Jews in the seventeenth century.[45]

In Germany on New Year's Eve, the thirty-first day of December, the Christian population were accustomed to consuming deep-fried pastries, while in Berlin jelly doughnuts (*Berliner Pfannkuchen*) were eaten. Having adopted this culinary tradition for the festival of Hanukkah, which usually occurred at the onset of winter, German Jews ate apricot-filled glazed doughnuts on Hanukkah, giving rise to similar customs in Poland and Israel. In Poland the Jews on Hanukkah enjoyed doughnuts fried in oil (*Paczki*) or pancakes (*Placki*) made from potato flour, which were again fried in oil. Of course, the Jews associated the frying of special foods in fat or oil with the miracle of the oil on Hanukkah. The German-Jewish immigrants to Israel, many of whom arrived in the 1930s, encouraged the rest of the population to enjoy munching jelly doughnuts (*sufganiyot*) on Hanukkah, the new Hebrew word *sufganiya* being derived from the Greek for sponge, *spongos*. Although Jews in Lithuania ate pancakes (*latkes*) made from potato flour on Hanukkah, having borrowed this culinary invention *Kartoflani platske* from the Ukrainians and other east European peoples, many Jews in these areas were accustomed to eating buckwheat *latkes* instead. The Yiddish author Mendele Sforim mentioned that *milkhic vareniki* were popular at Hanukkah, while Joachim Schoenfeld claimed that cracklings, *grieven*, were used at Hanukkah in Galicia to make *fleyshik vareniki*, defined as dough cooked and stuffed with mashed potatoes, fried onions, and goose cracklings.[46]

On Purim the Jews in eastern Europe prepared *Hamantashen*, three-cornered cakes filled with poppy seeds, a pastry of German origin. The name was derived from *Mohn* (poppy seed) and *Taschen*, pockets, which over the years was changed to *Hamantashen* because of the association of the food with Purim. In Bessarabia *Hamantashen* were alternatively filled with plums. In eastern Europe these baked goods were eaten in the evening and the next day for breakfast, while the noon meal consisted of soup and *kreplekh*, triangular pockets of dough filled with chopped meat. In Poland in the seventeenth century, as in the Jewish community in Prague, they kneaded the dough for the *kreplekh* with honey and spices, filling them with fruit or preserves; Rabbi Joel Sirkes (c. 1561–1640) added that people kneaded the *kreplekh* with goose fat and filled them with raisins and nuts. From ancient times nuts were a symbol of fertility. It is interesting to note how *kreplekh* changed from being filled with fruit and nuts in the seventeenth century to being filled with a meat mixture in the modern period, when the consumption of meat in Europe dramatically increased. Even so, in Galicia at the beginning of the century *Hamantashen* were still sometimes filled with nuts and honey. Just as the Gentiles in Germany and elsewhere consumed a variety of deep-fried pastries and pancakes (crêpes = *kreplekh*) on Shrove Tuesday, the Jews of eastern Europe ate *bubliki*, rings of choux pastry baked in oil or butter and sprinkled with poppy seed, and *rosalach*, thin cakes fried in oil on Purim. Whereas the Passover gift-exchange network comprised a system that tied the local Jewish community to their Gentile neighbors and customers, the Purim gift exchange of plates of delicacies tended on the whole to be confined to the Jewish community and led to a scrupulous reevaluation every year of each family's place in the local social hierarchy. Nonetheless, Rabbi Meir of Rothenburg held in the thirteenth century that "in a new town it is forbidden to introduce the custom of giving presents to Gentile servants on Purim . . .

However, in places where the custom has already been well rooted, it should not be discontinued lest it disturb peaceful relations with the Gentile neighbours." The custom still held sway in Germany in this century.[47]

In the past the Jewish communities in the Middle East and eastern Europe spent a long period of time making themselves ready for Passover. In Baghdad, "they began many months in advance, with the making of wine, *silan, matzot,* the pickling of vegetables and so on," while in Syria the Jews scrutinized their rice by spreading it on a white tablecloth to ensure that it had not become mixed with specks of wheat, after which it was packed into bags for Passover. In eastern Europe Jewish women started to prepare goose and chicken fat for Passover during December, often at the time of the festival of Hanukkah. After the fat had been fried and strained, it was poured into glazed earthenware jars for the festival, although some of it was offered for sale. After Purim most householders cleaned barrels with water, and red-hot stones were placed in them so as to scour them completely; then the beetroots were set to turn sour for the Passover *borscht,* while relatives and poor neighbors were offered brine to pickle their own beetroots and quantities of potatoes were prepared for the festival. Wheat flour was then purchased by individual families or, later, dealers for the baking of *matzah,* which commenced in earnest after Purim in bakeries that were hastily set up for this purpose, it being reckoned that ten pounds of wheat flour was sufficient to provide enough *matzah* for an individual during the festival. The richer customers tipped the workers in the bakery so as to secure thin and tasty *matzot,* which in the past were almost invariably round in shape. The men in the household then crushed some of the *matzah* with the aid of a special wooden mortar to make *matzah* meal and larger crumbs, or *farfel.* It was then customary for the Jews in central and eastern Europe on Passover to make their own raisin wine, which was yellowish-brown in color, despite the fact that there was no halachic basis for this. Probably the custom grew out of the rabbinic prohibition against using red wine on Passover, partly because of the association of such wine with blood, partly because this was the time of the year when ritual murder accusations were rife. The seventeenth-century Polish rabbi David Halevi declared that "nowadays we avoid the consumption of red wine because of false accusations [spread against us] on account of our numerous sins." Many families also made the ancient drink of mead by boiling hops in a pot, after which sugar and honey were added to the resulting mixture; the fermentation process was activated in an ingenious way, by dipping a length of coarse string into the white of an egg and inserting the string into the brew. *Haroset* (the Passover sauce) was made and distributed by wine dealers, rabbis, and wealthy members of the community, as it was too expensive for most householders to prepare. At the *Seder* in eastern Europe, instead of using lettuce for the bitter herbs, leaves of cabbage were dipped into the *haroset.*[48]

Prior to the First World War, *matzah* production in the United States was aimed at an exclusively Jewish market solely for the Passover festival; it was only in 1918 that a leading American firm, Horowitz Brothers, began producing *matzah* all the year round and tried attracting Gentile customers. At about the same time items such as tea and coffee were packaged in containers to which labels were added showing that these products were kosher for Passover, but this was a system that was easy to abuse, and from 1925 Horowitz Brothers started to package products in special containers under religious supervision. Square *matzahs,* later called American style *matzahs,* were first manufactured by machine in Austria around 1857, but as late as 1912 they were still not manufactured in London and had to be imported from the Continent. In the post-Second World War period in the United States rabbinical supervision was extended to the production of gefilte fish, *borscht,* and wine, as well as foods such as milk, coffee, salt, vegetable fat, frozen vegetables, and chocolate. By the 1980s in the United States, despite the limited market, large companies were willing to incur higher-than-normal production costs, amounting to $300,000 for Pepsi Cola in 1986 to take care of the Passover needs of their Jewish customers, to retain their regular customers throughout the year.[49]

In Russia in the late nineteenth century, milk supplies were in abundance in the summer in the dairy regions of the north and near the capital; we can appreciate how dairy pastries of Russian origin, *blini, knyshi,* and the *babka* were adapted by Jews for consumption on Shavuot (Pentecost), when there was a glut of milk. For Shavuot a big yellow *hallah* was baked that was glazed with saffron, just as a very large braided *hallah,* known as a *kitke* or *koyletsh,* which was decorated with raisins, adorned the table for the Purim banquet. According to Sholom Aleichem, for the main meal of the day of Shavuot a *milchic* feast was prepared consisting of a fish fried in butter, the fish being a potent symbol of leviathan and the luxurious fare awaiting the righteous at the messianic banquet, a message repeated in the special prayer recited on the festival, the *Akdamot millin.* Similarly, at the Purim banquet at Swislocz there was on the table a huge baked fish touched up with saffron, again a symbol of the feast of the righteous in the world to come, and in the center of the table were three plates of boiled chick-peas to commemorate the fact that Queen Esther lived in the palace on a vegetarian diet of beans and peas to observe the dietary laws, but the beans of Purim were also a symbol of fertility and resurrection.[50]

To return to Shavuot, a large variety of dairy foods were consumed on this festival because of the glut of milk in Europe and the Mediterranean at this time of the year: cheese *blintzes, kreplekh,* milk and *lokshen.* A variant of this meal was a *borscht* prepared with onions and *botvinya,* the green leafy parts of the beetroots that the Russians cooked, to which was added *smetana,* sour cream. Other dairy foods eaten at this time of the year were *knishes, blintzes* (buckwheat pancakes), and *khremzlekh* with cheese and butter, while Mendele Mokher Sforim mentioned fig cakes as well. *Knishes* were described by one rabbinic writer as being pastries filled with cheese, with cracklings (*gribenes*), with onions, or with cabbage, and sometimes with fruit, honey, and sugar; after this, they were baked. Sholom Aleichem suggested that *kneidlech* (dumplings), *latkes* (pancakes), *blintzes,* and an obscure type of pastry known as *palirtchkes* (perhaps *palatchinkin,* a variant of the *blintz*), all were enjoyed on Shavuot, probably in the Ukraine from where the author hailed. Joachim Schoenfeld referred to butter on *babkas* (soufflés), *blintzes* with cheese, sour cream, cheesecake, and fish as being foods eaten in Galicia on Shavuot. Mark Zborowski and Elizabeth Herzog, in their overall survey of the *shtetl* in eastern Europe, spoke of *blintzes, kreplekh* with cheese, cheese *strudel* with raisins and cinnamon, pot cheese, and sour cream as being among the culinary delights of the festival.[51]

CONCLUSION

During the biblical age, the Jews had a somewhat monotonous diet that included large quantities of parched corn, porridge, and bread eaten with vinegar, salt, oil, and wild bitter herbs to assist the digestive process. Although we have some knowledge of the daily diet and the festival food in the biblical age, we cannot reconstruct the total cuisine as we can for the talmudic age. In the latter period in Palestine the Jews followed the Graeco-Roman patterns both in their table manners, their vocabulary, in their choice of the daily bread, such as the *panis cibarius*, and in their addiction to *garum*, the fish sauce, which was available in a number of different guises. We have also seen how the *Seder* service at Passover was transformed from the shared Paschal sacrificial feast into a Graeco-Roman banquet or symposium. Obviously, the assimilated upper-class Jewish elite must have been attached to the same mores as the Romans were and must have had a belief in similar symbols, but the question to be asked is whether or not the Jewish masses, who shared the same mundane foods as the dominant imperial power, were equally moved by the same symbols as were the Romans. In certain of the Jewish ceremonies associated with wine there were messianic undertones and hints of a future life, but it is not clear whether this merely included the cup held at grace after meals or extended to the *Kiddush* itself, as Erwin Goodenough believed; the fish course, which was de rigueur on a Friday night, had definite messianic and eschatological connotations. Recently, archaeologists in the town of Sepphoris in Lower Galilee, which had a large Jewish population, have uncovered more mosaic floors with themes similar to the Beit Leontis mosaics. This shows how exposed the Jewish population was to the general eschatological beliefs of the Graeco-Roman world, while these beliefs in turn permeated Jewish rituals concerned with food. Further, the Talmud contains the first references to a number of important foods that appeared in medieval Arab cookery books some six hundred or more years later.

We discern considerable differences in the diet of the Ashkenazim in medieval Germany, England, France, and Italy on the one hand, and the Sephardim in medieval Spain with its Islamic inheritance on the other. Spain was a land of rice, pasta in a variety of shapes and sizes, olive oil, *sanbusaks,* and *ka'aks.* We now turn to the preeminent Jewish foods of the Middle Ages, *cholent* and *hallah.* We have established the evolution of the precursor of *cholent, harisa,* in the Islamic Middle Ages and have demonstrated how the dish migrated to North Africa and to Spain. From the latter country it emerged in France as *frumenty* and was either adopted or adapted by the German Jews, who had studied in France, in their perfection of *cholent.* Whereas *harisa* in the Middle East, North Africa, and Spain was a meat dish prepared with wheat, as it was in France in the dish known as *frumenty, cholent* in central and eastern Europe was a meat dish made with barley and later with potatoes. Nonetheless, there were many variants of the *harisa* and *cholent* dishes in the Middle East, North Africa, and Spain, depending on local cooking styles and recipes, the ingredients that were readily available, and the changing-world meat-consumption patterns over the centuries; perhaps this explains how early twentieth-century North African *harisa* was a meatless dish. In a similar fashion east European Jewish *cholent* differed from the *schalet* of the German Jews. In the modern age during the kosher meat boycott in 1902 in New York, women enforced the boycott by removing meat from the *cholent* pots of their neighbors who were visiting the local bakery.[1]

Hallah was adapted by the Jews in Austria and southern Germany in the latter Middle Ages, probably in the fifteenth century, from the Sunday loaf of their Gentile neighbors, although it may have been a century or two later when plaited loaves of bread became popular among the Jewish community. However, the special loaf of bread on the Sabbath was virtually unknown to the Middle Eastern and Spanish Jews. We conclude that neither the dish of *cholent* or *hamin,* nor the special Sabbath loaf, *hallah,* had come into use in the talmudic era or in the early Middle Ages. So, too, new evidence from medieval Spain and English culinary history makes it likely that R. Judah ben Kalonymos was already consuming a dish of real pasta on Friday night in the twelfth century.

We shall briefly summarize the further development of the Dietary Laws in the Middle Ages. Maimonides fixed a time limit of six hours for partaking of milky foods after consuming meat, which corresponded to the time interval between the morning and evening meals, the only two meals then eaten. However, the Tosafists, the medieval French commentators, held that it was sufficient to terminate the meat meal and recite grace, which gave rise to the custom of waiting for a shorter period of one hour. Rabbi Isserles, the Rema, wrote that in sixteenth-century Poland, the custom was to wait for one hour, although he considered this wrong. In Germany Rabbi Joseph Hahn (died 1637) wrote that "at large banquets it was the practice to eat cheese . . . after meat, which was called a lesser meal . . . [dessert]." Moreover, whereas the use of Gentile bread and butter was particularly widespread in western Europe, medieval Jews attached more importance to eating kosher cheese, although even here the French Jews were not strict, and there were individuals in Spain and Turkey who challenged these norms.[2]

We tried to present the respective dishes of the Spanish and east European Jews as total cuisines and not just as an odd assortment of unrelated foods, and we further tried to show how the range of dishes among the Sephardim was a fusion of the cooking styles of southern Spain and Turkey, and how the east European cuisine evolved in the late Middle Ages in southern Germany and Austria before spreading into Poland and Lithuania. Both these communities successfully preserved their distinctive cuisines for generation after generation; this leads inevitably to the question of how much of the cuisine of the Jews of the talmudic age and the Middle Ages has been preserved. For the talmudic era, the answers are the Friday-night fish dish, the *Kiddush* over wine, and the *Seder* service and some of its associated foods, such as *haroset,* and the ancient Jewish magical ceremony to assist adult memory retention called "Prince of the *Torah,*" which was brought by Jews from ancient Palestine into Italy and thence into France, culminating in the medieval ceremony of the child licking honey off his slate when he first attended *heder* to learn the *Torah.* For the Middle Ages, *cholent* and *hallah* are the answers, although few traces of the Friday-night pie, the *pastide,* remain, even if it still seems to be popular among the Sephardim.[3]

Moreover, when the Jews migrated from Poland and Lithuania and from other parts of eastern Europe from the 1880s, the cuisines of the migrants evolved differently in Britain, the United States, and South Africa. For instance, *knishes,* which were a pocket food of Russian origin, never achieved the degree of popularity in Britain that they attained in the United States. On the other hand, *teiglach,* which were small pastries steeped in honey and poppy seed, and *ingberlach,* which were made from grated carrots, ginger, and sugar, were preserved by South African Jews, even though these traditional pastries have almost been forgotten in Britain.[4]

Throughout this study we have tried to examine both the daily fare of the Jewish masses in different historical periods and to focus on the special Sabbath and festival foods. One Jewish Sabbath food to which we have devoted too little attention was chicken soup, which was endorsed by Maimonides and beloved by Middle Eastern Jewry from medieval times onward and by Ashkenazim a few centuries later; its service as a staple course of the meal before the fast of the Day of Atonement was widespread both in the East and the West; its history and multifarious recipes merit further research. Nor have we had the opportunity to discuss in detail the frugal fare of the Jews during famines, and we have omitted any mention of the starvation diets of the Jews in the concentration camps and occupied Europe. Even in the Warsaw Ghetto doctors made a meticulous scientific study of which ailments were most commonly associated with hunger disease and how the body reacted to prolonged starvation. Despite the fact Jews had an outstanding role as transmitters of new foods, such as oranges, chocolate, coffee, sugar, pita bread, and the bagel across national barriers and civilizations, much of this history remains to be unravelled.[5]

If the starvation diets of the concentration camps are sadly part of the agenda of Jewish food history, so too are the more joyful topics such as the different versions of the Passover *Seder*, a few of which we have caught a glimpse. Much research remains to be undertaken on the creative Jewish contributions to and adaptations and borrowings of the foods of their neighbors, particularly for celebrating the yearly cycle of festivals; but the interchange of culinary innovation was rarely in one direction or was discontinuous, and the tension often resulted in a creative symbiosis for two civilizations.

To some scholars authentic Jewish foods are very few in number, most of the typical Jewish dishes having been borrowed from neighbors in the countries to which Jews migrated. I would not agree with this minimalist viewpoint and instead would assert that the definition as to what constitutes Jewish food requires a formulation along the following lines: dishes that the Jews have utilized for their Sabbath and festival tables over the course of centuries have been thoroughly assimilated into Jewish cuisine; the recipes for preparing them have been subtly altered; and in the words of Stephen Stern, special "kinds and combinations of ingredients" have been selected for their preparation. In addition, only kosher oil and fat were used in the cooking process. All these factors contributed toward imparting a distinctive flavor to the dishes, and in the course of time these dishes, whatever their source of origin, have become authentic Jewish foods.[6]

Take the example of Spanish-Jewish cuisine: transplanted in part to Turkey, it had access to a wider range of fruit and vegetables and grains than that of the Ashkenazim in eastern Europe; it favored the employment of olive and sesame oil as a cooking medium, unlike that of the Ashkenazim, which relied on goose fat and butter; it prepared its dishes in a unique fashion with different ingredients quite unlike the cooking of its Turkish and other neighbors, so that vine leaves, *yaprak*, were made without beans, or lentils were added to a beef stew with onions instead of being made into a lentil soup. One essential feature of Sephardic cooking was to add tomato juice and onion to many dishes. Although the Sephardic cuisine had certain affinities to the cooking of other Mediterranean lands, the *bizcocho*, biscuit, and the *migina*, pie, were regarded by its adherents as special features of Sephardic baking. Again, there was a different rhythm in the Ashkenazic and Sephardic life-styles, and the Sephardim in the Mediterranean lands found their balmier climate more conducive to entertaining family and other guests.[7]

Claudia Roden has declared that what is typically a Jewish dish is that something which evokes a life, a community with its vibrant values and customs. She recounted that when she was a student in Paris, she and relatives adhered to a ritual in which they ate *ful medames,* Egyptian brown beans, every Sunday to conjure up memories of her hometown of Cairo, but we would suggest that this would not qualify as a Jewish dish because it had not become part of the Sabbath and festival cuisine. Yet a limited number of everyday foods such as the herring in eastern Europe and the despised eggplant or aubergine in Italy and *mulukhiya,* dubbed as a Jewish vegetable by Maimonides, which could be made into a thick soup beloved by the Egyptian peasantry—all these common foods could possibly be thought of as Jewish.[8]

In the past, there has been much research concentration on the folktales, folk songs, and customs of the Jews, but little attempt has been made to collect and map the regional variations in the cuisine of the Jews by observing it firsthand. Claudia Roden has pointed out the importance of undertaking this research in areas such as Turkey and Morocco, with their aging and dwindling communities.

Sydney Stahl Weinberg has stated that in the United States the synagogue, in contrast to eastern Europe, ceased to have a central role in Jewish life and that the generation of immigrant Jewish mothers' preservation of the Sabbath and festival rituals, chiefly through the traditional dishes that they prepared, fulfilled an important function by transmitting the Jewish heritage and sense of identity to their children. While assimilation resulted in the jettisoning of Jewish religious beliefs and values, the glowing memories of their mothers' cooking was the last Jewish vestige to be retained by the most assimilated persons of Jewish origin, such as the Marranos and the upper bourgeoisie in the Austro-Hungarian Empire. Food, on the other hand, was also the easiest point of entry into a culture. Moreover, food enjoyed at Sabbath and festival meals not only fostered the emotional closeness of members of the family but the simultaneous serving of the same prescribed festival dishes combined with the recitation of the authorized prayers at each family gathering promoted community bonding and solidarity. Food rekindled the unconscious memory of the primary contact with mother. Also, it could evoke a wider range of Proustian memories, retrieving and encapsulating family warmth, communal harmony, and shared religious values.

APPENDIX

The earliest extant Jewish recipes from the *Kitab al-tabih fi-l-Maghrib wa-al-Andalus fi 'asr al-Muwahhidin* (the *Cookery Book on North Africa and Andalusia in the time of the Almohades*), a thirteenth-century compilation by an anonymous author. Translated from the French of Professor Lucie Bolens and reproduced with her permission.

JEWISH RECIPE FOR HIDDEN STUFFING

Chop the meat, cutting it into little rounds. Take care that there are no more bones. Put it in a pot and pour in all the spices, except cumin, four spoonfuls of oil, some strong rose water, a little onion juice, and some salt. Cover it with a thick cloth. Put it on a moderate fire and watch the cooking with attention. The meat must be chopped as for making meatballs and well flavored. Make also all small balls and leave them to cook in the same way. When this is done, put in five beaten eggs, some salt, some pepper, some cinnamon; make a thin paste that you place in a frying pan. Do the same, if necessary, with five beaten eggs. Then take a new soup pot, put in a spoonful of oil, and let it simmer a little. At the bottom place one of the pastes; turn it over on the plate and cover with the second paste. Then beat three eggs with a little white flour, pepper, cinnamon, a little rose water, and put the rest of the minced meat on the side of the pot. Heat it gently until it is well roasted, paying attention that nothing burns. Afterward break the pot and place the entire dish on a plate. Cover it with some sprigs of mint, some pistachios, some pine nuts, and some sweet-smelling seasonings. Put in everything that has been indicated, remove the rose water, replace it with a spoonful of the juice of minced coriander and half a spoon of strong garum. Make this liquid like the other, God willing.

JEWISH PARTRIDGE [DISH]

Wash the partridge and salt it. Beat the entrails thoroughly with almonds and pine nuts and add to this mixture some macerated garum, some oil, a little coriander juice, some pepper, some cinnamon, Chinese cinnamon, spikenard, five eggs, and what remains of the meat. Cook two eggs and fill them with the stuffing. Cover them with the cooked eggs. The mince is put between the skin and the flesh and a little also into the partridge. Take another pan and pour into it four spoonfuls of oil, half a [spoonful] of shortened brine, and two of salt. Put the partridge there and place it on the fire, after having reinforced the lid with paste and having stirred it until it becomes even, which reduces the sauce. Lift the lid and pour in half a spoonful of vinegar, some slices of citron, and some mint, and add two or three eggs; put it above a saucepan of clay and a copper full of red embers until it has been roasted golden. Afterward turn it around until both sides are brown all over. Put it in a dish and arrange the mince all around and garnish [it] with the yolks of egg that have cooked with the mincemeat. Sprinkle with some pepper and cinnamon, then sugar, and serve, God willing.

DISH OF CHICKEN, A JEWISH RECIPE

Wash the chicken and remove the entrails. Cut the ends of the legs, ribs, and rump. Salt it and set it aside. Put the ends, the rump, and the giblets into a pot with selected spices and all the condiments: juice of green coriander and onion, whole pine nuts, a little vinegar and garum, some good oil, some citron leaves, and two sprigs of fennel. Place the pot on a moderate fire. When it is cooked enough and the major part of the sauce has been reduced, thicken it with three eggs, soft bread-crumbs from the inside of a loaf of bread, and fine flour. Mince the liver, place it in a pastry case, and roast it little by little until the liver and the pastry become firm. Then take a chicken, fry it, and break and beat two eggs over it. With oil and garum, baste it inside and outside. Next take a second pot and, with two spoonfuls of oil and a half [a spoon] of garum, one and a half of vinegar, and two of rose water, some juice of onion, spikenard, and condiments, put the chicken on the fire and simmer it. When it is cooked, allow the flavors to moisten it. Turn it next into another pot and garnish it with the yolks of egg. Sprinkle it with well-chosen spices and present the two dishes, God willing.

JEWISH CHICKEN RECIPE

Clean a chicken. Mince the offal with almonds and soft breadcrumbs, some flour, some salt, some fennel, some pounded coriander. Add six beaten eggs and four measures of water. Put the chicken on the fire in a clean pot with five spoonfuls of soft oil, and do not cease stirring until it is roasted all over evenly. Then mix it with the prepared stuffing so that the sauce is thickened and well seasoned. Pour the stuffing all around, garnish with some sprigs of fennel and rue, some sprigs of mint, some ground almonds, and you are able to present [it], God willing.

NOTES

INTRODUCTION

1. Dov Noy, "Dr. Max Grunwald: The Founder of Jewish Folkloristics," in Max Grunwald, *Tales, Songs, and Folkways of Sephardic Jews*, ed. Dov Noy (Jerusalem: Magnes Press, 1982), pp. ix–xiv.

2. Isaac Goss, "Rabbi J. L. Avida (Zlotnik)—An Assessment and a Tribute," in *Gleanings: Reflections on Judaism and Jewish Education* (Johannesburg: Kayor Publications, n.d.), pp. 80–85.

3. Barbara Kirschenblatt-Gimblett, "The Kosher Gourmet in the Nineteenth Century Kitchen: Three Jewish Cookbooks in Historical Perspective," *The Journal of Gastronomy* 2:4 (Winter 1986/1987): 51–89. Barbara Kirshenblatt-Gimblett, "Recipes for Creating Community: The Jewish Charity Cookbook in America, and Jewish Charity Cookbooks in the United States and Canada: A Bibliography of 201 Recent Publications," *Jewish Folklore and Ethnology Review* 9:1 (1987): 8–18. Barbara Kirshenblatt-Gimblett, "An Early Jewish Cookbook from the Antipodes," *Petits Propos Culinaires* 28 (April 1988): 11–21. *Aunt Babette's Cook Book* (Cincinnati: Bloch Publishing, 1889), pp. 323–325, Purim *Krapfen*. John M. Shaftesley, "Culinary Aspects of Anglo-Jewry," in *Studies in the Cultural Life of the Jews in England*, ed. Dov Noy and Isaachar Ben-Ami (Jerusalem: Magnes Press, 1975), pp. 367–399.

4. Hannah Glasse, *The Art of Cookery Made Plain* (Edinburgh, 1781), pp. 391, 392, 396, 420, 443.

5. Joëlle Bahloul, *Le Culte de la Table Dressée: Rites et traditions de la table juive algérienne* (Paris: Editions A. M. Métailié, 1983).

CHAPTER 1

1. William J. Darby, Paul Ghalioungui, and Louis Grivetti, *Food: The Gift of Osiris*, 2 vols. (London: Academic Press, 1977). See especially the preface to vol. 1, p. ix (hereafter cited as *Food: The Gift of Osiris*).

2. Henri Limet, "The Cuisine of Ancient Sumer," *Biblical Archaeologist* (September 1987): 132–147 (hereafter cited as Limet). Jean Bottéro, "The Cuisine of Ancient Mesopotamia," *Biblical Archaeologist* (March 1985): 36–47

(hereafter cited as Bottéro). A. Leo Oppenheim, *Ancient Mesopotamia: Portrait of a Dead Civilization* (Chicago: University of Chicago Press, 1964), p. 44 (hereafter cited as Leo Oppenheim).

3. Limet, p. 140. Bottéro, p. 46. Leo Oppenheim, p. 44.

4. R. J. Forbes, *Studies in Ancient Technology*, vol. 3 (Leiden: E. J. Brill, 1965), pp. 86–109. *The Times of London*, June 3, 1983, "Romans' diet provides food for thought."

5. Jacob Sapir, *Even Sapir* (Lyck ed., 1857; reprinted in Israel 1967), p. 58a. Naomi and Shimon Tzabar, *Yemenite and Sabra Cookery* (Tel Aviv: Sadan Publishing, 1979), pp. 11–12. Erich Brauer, *Ethnologie der Jemenitischen Juden* (Heidelberg: Carl Winters Universitat-Buchandlung, 1934), p. 105. Sidney W. Mintz, *Sweetness and Power* (Harmondsworth: Penguin Books, 1986), p. 10 (hereafter cited as Mintz).

6. Mintz, interview with Dr. Isaac Gottlieb, November 13, 1986, pp. 10–11.

7. However, a series of eleven excavations of sites from ancient Israel revealed a preponderance of sheep to goats by a ratio of 7:3. Nonetheless, it may be possible to reconcile this conflict of evidence, by suggesting that when Israelite society was more nomadic in the early stages of settlement the keeping of goats was more common and that the number of sheep increased when a more intensive form of agriculture was practiced. Magen Broshi, "The Diet of Palestine in the Roman Period—Introductory Notes," *The Israel Museum Journal* 5 (1986): 48. *Biblical Archaeology*, ed. Shalom M. Paul and William G. Dever (Jerusalem: Keter Publishing House, 1973), p. 220 (hereafter cited as *Biblical Archaeology*). Menahem Haran, "Seething a Kid in Its Mother's Milk," *Journal of Jewish Studies* 30: (Spring 1979): 32–33. E. W. Heaton, *Everyday Life in Old Testament Times* (London: B. T. Batsford, 1957), pp. 51–85.

8. Louis Rabinowitz, "Tora and Flora," *The Jerusalem Post International Edition*, March 27–April 2, 1983. Louis Rabinowitz, "Tora and Flora," *The Jerusalem Post*, August 28, 1981. Jack Goody, *Cooking, Cuisine and Class: A Study in Comparative Sociology* (Cambridge: Cambridge University Press, 1982), pp. 93, 145.

9. Michael Zohary, *Plants of the Bible* (Cambridge: Cambridge University Press, 1982), pp. 25, 74–76, 88 (hereafter cited as Zohary). Yehuda Feliks, *Nature and Man in the Bible* (London: Soncino Press, 1981), pp. 92–93 (hereafter cited as Feliks). *Encyclopaedia Judaica* (Jerusalem: Keter Publishing House, 1978), articles on barley and wheat. *Biblical Archaeology*, pp. 50–51. *The Jerusalem Post International Edition*, November 27–December 3, 1983. Report on an excavation of a fortress in Lower Galilee from the tenth century B.C.E.

10. Claude Lévi-Strauss, "The Culinary Triangle," *New Society*, December 22, 1966. R. Hubbard and A. al-Azim in *Journal of Archaeological Science* 17 (1991): 103–106. Oded Schwartz, *In Search of Plenty* (London: Kyle Kathie, 1992), pp. 25, 26, 273.

11. Fernand Braudel, *The Mediterranean and the Mediterranean World in the Age of Philip II*, vol. 1 (London: Fontana Collins, 1975), p. 242. Israel Abrahams, "The shape of *matzoth*," in *The Book of Delight and Other Papers* (Philadelphia: Jewish Publication Society of America, 1912), pp. 314–315. Naum Jasny, "Daily Bread of the Ancient Greeks and Romans," *Osiris* 9 (1950): 229–230 (hereafter cited as Jasny).

12. *Jewish Encyclopedia* (New York: Funk and Wagnalls Company, 1925), article on baking. *Encyclopaedia Judaica*, articles on cooking and baking and food. Hannah Trager, *Pioneers in Palestine* (London: G. Routledge & Sons, 1923), p. 17. Limet, p. 147. Eveline J. van der Steen, "Fiery Furnaces: Bread Ovens in the Ancient Near East," *Petits Propos Culinaires* 42 (December 1992): 45–52.

13. Leo Oppenheim, p. 315. Alexis Soyer, *The Pantropheon or a History of Food and Its Preparation in Ancient Times* (London: The Paddington Press, 1977), p. 31. Jasny, p. 249.

14. *Chicago Assyrian Dictionary: Massartu* (Chicago: The Oriental Institute of Chicago, 1966–1989). Jasny, p. 247.

15. Bottéro, p. 38. *Jewish Encyclopedia*, article on bread. Limet, p. 145. David Waines, "A Portrait of the Medieval Domestic Middle Eastern Kitchen," *First International Food Congress*, organized by Feyzi Halici (Ankara: Kultur ve Turizm Bakanligi Yayini, 1988), p. 316.

16. Baruch A. Levine and William W. Hallo, "Offerings to the Temple Gates at Ur," *H.U.C. Annual* 38 (1967): 17–58. *The Torah: A Modern Commentary*, ed. W. Gunther Plaut (New York: Union of American Hebrew Congregations, 1981), p. 762 (hereafter cited as *Torah: A Commentary*). R. A. Stewart Macalister, *The Excavations at Gezer*, vol. 2 (London: John Murray, 1912), p. 44.

17. *Jewish Encyclopedia*, article on showbread. *Encyclopaedia Judaica*, article on cult, the section dealing with the bread of display. *Torah: A Commentary*, p. 741. *Biblical Archaeology*, p. 220. Abraham Rabinovich, "True Coin," *The Jerusalem Post Magazine*, November 6, 1987.

18. Anton Jirku, *The World of the Bible* (London: Weidenfeld and Nicholson, 1967), p. 12. *A History of the Jewish People*, ed. H. H. Ben-Sasson (London: Weidenfeld and Nicholson, 1977), p. 232.

19. Zohary, pp. 40, 41, 83, 84. *The Times of London*, May 8, 1985, summarizing an article in *Science*, vol. 228. Y. Garfinkel, I. Carmi, and J. C. Vogel, "Dating of Horsebean and Lentil Seeds from Pre-Pottery Neolithic B Village of Yiftah'el," *Israel Exploration Journal* 37:1 (1987). Stephen Mennell, *All Manners of Food* (Oxford: Basil Blackwell, 1985), p. 42.

20. *Biblical Archaeology*, pp. 219–220. *Encyclopaedia Judaica*, article on biblical food. Bottéro, pp. 41–42. Louis Ginzberg, *On Jewish Law and Lore* (New York: Atheneum, 1981), p. 107.

21. Zohary, pp. 41, 73, 80, 85, 86, 93, 99, 100, 101. *Encyclopaedia Judaica*, article on melons. S. D. Goitein, *A Mediterranean Society: Daily Life*, vol. 4 (Los Angeles: University of California Press, 1983), pp. 232, 433. Herodotus, *The Histories*, trans. Aubrey de Selincourt (Harmondsworth: Penguin Books, 1954), pp. 151–152.

22. Zohary, pp. 56, 60, 64–70. Harold N. Moldenke and Alma L. Moldenke, *Plants of the Bible* (New York: Dover Publications, 1986), pp. 103–106 (hereafter cited as Moldenke). Louis Rabinowitz, *The Jerusalem Post*, Tora and Flora column on dates, March 25, 1983. Asaph Goor, "The History of the Pomegranate in the Holy Land," *Economic Botany* 21 (1967): 215. F. N. Hepper, "Plants and the Bible: Literary and Archaeological evidence," *Bulletin of the Anglo-Israel Archaeological Society*, 1987–1988, pp. 62–65.

23. Louis Rabinowitz, *The Jerusalem Post International Edition*, Tora and

Flora column on the apple, February 20–26, 1983. Moldenke, p. 186. Asaph Goor, "The History of the Pomegranate in the Holy Land," *Economic Botany*, p. 216.

24. R. J. Forbes, *Studies in Ancient Technology*, vol. 3 (Leiden: E. J. Brill, 1965), pp. 61–80. Don and Patricia Brothwell, *Food in Antiquity* (London: Thames and Hudson, 1969), pp. 164–171 (hereafter referred to as Brothwell). Ephraim Stern, "Excavations at Tell Mevorakh are a Prelude to a Tell Dor Dig," *Biblical Archaeology Review* 5:3 (May–June 1979): 36. E. W. Heaton, *Everyday Life in Old Testament Times* (London: B. T. Batsford, n.d.), p. 87. Louis Rabinowitz, *The Jerusalem Post*, Tora and Flora column on *shechar*, August 5, 1983.

25. Hogah Hareuveni, *Nature in Our Biblical Heritage* (Kiryat Ono: Neot Kedumin, 1980), pp. 11–12. Louis Ginzberg, *The Legends of the Jews*, vol. 3 (Philadelphia: Jewish Publication Society of America, 1947), p. 271. Menahem Haran, "Seething a Kid in Its Mother's Milk," *Journal of Jewish Studies* 30:1 (1979): 30–31. *Biblical Archaeology*, p. 222. *Interpreter's Dictionary of the Bible*, articles on cheese, curds, and milk (New York: Abingdon Press, 1962).

26. *Interpreter's Dictionary of the Bible*, article on honey. D'vora Ben Shaul, "Bee Good," *The Jerusalem Post Magazine*, July 22, 1988. Marjorie Shostack, *Nisa, The Life and Words of a ! Kung Woman* (Harmondsworth: Penguin Books, 1981), p. 97. L Valentine, *Palestine Past and Present* (London: Frederick Warne, 1893), p. 353.

27. F. S. Bodenheimer, "The Manna of Sinai," *The Biblical Archaeologist Reader*, ed. Noel Freedman and G. Ernest Wright (New York: Anchor Books, 1961), pp. 76–80. Zohary, pp. 142–143. Feliks, pp. 16–17.

28. Feliks, p. 16. *Food: The Gift of Osiris* 1:313–314. D'vora Ben Shaul, "Quailing," *The Jerusalem Post Magazine*, February 19, 1988.

29. Bottéro, pp. 39–47.

CHAPTER 2

1. S. Stein, "The Dietary Laws in Rabbinic and Patristic Literature," in *Studia Patristica*, vol. 2 (Berlin 1957), pp. 141–154 (hereafter cited as Stein, "Dietary Laws").

2. Fred Rosner, *Medicine in the Mishneh Torah of Maimonides* (New York: Ktav Publishing House, 1984), p. 243. *Encyclopaedia Judaica*, article on the Dietary Laws. Pinchas H. Peli, "Why Kashrut?" *The Jerusalem Post International Edition*, week ending April 20, 1985.

3. U. Cassuto, *A Commentary on the Book of Genesis, From Adam to Noah* (Jerusalem: Magnes Press, 1961), pp. 58–59. Jean Soler, "The Semiotics of Food in the Bible," in *Food and Drink in History: Selections from the Annales*, vol. 5 (Baltimore: Johns Hopkins University Press, 1979), pp. 126–138 (hereafter cited as Jean Soler). Louis Ginzberg, *The Legends of the Jews*, vol. 5 (Philadelphia: Jewish Publication Society of America, 1974), p. 93.

4. Mary Douglas, "The Abominations of Leviticus," in *Purity and Danger* (London: Ark Paperbacks, 1988), pp. 41–57 (hereafter sited as Mary Douglas). Stein, "Dietary Laws," p. 141.

5. Jean Soler, pp. 131–135. Mary Douglas, pp. 54–55. Sami Zubaida, "Explanations of Biblical Food Prohibitions." Paper delivered at the Oxford Food Symposium, 1985. Walter P. Zenner, "Kashrut & Rationality," *Jewish Folklore and Ethnology Newsletter* 1:1 (May 1977): 11–17.

6. Jean Soler, pp. 134–135. Mary Douglas, pp. 55–57. Naomi and Shimon Tzabar, *Yemenite & Sabra Cooking,* Introduction by H. Steckoll (Tel-Aviv: Sadan Publishing, 1979), p. 7. Abraham L. Udovitch and Lucette Valensi, *The Last Arab Jews: The Communities of Jerba, Tunisia* (New York: Harwood Academic Publishers, 1986), p. 18.

7. Marvin Harris, *Cannibals and Kings* (London: Fontana Collins, 1978), pp. 143–154. Norman Hammond, "Underwater Dig Reveals Neolithic Village," *The Times of London,* March 1, 1988. Norman Hammond, "Decapitated Bodies Found at Prehistoric Town in Jordan," *The Times of London,* December 22, 1987. Liora Kolska Horowitz, "Animal Offerings from two Middle Bronze Age Tombs," *Israel Exploration Journal* 37:4 (1987): 251–255.

8. John Ray, "Findings, Egyptology," *The Times of London,* November 19, 1985. Herodotus, *The Histories* (Harmondsworth: Penguin Edition, 1954), p. 121. Jacquetta Hawkes, *The First Great Civilizations* (Harmondsworth: Penguin Books, 1973), p. 127. Waverley Root, *Food,* article on pork (New York: Simon and Schuster, 1980), p. 372. Feliks, pp. 29–30. Abraham Rabinovich, "Canine Conundrum," *The Jerusalem Post Magazine,* August 26, 1988.

9. "Unique Biblical discovery on Mount Ebal," *The Jerusalem Post International Edition,* June 10–17, 1984. "The Artifacts of Life," *The Jerusalem Post International Edition,* September 25–October 1, 1983. Yigael Yadin, *Hazor* (London: Weidenfeld and Nicholson, 1975), pp. 183–184. Herodotus, *The Histories,* p. 122. Claus Westermann, *Isaiah 40–66* (London: S.C.M. Press, 1976), p. 3.

10. Herbert Chanan Brichto, "On Slaughter and Sacrifice, Blood and Atonement," *H.U.C. Annual,* 1976, pp. 19–51 (hereafter cited as Brichto). Jacob Milgrom, "Profane Slaughter and a Formulaic Key to the Composition of Deuteronomy," *H.U.C. Annual,* 1976, pp. 1–17 (hereafter cited as Milgrom).

11. *Torah: A Commentary,* p. 874.

12. Milgrom, pp. 13–15.

13. Dayan Dr. I. Grunfeld, *The Jewish Dietary Laws,* vol. 1 (London: Soncino Press, 1972), pp. 58–59 (hereafter cited as Grunfeld).

14. Grunfeld, pp. 65–67. Max Weinreich, *History of the Yiddish Language* (Chicago: University of Chicago Press, 1980), p. 82. Esther Levy, *Jewish Cookery Book,* facsimile ed. (Los Angeles: Pholiota Press, 1982), pp. 92–93. *Torah: A Commentary,* p. 766.

15. Rabbi Jacob Cohn, *The Royal Table: An Outline of the Dietary Laws of Israel* (Jerusalem: Feldheim Publishers, 1973), p. 75.

16. Salo Baron, *A Social and Religious History of the Jews,* vol. 1 (New York: Columbia University Press, 1952), pp. 159, 163. Max Weber, *Ancient Judaism* (New York: The Free Press, 1952), pp. 336, 353.

17. Martin Bernal, *Black Athena* (London: Free Association Books, 1987), pp. 445–450. "Canine Conundrum," *The Jerusalem Post Magazine,* August 26, 1988.

18. Jonathan A. Goldstein, *1 Maccabees.* The Anchor Bible (New York: Doubleday & Company, 1976), pp. 155–158.

19. *Encyclopaedia Judaica,* article on the Dietary Laws. Ernest Weisenberg, "Related Prohibitions: Swine Breeding and the Study of Greek," *H.U.C. Annual,* 1956, pp. 213–233.

20. Morton Smith, "On the Wine God in Palestine," in the *Salo Baron Jubilee Volume,* vol. 2 (New York: Columbia University Press, 1974), pp. 815–829. Gedaliah Alon, *The Jews in Their Land in the Talmudic Age,* vol. 1 (Jerusalem: Magnes Press, 1980), p. 164. Alon, *Jews, Judaism and the Classical World* (Jerusalem: Magnes Press, 1977), p. 157.

21. Alon, *Jews, Judaism and the Classical World,* p. 157. Martin Goodman, *The Ruling Class of Judaea* (Cambridge: Cambridge University Press, 1987), pp. 82, 83, 102 (hereafter cited as Martin Goodman). Jacob Neusner, *Judaism, the Evidence of the Mishnah* (Chicago: University of Chicago Press, 1981), pp. 50, 51, 70, 71 (hereafter cited as Neusner).

22. Heinrich Graetz, *History of the Jews,* vol. 2 (Philadelphia: Jewish Publication Society of America, 1946), pp. 269–270. Gedaliah Alon, *Jews, Judaism and the Classical World,* pp. 146–234, particularly pp. 156, 157, 181, 182, 187. Jacob Katz, *Exclusiveness and Tolerance* (New York: Behrman House, 1983), p. 30. Martin Goodman, pp. 102, 103, 108. Neusner, pp. 50, 51, 70, 71.

23. *The Jerusalem Post International Edition,* May 10, 1986. Nachman Avigad, *Discovering Jerusalem: Recent Archaeological Excavations in the Upper City* (Oxford: Basil Blackwell, 1984), pp. 79, 88. Daniel Sperber, "On Pubs and Policemen in Roman Palestine," *Zeitschrift der deutschen morgenländischen Gesellschaft* 120:2 (1971): 257–263.

24. E. P. Sanders, *Jewish Law from Jesus to the Mishnah* (London: S.C.M. Press, 1990), pp. 272–283. Walter Burkert, *Greek Religion* (Oxford: Basil Blackwell, 1987), p. 57.

25. Gedaliah Alon, *The Jews in Their Land in the Talmudic Age,* vol. 2 (Jerusalem: Magnes Press, 1984), pp. 735–736.

26. Louis Dumont, *Homo Hierarchicus* (London: Paladin, 1972), pp. 90, 91, 182. Martin Goodman, p. 104.

27. Menahem Haran, "Seething a Kid in Its Mother's Milk," *Journal of Jewish Studies* 30:1 (1979): 23–35. Robert Ratner and Bruce Zuckerman, "A Kid in Milk?" New Photographs of KTU 1.23, Line 14, *H.U.C. Annual,* 1986, pp. 15–52. A third but equally inconclusive interpretation of the passage is, "A kid in milk, *annh-* plant in butter."

28. Menahem Haran, "Seething a Kid in Its Mother's Milk," pp. 29, 30, 34, 35. Robertson Smith, *The Religion of the Semites* (London: A. & C. Block, 1927), pp. 576–577. Jacob Milgrom, "The Biblical Diet Laws as an Ethical System," *Interpretation,* 1963, pp. 288–301.

29. Louis Finkelstein, *The Pharisees,* vol. 1 (Philadelphia: Jewish Publication Society of America, 1946), pp. 58–60. *The Pentateuch and Haftorahs,* ed. J. H. Hertz (London: Soncino Press, 1947), p. 318.

30. Brichto, p. 53. Jean Soler, pp. 133–134.

31. Robertson Smith, *The Religion of the Semites,* pp. 221, 577. Grunfeld, vol. 1, p. 23. R. Po-chia Hsia, *The Myth of Ritual Murder: Jews and Magic in*

Reformation Germany (New Haven: Yale University Press, 1988), p. 127. Alan Davidson, *On Fasting and Feasting* (London: MacDonald Orbis, 1988), p. 186.

CHAPTER 3

1. Louis Ginzberg, *On Jewish Law and Lore* (New York: Atheneum, 1981), p. 104. Hillel A. Fine, "The Haggadah of Rabban Gamaliel," *Central Conference of American Rabbis Journal*, Spring 1975, p. 28.

2. *Encyclopaedia Judaica*, "The Five Species."

3. *Encyclopaedia Judaica*, "Barley." Louis Rabinowitz, *The Jerusalem Post*, Tora and Flora columns, April 16, 1982, and April 1, 1983. Salo Wittmayer Baron, *A Social and Religious History of the Jews*, vol. 5 (New York: Columbia University Press, 1957), p. 217.

4. Magen Broshi, "The Diet of Palestine in the Roman Period—Introductory Notes," *The Israel Museum Journal* 5 (Spring 1986): 41–42 (hereafter cited as Broshi, "Palestinian Diet"). Wilhelm Abel, *Agricultural Fluctuations in Europe from the thirteenth to the twentieth centuries* (London: Methuen & Company, 1986), pp. 142–143.

5. Saul Lieberman, "Grain mills and those who work with them," *Tarbiz* 50 (1980–1981). J. Newman, *Agricultural Life of the Jews in Babylonia* (London: Oxford University Press, Humphrey Milford, 1932), pp. 144, 146 (hereafter cited as Newman, *Agricultural Life*). L. Sprague de Camp, *Ancient Engineers* (London: Tandem Publishing, 1977), pp. 226–228.

6. Samuel Krauss, *Talmudische Archaologie*, vol. 1 (Hildesheim: Georg Olms Verlags-Buchandlung, 1966), pp. 467–469 and nn. 400, 406, 407, 407a (hereafter cited as Krauss, *Talmudic Archaeology*). Daniel Sperber, "*Cibar*, Bread" (Hebrew), *Tarbiz* 36:2 (1966): 199–201. Eliyahu Ashtor, "An essay on the Diet of the Various Classes in the Medieval Levant," *Biology of Man*, ed. Robert Forster and Orest Ranum (Baltimore: Johns Hopkins University Press, 1975), *khushkar*, p. 127. Marcus Jastrow, *A Dictionary of the Targumim, Talmud Babli, Yerulshalmi and Midrashic Literature* (New York: The Judaica Press, 1985), pp. 228, *gushkrah*, and 1354, *cibar* (hereafter cited as Jastrow, *Dictionary*).

7. Erwin R. Goodenough, *Jewish Symbols in the Greco-Roman Period*, vol. 5 (New York: Pantheon Books, 1956), pp. 6, 69, 70, 71 and figs. 65, 80. Krauss, *Talmudic Archaeology* 1:103. David L. Gold, "The Etymology of the English Bread name *pita*: A Study in Jewish Intralinguistics," *Jewish Language Review* 4 (1984).

8. Krauss, *Talmudic Archaeology* 1:105.

9. *The Works of Josephus*, trans. William Whiston (London: William Milner, 1866), *Antiquities of the Jews*, Book 15, 9:2, p. 341. H. H. Ben-Sasson, *A History of the Jewish People* (1977), p. 269. Newman, *Agricultural Life*, p. 90. For other examples of grass eating: Daniel Sperber, *Roman Palestine 200–400 The Land* (Ramat Gan: Bar-Ilan University Press, 1978), pp. 59, 85 (hereafter cited as Sperber, *The Land*). Piero Camporesi, *Bread of Dreams* (Oxford: Polity Press, 1989), pp. 28, 62, 110, 111.

10. Louis Rabinowitz, *The Jerusalem Post International Edition*, Tora and

Flora columns, March 6–12, 1983, and April 16, 1982. Louis Ginzberg, *The Legends of the Jews*, vol. 6 (Philadelphia: Jewish Publication Society of America, 1946), p. 169.

11. Leo Oppenheim, p. 44. Newman, *Agricultural Life*, pp. 22, 23, 107–110, 136, 139. Salo Wittmayer Baron, *A Social and Religious History of the Jews*, vol. 1 (New York: Columbia University Press, 1952), p. 247, 249. R. J. Forbes, *Studies in Ancient Technology*, vol. 3 (Leiden: E. J. Brill, 1965), pp. 60–72.

12. Newman, *Agricultural Life*, p. 91. Jastrow, *Dictionary*, p. 457. Barbara Flower and Elisabeth Rosenbaum, *The Roman Cookery Book: A Critical Translation of the Art of Cooking by Apicius* (London: Harrap, 1958), pp. 63, 65 (hereafter cited as Apicius). Leo Oppenheim, p. 44. Leguminous plants were not of much dietary significance in Mesopotamia, being rarely mentioned in first-millennium texts.

13. Jastrow, *Dictionary*, p. 627. Mishnah *Pesahim* 3:1. Copeland Marks, *The Varied Kitchens of India* (New York: M. Evans & Company, 1986), p. 65. Charles Perry, "Tracta, Trahanas, Kishk," *Petits Propos Culinaires* 14 (1983): 58–59. Nassrollah Islami, *Persian Cookery* (privately printed), pp. 45–46. Lesley Chamberlain, *The Food and Cooking of Russia* (Harmonsworth: Penguin Books, 1983), pp. 173–178.

14. Carol Meyers and Eric Meyers, "Talmudic village life in the Galilean Highlands," *Bulletin of the Anglo-Israel Archaeological Society*, 1982–1983, pp. 32–36. Eric M. Myers and Carol L. Myers, "Digging the Talmud in Ancient Meiron," *Biblical Archaeology Review* 4:2 (June 1978): 39–41. Jacob Neusner, ed., *The Talmud of the Land of Israel: Abodah Zarah* (Chicago: University of Chicago Press, 1982), p. 195.

15. *Encyclopaedia Judaica*, article on legumes.

16. *Encyclopaedia Judaica*, articles on vegetables and beet. Jean Bottéro, "The cuisine of Ancient Mesopotamia," *Biblical Archaeologist*, March 1985, p. 42.

17. M. Avi Yonah, *The Jews of Palestine: A Political History from the Bar Kochba War to the Arab Conquest* (Oxford: Basil Blackwell, 1976), pp. 104–106.

18. *Encyclopaedia Judaica*, articles on cabbage, vegetables, legumes, the melon, and cucumber. Salo Wittmayer Baron, *A Social and Religious History of the Jews* 2:246. *Jewish Encyclopedia*, article on food. S. D. Goitein, *A Mediterranean Society: Daily Life*, vol. 4 (Los Angeles: University of California Press, 1983), p. 434.

19. *Encyclopaedia Judaica*, article on vegetables. Newman, *Agricultural Life*, pp. 110–111. Broshi, "Palestinian Diet," p. 47.

20. Nahman Avigad, *Discovering Jerusalem* (1984), p. 106, 107, 168, 170, 171, 189–191.

21. Krauss, *Talmudic Archaeology* 1:116–117. Daisy Iny, *The Best of Baghdad Cooking with Treats from Teheran* (New York: Saturday Review Press/E.P. Dutton & Company, 1976), p. 113.

22. Louis Ginzberg, *On Jewish Law and Lore*, p. 107. I. A. Agus, *Urban Civilization in Pre-Crusade Europe*, vol. 1 (New York: Yeshiva University Press/Bloch Publishing Company, 1965), p. 308.

23. Louis Rabinowitz, *The Jerusalem Post*, International Editions, Tora and

Flora columns, September 5–11, 1982, and January 17–23, 1982. Also the International Edition of *The Jerusalem Post* on the Ekron excavations, January 10, 1987. Sperber, *The Land*, p. 29. Gedaliah Alon, *The Jews in Their Land in the Talmudic Age*, vol. 1 (Jerusalem: Magnes Press, 1980), pp. 163–164 (hereafter cited as Alon, *Talmudic Age*).

24. Yigael Yadin, *Massada* (London: Weidenfeld and Nicholson, 1966), p. 132. Sperber, *The Land*, p. 29. Alon, *Talmudic Age* 1:166–167. Asaph Goor, "History of the Date Through the Ages," *Economic Botany* 21 (1967): 332–334.

25. S. Tolkowsky, *Hesperides: A History of the Culture and Use of Citrus Fruits* (London: John Bale Sons & Curnow, 1938), pp. 48–110. *Encyclopaedia Judaica*, articles on citrus and the *etrog*. G. Widengren, *The King and the Tree of Life in Ancient Near Eastern Religion* (Uppsala: Universitets Arsskrift, 1951), pp. 15–59. Apicius, p. 53.

26. *Encyclopaedia Judaica*, article on cheese. *Jewish Encyclopedia*, article on cheese. Victor Tcherikover, *Hellenistic Civilization and the Jews* (Philadelphia: Jewish Publication Society of America, 1959), p. 70. Heinrich Graetz, *History of the Jews*, vol. 2 (Philadelphia: Jewish Publication Society of America, 1946), p. 270. Harold P. Gastwirt, *Fraud, Corruption and Holiness* (Port Washington, New York: National University Publications/Kennikat Press, 1974), p. 15. But see Gedaliah Alon, *Jews, Judaism and the Classical World* (Jerusalem: Magnes Press, 1977), pp. 146–189, but especially pp. 187–188, where the prohibitions against the use of non-Jewish wine, oil, and bread were said to be from the time of the Hasmonaeans.

27. Jean Bottéro, "The Cuisine of Ancient Mesopotamia," *Biblical Archaeologist*, March 1985, p. 38.

CHAPTER 4

1. *The Jerusalem Post* International Edition, "Yigal Shiloh on City of David excavations," September 25–October 1, 1983. Broshi, "Palestinian Diet," p. 48. Krauss, *Talmudic Archaeology*, vol. 1, pp. 108–110. *Jewish Encyclopedia*, articles on hen, poultry, and goose.

2. Krauss, *Talmudic Archaeology* 1:108–110. *Bezah* 28b. John M. Allegro, *The Dead Sea Scrolls* (Harmondsworth: Penguin Books, 1956), p. 116. Yakov Yehoshua, *Ha-Bayit Ve Ha Rechov Bi-Yerushalayim Ha-Yeshana* (*Home and Street in Jerusalem in the Old Days*), vol. 2 (Jerusalem: Rubin Mass, 1966), pp. 47–48. Viviane and Nina Moryousseff, *Moroccan Jewish Cookery* (Paris: J.P. Taillandier/Sochepress, 1983), pp. 65–69. Jill Tilsey-Benham, "Bringing Their Tails Behind Them: Some notes on Sheeps' Tail-Fat as used in the Middle Eastern Kitchen," *First International Food Congress*, ed. Feyzi Halici (Ankara: Kultur ve Turizm Bakanligi Yayini, 1988), pp. 303–308.

3. Louis Finkelstein, *The Pharisees*, vol. 1 (Philadelphia: Jewish Publication Society of America, n.d.), pp. 9, 109. *Bava Batra* 60b. Pinhas H. Peli, *The Jerusalem Post* International Edition, "Tora Today: Taking the Nazarites Vow," week ending June 14, 1986. Gedaliah Alon, *The Jews in Their Land in*

the Talmudic Age, vol. 1 (Jerusalem Press, 1980), pp. 51–52 (hereafter cited as Alon, *Talmudic Age*). Jeremiah Berman, *Shehita* (New York: Bloch Publishing Company, 1941), pp. 32–33.

4. Jeremiah Berman, *Shehita,* pp. 33–34. Leon Nemoy, *Karaite Anthology* (New Haven: Yale University Press, 1952), p. 351.

5. Avi-Yonah, *The Jews of Palestine: A Political History from the Bar Kokhba War to the Arab Conquest* (Oxford: Basil Blackwell, 1976), pp. 22, 167 (hereafter cited as Avi-Yonah). Salo Wittmayer Baron, *A Social and Religious History of the Jews,* vol. 1 (New York: Columbia University Press, 1952), pp. 205, 407. *Interpreter's Dictionary of the Bible,* article on fishing. J. J. Janssen, "The Economic System of a Single Village," *Royal Anthropological Institute News* 15 (August 1976): 17–19. R. J. Forbes, *Studies in Ancient Technology,* vol. 3 (Leiden: E. J. Brill, 1965), pp. 191–196. Krauss, *Talmudic Archaeology* 1:110–112. Daniel Sperber, "Some Observations of Fish and Fisheries in Roman Palestine," *Zeitschrift der deutschen morgenländischen Gesellschaft* (1969), pp. 265–269 (hereafter cited as Sperber, *Fish*).

6. Newman, *Agricultural Life,* pp. 136–140.

7. Sperber, *Fish,* pp. 265–269. Jastrow, *Dictionary,* p. 643. Chalkis = small fish resembling a sardine. May H. Beattie, *Recipes from Baghdad* (Baghdad: The Iraq Red Crescent Society, Women's Branch, 1952), p. 104. *Interpreter's Dictionary of the Bible,* article on kinds of fish (in the sea of Galilee). Cichlidae = *musht* of the Arabs. Cyprinidae = bigger species of carp which belong to the barbels. Alan Davidson, *Mediterranean Seafood* (Harmondsworth: Penguin Books, 1981). Mishnah *Hullin* 8:1. Solomon Zeitlin, *The Rise and Fall of the Judaean State* (Philadelphia: Jewish Publication Society of America, 1969), p. 287.

8. Krauss, *Talmudic Archaeology* 1:112. Apicius, pp. 21–23, 59. Thomas H. Corcoran, "Roman Fish Sauces," *Classical Journal* 58 (1968): 204–210 (hereafter cited as Corcoran, "Roman Fish Sauces"). Avi-Yonah, pp. 24; 59. *Yoma* 76a. Robin Howe, *The Mediterranean Diet* (London: Weidenfeld and Nicholson, 1985), p. 47.

9. Corcoran, "Roman Fish Sauces." Robert I. Curtis, "In Defence of Garum," *Classical Journal* 78 (1983): 232–240. Sperber, *Fish,* pp. 265–269. Daniel Sperber, *Roman Palestine 200–400: Money and Prices* (Ramat Gan: Bar-Ilan University Press, 1974), pp. 129–131.

10. Genesis 14:18–19. Krauss, *Talmudic Archaeology* 1:467–468 and n. 401.

11. Erwin R. Goodenough, *Jewish Symbols of the Greco-Roman Period,* vol. 6 (New York: Pantheon Books, 1956), pp. 6, 9 (hereafter cited as Goodenough, *Symbols*). Siegfried Stein, "The Influence of Symposia Literature on the Literary Form of the Pesah Haggadah," *The Journal of Jewish Studies* 7 (1957): 25–26 (hereafter cited as Stein, "Symposia").

12. Abraham P. Bloch, *The Biblical and Historical Background of Jewish Customs and Ceremonies* (New York: Ktav Publishing House, 1980), p. 118. Jacob Neusner, *Rabbinic Traditions about the Pharisees before 70,* vol. 2 (Leiden: E. J. Brill, 1971), pp. 145–146. Goodenough, *Symbols* 6:135. Baruch M. Bokser, *The Origins of the Seder* (Berkeley: University of California Press, 1984), pp. 63, 130–131, nn. 49–50. J. Elbogen, "Eingang und Ausgang des

Sabbats," *Fetschrift zu Israel Lewys 70tem Geburstag* (Breslau: Verlag von M.&H. Marcus, 1911), p. x.

13. Goodenough, *Symbols* 1, 6:202–203. Hyam Maccoby, *Paul and Hellenism* (London: S.C.M. Press, 1991), pp. 90–128. Arthur Darby Nock, *Essays on Religion and the Ancient World*, ed. Zeph Stewart, vol. 2 (Oxford: Clarendon Press, 1972), pp. 900–901 (hereafter cited as Nock, *Essays*). F. Gavin, *The Jewish Antecedents of the Christian Sacraments* (London: S.P.C.K., 1928), pp. 59–87. *Interpreter's Dictionary of the Bible*, article on the Lord's Supper.

14. Erwin R. Goodenough, "Symbolism," *Encyclopaedia Judaica*. Goodenough, *Symbols* 6:141, 216, 217. Nock, *Essays* 2: 885.

15. Goodenough, *Symbols* 6: 133. John G. Gager, *The Origins of Anti-Semitism* (New York: Oxford University Press, 1985), pp. 79, 280 n. 29. Morton Smith, "On the Wine God in Palestine," in *Salo Baron Jubilee Volume*, ed. S. Lieberman, vol. 2 (New York: Columbia University Press, 1974), pp. 815–827 and particularly p. 826. Robin Lane Fox, *Pagans and Christians* (Harmondsworth: Penguin Books, 1988), pp. 486–487. Eric M. Meyers, Ehud Netzer, and Carol L. Myers, "Artistry in Stone: The Mosaics of Ancient Sepphoris," *Biblical Archaeologist*, December 1987.

16. Goodenough, *Symbols* 6: 141, 187–190.

17. Gabrielle Sed-Rajna, *Ancient Jewish Art* (New Jersey: Chartwell Books, 1985), pp. 69, 115. Gary G. Porton, "The Grape Cluster in Jewish Literature and Art of late Antiquity," *Journal of Jewish Studies* 27 (1976): 159–176.

18. Goodenough, *Symbols* 5: 42, 45.

19. Angelo S. Rappoport, *The Folklore of the Jews* (London: Soncino Press, 1937), p. 28. Stith Thompson, *The Folktale* (Berkeley: University of California Press, 1977), p. 142.

20. Goodenough, *Symbols* 5: 32, 46, 51. N. G. L. Hammond and H. H. Scullard, *The Oxford Classical Dictionary*, article on fish (Oxford: Clarendon Press, 1970), p. 440. Louis Ginzberg, *The Legends of the Jews* (Philadelphia: Jewish Publication Society of America, 1947), vol. 1, pp. 26–30, and vol. 5, pp. 43–46. *Jewish Encyclopedia*, "Leviathan." Lucille Roussin, "The Beit Leontis Mosaic: An Eschatological Interpretation," *Journal of Jewish Art* 8 (1981): 6–19. Nock, *Essays* 2: 904–906.

21. Angelo S. Rappoport, *The Folklore of the Jews* (London: Soncino Press, 1937), pp. 28, 38.

22. Louis Ginzberg, *The Legends of the Jews* 1: 29.

23. Jacob Z. Lauterbach, "Development of Two Sabbath Ceremonies," in *Studies in Jewish Law, Custom and Folklore* (New York: Ktav Publishing, 1970), pp. 77–97. Mordechai Narkiss, "Origins of the Spice Box," *Journal of Jewish Art* 8 (1981): 28–41. Bloch, *Biblical and Historical Background of Jewish Customs and Ceremonies*, p. 121. S. D. Goitein, *A Mediterranean Society*, vol. 4 (Berkeley and Los Angeles: University of California Press, 1983), pp. 137, 149, 229, 230. Ginzberg, *Legends of the Jews* 1: 19–20.

24. "The Jews of Kurdistan," *The Jerusalem Post Magazine*, August 21, 1981. Shifra Epstein, "The Jews of Kurdistan," *Ariel* 51 (1982).

25. Louis Ginzberg, *Geonica*, vol. 2 (New York: Jewish Theological Seminary of America, 1909), p. 156. Max Weinreich, *History of the Yiddish Language* (Chicago: University of Chicago Press, 1980), p. 400. Samuel Bacchiocchi, *From*

Sabbath   to Sunday (Rome: Pontifical Gregorian University Press, 1977), p. 216.

26. Baruch M. Bokser, *The Origins of the Seder: The Passover Rite and Early Rabbinic Judaism* (Berkeley: University of California Press, 1984), pp. 12–19 (hereafter cited as Bokser, *Origins*). Alon, *Talmudic Age*, p. 261. Roland de Vaux, *Ancient Israel: Its Life and Institutions* (London: Darton, Longman, & Todd, 1976), pp. 489–491. Naum Jasny, "The Daily Bread of the Ancient Greeks and Romans," *Osiris* 9: (1950): 244, 247–249.

27. Theodor H. Gaster, *Passover: Its History and Traditions* (New York: Henry Schuman, 1949), pp. 77–83. Zev Garber, "The Samaritan Passover," *Central Conference of American Rabbis Journal*, Spring 1975, pp. 41–44. Siegfried Stein, "The Influence of Symposia Literature on the Literary Form of the Pesah Haggadah," *Journal of Jewish Studies* 7 (1957): 14 (hereafter cited as Stein, "Symposia"). Bokser, *Origins*, p. 21.

28. Philip Goodman, *The Passover Anthology* (Philadelphia: Jewish Publication Society of America, 1962). Jacques Faitlovitch, "The Passover as Observed by the Falashas," pp. 35–36. Wolf Leslau, *Falasha Anthology* (New Haven: Yale University Press, 1951), p. xxxi. Jacob Lauterbach, "Tashlik," *Hebrew Union College Annual* 11 (1936): 214–218.

29. Manashe Har-El, "Paths to Jerusalem," *The Jerusalem Post*, March 28, 1983. Hillel A. Fine, "The Haggadah of Rabban Gamaliel," *Central Conference of American Rabbis Journal* (Spring 1975), pp. 28–31. Alon, *Talmudic Age* 1:263–265. Bokser, *Origins*, pp. 89, 90, 103, 101–106. Marcel Simon, *Versus Israel: A Study of the Relations Between Christians and Jews in the Roman Empire* (Oxford: Oxford University Press for Littman Library, 1986), pp. 325, 494. The sacrifice of the Paschal lamb was well known in the Byzantine and Armenian Churches. Waverley Root, *Food* (New York: Simon and Schuster, 1980), pp. 212–213. Rena Salaman, *Greek Food* (London: Fontana Paperbacks, 1984), pp. 265–267.

30. Stein, "Symposia," p. 16. *Athenaeus: Deipnosophists*, trans. Charles Burton Gullick, Loeb Classical Library 4, 9: 408e. Andrew Dalby, "The Banquet of Philoxenus," *Petits Propos Culinaires* 26 (1987): 30.

31. Stein, "Symposia," p. 31. Bokser, *Origins*, pp. 62, 130. Oswyn Murray, *Early Greece* (London: Fontana Paperbacks, 1980), pp. 80, 198. Oswyn Murray, "The Greek Symposium in History," *Times Literary Supplement*, November 6, 1981. Oswyn Murray, "Days of Wine and Sofas," *Oxford Today*, Trinity Issue (1991). Jerome Carcopino, *Daily Life in Ancient Rome* (Harmondsworth: Penguin Books, 1956), pp. 264–265. The diners reclined on these couches by leaning on their left elbow and taking food from the table with their right hand. Athenaeus 1,2: 47.

32. Stein, "Symposia," p. 26.

33. Nahum N. Glatzer, ed., *The Passover Haggadah* (New York: Schocken Books, 1969), pp. 6–7. Nahman Avigad, *Discovering Jerusalem* (Oxford: Basil Blackwell, 1984), pp. 106, 107, 168, 170–172. S. D. Goitein, *A Mediterranean Society: Daily Life*, vol. 4 (Berkeley and Los Angeles: University of California Press, 1983), pp. 144–145. Joseph Tabory, "The Household Table in Rabbinic Times," *Association for Jewish Studies Review* 4 (1979). Edward William Lane, *An Account of the Manners and Customs of the Modern Egyptians* (London: Ward, Lock, and Bowden, 1889), pp. 130–131.

34. Rabbi Menachem M. Kasher, *Israel Passover Haggadah* (New York: Shengold Publishers, 1964), p. 333. Athenaeus 1:2: 49b, 49c. Oswyn Murray, *Early Greece* (London: Fontana Paperbacks, 1980), p. 198. Venetia Newall, *An Egg at Easter: A Folklore Study* (London: Routledge & Kegan Paul, 1984), pp. 159–164. Stein, "Symposia," pp. 16–17. Athenaeus 2:19. Apicius, p. 171. Charles Perry, "The Sals of the Infidels," *Petits Propos Culinaires* 26 (1987): 55–59. Ya'acov Friedler, "Alternative bitter herbs," *Contact: The Jerusalem Post Magazine*, March 29, 1991. *Hazeret* = lettuce such as the compass lettuce, *olshin* = chicory, *tamha* = not yet identified, *harhavina* = wild eryngo. The *maror hagina* = sow thistle, most likely biblical-talmudic *maror*.

35. Stein, "Symposia," pp. 24, 28. Jastrow, *Dictionary*, p. 554, *triclinium*. Bokser, *Origins*, pp. 41, 119 n. 11, pp. 123–124.

36. Bokser, *Origins*, pp. 63, 65, 66. Stein, "Symposia," pp. 29, 30, 36. Athenaeus 1:2:69c, 69e, 303. "Aphrodite hid Adonis in a lettuce-bed, since the poets mean by this allegory that the constant eating of lettuce produces impotence." Further, . . . lettuce is wholesome, cooling, a good regulatory and soporific, juicy, and checks sexual desire."

37. Krauss, *Archaeology* 1:107, 476 n. 458. Jastrow, *Dictionary*, p. 43, *Itri*. Charles Perry, "The Oldest Mediterranean Noodle: A Cautionary Tale," *Petits Propos Culinaires*, no. 9, pp. 42–45. Charles Perry, "Notes on Persian Pasta," *Petits Propos Culinaires*, no. 10, pp. 48–49. Maxine Rodinson, "On the Etymology of 'Losange,' " *Petits Propos Culinaires* 23 (1986).

38. Jastrow, *Dictionary*, p. 419. Maxine Rodinson, *"Reserches Sur Les Documents Arabes Relatifs A La Cuisine,"* *Revue des Etudes Islamiques* 17–18 (1949): 103, 150. Greek *Laganon* was derived from Persian *Lakshah*.

39. Patti Shosteck, *A Lexicon of Jewish Cooking* (Chicago: Contemporary Books, 1981), p. 217. Jastrow, *Dictionary*, p. 681. A. J. Arberry, "A Baghdad Cookery Book," *Islamic Culture* 13 (1939). Jastrow, *Dictionary*, p. 656, *Ka'ak*. Krauss, *Archaeology* 1:107, 477. Jastrow, *Dictionary*, p. 1296, "Waffle." Jastrow, *Dictionary*, p. 128, *Ashishim*. *Encyclopaedia Judaica*, article on lentils for *Ashishim*. Jastrow, *Dictionary*, p. 554, *Tracta*. Jon Solomon, "Tracta: a versatile Roman pastry," *Hermes* 106 (1978): 539–556. Charles Perry, "What Was Tracta?" *Petits Propos Culinaires* 12:37–39. Jastrow, *Dictionary*, p. 695, *Ludit*.

CHAPTER 5

1. Dovid Katz, "The Proto Dialectology of Ashkenaz," in *Origins of the Yiddish Language* (Oxford: Pergamon Press, 1987), pp. 47–60. Max Weinreich, *History of the Yiddish Language* (Chicago: University of Chicago Press, 1980) (hereafter cited as Weinreich).

2. Mordecai Kosover, *Yiddishe Maykholim* (New York: Yivo, 1958), pp. 80–97 (hereafter cited as Kosover, *Maykholim*). Louis Rabinowitz, *The Social Life of the Jews of Northern France in XII–XIV Centuries* (London: Edward Goldston, 1938), p. 71 (hereafter cited as Rabinowitz). *Or Zarua: Piskei Avoda Zara* (Zhitomir, 1862), 194, p. 53. B. Irving A. Agus, *Rabbi Meir of Rothenburg* (New York: Ktav Publishing House, 1970), p. 209 (hereafter cited as Agus).

Bridget Ann Henisch, *Fast and Feast* (Philadelphia: Pennsylvania State University Press, 1978) (hereafter cited as Henisch). Barbara Ketcham Wheaton, *Savouring the Past: The French Kitchen and Table from 1300 to 1789* (London: Chatto & Windus, 1983), pp. 7, 26, 174–175 (hereafter cited as Wheaton). J. F. Niermeyer, *Mediae Latinitatis Lexicon Minus* (Leiden: E. J. Brill, 1976), p. 770. Medieval Latin *pasticium* = pâté, pasty, dough, paste, thirteenth century. Modern Italian *pasticcio* = pie (hereafter cited as Niermeyer).

3. *Or Zarua: Piskei Avoda Zara* sec. 256, p. 67. Kosover, *Maykholim, Floden*, pp. 97–100, and *Torte*, pp. 107–109. Patti Shosteck, *Lexicon of Jewish Cooking* (Chicago: Contemporary Books, 1981), pp. 64–65, 215. Waverley Root, *The Food of Italy* (New York: Vintage Books, 1977), pp. 118, 198, 199. Niermeyer, p. 437, *Flado*. Frédéric Godefroy, *Dictionaire Du IX au XV siècle*, vol. 4 (Paris: F. Vieweg Libraire-Editeur, 1885), p. 24, *Flaoncel*. Enrst Gamillscheg, *Ethymologisches Wörterbuch der Französischen Sprache*, vol. 1 (Heidelberg: Carl Winter Universitatsverlag, 1969), p. 430, Flan (hereafter cited as Gamillscheg). Modern German *Fladen* = flat cake. Cecil Roth, "Elijah of London," in *Transactions of the Jewish Historical Society of England*, vol. 15 (1939–1945), p. 50 (hereafter cited as Roth, *Elijah of London*).

4. Charles Perry, "The Oldest Mediterranean Noodle: A Cautionary Tale," *Petits Propos Culinaire* (P.P.C.) 9: 42–45 (hereafter cited as Perry, "Cautionary Tale"). Charles Perry, "Notes on Persian Pasta," *P.P.C.* 10. K. C. Chang, ed., *Food in Chinese Culture* (New Haven: Yale University Press, 1977), p. 338 (hereafter cited as Chang). Waverley Root and the editors of Time-Life Books, *The Cooking of Italy* (New York: Time-Life, 1968), pp. 21, 24. Israel Davidson, *Parody in Jewish Literature* (New York, 1907), p. 22 (hereafter cited as Davidson). Vincenzo Buonassisi, *Pasta* (London: Futura, 1977), p. 8.

5. Max Grunwald, *History of Jews in Vienna* (Philadelphia: Jewish Publication Society of America, 1936), p. 56. Kosover, *Maykholim*, pp. 61–70. Perry, "Cautionary Tale," pp. 42–45. Constance B. Hieatt and Robin F. Jones, "Two Anglo-Norman Culinary Collections Edited from British Library Manuscripts Additional 32085 and Royal 12 C. XII," *Speculum, American Medieval History Journal* 61:4 (1986).

6. Chang, p. 338. Root, *Food of Italy*, pp. 156, 196, 200, 204. Edda Servi Machlin, *The Classic Cuisine of the Italian Jews* (New York: Everest House, 1981), p. 124 (hereafter cited as Machlin).

7. Weinreich, p. 637. Gamillscheg, 1:282, *Crêpe*. Niermeyer, *Crispa, Crespa*. Kosover, *Maykholim*, pp. 71–74. Wheaton, pp. 21, 174. Jacob Grimm and Wilhelm Grimm, *Deutsches Wörterbuch*, vol. 5 (Leipzig, Verlag von S. Hirzel, 1873), *Krapfe, Krapfen*. Fifteenth century; older texts gave the spelling *crespida, crapfe*.

8. Agus, pp. 273–274. Lesley Chamberlain, *The Food and Cooking of Eastern Europe* (Harmondsworth: Penguin Books, 1989), p. 22 (hereafter cited as Chamberlain, *Eastern Europe*).

9. Sidney W. Mintz, *Sweetness and Power: The Place of Sugar in Modern History* (Harmondsworth: Penguin Books, 1986), pp. 88, 242. Sarah Kelly, *Festive Baking in Austria, Germany, and Switzerland* (1985), p. 97. Kosover, *Maykholim*, pp. 113–114. Cecil Roth, *The Jews in the Renaissance* (New York: Harper & Row, 1965), p. 21. Mozes Heiman Gans, *Memorbook: A Pictorial*

History of Dutch Jewry from the Renaissance to 1940 (London: George Prior Associated Publishers, 1977), p. 216.

10. Cecil Roth, *The History of the Jews of Italy* (Philadelphia: Jewish Publication Society of America, 1946), p. 350. Root, *Food of Italy*, pp. 86, 87, 499, 500. Machlin, pp. 216–217. Irene Roth, *Cecil Roth: Historian Without Tears: A Memoir* (New York: Sepher-Hermon Press, 1982), p. 241. David L. Gold, "The Ethymology of the English Bread Name *Pita:* A Study in Jewish Intralinguistics," *Jewish Language Review* 4 (1984). Alan Davidson, *On Fasting and Feasting* (London: MacDonald Orbis, 1988), p. 115. Antonio Frugoli described in 1631 the eggplant as a base class of food relished by Jews.

11. Davidson, p. 22.

12. Harry Friedenwald, *The Jews and Medicine: Essays*, vol. 2 (New York: Ktav Publishing House, 1967), pp. 395, 399.

13. H. J. Zimmels, *Sephardim and Ashkenazim* (London: Marla Publishers, 1976), pp. 268, 274. Agus, pp. 272–273. Esra Shereshevsky, *Rashi the Man and his World* (New York: Sepher-Hermon Press, 1982), pp. 227–236 (hereafter cited as Shereshevsky). Leon Poliakov, *The History of Anti-Semitism*, vol. 1 (London: Elek Books, 1966), p. 143. H. H. Ben-Sasson, ed., *A History of the Jewish People* (London: Weidenfeld and Nicholson, 1977), p. 401. Rabinowitz, pp. 69–73. Kosover, *Maykholim*, p. 64 on *Trijes;* also S. Krauss, *Aus der jüdischen Volksküche: Mittelungen zur jüdischen Volkskunde* (Vienna 1915), pp. 28–29 (hereafter cited as Krauss, *Volksküche*).

14. Chamberlain, *Eastern Europe*, p. 321. Kosover, *Maykholim*, pp. 77–79, 131–134. Henisch, p. 123. Shereshevsky, pp. 229, 235. Apicius, *The Roman Cookery Book*, The Barbara Flower and Elisabeth Rosenbaum Edition (London: Harrap, 1974), p. 34. Rabinowitz, p. 70. Krauss, *Volksküche*, "Waffles," see p. 27. Herman Pollack, *Jewish Folkways in Germanic Lands 1648–1806* (Cambridge, MA: M.I.T. Press, 1971), pp. 98, 270, 271. Salo Wittmayer Baron, *A Social and Religious History of the Jews*, vol. 11 (New York: Columbia University Press, 1967), p. 186. William Woys Weaver, *Sauerkraut Yankees* (Philadelphia: University of Pennsylvania Press, 1983), pp. 133–134. "Wafler irons are required and can be obtained at any good ironmongers of the Hebrew persuasion," *The Jewish Manual* (1846), Facsimile Edition (New York: Nightingale Books, 1983), p. 124. Waffles were popular among Jews in Germany, Czechoslovakia, and Holland and even in Italy under the name of *cialdone*.

15. Israel Abrahams, *Hebrew Ethical Wills*, vol. 2 (Philadelphia: Jewish Publication Society of America, 1948), pp. 171, 172, 212, 222. Simon Dubnov, *History of the Jews*, vol. 4 (New York: Thomas Yoseloff, 1971), p. 239.

16. Reay Tannahill, *Food in History* (Harmondsworth: Penguin Books, 1988), pp. 184, 267. Stephen Mennell, *All manners of Food* (Oxford: Basil Blackwell, 1985), pp. 42, 46, 47. For bread see: Kosover, *Maykholim*, p. 56, and Pollack, p. 269, 270. *Sefer Maharil* (Lublin, 1904), pp. 17, 28. Latter section forbidding the taking of pulse and beans out of their pods on the Sabbath. For soup see: Kosover, *Maykholim*, pp. 41, 44, 47, 50, 51. Pollack, pp. 267–268. Immanuel Loew, "Gloses Romanes Dans Les Écrits Rabbiniques," *Revue des Études Juives* (*R.E.J.*) 27 (1893): 266. Foreign words in Schibbole Halleket composed in Italy around 1230. M. Kayserling, "Mots Espagnols Dans Le Schibbole Halleket," *R.E.J.* 29 (1894). Agus, p. 205. Eugen Weber, *Peasants*

into Frenchmen (London: Chatto and Windus, 1979), pp. 131, 132. Iris Origo, *The Merchant of Prato* (Harmondsworth: Penguin Books, 1979), p. 287, *la minestra*. Shlomo Eidelberg, *Jewish Life in Austria in the XVth Century* (Philadelphia: Dropsie College, 1962), p. 120.

17. Stephen Mennell, *All Manners of Food* (Oxford: Basil Blackwell, n.d.), pp. 42–43, 46. J. G. Pounds, *Hearth and Home* (Bloomington, IN: Indiana University Press, 1989), pp. 166, 169. Simon Schama, *The Embarrassment of Riches: An Interpretation of Dutch Culture in the Golden Age* (London: Fontana Press, 1988), pp. 163, 174. Shereshevsky, p. 230. Rabinowitz, pp. 72–73. Jacques Revel, "A Capital City's Privileges: Food Supplies in Early-Modern Rome," in *Food and Drink in History*, Robert Forster and Orest Ranum, ed. (Baltimore: Johns Hopkins University Press, 1979), pp. 37–40. Ariel Taoff and Simon Schwarzfuchs, *The Mediterranean and the Jews* (Ramat Gan: Bar-Ilan University Press, 1989), p. 244. Max Weinreich, p. 197. S. D. Goitein, *A Mediterranean Society: Daily Life*, vol. 4 (Berkeley and Los Angeles: University of California Press, 1983), p. 252.

18. Rabinowitz, p. 69.

19. Elkan Nathan Adler, *Jewish Travellers in the Middle Ages* (New York: Dover Publications, 1987), pp. 169, 194, 195 (hereafter cited as Adler, *Travellers*). Jacob M. Landau, *Jews in Nineteenth Century Egypt* (New York: New York University Press, 1969), p. 171.

20. Adler, *Travellers*, pp. 194, 237. Itzhak Ben-Zvi, "Eretz Yisrael Under Ottoman Rule 1517-1917," in *The Jews Their History*, Louis Finkelstein ed. (New York: Schocken Books, 1974), pp. 403, 406, 414.

21. S. D. Goitein, *A Mediterranean Society*, vol. 2 (Berkeley and Los Angeles: University of California Press, 1971), pp. 105, 126, 127 and vol. 4 (1983), pp. 234–246. Eliyahu Ashtor, "An Essay on the Diet of the Various Classes in the Medieval Levant," in *Biology of Man in History*, Robert Forster and Orest Ranum ed. (Baltimore, 1975), pp. 125–162 (hereafter cited as Ashtor).

22. Ashtor, pp. 133–135, 136, 139, 142. Goitein, *Mediterranean Society* 1:120, 121, 124, 126; 4:246, 247, 251, 252. Salo Wittmayer Baron, *A Social and Religious History of the Jews*, vol. 4 (New York: Columbia University Press, 1957), p. 163. Mike Rogoff, "Hellenistic Ashkelon," *Jerusalem Post Magazine*, September 6, 1988.

23. Erich Isaac, "Influence of Religion in the Spread of Citrus Fruit," *Science* 129 (January 23, 1959): 179–186 (hereafter cited as Erich Isaac). S. Tolkowsky, *Hesperides: A History of the Culture and Use of Citrus Fruits* (London: John Bale Sons & Curnow, 1938), pp. 110, 140, 165, 286 (hereafter cited as Tolkowsky). S. D. Goitein 1:121, 4:230. Iris Origo, *The Merchant of Prato* (Harmondsworth: Penguin Books, 1979), p. 294. Todd M. Endelman, *The Jews of Georgian England 1714–1830* (Philadelphia: Jewish Publication Society of America, 1979), pp. 180–181.

24. Tolkowsky, pp. 170, 171, 284, 285, 286. Salo Wittmayer Baron, *A Social and Religious History of the Jews*, vol. 11 (New York: University of Columbia Press, 1967), p. 310. Erich Isaac, p. 185. Nahum Sokolow, *Hibbath Zion (The Love of Zion)* (Jerusalem: Rubin Mass, 1941), p. 220.

25. Adler, *Travellers*, pp. 228, 236, 237. "The Jew can buy everything that is necessary . . . in the Jews' street; this is also the case in Palermo, but there it is not the same as in Cairo, for in the latter place the Jews cook at home only for

the Sabbath, since men as well as women are occupied during the whole week and can therefore buy everything in the market."' S. D. Goitein, 4:227, 248. S. D. Goitein, 1:81, 114–115, 126, 424. A. J. Arberry, "A Baghdad Cookery Book," *Islamic Culture*, vol. 13 (1939): 29. There is also the spelling *qata'if* for *kadaif*.

26. L. Nemoy, *Karaite Anthology* (New Haven: Yale University Press, 1952), p. 110. Joseph Sutton, *Magic Carpet: Aleppo-in-Flatbush* (New York: Thayer-Jacoby, 1986), pp. 190–191.

CHAPTER 6

1. Louis Rabinowitz, *The Social Life of the Jews of Northern France in XII–XIV Centuries* (London: Edward Goldston, 1938), pp. 70–71 (hereafter cited as Rabinowitz). Herman Pollack, *Jewish Folkways in Germanic Lands 1648–1806* (Cambridge, MA: M.I.T. Press, 1971), pp. 97, 268 (hereafter cited as Pollack, *Folkways*). Benjamin R. Gumpel, *The Last Jews on Iberian Soil: Navaresse Jewry 1479–1498* (Berkeley and Los Angeles: University of California Press, 1989), pp. 31–33, 43. J. David Bleich, *Contemporary Halachic Problems*, vol. 3 (New York: Ktav Publishing House, 1989), pp. 60–65.

2. Esra Shereshevsky, *Rashi: The Man and His World* (New York: Sepher-Hermon Press, 1982), pp. 227, 228, 232. Terence Scully, ed., *The Viandier of Taillevent* (Ottawa: University of Ottawa Press, 1988), pp. 132, 133, 169. Irving A. Agus, *Urban Civilization in Pre-Crusade Europe*, vol. 1 (New York: Yeshiva University Press, 1965), p. 84. Max Grunwald, *Vienna* (Philadelphia: Jewish Publication Society of America, 1936), p. 59. Irving A. Agus, *Rabbi Meir of Rothenburg: His Life and his works as sources for the religious, legal and social history of the Jews of Germany in the thirteenth century* (New York: Ktav Publishing House, 1970), p. 210 (hereafter cited as *Rabbi Meir of Rothenburg*).

3. Rabinowitz, p. 179. Meyer S. Lew, *The Jews of Poland* (London: Edward Goldston, 1944), pp. 131, 163.

4. Salo Wittmayer Baron, *The Jewish Community: Its History and Structure to the American Revolution*, vol. 2 (Philadelphia: Jewish Publication Society of America, 1948), pp. 160–161. Morris S. Goodblatt, *Jewish Life in Turkey in the XVI Century* (New York: Jewish Theological Seminary of America, 1952), p. 54.

5. *Sefer Maharil* (Lublin, 1904), p. 28a (hereafter cited as *Sefer Maharil*). *Rabbi Meir of Rothenburg*, pp. 186–187. Shlomo Eidelberg, *Jewish Life in Austria in the XVth Century* (Philadelphia: Dropsie College, 1962), pp. 118–119 (hereafter cited as Eidelberg, *Austria*). Pollack, *Folkways*, p. 275.

6. Mordechai Kosover, *Yiddishe Maykholim* (New York: Yivo, 1958), pp. 80–81. Israel Abrahams, *Jewish Life in the Middle Ages* (London: Edward Goldston, 1932), p. 167. *Vallentine's Jewish Encyclopaedia* (London: Shapiro, Vallentine & Company, 1938), article on cookery by Max Grunwald, p. 157. Harry Friedenwald, *The Jews and Medicine: Essays*, vol. 1 (New York: Ktav Publishing House, 1967), p. 384.

7. Elizabeth E. Bacon, *Central Asians Under Russian Rule: A Study in Culture Change* (Ithaca, NY: Cornell University Press, 1980), p. 59. Samuel Bacchiocchi, *From Sabbath to Sunday. Divine Rest for Human Restlessness* (Rome: Pontifical Gregorian University Press, 1977), pp. 217, 239.

8. Adler, *Travellers,* p. 221.

9. Adler, *Travellers,* pp. 220, 221. Israel Cohen, *The Journal of a Jewish Traveller* (London: John Lane, 1925), p. 125. Naomi and Shimon Tzabar, *Yemenite and Sabra Cookery* (Tel-Aviv: Sadan Publishing, 1979), p. 8.

10. Samuel Bacchiocchi, *From Sabbath to Sunday: Divine Rest for Human Restlessness,* p. 216. S. D. Goitein, *A Mediterranean Society, vol. 1, Economic Foundations* (Berkeley and Los Angeles: University of California Press, 1967), p. 72. S. D. Goitein, *A Mediterranean Society, vol. 4, Daily Life* (Berkeley and Los Angeles: University of California Press, 1983), pp. 227, 243 (hereafter cited as S. D. Goitein, *Daily Life*). S. D. Goitein, "Jewish Matters in Baladhuri's Ansab al Ashraf," *Zion* 1 (1936): 75–81.

11. Salo Wittmayer Baron, *A Social and Religious History of the Jews,* vol. 5 (New York: Columbia University Press, 1957), p. 244. *Talmudic Encyclopaedia,* vol. 9 (Jerusalem: Talmudic Encyclopedia Publ., 1959), "*Hatmanah,*" columns Heh and Vav.

12. "The Jews of Kurdistan," *The Jerusalem Post Magazine,* August 21, 1981. Shifra Epstein, "The Jews of Kurdistan," *Ariel,* no. 51 (Jerusalem 1982). Laurence D. Loeb, *Outcaste: Jewish Life in Southern Iran* (New York: Gordon and Breach, 1977), p. 179.

13. S. D. Goitein, *Daily Life,* pp. 227, 431. Ambrosio Huica Miranda, *La Cocina Hispano-Magribi durante la epoca Almohade. Revista del Instituto de Estudios Islamicos en Madrid* 5 (1957): 139. W. Marcais, *Textes Arabes de Tanger* (Paris: Imprimerie National, 1911), pp. 149–150 (hereafter cited as Marcais).

14. Lucie Bolens, *La cuisine andalouse, un art de vivre XIe–XIIIe siècle* (Paris: Albin Michel, 1990), pp. 57–59, 62, 164, 165. Other medieval Spanish recipes described by Bolens are Sabbath with fat, p. 64, a Jewish recipe for stuffing, pp. 77–78, a Jewish partridge recipe, p. 110, and Jewish chicken recipes, pp. 123–124. Bridget Ann Henisch, *Fast and Feast: Food in Medieval Society* (Philadelphia: Pennsylvania State University Press, 1978), p. 130. Reay Tannahill, *Food in History* (Harmondsworth: Penguin Books, 1988), p. 182. M. Rodinson, *Reserches Sur les Documents Arabes Relatifs a la cuisine. Revue Des Etudes Islamiques* (1949), pp. 135, 157. Abraham Ben-Yacob, *Iraqi Jewish Customs* (Hebrew) (Jerusalem, 1967), p. 18.

15. Malvina W. Liebman, *Jewish Cookery from Boston to Baghdad* (Florida: E. E. Seeman Publishing, 1975), p. 14. Paul Wexler, "The Term 'Sabbath Food': A Challenge for Jewish Interlinguistics," *Journal of the American Oriental Society* 98:4 (Oct.–Dec. 1978): 462 (hereafter cited as Paul Wexler). Joëlle Bahloul, *Le Culte de la Table Dresslée: Rites et traditions de la table juive algerienne* (Paris, Éditions A.M. Metailié, 1983), p. 182.

16. Richard Ford, *Gatherings from Spain* (London: J.M. Dent, 1970), pp. 132, 137. Penelope Casas, *The Foods and Wines of Spain* (Harmondsworth: Penguin Books, 1985), p. 76 (hereafter cited as Penelope Casas).

17. Lucien Wolf, *Jews in the Canary Islands* (London: Spottiswoode, Ballantyne & Company, 1926), pp. 86, 99.

18. Penelope Casas, pp. 138–139. Peter S. Feibleman, *The Cooking of Spain and Portugal* (New York: Time-Life Books, 1985), p. 23.

19. Marcais, p. 149. Paul Wexler, p. 462. *Glossairé Judeo-Arabe de Fès*, p. 60. Captain James Riley, *Narrative of the loss of the American Brig Commerce wrecked on the Western coast of Africa in the month of August 1815 with . . . observations historical, geographical, & C* (New York, Published by the author, 1817), pp. 414–415.

20. Penelope Casas, p. 138. Richard Ford, *Gatherings from Spain*, p. 148. Mordecai Kosover, "Gleanings from the Vocabulary of a 15th Century Yiddish Manuscript Collection of Customs," in *For Max Weinreich on his Seventieth Birthday. Studies in Jewish Languages, Literature and Society* (The Hague: Mouton, 1964), p. 356 (hereafter cited as Kosover, "15th Century"). Max Weinreich, *History of the Yiddish Language* (Chicago: University of Chicago Press, 1980), p. 400.

21. *Or Zarua*, part 2, *Hilchos Erev Shabbos* (Zhitomir, 1862), sec. 8, p. 6, column Bes. Jacob Katz, *The 'Shabbos Goy'* (Philadelphia: Jewish Publication Society of America, 1989), pp. 56–58, 63, 66. *Sefer Maharil*, p. 28(b). Israel Abrahams, *Jewish Life in the Middle Ages* (London: Edward Goldston, 1932), p. 173. *Rabbi Meir of Rothenburg*, p. 184.

22. Waverley Root, *The Food of France* (London: Macmillan, 1983), pp. 11, 302, 303–305. George Lang, *The Cuisine of Hungary* (Harmondsworth: Penguin Books, 1985), pp. 211–223. Kosover, *Maykholim*, p. 10.

23. Shlomo Eidelberg, *Jewish Life in Austria in the XVth Century* (Philadelphia: Dropsie College, 1962), p. 73. *Sefer Maharil*, p. 28(b). Kosover, "15th Century," p. 359.

24. S. D. Goitein, *Daily Life*, pp. 229, 432. Sidney Steiman, *Custom and Survival: A Study of the Life and work of Rabbi Jacob Molin (Moelln) known as the Maharil c. 1340–1427 . . .* (New York: Bloch Publishing Company, n.d.), p. 68 (hereafter cited as Steiman, *Maharil*).

25. Fernand Braudel, *Capitalism and Material Life 1400–1800* (London: Weidenfeld and Nicholson, 1943), pp. 66–67, 127–135.

26. Salo Wittmayer Baron, *A Social and Religious History of the Jews*, vol. 12 (New York: Columbia University Press, 1967), pp. 68–74, 276–277.

27. Salo Wittmayer Baron, *A Social and Religious History of the Jews*, vol. 9 (New York: Columbia University Press, 1965), pp. 210–211. Bernard D. Weinryb, *The Jews of Poland: A Social and Economic History of the Jewish Community in Poland from 1100 to 1800* (Philadelphia: Jewish Publication Society of America, 1973), p. 145. Salo Wittmayer Baron, *A Social and Religious History of the Jews*, vol. 16 (New York: Columbia University Press, 1976), pp. 231, 256–257, 425–426. Fernand Braudel, *Capitalism and Material Life 1400–1800* (London: Weidenfeld and Nicholson, 1973), p. 135. Leon Poliakov, *The History of Anti-Semitism*, vol. 1 (London: ELEK Books, 1966), p. 151. Yitzhak Baer, *A History of the Jews in Christian Spain*, vol. 1 (Philadelphia: Jewish Publication Society of America, 1978), pp. 92, 397. Max Grunwald, *Vienna* (Philadelphia: Jewish Publication Society of America, 1936), p. 55.

28. Jeremiah J. Berman, *Shehitah* (New York: Bloch Publishing Company, 1941), p. 91. Rabinowitz, p. 113. Alfred Krober, *Cologne* (Philadelphia: Jewish Publication Society of America, 1940), p. 106. Max Grunwald, *Vienna* (Philadelphia: Jewish Publication Society of America, 1936), p. 56. Dr. Aaron Owen,

"The References to England in the Responsa of Rabbi Meir Ben Baruch of Rothenburg (1215–1293)." *Transactions of the Jewish Historical Society of England* 17 (1953): 75. Pollack, *Folkways*, p. 267. Eidelberg, *Austria*, p. 119.

29. S. D. Goitein, *A Mediterranean Society: The Community*, vol. 2 (Berkeley and Los Angeles: University of California Press, 1971), pp. 227–228. Fred Rosner and Suessman Muntner, eds., *The Medical Aphorisms of Moses Maimonides*, vols. 1, and 2 (New York: Bloch Publishing Company for Yeshiva University Press, 1970), p. 77. S. D. Goitein, *A Mediterranean Society: Economic Foundations*, vol. 1 (Berkeley and Los Angeles: University of California Press, 1967), p. 429 n. 69. S. D. Goitein, *Daily Life*, pp. 231–234, 245, 249–250. Eliyahu Ashtor, "An Essay on the Diet of the Various Classes in the Medieval Levant," in *Biology of Man in History*, ed. Robert Forster and Orest Ranum (Baltimore: Johns Hopkins University Press, 1975), p. 130. Charles Perry, "Buran: 1100 Years in the Life of a Dish," *The Journal of Gastronomy* 1 (Summer 1984): 67–77.

30. Berman, *Shehitah*, pp. 208–227. Salo Wittmayer Baron, *The Jewish Community: Its History and Structure to the American Revolution*, vol. 2 (Philadelphia: Jewish Publication Society of America, 1948), pp. 157–160. Irving A. Agus, *The Heroic Age of Franco-German Jewry* (New York: Yeshiva University Press, 1969), pp. 350–351.

31. Irving A. Agus, *The Heroic Age of Franco-German Jewry* (New York: Yeshiva University Press, 1969), p. 352. H. J. Zimmels, *Ashkenazim and Sephardim* (London: Marla Publications, 1976), pp. 200–201. Berman, *Shehitah*, pp. 228–233.

32. Cecil Roth, *The Jews in the Renaissance* (New York: Harper and Row, 1965), p. 30. Grunwald, *Vienna*, p. 56. Rabbi David Goldberg, "Shared eating leads to a shared belief," *The Independent*, July 21, 1990.

33. Krauss, *Volksküche*, p. 11. S. D. Goitein, *Daily Life*, p. 251. Cecil Roth, "Folklore of the Ghetto," in *Personalities and Events in Jewish History* (Philadelphia: Jewish Publication Society of America, 1953), pp. 78–90 but particularly pp. 82–83. Salo Wittmayer Baron, *A Social and Religious History of the Jews*, vol. 6 (New York: Columbia University Press, 1958), p. 125.

34. Philip Goodman, *The Rosh Hashana Anthology* (Philadelphia: Jewish Publication Society of America, 1973), p. 282. Therese and Mendel Metzger, *Jewish Life in the Middle Ages* (London: Alpine Fine Arts Collecetion, 1985), p. 246. *Sefer Maharil*, p. 38a. Steiman Maharil, p. 69. Pollack, *Folkways*, pp. 101, 102, 276.

35. Krauss, *Volksküche*, p. 11. Eidelberg, *Austria*, pp. 119–120. Pollack, *Folkways*, pp. 101, 102, 276.

36. "Decoration of the Sukka with Fruits and Vegetables," *Journal of Reform Judaism*, Summer 1985, p. 117. Anita Engle, "Fragile Reminders of the Past," *The Jerusalem Post*, October 9, 1987. Solomon B. Freehof, "Home Rituals and the Spanish Synagogue," in *Studies and Essays in honor of Abraham A. Neuman*, ed. Meir Ben-Horin (Leiden: E. J. Brill, 1962), pp. 225–226 (hereafter cited as Solomon B. Freehof). Weinreich, p. 182.

37. Joshua Trachtenberg, *The Devil and the Jews* (Philadelphia: Jewish Publication Society of America, 1983), p. 89.

38. *The Passover Haggadah*, ed. Nahum N. Glatzer (New York, 1969), pp.

6–7. *Mishnah Torah: Zemanim Hilchos Hametz Vematza,* ed. Rabbi S. Frankel (Jerusalem, 1975), chaps. 8:1–2. *Shulchan Aruch: Orach Hayim. Hilchos Pesach* (Vilna Edition, 1879), Karo 473:3 and Isserles commentary.

39. Haim Shapiro, "Seder Plates through the ages," *The Jerusalem Post Supplement,* April 13, 1987. David George, "*Pessah* Treasures," *The Jerusalem Post International Edition,* April 14, 1990.

40. Philip Goodman, *The Passover Anthology* (Philadelphia: Jewish Publication Society of America, 1962), pp. 86–88.

41. Viviane and Nina Moryoussef, *Moroccan Jewish Cookery* (Paris: J. P. Taillandier/Soche Press, 1983), pp. 65–66. Waverley Root, *Food* (New York: Simon & Schuster, 1980), p. 213, and Rena Salaman, *Greek Food* (London: Fontana Paperbacks, 1984), pp. 265–267). Gedaliah Alon, *The Jews in Their Land in the Talmudic Age,* vol. 1 (Jerusalem: Magnes Press, 1980), pp. 231–232. *Mishnah Torah: Zemanim. Hilchos Hametz Vematza* 8:1. Commentary of Rabbi Moses Hacohen of Lunel. *Shulchan Aruch: Orach Hayim, Hilchos Pesach* 473:4 and Isserles commentary.

42. Venetia Newell, *An Egg at Easter: A Folklore Study* (London: Routledge & Kegan Paul, 1984), pp. 160–162. Ruth Gruber Fredman, *The Passover Seder: Afikoman in Exile* (Philadelphia: University of Pennsylvania Press, 1981), pp. 138–139.

43. Marc J. Rosenstein, "Legumes in Passover," *Central Conference of American Rabbis Journal,* Spring 1975, pp. 32–40.

44. Salo Wittmayer Baron, *A Social and Religious History of the Jews,* vol. 11 (New York: Columbia University Press, 1967), pp. 151–152. Louis Rabinowitz, "Horse-radish History," Tora and Flora column summarizing Arthur Schaffer, "The History of the Horse-radish as the Bitter Herb of Passover," *Gesher,* vol. 8 (1981), *The Jerusalem Post* (March 18, 1983). Thérèse and Mendel Metzger, *Jewish Life in the Middle Ages* (London: Alpine Fine Arts Collection, 1985), pp. 212–214. Cecil Roth, "Elijah of London," *Transactions of the Jewish Historical Society* 14:48. Cecil Roth, "New Notes on Pre-Expulsion Anglo-Jewish Scholars," *The Journal of Jewish Studies* 3:2 (1952): 56–61.

45. H. J. Zimmels, *Ashkenazim and Sephardim* (London: Marla Publications, 1976), p. 196. Solomon B. Freehof, pp. 219–220. Yakov Marmonstein, "The Communal Seder: Historical and Halachic Perspectives," *L'Eylah* 23 (Pesach 1987): 37–41. Brian Pullan, *The Jews of Europe and the Inquisition of Venice 1550–1670* (Oxford: Basil Blackwell, 1983), pp. 163–164.

46. Hayyim Schauss, *The Lifetime of a Jew* (New York: Union of American Hebrew Congregations, 1967), pp. 101–102. H. H. Ben-Sasson, ed., *A History of the Jewish People* (London: Weidenfeld and Nicholson, 1977), p. 522.

47. H. I. Marrou, *A History of Education in Antiquity* (New York: Mentor Books, 1956), pp. 367, 557. Diane Roskies, "Alphabet Instruction in the East European Heder," *Yivo Annual* 17 (1978) (hereafter cited as Diane Roskies).

48. Sarah Kelly, *Festive Baking in Austria, Germany and Switzerland* (1985), p. 43. Krauss, *Volksküche,* p. 27.

49. Eric Zimmer, "Rabbi David B. Isaac of Fulda: The Trials and Tribulations of a Sixteenth Century German Rabbi," *Jewish Social Studies* 45:3–4 (1983). Isidore Fishman, *Jewish Education in Central Europe XVI–XVIII Centuries* (London: Edward Goldston, 1944), pp. 77–78. Diane Roskies, pp. 26–28.

50. *Rabbi Meir of Rothenburg,* p. 192. Cecil Roth, *Jüdische Bräuche in Comtat Venaissin: Mittelungen zur Jüdische Volkskunde* 30 (1927): 18–19. Israel Abrahams, *Festival Studies* (London: Macmillan & Company, 1905), p. 11. Israel Abrahams, *Jewish Life in the Middle Ages* (London: Edward Goldston, 1932), p. 167).

51. Theodor H. Gaster, *Festivals of the Jewish Year* (New York: William Sloane Associates, 1966), pp. 76–77. Kosover, *Maykholim,* pp. 97–99.

52. *Sefer Maharil,* 61a. Eidelberg, *Austria,* p. 119. Hayyim Schauss, *The Jewish Festivals* (New York: Union of American Hebrew Congregations, 1986), pp. 234, 270, 311 n. 272, 312. Hanna Goodman, *Jewish Cooking Around the World* (Philadelphia: Jewish Publication Society of America, 1973), p. 167.

CHAPTER 7

1. Salo Wittmayer Baron, *A Social and Religious History of the Jews,* vol. 12 (New York: Columbia University Press, 1967), p. 25 (hereafter cited as Baron, *History*). John M. Shaftesley, "Culinary Aspects of Anglo-Jewry," in *Studies in the Cultural Life of Jews in England,* ed. Dov Noy and Issacher Ben-Ami (Jerusalem: Magnes Press, 1975), pp. 375, 376. Barbara Kirschenblatt-Gimblett, "The Kosher Gourmet in the Nineteenth Century Kitchen: Three Jewish Cookbooks in Historical Perspective," *The Journal of Gastronomy* 2:4 (Winter 1986/1987), footnote 10. Jean Anderson, *The Food of Portugal* (London: Robert Hale, 1987), p. 42. Mary Hillgarth, *The International Wine & Food Society's Guide to Spanish Cookery* (Newton Abbot: David & Charles, 1970), pp. 144–145 (hereafter cited as Hillgarth). Elizabeth Cass, *Spanish Cooking* (London: André Deutsch, 1968), p. 139 (hereafter cited as Cass).

2. Yakov Yehoshua, *Ha-Bayit Ve Ha Rechov Bi-Yerushalayim Ha-Yeshunah* (*Home and Street in Jerusalem in the Old Days*) (Jerusalem: Rubin Mass, 1966), p. 55 (hereafter cited as Yehoshua, *Old Jerusalem*). Avraham Yaari, *The Goodly Heritage* (Jerusalem: Youth and Hechalutz Department of the Zionist Organization, 1958), p. 106 (hereafter cited as Yaari). Emile de Vidas Levy, *Sephardic Cookery* (New York: Women's Division of the Central Sephardic Jewish Community of America, 1983), Introduction. Leon Sciaky, *Farewell to Salonica* (London: W. H. Allen, 1946), pp. 50–51.

3. Yehoshua, *Old Jerusalem,* p. 54. Elie Eliachar, *Living With Jews* (London: Weidenfeld and Nicholson, 1983), p. 54 (hereafter cited as Eliachar). Jane Grigson, *The Observer Guide to European Cookery: Portugal* (London: Michael Joseph, 1983). C. Anne Wilson, *The Book of Marmalade* (London: Constable, 1985), pp. 15–29.

4. Eliachar, p. 56. Yaari, p. 107.

5. Yaari, pp. 74, 106. Yehoshua, *Old Jerusalem,* pp. 50–52. Viviane Alchech Miner and Linda Krinn, *From My Grandmother's Kitchen: A Sephardic Cookbook* (Gainesville, FL: Triad Publishing Company, 1984), p. 31. Hillgarth, p. 12. Cass, p. 267. Sarah Bergner-Rabinowitz, "Hygiene, Education and Nutrition Among Kurdish, Persian and Ashkenazic Jews in Jerusalem," *Edoth* 3 (1947).

6. Interview with Mr. Solomon Cikurel. Yehoshua, *Old Jerusalem,* pp.

52–53. Juan Manuel Figueras, "Man sleeps, but in his dreams sees Spain," *Lookout Magazine*, April 1969. Hillgarth, p. 12.

7. Yehoshua, *Old Jerusalem*, pp. 52–54, 56, 57. H. J. Zimmels, *Ashkenazim and Sephardim* (London: Marla Publications, 1976), p. 274. Allicia Rios, "The Culinary Culture of Olive Oil in Spain," *First International Food Congress*, Turkey 1986, organized by Feyzi Halici (Ankara: Kultur ve Turizim Bakanligi Yayini, 1988), p. 244 (hereafter cited as Rios, "Olive Oil"). Between the eleventh and thirteenth centuries, the use of different types of pasta spread across the Mediterranean from North Africa into Spain and Italy, where in the latter country one of the Arabic words for pasta, *Atriya*, was transformed into *Trii*, and in France, where it possibly became known as *trijes*. See Lucie Bolens, *La cuisine andalouse, un art de vivre XIe–XIIIe siècle* (Paris: Albin Michel, 1990), pp. 160–161.

8. Bridget Ann Henisch, *Fast and Feast: Food in Medieval Society* (Philadelphia: Pennsylvania State University Press, 1978), pp. 44–45. C. Anne Wilson, "The Saracen Connection: Arab Cuisine and the Medieval West," *Petits Propos Culinaires* 7:18, Persian *Isfidbaja* (white gruel). Yehoshua, *Old Jerusalem*, pp. 45–46. Jacob M. Landau, *Abdul Hamid's Palestine* (London: André Deutsch, 1979), pp. 138–139. Patricia Smouha, *Middle Eastern Cooking* (London: André Deutsch, 1955), p. 15.

9. Yehoshua, *Old Jerusalem*, pp. 49–50. Alan Davidson, *Mediterranean Seafood* (Harmondsworth: Penguin Books, 1987), pp. 140–143. Grey mullet = *Bouri* (Arabic).

10. Yaari, p. 72. Jeremiah J. Berman, *Shehitah* (New York: Bloch Publishing Company, 1941), pp. 232–233.

11. Interview with Mr. Solomon Cikurel. Yehoshua, *Old Jerusalem*, pp. 47–49, 56. Viviane and Nina Moryousseff, *Moroccan Jewish Cookery* (Paris: J.P. Taillandier/Soche Press, 1983), pp. 65–69. Joseph A. Sutton, *Magic Carpet Aleppo-in-Flatbush* (New York: Thayer-Jacoby, 1986), p. 161.

12. Yehoshua, *Old Jerusalem*, pp. 48, 57. Raphael Patai, *On Jewish Folklore* (Detroit: Wayne State University Press, 1983), pp. 308–312.

13. The responsa of Rabbi Solomon ben Abraham Adret (1235–1310), particularly numbers 67, 133, 228, 248, 554, 623, 709 (Bnei Brak, 1958). A. Cohen, *An Anglo-Jewish Scrapbook 1600–1840: The Jew through English Eyes* (London: M.L. Cailingold, 1943), p. 77. Yehoshua, *Old Jerusalem*, p. 83. Reginetta Haboucha, "Societal Values in the Judeo-Spanish Folktales," in *Studies in Jewish Folklore*, ed. Frank Talmadge (Cambridge, MA: Association for Jewish Studies, 1980), p. 160. Mordecai Kosover, *Arabic Elements in Palestinian Yiddish* (Jerusalem: Rubin Mass, 1966), p. 247. David M. Bunis, "Food Terms and Traditions in Sefer Damesek Eliezer," *Jerusalem Studies in Jewish Folklore* 5–6 (1984): 189 (hereafter cited as Bunis).

14. Don Salvador de Madariaga, *Spain and the Jews* (London: Jewish Historical Society of England, 1946), p. 23. Léon Poliakov, *The History of Anti-Semitism: From Mohammed to the Marranos*, vol. 2 (London: Routledge & Kegan Paul, 1974), p. 180. Rios, "Olive Oil," pp. 308–312.

15. Mordecai Kosover, *Arabic Elements in Palestinian Yiddish*, p. 248. Alexander Russell, *The Natural History of Aleppo*, vol. 2 (London: Ward, Lock, and Bowden, 1794), p. 61. Edward William Lane, *An Account of the Manners*

and Customs of the Modern Egyptians (London: Ward, Lock and Bowden, n.d.), p. 512. Lucy M. J. Garnett, *The Women of Turkey and their Folk-Lore*, vol. 2 (London: David Noble, 1891), p. 46.

16. Yehoshua, *Old Jerusalem*, p. 54. Hillgarth, p. 12. Aryeh Shmuelevitz, *The Jews of the Ottoman Empire* (Leiden: E. J. Brill, 1984), p. 140.

17. Yehoshua, *Old Jerusalem*, p. 53. Herbert C. Dobrinsky, *A Treasury of Sephardic Laws and Customs* (New York: Ktav Publishing House/Yeshiva University Press, 1986), p. 240 (hereafter cited as Dobrinsky). Interview with Mr. Solomon Cikurel. David M. Bunis, "The Culinary Terminology and Traditions of the Sephardim in the Sixteenth Through the Nineteenth Centuries: A Historical Study based on Rabbinical Sources," *Jewish Folklore and Ethnology Review* 9:1 (1987): 22 (hereafter cited as Bunis, "Historical Study"). Gunay Kut, "On the Additions by Shirwani (15th Century?) to his Translation of a Cookery Book (13th Century)," *First International Food Congress*, organized by Feyzi Halici (Ankara, 1988), p. 178.

18. Michael Molho, *Usos Y Costumbres de Los Sefardies de Salonica* (Madrid-Barcelona: Instituto Arias-Montero, 1950), pp. 204–205 (hereafter cited as Molho, *Sefardies*). Dobrinsky, p. 240. Marc D. Angel, *The Jews of Rhodes* (New York: Sepher-Hermon Press, 1978), p. 123 (hereafter cited as Angel, *Rhodes*). Miner and Krinn, *From My Grandmother's Kitchen*, pp. 41–42.

19. Dobrinksy, p. 242. Israel M. Goldman, *The Life and Times of Rabbi David Ibn Abi Zimra* (New York: Jewish Theological Seminary of America, 1970), p. 143. Barbara Kirshenblatt-Gimblett, "The Kosher Gourmet in the Nineteenth-Century Kitchen: Three Jewish Cookbooks in Historical Perspective," *The Journal of Gastronomy* 2:4 (Winter 1986/1987), footnote 27. Rudolph Grewe, "Catalan Cuisine in an Historical Perspective," *National & Regional Styles of Cookery*, Oxford Symposium, 1981 (London: Prospect Books, 1981), pp. 174–176. Samuel G. Armistead and Joseph H. Silverman, "Rare Judeo Spanish Ballads from Monastir (Yugoslavia)," *The American Sephardi* 7, 8 (1975).

20. Max Grunwald, "Jewish Cookery," *Vallentine's Jewish Encyclopaedia* (London: Shapiro, Vallentine & Company, 1938), p. 157 (hereafter cited as Grunwald, "Jewish Cookery"). Miner and Krinn, *From My Grandmother's Kitchen*, pp. 24–25.

21. Interview with Mr. Solomon Cikurel. Angel, *Rhodes*, p. 69. Levy, *Sephardic Cookery*, p. 35. Claudia Roden, *A Book of Middle Eastern Food* (Harmondsworth: Penguin Books, 1970), pp. 20, 309 (hereafter cited as Claudia Roden). Molho, *Sefardies*, p. 205. David L. Gold, "The Etymology of the English Bread Name *pita:* A Study in Jewish Intralinguistics," *Jewish Language Review* 4 (1984): 58–76. David L. Gold, "More on the Origins of the English Bread Name *pita,*" *Jewish Linguistic Studies* (1989), pp. 42–52 but particularly pp. 47–48. Sandra Debenedetti Stow wrote that the earliest citation for the bread was *pizza* in a fourteenth-century Jewish-Italian text. Pita bread derived its name from medieval Italian *pizza* > Greek *pitta* > Italian *pitta*. Southeastern Judezmo pita bread was not only of Greek origin but of "immediate Jewish Italian origin," as Italian Jews may have diffused this type of bread throughout the Balkans.

22. Eliachar, p. 54. Yehoshua, *Old Jerusalem*, pp. 46, 47, 56.

23. Eliachar, p. 54. Miner and Krinn, *From My Grandmother's Kitchen*, pp. 131, 159. Hillgarth, pp. 182–183. Claudia Roden, pp. 95–96, 101–102. Bunis *Historical Study*, pp. 22–23. Lucie Bolens, *La cuisine andalouse un art de vivre XIe–XIIIe siècle*, pp. 167, 299, 300. *Sanbusaks* were known to the Sephardim in Spain.

24. Patti Shosteck, *A Lexicon of Jewish Cooking* (Chicago: Contemporary Books, 1981), pp. 5, 6, 213. *The Jewish Manual*, pp. 32–35. Ambrosio Huici Miranda, *La Cocina Hispano-Magribi Durante La Epoca Almonhade: Revista Del Instituto De Estudios Islamics en Madrid* 5 (1957): 137. Martin Alonso, *Dictionario Medieval Español*, vol. 1 (Salamanca: Universidad Pontificia de Salamanca, 1986), *Albondiga*.

25. Eliachar, p. 54.

26. Dobrinsky, p. 325. Rabbi Shemtob Gaguine, *Keter Shem Tob*, vol. 6 (London, 1957), p. 54.

27. Dobrinsky, pp. 326–327. Reay Tannahill, *Food in History* (Harmondsworth: Penguin Books, 1988), p. 147.

28. In Salonika the chicken was cooked in tomato sauce for the meal prior to the fast of Yom Kippur. Lucette Valensi and Nathan Wachtel, *Jewish Memories* (Berkeley and Los Angeles: University of California Press, 1991), p. 65. H. J. Zimmels, *Ashkenazim and Sephardim* (London: Marla Publications, 1976), p. 267. Eliachar, p. 55. Yehoshua, *Old Jerusalem*, p. 47. Angel, *Rhodes*, p. 127. Dobrinsky, p. 360.

29. Dobrinsky, pp. 280–283. "Ask the Rabbi," *Jewish Chronicle*, March 11, 1983. Rev. P. Beaton, *The Jews in the East*, vol. 1 (Westport, CT: Greenwood Press, 1975), p. 103. *Sephardi Bulletin* (March/April 1988). Herbert C. Dobrinsky, *Selected Laws & Customs of Sephardic Jewry*, vol. 2 (Ann Arbor, MI: University Microfilms International, 1980), p. 475. Gaguine, *Keter Shem Tob* 3:166.

30. Dobrinsky, p. 278. Eliachar, p. 56. Carlos Carrete Parrondo, "Fraternization between Jews and Christians in Spain before 1492," *The American Sephardi* 9 (1978): pp. 16, 17.

31. Dobrinksy, p. 291.

32. Eliachar, p. 52. Bunis, "Historical Study," p. 23. Martin Alonso, *Dictionario Medieval Español*, vol. 1, *Bunuelo* (Salamanca: Universidad Pontificia de Salamanca, 1986). Penelope Casas, *The Foods and Wines of Spain* (Harmondsworth: Penguin Books, 1982), p. 346–347.

33. Eliachar, pp. 54, 56. Dobrinsky, pp. 385–388. Angel, *Rhodes*, pp. 129–130. Jose M. Estrugo, *Los Sefardies* (Havana, 1958), p. 66. Maria Johnson, "Notes on Turkish contributions to Balkan Flour Confectionery," *First International Food Congress*, Halici, pp. 153–162. Bunis, p. 175. Charles Perry, "Baklava Not Proven Greek," *Petits Propos Culinaires* 27 (October 1987): 47–48.

34. Yehoshua, *Old Jerusalem*, pp. 44, 54. Iris Origo, *The Merchant of Prato* (Harmondsworth: Penguin Books, 1979), p. 295.

35. Estrugo, *Los Sefardies*, p. 66. Bunis, p. 181. Yehoshua, *Old Jerusalem*, p. 57. Maxime Rodinson, "On the Etymology of 'Losange,' " *Petits Propos Culinaires* 23 (July 1986): 15–22.

36. Max Grunwald, "Jewish Cookery," in *Vallentine's Jewish Encyclo-*

paedia (London: Shapiro, Vallentine & Company, n.d.), pp. 156–157. Yehoshua, *Old Jerusalem*, p. 68. Mair Jose Benardete, *Hispanic Culture and Character of the Sephardic Jews* (New York: Hispanic Institute in the United States, 1952), pp. 117–118.

37. Penelope Casas, *Foods and Wines of Spain* (Harmondsworth: Penguin Books, n.d.), p. 119, Pickled Eggplant, Almagro Style. Jose M. Estrugo, *Los Sefardies*, pp. 67–68. Charles Perry, "Puff paste is Spanish," *Petits Propos Culinaires* 17 (June 1984): 57–62. Charles Perry, "Buran 1100 Years in the Life of a dish," *The Journal of Gastronomy* 1 (Summer 1984): 67–75, particularly pp. 71, 73.

38. Dobrinsky, pp. 293, 329. Abraham Cardozo, "A Lyrical Excursion into Sephardic Gastronomy," *American Sephardi* 5 (1971): 1–2. *The Jewish Manual*, ed. Ruth L. Gales and Lila T. Gold (New York: Nightingale Books, 1983), pp. 114–117, 124.

39. *Jewish Manual*, pp. 34, 84, 114–117, 119–120. Barbara Kirshenblatt-Gimblett, "The Kosher Gourmet in the Nineteenth Century Kitchen: Three Jewish Cookbooks in Historical Perspective," *Journal of Gastronomy* 2:4 (Winter 1986/1987): footnote 24. Jean Anderson, *The Food of Portugal* (London: Robert Hale, 1986), pp. 48, 84, 85, 246–248. *The Jewish Manual*, p. 152. Lucie Bolens, *La cuisine andalouse, un art de vivre XI–XIIIe siècle*, pp. 94 (*sikbaj*), 295. *Escabeche* comes from the Persian *sikbaj*.

40. Henry Mayhew, *Mayhew's London*, ed. Peter Quennell (London: Bracken Books, 1984), p. 297. *The Jewish Manual*, pp. 40, 46, 47, 87, 126, 156.

41. Barbara Kirshenblatt-Gimblett, "Hebrew Cookery: An Early Jewish Cookbook from the Antipodes," *Petits Propos Culinaires* 28 (April 1988): 11–21. Letter of Lionel Simmonds, *Jewish Chronicle*, October 22, 1982. Bea Polak, *Recepten uit de joodse keuken van toen en nu* (Amsterdam: Amphora Books, 1986), *Boterkoek*, p. 90, *Botercake*, p. 93, *Orgeadebolus*, p. 98.

42. Noah Shapiro, "Sugar and Cane Sugar in Hebrew Literature," *Hebrew Medical Journal* 2 (1957): 128–130. S. D. Goitein, *A Mediterranean Society: Economic Foundations*, vol. 1 (Berkeley and Los Angeles: University of California Press, 1967), pp. 81, 125, 126, 367. Alfred Crosby, *Columbian Exchange* (Westport, CT: Greenwood Press, 1973), pp. 178–181. Marcus Arkin, *Aspects of Jewish Economic History* (Philadelphia: Jewish Publication Society of America, 1975), pp. 199, 200, 206. Herbert I. Bloom, *The Economic Activities of the Jews of Amsterdam in the Seventeenth and Eighteenth Centuries* (Port Washington, NY: Kennikat Press, 1969), pp. 36–39. Stephen Alexander Fortune, *Merchants & Jews: The Struggle for British West Indian Commerce 1650–1750* (Florida: University of Florida Press, 1984), p. 72 (hereafter cited as Fortune).

43. Fortune, pp. 75–77. Salon Baron, Arcadius Kahan, et al., *Economic History of the Jews* (New York: Schocken Books, 1976), p. 190. Jonathan I. Israel, *European Jewry in the Age of Mercantilism* (Oxford: Clarendon Press, 1989), pp. 161, 177 (hereafter cited as Israel, *Mercantilism*).

44. Israel, *Mercantilism*, p. 179. Isaiah Sachar, "The Emergence of the Modern Pictorial Stereotype of The Jews in England," in *Studies in the Cultural Life of the Jews in England*, ed. Dov Noy and Issachar Ben-Ami (Jerusalem: Magnes Press, 1975), p. 362. Israel Abrahams, *Jewish Life in the Middle Ages* (London: Edward Goldston, 1932), p. 154. Cecil Roth, *The Jewish*

Contribution to Civilization (London: Macmillan & Company, 1938), pp. 222–223. Jean Leclant, "Coffee and Cafes in Paris 1644–1693," in *Food and Drink in History* (Baltimore: Johns Hopkins University Press, 1979), pp. 86–97. Oswald O. Dutch, "Seeds of a Noble Inheritance," in *Jews of Austria*, ed. Josef Fraenkel (Vallentine, Mitchell, 1967), pp. 189–190.

45. Anita Libman Lebeson, "The American Jewish Chronicle," in *The Jews: Their History*, ed. Louis Finkelstein (New York: Schocken Books, 1974), pp. 488–489. Abraham David, "The Integration of the Jews of the Land of Israel in Mediterranean Trade in the Early Ottoman Period," in *The Mediterranean and The Jews: Banking, Finance and International Trade (XVI–XVIII Centuries)*, ed. Ariel Toaff and Simon Schwarzfuchs (Ramat Gan: Bar-Ilan University Press, 1989).

CHAPTER 8

1. B. E. F. Smith and D. Christian, *Bread and Salt: A Social and Economic History of Food and Drink in Russia* (Cambridge: Cambridge University Press, 1984), pp. 9, 255, 256 (hereafter cited as Smith and Christian). Herman Pollack, *Jewish Folkways in Germanic Lands (1648–1806)* (Cambridge, MA: M.I.T. Press, 1971), pp. 98, 270 (hereafter cited as Pollack, *Folkways*). Myer S. Lew, *The Jews of Poland: Their Political, Economic, Social and Communal Life as reflected in the works of Rabbi Moses Isserles* (London: Edward Goldston, 1944), p. 97. Salo Wittmayer Baron, *A Social and Religious History of the Jews*, vol. 16 (New York: Columbia University Press, 1976), p. 113. Leo W. Schwarz, *Memoirs of My People* (New York: Schocken Books, 1963), pp. 106, 111, 112 (hereafter cited as Schwarz, *Memoirs*).

2. Solomon Maimon, *An Autobiography*, trans. J. Clark Murray (London: Alexander Gardner, 1888), pp. 10, 145, 146.

3. *A Jewish Life under the Tsars: The Autobiography of Chaim Aronson 1825–1888*, trans. from the Hebrew by Norman Marsden (Totowa, NJ: Allan-held Osmun, 1983), pp. 98–100 (hereafter cited as *Aronson Autobiography*). Schwarz, *Memoirs*, p. 222. Israel Kasovich, *The Days of Our Years: Personal and General Reminiscences 1859–1929* (New York: Jordan Publishing Company, 1929), pp. 4, 13 (hereafter cited as Kasovich, *Days*).

4. Smith and Christian, pp. 9, 75. Seymour Siegel, "The War of the *Kitniyot* (Legumes)," in Arthur A. Chiel, ed., *Perspectives on Jews and Judaism: Essays in Honour of Wolfe Kelman* (New York: The Rabbinical Assembly of America, 1978), pp. 383–393. Louis Greenberg, *The Jews in Russia*, vol. 1 (New York: Schocken Books, 1976), p. 67. *Jewish Chronicle*, April 13, 1984.

5. Hirsh Abramowicz, *Fashvundene Geshalten* (Buenos Aires, 1958), pp. 468–469 (hereafter cited as Abramowicz). Interview with Mr. Chaim Berlin, formerly of Vilna. *The Samurai of Vishogrod: The Notebooks of Jacob Mara-teck*, retold by Shimon and Anita Wincelberg (Philadelphia: Jewish Publication Society of America, 1976), p. 64 (hereafter cited as *The Samurai*). Israel Cohen, *Jewish Life in Modern Times* (London: Methuen & Company, 1929), p. 49.

6. Abramowicz, pp. 468–469. Smith and Christian, p. 258.

7. Abramowicz, p. 470. Jacob A. Riis, *How the Other Half Lives* (Cambridge, MA: Harvard University Press, 1970), p. 84.

8. Abraham Ain, "Swislocz: Portrait of a Shtetl," in *Voices from the Yiddish*, ed. Irving Howe and Eliezar Greenberg (New York: Schocken Books, 1975), p. 104 (hereafter cited as Ain, "Swislocz"). Sholom Aleichem, *Tevye's Daughters* (New York: Crown Publishers, 1949), p. 31. Lesley Chamberlain, *The Food and Cooking of Russia* (Harmondsworth: Penguin Books, 1983), p. 250 (hereafter cited as Chamberlain, *Food of Russia*). Azia Yezierska, *Hungry Hearts and Other Stories* (London: Virago, 1987), p. 256. Louis Wirth, *The Ghetto* (Chicago: University of Chicago Press, 1956), p. 224. Irving Howe, *The Immigrant Jews of New York* (London: Routledge & Kegan Paul, 1976), p. 73. Manès Sperber, *God's Water-Carriers* (New York: Holmes & Meier, 1987).

9. Mordechai Kosover, *Yiddishe Maykholim* (New York: Yivo Institute for Jewish Research; reprinted from the Judah J. Joffe Bukh, 1958), pp. 116, 129 (hereafter cited as Kosover, *Maykholim*). Molly Lyons Bar-David, *The Israel Cookbook* (New York: Crown Publishers, 1964), p. 26. William Woys Weaver, *Sauerkraut Yankees* (Philadelphia: University of Pennsylvania Press, 1983), pp. 135–136. Evelyn Rose, *The Complete International Jewish Cookbook* (London: Pan Books, 1976), p. 290. Waverley Root, *The Food of Italy* (New York: Vintage Books, 1977), pp. 183–184. Edda Servi Machlin, *The Classic Cuisine of the Italian Jews* (New York: Everest House, 1981), p. 54. Anita Moesli, *Know Austria by Cooking* (Glasgow: Ossian Publishers, 1984), p. 22, Pressburger [Bratislava] *Nussbeugel* (croissants with nut filling). The bagel was not imported into Austria from Italy. An examination of recipes in Italian Renaissance cookery books kindly provided by Dr. Claudio Benporat shows that there is little to commend the hypothesis that the bagel was of Italian origin and developed out of the *ciambelle* (French, *gimblettes*; English, *jumbles*). See Bartolemeo Scappi, *Opera* (Venice, 1570), pp. 372–373. To make a stuffed *ciambelle*, see Roroli, *Singolar Dottrina* (Rome, 1560), p. 192. To make *ciambelle* and small biscuits from sugar and almonds, see Pollack, *Folkways*, pp. 275, 277.

10. William Woys Weaver, "Food with a Twist: The Pretzel Family Tree," *The World & I*, April 1991, pp. 616–623. Letter from William Woys Weaver to the author.

11. Yehuda Elzet [Zlotnik], *Yiddishe Maykholim* (Warsaw 1920), pp. 98–99 (hereafter cited as Elzet, *Maykholim*). Isaac Goss, *Gleanings* (Johannesburg: Kayor Publishers, n.d.), chapter on Rabbi J. C. Avida (Zlotnik)—an assessment and tribute, pp. 80–85. Shmarya Levin, *Childhood Exile* (London: George Routledge & Sons, 1935), pp. 110, 142. Diane K. Roskies and David G. Roskies, *The Shtetl Book* (New York: Ktav Publishing House, 1975), pp. 119, 121, 122 (hereafter cited as Roskies, *Shtetl*). Schwarz, *Memoirs*, p. 273. Patti Shosteck, *A Lexicon of Jewish Cooking* (Chicago: Contemporary Books, 1981), pp. 17–19. Stanley Regelson cited in Walter Zenner, "Kashrut and Rationality: The Dietary Laws in Recent Anthropological writing," *Jewish Folklore and Ethnology Newsletter* 1:1 (May 1977): 15.

12. Abramowicz, p. 462. Ben-Sasson, ed., *A History of the Jewish People* (London: Weidenfeld and Nicholson, 1977), p. 790. Waverley Root, *Food* (New York: Simon & Schuster, 1980), pp. 378–387. Redcliffe Salaman, *The History and Social Influence of the Potato* (Cambridge: Cambridge University Press,

1985), pp. 122–123 (hereafter cited as Salaman, *Potato*). Peter Stearns, *European Society in Upheaval: Social History Since 1750* (New York: Macmillan Publishing Company, 1975), pp. 66–67.

13. Alfred W. Crosby, *The Colombian Exchange: Biological and Ecological Consequences of 1492* (Westport, CT: Greenwood Press, 1973), p. 184. Jerome Blum, *Lord and Peasant in Russia* (New York: Atheneum, 1966). V. L. Benes and N. G. Pounds, *Poland* (London: Benn, 1970), p. 97. Smith and Christian, p. 286. Abramowitz, pp. 466–467. Nathan Goldenberg, *Thought for Food* (Orpington Kent: Food Trade Press, 1989), p. 2. "There was also a very large storage room and loft where wood and reserve foods could be stored for the winter; it was also used as a toilet during the winter months."

14. Raphael Mahler, *Hasidim and the Enlightenment* (Philadelphia: Jewish Publication Society of America, 1985), p. 186 (hereafter cited as Mahler, *Hasidim*). Greenberg, *Jews in Russia* 1:160. Schwarz, *Memoirs*, p. 276. Ruth Rubin, *Voices of a People* (Philadelphia: Jewish Publication Society of America, 1979), p. 279 (hereafter cited as Rubin, *Voices*).

15. Abramowicz, pp. 462, 465. Don Gussow, *Chaia Sonia* (New York: Bantam Books, 1981), pp. 36–37. Ain, *Swislocz*, p. 100. Mark Zborowski and Elizabeth Herzog, *Life Is With People* (New York: Schocken Books, 1978), p. 257 (hereafter cited as Zborowski and Herzog). Smith and Christian, p. 257. Abraham Cohen, *An Anglo-Jewish Scrapbook* (London: M. Cailingold, 1943), p. 156. Charlotte Baum, Paula Hyman, and Sonya Michel, *The Jewish Woman in America* (New York: New American Library, 1977), p. 66.

16. Abramowicz, pp. 462–464. Marta Ochorowicz-Monatowa, *Polish Cooking* (London: André Deutsch, 1960), pp. 203, 255. Lesley Chamberlain, *The Food of Eastern Europe* (Harmondsworth: Penguin Books, 1989), p. 315, Dumpling; South German *Knodel*; Czech *Knedlicky*; Polish *Knedle*. Pollack, *Folkways*, p. 268.

17. Ain, *Swislocz*, p. 100. Abramowicz, pp. 463, 470. Elzet, *Maykholim*, p. 1, pp. 11. Smith and Christian, p. 258. Charles Perry, "Tracta, Trahanas, Kishk," *Petits Propos Culinaires* 19:61. Kosover, *Maykholim*, p. 143. Roskies, *Shtetl*, p. 38.

18. Smith and Christian, p. 176. Abramowicz, pp. 460, 461. Rosalind B. Schwartz, "The Geography of Two Food Terms: A Study in Yiddish Lexical Variation," in *The Field of Yiddish*, Third Collection, ed. Marvin I. Herzog, Wita Ravid, and Uriel Weinreich (The Hague: Mouton & Company, 1969), pp. 240–266. Jack Lang and Lis Leigh, *The Definitive Borshch Recipe* in a paper to the First Oxford Symposium of Jewish Food in 1989; suggested that borscht was an ancient Ukrainian peasant food, but possibly it is of only medieval origin. I. J. Singer, *The Brothers Ashkenazi* (New York: Antheum, 1980), p. 179.

19. Abramowicz, pp. 459–460. Kim Chernin, *In My Mother's House* (London: Virago, 1985), p. 3. Chaim Grade, *The Yeshiva*, vol. 2 (New York: Menorah Publishing, 1979), p. 59. Patti Shosteck, *A Lexicon of Jewish Cooking* (Chicago: Contemporary Books, 1981), pp. 189–190. Lesley Chamberlain, *The Food and Cooking of Russia* (Harmondsworth: Penguin Books, 1983), pp. 74–75. I. J. Singer, *Of a World That Is No More* (London: Faber and Faber, 1987), p. 14. Gussow, *Chaia Sonia*, p. 36.

20. William Woys Weaver, *Sauerkraut Yankees* (Philadelphia: University of Pennsylvania Press, 1983), pp. 153, 154, 174, 175. Shmarya Levin, *Childhood in Exile* (London: George Routledge & Sons, 1935), p. 110. Molly Lyons Bar-David, *The Israeli Cookbook* (New York: Crown Publishers, 1964), p. 220. Abramowicz, p. 461.

21. Arthur Michael Samuel, *The Herring, and its effect on the History of Britain* (London: John Murray, 1918), pp. 108, 170, 171.

22. Harry Finkelstein, *Memoirs* (Hebrew University Library, MS VAR 380), pp. 75, 189, 246, 247, 248, 249. Clifford R. Barnett, *Poland: Its People, its Society and Culture* (New Haven: MRAF Press, 1958), p. 245. *Jewish Chronicle*, March 28, 1986.

23. Chaim Bermant, "How herrings have become the rich man's delicacy," *Jewish Chronicle*, October 19, 1984. Edouard de Pomiane, *The Jews of Poland: Recollections and Recipes* (Garden Grove, CA: Pholiota Press, 1985), p. 123. Schwarz, *Memoirs*, p. 276. Zborowski and Herzog, p. 257.

24. Smith and Christian, pp. 262, 266, 268. Levin, *Childhood in Exile*, pp. 110–111. Mahler, *Hasidim*, p. 186. *Aronson Autobiography*, p. 99. Kasovich, *Days*, pp. 4, 86. Chaim Weizmann, *Trial and Error* (London: Hamish Hamilton, 1949), p. 15. Interview with Mr. Ralph Cain.

25. Abramowicz, pp. 466–467. Kasovich, *Days*, p. 112. Jack Kugelmass and Jonathan Boyarin, *From a Ruined Garden: The Memorial Books of Polish Jewry* (New York: Schocken Books, 1983), p. 78. Isaac Bashevis Singer, *In My Father's Court* (Harmondsworth: Penguin Books, 1980), pp. 140–141. Joachim Schoenfeld, *Shtetl Memoirs* (Hoboken, NJ: Ktav Publishing House, 1985), pp. 31–32 (hereafter cited as *Shtetl Memoirs*).

26. Redcliffe Salaman, *The History and Social Influence of the Potato* (Cambridge: Cambridge University Press, 1985), p. 123–124. Abramowicz, p. 467.

27. *Shtetl Memoirs*, p. 95. Shosteck, *Lexicon of Jewish Cooking*, pp. 144–146. Crosby, *The Columbian Exchange*, pp. 179–181. I. J. Singer, *Of a World That Is No More*, p. 85. Abramowicz, p. 470. Sholom Aleichem, *Tevye's Daughters* (New York: Crown Publishers, 1949), p. 5. Chamberlain, *Food of Russia*, p. 280. Joan Nathan, *The Jewish Holiday Kitchen* (New York: Schocken Books, 1979), pp. 225, 243. K. C. Chang, *Food in Chinese Culture* (New Haven, CT: Yale University Press, 1977), p. 338. Nicolae Dunare, *Fromagers Juifs Dans Les Carpathes Nordiques De La Roumanie (1860–1940)*, *Folklore Research Center Studies*, vol. 3, ed. Issachar Ben-Ami (Jerusalem: Magnes Press, 1972), pp. 242–243. Isaac Bashevis Singer, *In My Father's Court*, p. 217.

28. Levin, *Childhood in Exile*, p. 119. Abraham Cahan, *The Education of Abraham Cahan* (Philadelphia: Jewish Publication Society of America, 1969), p. 82. Marvin I. Herzog, *The Yiddish Language in Northern Poland: Its Geography and History* (The Hague: Mouton & Company, 1965), p. 28. Kim Chernin, *In My Mother's House* (London: Virago, 1985), p. 35. Irving Howe, *The Immigrant Jews of New York* (London: Routledge & Kegan Paul, 1976), p. 175. *The Samurai*, p. 59.

29. Interview with Mr. Ralph Cain. Hanna Goodman, *Jewish Cooking*

Around the World (Philadelphia: Jewish Publication Society of America, 1981), p. 18. Kim Chernin, *In My Mother's House*, p. 21. Ain, *Swislocz*, p. 103. *Shtetl Memoirs*, pp. 29–30. Sholom Aleichem, *Tevye's Daughters* (New York: Crown Publishers, 1949), pp. 85, 87–89. Grade, *Yeshiva* 1:159. Esther Kreitman, *Deborah* (London: Virago, 1983), pp. 41, 121. Zalman Shazar, *Morning Stars* (Philadelphia: Jewish Publication Society of America, 1967), p. 35.

30. *Aronson Autobiography*, pp. 69, 80, 297. Louis Greenberg, *The Jews in Russia* 1:58. Abraham Menes, "Patterns of Jewish Scholarship in Eastern Europe," in *The Jews: Their Religion and Culture*, ed. Louis Finkelstein, vol. 2 (New York: Schocken Books, 1975), pp. 205, 208.

31. Kasovich, *Days*, pp. 24, 25, 36, 38, 53. Finkelstein, *Memoirs*, p. 17.

32. Raphael Mahler, *A History of Modern Jewry 1780–1815* (London: Vallentine Mitchell, 1971), p. 250. Zborowski and Herzog, p. 253. Jack Kugelmass and Jonathan Boyarin, *From a Ruined Garden* (New York: Schocken Books, 1983), pp. 71, 83, 84. Steven Hertzberg, *Strangers Within the Gate: The Jews of Atlanta 1845–1915* (Philadelphia: Jewish Publication Society of America, 1978), p. 91. Alex M. Jacob, "The Jews of Falmouth," *Transactions of the Jewish Historical Society of England* 17:65. In 1780 a bailiff described the condition of the Jewish peddlers in Alsace Lorraine as living all day "on a piece of bread, or a few apples, or another fruit, depending on the season." Zosa Szajkowski, *The Economic Status of Jews in Alsace, Metz and Lorraine (1648–1789)* (New York: Editions Historiques Franco-Juive, 1954), p. 62.

33. *The Samurai*, p. 59. De Pomiane, *Jews of Poland*, p. 65. Ruth Rubin, *Voices of a People* (Philadelphia: Jewish Publication Society of America, 1979), p. 281. Mahler, *Hasidism*, p. 192.

34. Roskies, *Shtetl*, pp. 38, 39, 40.

35. N. Shapiro, "Sugar and cane sugar in Hebrew Literature," *Hebrew Medical Journal* 2 (1957): 89–94, 128–130. Sidney W. Mintz, *Sweetness and Power* (Harmondsworth: Penguin Books, 1986), pp. 73, 190, 191.

36. Salo W. Baron, *The Russian Jew Under the Tsars and Soviets* (New York: Schocken Books, 1987), pp. 89–90. Salo W. Baron, "Arcadius Kahan and Others," in *Economic History of the Jews* (New York: Schocken Books, 1976), p. 190. V. L. Benes and N. G. J. Pounds, *Poland* (London: Benn, 1970), p. 97. Interview with Mr. Kazmierczak.

37. De Pomiane, *Jews of Poland*, pp. 65, 173.

38. *Encyclopaedia Judaica*, article on the *Korobka*. Mahler, *Hasidism*, pp. 4, 177. Mahler, *History of Modern Jewry 1780–1815*, p. 355.

39. I. J. Singer, *The Brothers Ashkenazi*, p. 179. Isaac Bashevis Singer, *In My Father's Court*, pp. 118–119.

40. *Encyclopaedia Judaica*, article on the *Korobka*. Mahler, *A History of Modern Jewry 1780–1815*, pp. 355–356. Isaac Bashevis Singer, *In My Father's Court*, p. 119.

41. Mahler, *Hasidism*, pp. 142–143. Chone Szmeruk, "The Social Significance of Hassidic Shekhita," *Zion* 20 (1955): 47–72. Rebecca Himber Berg, "Childhood in Lithuania," in *Memoirs of My People*, ed. Leo W. Schwarz (New York: Schocken Books, 1963), pp. 271–274. Ain, *Swislocz*, p. 92.

42. Zosa Szajkowski, *Jews and the French Revolution of 1789, 1830 and*

1848 (New York: Ktav Publishing House, 1970), p. 1151. Howe, *Immigrant Jews of New York*, pp. 27, 175. Robert Weisbrot, *The Jews of Argentina* (Philadelphia: Jewish Publication Society of America, 1979), p. 54.

CHAPTER 9

1. Hayyim Schauss, *The Jewish Festivals* (London: Jewish Chronicle Publications, 1986), p. 21 (hereafter cited as Schauss). Mark Zborowski and Elizabeth Herzog, *Life Is With People* (New York: Schocken Books, 1978), pp. 38–39 (hereafter cited as Zborowski and Herzog). Joachim Schoenfeld, *Shtetl Memoirs* (Hoboken, NJ: Ktav Publishing House, 1985), pp. 85–86 (hereafter cited as *Shtetl Memoirs*). Edouard de Pomaine, *The Jews of Poland: Recollections and Recipes*, trans. Josephine Bacon (Garden Grove, CA: Pholiota Press, 1985), pp. 45, 46, 123 (hereafter cited as de Pomaine). I. J. Singer, *Of a World That Is No More* (London: Faber & Faber, 1987), p. 118. Asher Barash, *Pictures from a Brewery* (London: Peter Owen, 1972), p. 21. Nicholas Stavroulakis, *Cookbook of the Jews of Greece* (Port Jefferson, NY: Cadmus Press, 1986), pp. 60–61). Herman Pollack, *Jewish Folkways in Germanic Lands 1648–1806* (Cambridge, MA: M.I.T. Press, 1971), pp. 96, 158, 268 (hereafter cited as Pollack).

2. *Shtetl Memoirs*, pp. 85–86. Louis Wirth, *The Ghetto* (Chicago, 1956), p. 224.

3. Schauss, pp. 21–22. Zborowski and Herzog, pp. 38–39. Yehuda Elzet (Zlotnick), "Customs of Israel," *Reshumot* 1 (1918): 338–339 (hereafter cited as Elzet, *Reshumot*). Esther Kreitman, *Deborah* (London: Virago, 1983), p. 122. Chaim Grade, *My Mother's Sabbath Days* (New York: Schocken Books, 1987), p. 131 (hereafter cited as Grade).

4. Pollack, pp. 162–163. Kreitman, *Deborah*, p. 123. Zborowski, p. 40. Rina Valero, *Delights of Jerusalem* (Tel-Aviv: Namar Publishing House, 1985), pp. 11–12.

5. Mishnah Berurah, *Shulchan Aruch: Orach Chayim*, vol. 3 (Jerusalem: Feldheim Publishers, 1980), Laws of Shabbos 249 (2) and (3). E. J. Schochet, *Bach: Rabbi Joel Sirkes* (Jerusalem: Feldheim Publishers, 1971), pp. 36, 192. Bella Chagall, *First Encounter* (New York: Schocken Books, 1983), p. 24. Abraham Ain, "Swislocz, Portrait of a *Shtetl*," in Irving Howe and Eliezar Greenberg, *Voices from the Yiddish* (New York: Schocken Books, 1975), p. 100. Hirsch Abramowicz, *Fashvundene Geshtalten* (Buenos Aires, 1958), p. 471. I. J. Singer, *Of a World That Is No More*, pp. 116–117.

6. Dovid Katz, "The Proto Dialectology of Ashkenaz," in *Origins of the Yiddish Language* (Oxford: Pergamon Press, 1987), pp. 47–60. David L. Gold, "Towards a Study of the Origins of the Two Synonymous Yiddish Adjectives: *pareve* and *minikh*," *Jewish Language Review* 5 (1985): 128–139.

7. Israel Cohen, *Journal of a Jewish Traveller* (London: John Lane, 1925), p. 125. Max Grunwald, "Aus dem jüdischen Kochbuch," *Menorah* 6 (1920): 519 (hereafter cited as Grunwald). Samuel Krauss, "Aus der jüdischen Volksküche," *Mitteleilungen zur jüdischen Volkskunde* 18 (1915): 2, 5 (hereafter cited as Krauss, *Volksküche*). David L. Gold, "The Etymology of the English

Bread name *pita:* A Study in Jewish Intralinguistics," *Jewish Language Review* 4 (1984): 62, 64. Lawrence D. Loeb, *Outcaste Jewish Life in Southern Iran* (New York: Gordon and Breach, 1977), p. 178. Erich Brauer, *The Jews of Kurdistan* (Jerusalem: Institute of Ethnology and Folklore, 1947), p. 219. Abraham P. Bloch, *The Biblical and Historical Background of Jewish Customs and Ceremonies* (New York: Ktav Publishing House, 1980).

8. Joan Nathan, *The Jewish Holiday Kitchen* (New York: Schocken Books, 1979), p. 21 (hereafter cited as Nathan). Zorica Herbst-Kraucz, *Old Jewish Dishes* (Budapest: Corvina, 1988), p. 21. Grunwald, p. 519. Krauss, *Volksküche,* pp. 1–7. Schauss, p. 31. Theodore H. Gaster, *Festivals of the Jewish New Year* (New York: William Sloane Associates, 1966), pp. 278–279. Freddy Raphael and Robert Wey, *Juifs en Alsace* (Toulouse: Privat, 1977), p. 338. Sabbath Bread = *Berchess* (hereafter cited as Raphael and Weyl).

9. *Jewish Language Review,* 1984, pp. 106, 287, 288. Pollack, pp. 101, 275.

10. Joseph Bar Moses, *Leket Yosher,* vol 1, ed. Dr. J. Freimann (Berlin: Von Itzkowski, 1903), p. 49. Joseph Karo, *Shulchan Aruch: Orach Hayim,* ed. with commentaries of the Rema and the Baer Hetev (Jerusalem, 1983). *Hilchos Shabbos* 242 (hereafter cited as Rema).

11. Elzet, *Reshumot,* pp. 338–339. Yehuda Elzet, *Yiddishe Maykholim (Jewish Foods)* (Warsaw, 1920), part 1, pp. 26–27 (hereafter cited as Elzet, *Maykholim).* Interviews with Mr. C. Berlin and Mrs. Kitty Cooper. *In Praise of the Baal Shem Tov,* ed. Dan Ben-Amos and Jerome R. Mintz (New York: Schocken Books, 1984), p. 29. Sarah Kelly, *Festive Baking in Austria, Germany and Switzerland* (Harmondsworth: Penguin Books, 1985), pp. 168–169.

12. S. S. Prawer, *Heine's Jewish Comedy: A Study of His Portraits of Jews and Judaism* (Oxford: Clarendon Press, 1985), p. 398 (hereafter cited as Prawer). *Rieder-Sachsisches Koch-Buch* (Altona and Lubeck: David Iverson, 1758), p. 286. *Neues Hannoverisches Kochbuch* (Hanover: Brothers Hahn, 1800), p. 146. *Die Colner Kochinn* (Cologne: Arnold Christian Hass, 1806), p. 90. I owe these references to German fish recipes and other similar references to the generosity of Herr Ulf Löchner, who made photostats of the relevant sections of German cookery books available to me.

13. *Neues Hannoverisches Kochbuch,* p. 146. Nathan, p. 71. De Pomaine, p. 126. Rebecca Wolf, *Kochbuch für Israelitische Frauen* (Berlin: Wolf Cohn Verlag & Antiquariat, 1875), pp. 111–112 (hereafter cited as Wolf). Raphael and Weyl, p. 303. Esther Levy, *Jewish Cookery Book,* Josephine Bacon Facsimile Edition (Garden Grove, CA: Pholiota Press, 1982), pp. 20, 176.

14. *Daz Buoch Von Guoter Spise* (1350), ed. Gerold Hayer (Göppingen: Alfred Kummerle, 1976), pp. 17, 27. *Von Speisen,* 1531, recipe for *Dreierlei Essen von Einem Fisch. Koch und Kellermeistern* (Frankfurt on Main: Thomas Rebart, 1566), recipe for *Dreierlen Essen von Einem Fisch. Koch und Kellermeisteren* (Frankfurt on Main: Sigmund Feyrabend, 1581), p. 29. *Sefer Maharil, Hilchos Shabbos* (Lublin, 1904), p. 28b. Pollack, p. 97. Wolf, pp. 118–119.

15. K. C. Chang, ed., *Food in Chinese Culture* (New Haven: Yale University Press, 1977), pp. 30, 67, 102–103, 115, "fine minced fresh carp" (Han period). Waverley Root, *Food* (New York: Simon & Schuster, 1980), p. 49. J. Litman,

240	*Notes for pages 179–182*

Yitzhak Schipper's Contributions to the Understanding of the Economic Role of the Jews in Medieval Poland (Ann Arbor, MI: University Microfilms International, 1968), p. 268. I owe this idea to Josephine Bacon.

16. Massialot, *Le Cuisinier Roial et Bourgeois* (Paris, 1698), p. 177. Massialot, *Le Nouveau Cuisinier Royal et Bourgeois,*vol. 1 (Paris, 1722), pp. 205, 207. German edition, *Allneueste Anweisung zum Kochen* (Halberstadt and Leipzig: Christian Friedrich Schopp, 1739), p. 758. Nathan, pp. 26–29. Evelyn Rose, *The Complete International Jewish Cookbook* (London: Pan Books, 1982), p. 58. In eastern Europe and in Edwardian England sometimes more than one fish was used in making gefilte fish. Interviews with Mr. C. Berlin and Mrs. Kitty Cooper. Waverley Root, *The Food of France* (London: Macmillan, 1983), p. 250.

17. Patti Shosteck, *A Lexicon of Jewish Cooking* (Chicago: Contemporary Books, 1981), p. 73.

18. *Koch und Kellermeistern,* 1566, recipe for *Küchlin von Fischen. Von Speisen,* 1531, similar recipe for *Küchlin von Fischen.* Wolf, p. 119. Levy, *Jewish Cookery Book,* p. 20. In Lithuania poor Jews made gefilte fish balls from little fish known as "stinkers." Interview with Mr. Berlin.

19. De Pomiane, pp. 123, 126. Marvin I. Herzog, *The Yiddish Language in Northern Poland: Its Geography and History* (The Hague: Mouton & Company, 1965), p. 47. Marta Ochorowicz-Monatowa, *Polish Cooking* (London: André Deutsch, 1960), pp. 53, 55, 56, 61.

20. Max Weinreich, *History of the Yiddish Language* (Chicago: University of Chicago Press, 1980), pp. 540–541. Hans Wiswe, *Kulturgeschichte der Kochkunst* (Munich: Heinz Moos, 1970), p. 201. Root, *Food,* p. 186. Lesley Chamberlain, *The Food and Cooking of Russia* (Harmondsworth: Penguin Books, 1983), pp. 109–110.

21. Israel Zangwill, *Children of the Ghetto* (London: William Heinemann & Company, 1893), pp. 48–49. Cecil Roth, "The Middle Period of Anglo-Jewry (1290–1655) Reconsidered," *Transactions of the Jewish Historical Society of England* 19 (1960): 5. John M. Shaftesley, "Culinary Aspects of Anglo-Jewry in Dov Noy and Issachar Ben-Ami," in *Studies in the Cultural Life of Anglo-Jewry* (Jerusalem: Magnes Press, 1975), p. 392 (hereafter cited as Shaftesley). Lucien Wolf, *Jews in the Canary Islands* (London: Spottiswoode, Ballantyne & Company, 1926), pp. 86, 99. *The Jewish Encyclopedia,* article on cookery.

22. Hannah Glasse, *The Art of Cookery Made Plain and Easy* (Edinburgh and London: Alexander Donaldson, 1781), p. 295. Nathan, pp. 222–223. Alexis Soyer, *A Shilling Cookery for the People* (London: George Routledge & Company, 1855), p. 28. Eliza Acton, *Modern Cookery for Private Families* (London: Longmans Green & Company, 1887), p. 607. Shaftesley, pp. 292–293. Judith Montefiore, *The Jewish Manual,* Facsimilie Edition (New York: Nightingale Books, 1983), p. 38 (hereafter cited as *Jewish Manual*). Sholom Aleichem, "London why don't you burn?"

23. Shlomo Eidelberg, *Jewish Life in Austria in the XV Century* (Philadelphia: Dropsie College, 1962), p. 119 (hereafter cited as Eidelberg). Pollack, p. 267. Jeremiah J. Berman, *Shehita* (New York: Bloch Publishing Company, 1941), pp. 89–91. *Code of Jewish Law,* trans. Hyman E. Goldin (New York: Hebrew Publishing Company, 1927), vol. 2, pp. 64–65 (hereafter cited as *Code of Jewish Law*).

24. Sholom Aleichem, *The Old Country* (New York: Crown Publishers, 1953), p. 71. Prawer, p. 398. Schauss, p. 24. Abraham Cahan, *The Education of Abraham Cahan* (Philadelphia: Jewish Publication Society of America, 1969), pp. 27, 37. Ruth Rubin, *Voices of a People* (Philadelphia: Jewish Publication Society of America, 1979), pp. 137, 214, 215. Zborowski and Herzog, p. 46. I. J. Singer, *Of a World That Is No More*, p. 116.

25. Mordecai Kosover, *Yiddishe Maykholim* (New York: Yivo Institute for Jewish Research, 1958), pp. 61, 62, 64, 67, 70. Shosteck, pp. 51–52. Vincenzo Buonassisi, *The Classic Book of Pasta* (London: Futura, 1985), pp. 7–9. Grunwald, p. 56. Charles Perry, "Notes on Persian pasta," *Petits Propos Culinaires* 10:48–49. Charles Perry, "The Oldest Mediterranean Noodle: a Cautionary Tale," *Petits Propos Culinaires* 9:42–45. "Linguistic Remarks on Esther Levy's Cookery Book 1871," *Jewish Language Review* 6 (1986): 166.

26. Grunwald, p. 250. *Jewish Language Review* 6:169. *Jewish Language Review*, 1984, p. 106. *Jewish Language Review*, 1982, p. 121. Mordecai Kosover, "Gleanings from the Vocabulary of a Fifteenth Century Yiddish Manuscript Collection of Customs," in *For Max Weinreich on His Seventieth Birthday* (The Hague: Mouton & Company, 1964), pp. 360–355 (hereafter cited as Kosover, "Gleanings"). *Or Zarua*, part 2, Hilchos Erev Shabbos (Zhitomir, 1862), p. 6/column *Bes*, sec. 8 (hereafter cited as *Or Zarua*). Rema, Hilchos Shabbos 257.8.

27. Eidelberg, p. 73. Rabbi L. I. Halpern, *Shabbat and the Modern Kitchen* (Jerusalem: Gefen Publishing House, 1986), pp. 33–34. Louis Wirth, *The Ghetto* (Chicago: Chicago University Press, n.d.), pp. 154–155. *Code of Jewish Law* 2:67.

28. Shlomo Noble, "Rabbi Yehiel Mikhel Epstein, Educator and Advocate of Yiddish in the Seventeenth Century," *Yivo Annual of Jewish Social Science* 6 (1951): 313–314. Gabriel Ben Pedhazur (Abraham Mears), *The Book of Religion, Ceremonies, and Prayers of the Jews as practised in their Synagogues and Families On All Occasions: On their Sabbaths and other Holy-days Throughout the Year* (London, 1738), pp. 60–61. *Or Zarua*, sec. 8. Raphael and Weyl, p. 338. Freddy Raphael and Robert Weyl, *Regards nouveaux sur les juifs d'Alsace* (Strasbourg: Libraire Istra, 1980), p. 211.

29. Hugo Mandelbaum, *Jewish Life in the Village Communities of Southern Germany* (Jerusalem: Feldheim Publishers, 1958), p. 58 (hereafter cited as Mandelbaum).

30. Harry Blacker, *Just Like It Was: Memoirs of the Mittel East* (London: Vallentine Mitchell, 1982), pp. 19–20. *Jewish Chronicle*, London Extra, September 30, 1988.

31. Mozes Heiman Gans, *Memorbook: A Pictorial History of Dutch Jewry from the Renaissance to 1940* (London: George Prior Associated Publishers, 1977), p. 643. David Toback's Memoirs. I am grateful to Carole Malkin for permission to see part of her grandfather's unpublished autobiography. *Jüdisches Lexikon*, vol. 4/2, article on *Schalet* (Berlin: Judischer Verlag, 1927).

32. Joseph Sutton, *Magic Carpet: Aleppo-in-Flatbush* (New York: Thayer-Jacoby, 1986), p. 196. Interview with Mr. Rimock about the town of Fez in Morocco.

33. Mandelbaum, p. 58. Raphael and Weyl, p. 338. George Lang, *The Cuisine of Hungary* (Harmondsworth: Penguin Books, 1985), pp. 221–223.

34. Grunwald, p. 520. Prawer, p. 271. Molly Lyons Bar-David, *The Israeli Cook Book* (New York: Crown Publishers, 1964), p. 130 (hereafter cited as Bar-David).

35. De Pomiane, p. 43. Don Gussow, *Chaia Sonia* (New York: Bantam Books, 1981), p. 37. Dennis Eisenberg, Uri Dan, and Eli Landau, *Meyer Lansky: Mogul of the Mob* (New York: Paddington Books, 1979), pp. 33–34.

36. Kosover, *Fifteenth Century*, p. 358. Wolf, pp. 158–159. De Pomaine, pp. 116–117. Nathan, pp. 127–129, 210–211. Max Grunwald, *Vienna* (Philadelphia, 1936), p. 56. Bar-Lyons, pp. 278, 287–288. William Woys Weaver, *Sauerkraut Yankees* (Philadelphia: University of Pennsylvania Press, 1983), pp. 103, 114–117, 120 (hereafter cited as Weaver).

37. Elzet, *Maykholim*, p. 36. De Pomiane, pp. 115–119, 188–191. Weaver, p. 106. Adele Mondry, *Wyszkowo, a Shtetl on the Bug River* (New York: Ktav Publishing House, 1910), p. 25). Kosover, *Maykholim*, p. 10. Barbara Ketcham Wheaton, *Savouring the Past: The French Kitchen Table from 1300–1789* (London: Chatto & Windus, 1983), pp. 168, 200, 206, 295 (hereafter cited as Wheaton).

38. Kelly, pp. 169–171. Wolf, pp. 158–159. *Grimm's Deutsches Worterbuch, Gugelhupf, Gogelhopf* (Leipzig: Verlag S. Hirzel, 1935).

39. *Jewish Language Review* 2:201. Kosover, *Fifteenth Century*, p. 356. Shaftesley, pp. 385–386. Waverley Root, *The Food of France* (1983), p. 246. Maguelonne Toussaint-Samat, *A History of Food* (Oxford: Blackwell, 1992).

40. David Toback's memoirs. Elzet, *Maykholim*, pp. 34–35. *A Jewish Life Under the Tsars: The Autobiography of Chaim Aronson, 1825–1888* (Totowa, NJ: Allanheld Osmun, 1983), p. 33.

41. Weaver, p. 112. Elzet, *Maykholim*, p. 35. Nathan, p. 43. Shosteck. pp. 173–174. *The Jewish Manual*, p. 145. Iris Origo, *The Merchant of Prato* (Harmondsworth: Penguin Books, 1979), p. 174. Bridget Ann Henisch, *Fast and Feast: Food in Medieval Society* (Philadelphia: Pennsylvania State University Press, 1978), p. 131. Wheaton, p. 33. *The Viandier of Taillevent*, ed. Terence Scully (Ottawa: University of Ottawa Press, 1988), pp. 128–129.

42. Sarah Kelly, *Festive Baking in Austria, Germany and Switzerland* (Harmondsworth: Penguin Books, 1985), pp. 12, 140, 171. Wheaton, pp. 26, 66. Herzog, *The Yiddish Language in Northern Poland*, p. 48. Krauss, *Volksküche*, p. 34. Pollack, pp. 97, 267, 268, 276. Elzet, *Maykholim*, p. 44. Weinreich, p. 5.

43. Shmarya Levin, *Childhood in Exile* (London: George Routledge & Sons, 1935), p. 90.

44. Nathan, p. 116. Shosteck, p. 103. Barash, *Pictures from a Brewery*, p. 207. Claudia Roden, *A Book of Middle Eastern Food* (Harmondsworth: Penguin Books, 1970), pp. 20, 309–311. George Lang, *The Cuisine of Hungary* (Harmondsworth: Penguin Books, 1985), p. 30. Chamberlain, *Food of Russia*, p. 140.

45. Nathan, p. 141. Elzet, *Reshumot*, pp. 342–343. Dayan I. Grunfeld, *The Jewish Dietary Laws*, vol. 1 (London: Soncino Press, 1972), p. 99. Barbara Kirschenblatt-Gimblett, "The Kosher Gourmet in the Nineteenth-Century Kitchen: Three Jewish Cookbooks in Historical Perspective," *The Journal of Gastronomy* 2:4 (Winter 1986/1987), footnote 21.

46. Sarah Kelly, *Festive Baking in Austria, Germany and Switzerland*

(Harmondsworth: Penguin Books, 1985), p. 14. Nathan, p. 151. Elzet, *Reshumot*, p. 342. Sholom Aleichem, *Stories and Satires* (London: Collier Books, 1970), p. 122. Elzet, *Maykholim*, p. 45. *Shtetl Memoirs*, p. 103.

47. Philip Goodman, *The Purim Anthology* (Philadelphia: Jewish Publication Society of America, 1973), pp. 415–420. Elzet, *Maykholim*, pp. 45–48. Kosover, *Maykholim*, pp. 75–76. Pollack, pp. 276–277. Kelly, *Festive Baking*, p. 11. Hayyim Schauss, *The Jewish Festivals* (London: Jewish Chronicle Publications, 1986), p. 270. Elzet, *Reshumot*, p. 343. Irving A. Agus, *Rabbi Meir of Rothenburg* (New York: Katv Publishing House, 1970), p. 197. Herman Schwab, *A World in Ruins* (London: Edward Goldston, 1946), p. 206.

48. *The Scribe: Journal of Babylonian Jewry*, August 1988. Letter from Samuel Lyons. Beatrice Weinreich, "The Americanization of Passover," in *Studies in Biblical and Jewish Folklore*, ed. Raphael Patai, Francis Lee Utley, and Dov Noy (Bloomington, IN: Indiana University Press, 1960), pp. 332–339. Levin, *Childhood in Exile*, p. 33. Salo Wittmayer Baron, *A Social and Religious History of the Jews*, vol. 11 (New York: Columbia University Press, 1967), p. 151. Jonathan D. Sarna, "Passover Raisin Wine, The American Temperance Movement and Mordecai Noah," *Jewish Folklore and Ethnology Review* 9:1 (1987): 34. Flora Brodie, "Seder mead not a drink for the meek!" *Jewish Chronicle*, April 21, 1989.

49. Harold P. Gastwirt, *Fraud, Corruption and Holiness* (Port Washington, NY: Kennikat Press, 1974), pp. 9–10. Israel Abrahams, "The Shape of Matzoth," in *The Book of Delight and Other Papers* (Philadelphia: Jewish Publication Society of America, 1912), pp. 291–315. Weinreich, "Americanization of Passover," pp. 341–350. Rifka Rosenwein, "Passover makes much work for Kosher-Conscious Firms," *The Wall Street Journal*, April 24, 1986.

50. R. E. F. Smith and D. Christian, *Bread and Salt: A Social and Economic History of Food and Drink in Russia* (Cambridge: Cambridge University Press, 1984), p. 268. Elzet, *Maykholim*, pp. 42, 44. Philip Goodman, *The Purim Anthology* (Philadelphia: Jewish Publication Society of America, 1973), p. 417. Levin, *Childhood in Exile*, p. 158.

51. Elzet, *Maykholim*, pp. 42–43. Bar-David, p. 36. *Shtetl Memoirs*, p. 95. Kosover, *Maykholim*, p. 138. Abramowicz, *Fashvundene Geshtalten*, p. 469. Zborowski and Herzog, p. 391. Chaim Grade, *The Yeshiva*, vol. 2 (New York: Menorah Publishing House, 1979), p. 59.

CONCLUSION

1. Paula E. Hyman, "Immigrant Women and Consumer Protest: The New York Kosher Meat Boycott of 1902," *American Jewish History* 70 (September 1980).

2. Dayan I. Grunfeld, *The Jewish Dietary Laws*, vol. 1 (London: Soncino Press, 1972), pp. 123–124. Herman Pollack, "The Minhag: Some Examples of its Characteristics," in *Go and Study: Essays and Studies in Honor of Alfred Jospe*, ed. Rahel Jospe and Samuel Z. Fishman (Washington: B'nai B'rith Hillel Foundation, 1980), pp. 341–344.

3. Ivan G. Marcus, "Jewish Schools in Medieval Europe," *The Melton Journal,* Winter 1987, p. 5.

4. *The New International Goodwill Recipe Book,* ed. Hazel Levin and Mimi Sacks (Johannesburg: The Johannesburg Women's Zionist League, 1981), pp. 127–129.

5. *Hunger Disease,* ed. Myron Winnick (New York: John Wiley & Sons, 1979). *The Martyrdom of the Jewish Physicians in Poland,* ed. Louis Falstein (New York: Exposition Press, 1963). Henri Van Der Zee, *The Hunger Winter: Occupied Holland 1944–5* (London: Jill Norman and Hobhouse, 1982). Elie A. Cohen, *Human Behaviour in the Concentration Camp* (London: Free Association Books, 1988), pp. 51–58.

6. Stephen Stern, *The Sephardic Jewish Community of Los Angeles* (New York: Arno Press, 1980), p. 263.

7. Ibid., pp. 261–285. Rudolf Grewe, "The Arrival of the Tomato in Spain and Italy Early Recipes," *First International Food Congress* (Turkey, 1986). These recipes were incorporated into Sephardic cuisine in the nineteenth century.

8. Claudia Roden, *A Book of Middle Eastern Food* (Harmondsworth: Penguin Books, 1970), pp. 11–12, 280–281.

FOR FURTHER
READING

Abramowicz, Hirsh. *Fashvundene Geshtalten*. Buenos Aires, 1958.

Adler, Nathan Elkan. *Jewish Travellers in the Middle Ages*. New York: Dover Publications, 1987.

Agus, Irving A. *Rabbi Meir of Rothenburg*. New York: Ktav Publishing House, 1970.

Alon, Gedaliah. *Jews, Judaism and the Classical World*. Jerusalem: Magnes Press, 1977.

———. *The Jews in Their Land in the Talmudic Age*. Vol. 1. Jerusalem: Magnes Press, 1980.

Anderson, Jean. *The Food of Portugal*. London: Robert Hale, 1987.

Ashtor, Eliyahu. "An Essay on the Diet of the Various Classes in the Medieval Levant." In *Biology of Man in History: Selections from the Annales*, ed. Robert Forster and Orest Ranum, pp. 125–62. Baltimore: Johns Hopkins University Press, 1975.

Bahloul, Joëlle. *Le culte de la Table Dressée Rites et traditions de la table juive algerienne*. Paris: Éditions A. M. Métailié, 1983.

Benbassa, Esther. *Cuisine judeo-espagnole: Recettes et Traditions*. Paris: Editions du Scribe, 1984.

Berman, Jeremiah. *Shehita*. New York: Bloch Publishing Company, 1941.

Bokser, Baruch M. *The Origins of the Seder*. Berkeley and Los Angeles: University of California Press, 1984.

Bolens, Lucie. *La cuisine andalouse, un art de vivre XIè-XIIIès*. Paris: Albin Michel, 1990.

Braudel, Fernand. *Capitalism and Material Life 1400–1800*. London: Weidenfeld and Nicholson, 1973.

Broshi, Magen. "The Diet of Palestine in the Roman Period—Introductory Notes." *The Israel Museum Journal* (Spring 1986).

Budd, Philip J. "Holiness and Cult." In *The World of Ancient Israel: Sociological, Anthropological and Political Perspectives*, ed. R. E. Clements. Cambridge: Cambridge University Press, 1989.

Bunis, David M. "Food Terms and Traditions in Sefer Damesek Eliezer. *Jerusalem Studies in Folklore* 5–6 (1984): 151–195.

———. "The Culinary Terminology and Traditions of the Sephardim in the Sixteenth Through the Nineteenth Centuries: A Historical Study Based on Rabbinical Sources." *Jewish Folklore and Ethnology Review* 9:1 (1987).

Cardozo, Abraham. "A Lyrical Excursion into Sephardic Gastronomy." *American Sephardi* V (1971):1–2.

Casas, Penelope. *The Foods and Wines of Spain.* Harmondsworth: Penguin Books, 1985.

Chamberlain, Lesley. *The Food and Cooking of Russia.* Harmondsworth: Penguin Books, 1983.

———. *The Food and Cooking of Eastern Europe.* Harmondsworth: Penguin Books, 1989.

Cosman, Madelaine Pelner. *Fabulous Feasts: Medieval Cookery and Ceremony.* New York: George Braziller, 1989.

Crosby, Alfred. *Columbian Exchange.* Westport, CT: Greenwood Press, 1972.

Davidson, Alan. *On Fasting and Feasting.* London: MacDonald Orbis, 1988.

De Pomiane, Edouard. *The Jews of Poland: Recollections and Recipes.* Trans. Josephine Bacon. Garden Grove, CA: Pholiota Press, 1985.

Dobrinsky, Herbert C. *A Treasury of Sephardic Laws and Customs.* New York: Ktav Publishing Company, 1986.

Douglas, Mary. *Purity and Danger.* London: Ark Paperbacks, 1988.

Eidelberg, Shlomo. *Jewish Life in Austria in the XVth Century.* Philadelphia: Dropsie College, 1962.

Eliachar, Elie. *Living With Jews.* London: Weidenfeld and Nicholson, 1983.

Elzet (Zlotnik), Yehuda. *"Minhagai Yisroel"* ("Customs of Israel"). *Reshumot* 1 (1918).

———. *Yiddishe Maykholim: Folkstimlikhe Rednsartn, Glaykhvertlekh, Un Anekdotn: Der Vunderoytser Fun Der Yiddisher Shprakh.* 2 parts. Warsaw: Lewin Epstein, 1920.

Estrugo, Jose M. *Los Sefardies.* Havana, 1958.

Feliks, Yehuda. *Nature and Man in the Bible.* London: Soncino Press, 1981. See also articles by him on biblical and talmudic foods in the *Encyclopaedia Judaica.* Jerusalem: Keter Publishing House, 1978.

First International Food Congress, Turkey 1986, organized by Feyzi Halici. Ankara: Kultur ve Turiym Bakanligi Yayini, 1988.

Flower, Barbara, and Elisabeth Rosenbaum. *The Roman Cookery Book: A critical translation of the Art of Cooking by Apicius for use in the study and kitchen.* London: Harrap, 1958.

Forbes, R. J. *Studies in Ancient Technology.* Vol. 3. Leiden: E. J. Brill, 1965.

Gastwirt, Harold P. *Fraud, Corruption, and Holiness.* Port Washington, NY: Kennikat Press, 1974.

Goitein, S. D. "Jewish Matters Baladhuri's Ansab al Ashraf." *Zion* 1 (1936): 75–81.

———. *A Mediterranean Society.* Vol. 1. *Economic Foundations.* Berkeley and Los Angeles: University of California Press, 1967.

———. *A Mediterranean Society.* Vol. 2. *The Community.* Berkeley and Los Angeles: University of California Press, 1971.

———. *A Mediterranean Society.* Vol. 4. *Daily Life.* Berkeley and Los Angeles: University of California Press, 1983.

Gold, David L. "The Etymology of the English Bread Name *pita:* A Study in Jewish Intralinguistics." *Jewish Language Review* 4 (1984): 58–76.

———. "Towards a Study of the Origins of Two Synonymous Yiddish Adjectives: *pareve* and *minikh.*" *Jewish Language Review* 5 (1985).

_____. "More on the Origins of the English Bread Name *pita.*" *Jewish Linguistic Studies* (1989).

Goodenough, Erwin R. *Jewish Symbols in the Greco-Roman Period.* Vols. 5–6. New York: Pantheon Books, 1953–1965.

Grewe, Rudolph. "Catalan Cuisine in an Historial Perspective." *National & Regional Styles of Cookery.* Oxford Symposium, 1981.

Grunfeld, Dayan I. *The Jewish Dietary Laws.* 2 vols. London: Soncino Press, 1982.

Grunwald, Max. "*Aus dem jüdischen Kochbuch.*" *Menorah* 6:9 (1920): 518–520.

Haran, Menahem. "Seething a Kid in Its Mother's Milk." *Journal of Jewish Studies* 30:1(1979).

Harris, Marvin. *Cannibals and Kings.* London: Fontana Collins, 1978.

Henisch, Bridget Ann. *Fast and Feast: Food in Medieval Society.* Philadelphia: Pennsylvania State University Press, 1978.

Herzog, Marvin I. *The Yiddish Language in Northern Poland: Its Geography and History.* The Hague: Mouton & Company, 1965.

Isaac, Erich. "Influence of Religion in the Spread of Citrus Fruit." *Science* 129 (January 23, 1959): 179–186.

Jasny, Naum. "The Daily Bread of the Ancient Greeks and Romans." *Osiris* 9 (1950).

Kasovich, Israel. *The Days of Our Years: Personal and General Reminiscences 1859–1929.* New York: The Jordan Publishing Company, 1929.

Kelly, Sarah. *Festive Baking in Austria, Germany and Switzerland.* Harmondsworth: Penguin Books, 1985.

Kirshenblatt-Gimblett, Barbara. "The Kosher Gourmet in the Nineteenth Century Kitchen: Three Jewish Cookbooks in Historical Perspective." *Journal of Gastronomy* 2:4 (Winter 1986/1987): 51–89.

Kosover, Mordecai. *Yiddishe Maykholim: A Shtudye in Kultur, Geshikhte un Shprakhforshung.* New York: VIVO Institute for Jewish Research. Reprinted from the Judah J. Joffe Bukh.

_____ "Gleanings from the Vocabulary of a Fifteenth Century Yiddish Manuscript Collection of Customs." In *For Max Weinreich on His Seventieth Birthday: Studies in Jewish Languages, Literature and Society.* The Hague: Mouton & Company, 1964.

Krauss, Samuel. *Aus der jüdischen Volksküche: Mitteilungen zur Jüdischen Volkskunde* 18,1–2 (Vienna, 1915), pp. 1–40.

_____. *Talmudische Archaologie.* Vol. 1. Hildesheim: Georg Olms Verlagsbuchhandlung, 1966.

Lauterbach, Jacob Z. "Development of Two Sabbath Ceremonies." In *Studies in Jewish Law, Custom and Folklore,* pp. 77–97. New York: Ktav Publishing House, 1970.

Levy, Esther. *Jewish Cookery Book.* Facsimile Edition. Garden Grove, CA: Pholiota Press, 1982.

Milgrom, Jacob. "Profane Slaughter and a Formulaic Key to the Composition of Deuteronomy." *H.U.C. Annual,* 1976.

Miner, Viviane Alchech, and Linda Krinn. *From My Grandmother's Kitchen: A Sephardic Cookbook.* Gainesville, FL: Triad Publishing Company, 1984.

Mintz, Sidney W. *Sweetness and Power: The Place of Sugar in Modern History.* Harmondsworth: Penguin Books, 1986.

Moldenke, Alma L. *Plants of the Bible.* New York: Dover Books, 1986.

Narkiss, Mordechai. "Origins of the Spice Box." *Journal of Jewish Art* 8 (1981): 28–41.

Nathan, Joan. *The Jewish Holiday Kitchen.* New York: Schocken Books, 1979.

Newman, J. *Agricultural Life of the Jews in Babylonia.* London: Oxford University Press, 1932.

Perry, Charles. "The Oldest Mediterranean Noodle: A Cautionary Tale." *Petits Propos Culinaires* 9: 42–45.

———. "Notes on Persian Pasta." *Petits Propos Culinaires* 10: 48–49.

———. "What Was Tracta?" *Petits Propos Culinaires* 12: 37–39.

———. "Tracta? Trachanas/Kishk." *Petits Propos Culinaires* 14: 58–59.

———. "1100 Years in the Life of a Dish." *The Journal of Gastronomy* 1 (Summer 1984): 67–77.

———. "Puff Paste Is Spanish." *Petits Propos Culinaires* 17 (1984): 57–62.

———. "The Sals of the Infidels." *Petits Propos Culinaires* 26 (1987): 55–59.

———. "Baklava not Proven Greek." *Petits Propos Culinaires* 27 (1987): 47–48.

Pollack, Herman. *Jewish Folkways in Germanic Lands 1648–1806.* Cambridge, MA: M.I.T. Press, 1971.

———. "The Minhag: Some Examples of Its Characteristics." In *Go and Study: Essays and Studies in Honor of Alfred Jospe,* ed. Rahel Jospe and Samuel Z. Fishman. Washington: B'nai Brith Hillel Foundation, 1980.

Rabinowitz, Louis. *The Social Life of the Jews of Northern France in the XII–XIV Centuries as Reflected in the Rabbinical Literature of the Period.* London: Edward Goldston, 1938.

———. *Torah and Flora.* New York: Sanhedrin Press, 1977. See also his Tora and Flora column that appeared in the *Jerusalem Post* for many years.

Ratner, Robert, and Bruce Zuckerman. "A Kid in Milk?" New Photographs of KTU I.23, Line 14. *H.U.C. Annual,* 1986, pp. 15–52.

Rodin, Claudia. *A Book of Middle Eastern Food.* Harmondsworth: Penguin Books, 1970.

Rodinson, Maxime. "Reserches sur les Documents Arabes Relatifs a la Cuisine." *Revue Des Etudes Islamiques* 17–18 (1949): 95–165.

———. "On the Etymology of 'Losange.' " *Petits Propos* Culinaires 23 (1986).

Rose, Evelyn. *The Complete International Jewish Cookbook.* London: Pan Books, 1976.

Roskies, Diane. "Alphabet Instruction in the East European Heder." *Yivo Annual* (1978).

Root, Waverley. *The Food of Italy.* New York: Vintage Books, 1977.

———. *Food.* New York: Simon and Schuster, 1980.

———. *The Food of France.* London: Macmillan, 1983.

Salaman, Redcliffe. *The History and Social Influence of the Potato.* Cambridge: Cambridge University Press, 1985.

Schauss, Hayyim. *The Lifetime of a Jew.* New York: Union of American Hebrew Congregations, 1967.

———. *The Jewish Festivals.* London: Jewish Chronicle Publications, 1986.

Schwartz, Oded. *In Search of Plenty: A History of Jewish Food.* London: Kyle Kathie, 1992.

Schwartz, Rosaline B. "The Geography of Two Food Terms: A Study in Yiddish Lexical Variation." In *The Field of Yiddish. Third Collection,* ed. Marvin I. Herzog, Wita Ravid, and Uriel Weinreich. The Hague: Mouton & Company, 1969.

Shosteck, Patti. *A Lexicon of Jewish Cooking.* Chicago: Contemporary Books, 1981.

Smith, B. E. F., and D. Christian. *Bread and Salt: A Social and Economic History of Food and Drink in Russia.* Cambridge: Cambridge University Press, 1984.

Soler, Jean. "The Semiotics of Food in the Bible." In *Food and Drink in History: Selections from the Annales,* ed. Robert Forster and Orest Ranum. Baltimore: Johns Hopkins University Press, 1979.

Sperber, Daniel. "*Cibar* Bread (Hebrew)." *Tarbiz* 36:2 (1966): 199–201.

———. "Some Observations of Fish and Fisheries in Roman Palestine." *Zeitschrift der deutschen morgenländischen Gesellschaft,* 1969, pp. 265–269.

Stein, Siegfried. "The Influence of Symposia Literature on the Literary Form of Pesah Haggadah." *The Journal of Jewish Studies* 7 (1957): 13–44.

Stern, Stephen. *The Sephardic Community of Los Angeles.* New York: Arno Press, 1980.

Tannahill, Reay. *Food in History.* Harmondsworth: Penguin Books, 1988.

Tolkowsky, Samuel. *Hesperides: A History of the Culture and Use of Citrus Fruits.* London: John Bale Sons & Curnow, 1938.

Toussaint-Samat, Maguelonne. *A History of Food.* Oxford: Blackwell, 1992.

Weaver, William Woys. *Sauerkraut Yankees.* Philadelphia: University of Pennsylvania Press, 1983.

———. "Food with a Twist: The Pretzel Family Tree." *The World & I* (April 1991): 616–623.

Weinreich, Beatrice. "The Americanization of Passover." In *Studies in Biblical and Jewish Folklore,* ed. Raphael Patai, Francis Lee Utley, and Dov Noy. Bloomington, IN: Indiana State University Press, 1960.

Wexler, Paul. "The Term 'Sabbath Food': A Challenge for Jewish Interlinguistics." *Journal of the American Oriental Society* 98 (Oct.–Dec. 1978).

Wheaton, Barbara Ketcham. *Savouring the Past: The French Kitchen and Table from 1300 to 1789.* London: Chatto and Windus, 1983.

Yehoshua, Yakov. *Ha-Bayit Ve Ha Rechov Bi-Yerushalayim Ha-Yeshanah.* Jerusalem: Rubin Mass, 1966.

INDEX

About the Author

Through extensive research in libraries in the United States, London, and Jerusalem, John Cooper has become a pioneer in the field of Jewish culinary history. He was a lecturer at the first Oxford Symposium on Jewish Food and at the Spiro Jewish Food Conference. Cooper studied history at Balliol College at Oxford University, where he received an M.A. He is an attorney in London, where he lives with his wife and two children.